MW01155964

The Endless Sky

Also by Steven Forrest

The Inner Sky

The Changing Sky

The Night Speaks

The Book of Pluto

Measuring the Night (with Jeffrey Wolf Green)

Measuring the Night Vol. 2 (with Jeffrey Wolf Green)

Stalking Anubis

Skymates (with Jodie Forrest)

Skymates II (with Jodie Forrest)

Yesterday's Sky

The Book of the Moon

The Book of Neptune

The Book of Fire

The Book of Earth

The Book of Air

The Book of Water

The Endless Sky

Collected Astrological Essays
2002-2021

by Steven Forrest

Seven Paws Press, Inc.
Borrego Springs, CA

Published in 2021 by Seven Paws Press, Inc.
PO Box 82
Borrego Springs, CA 92004
www.sevenpaws.com

Copyright © 2021 by Steven Forrest

All rights reserved. No part of this publication may be reproduced or transmitted in any form or by any means, electronic or mechanical, including mimeographing, recording, taping, scanning, via Internet download, or by any information storage and retrieval systems, without permission in writing from Seven Paws Press, Inc.
Reviewers may quote brief passages.

ISBN for print: 978-1-939510-11-2
ISBN for ebook: 978-1-939510-12-9

Cover art by Simon Avery

Printed in the United States of America
LCCN 2021949560

ACKNOWLEDGEMENTS

Over the past few years, my life has changed dramatically. I am no longer traveling so much, no longer running my apprenticeship programs, no longer seeing as many clients for private work. Despite those "deletions," I am miles away from anything resembling retirement. The vacuum has been filled by legacy projects, most of them involving levels of teamwork and support that I've never before experienced. I want to thank Jeff Parrett and Catie Cadge for helping me build the Forrest Center for Evolutionary Astrology. I've already dedicated this book to them and to our able staff and our dedicated students. I've also been doing most of the writing for an astrological cell phone application called *Lila*. Many hands are involved in that work. I am grateful to all of them, but I would particularly like to name Ricky Willams and Linnea Miron, who conceived the idea with me, along with Matt Cohen, and the indomitable AstroTwins, Ophira and Tali Edut. Meanwhile, my webmaster and right-hand man, Tony Howard, continues to be an irreplaceable gem to whom I owe an incalculable and growing debt of gratitude.

A profound thank you to the people who have run my various Apprenticeship Programs around the world over the years. I learned so much astrology by teaching it there. Here, in no particular order, are their names: Ingrid Coffin and her team at the Blue Sky Ranch Fellowship, with special thanks to Cristina Smith, Jonathan Sacks, Paula Wansley, and Carey Nash. Felicia Jiang and David Railey, along with the amazing NoDoor team in Beijing. Kathy Hallen and her able assistants, Carol McLauren and Tricia Mickleberry. Lisa Jones and Christine Murfitt. Joyce Van Horn and Deni Mateer. My Apprenticeship Programs have come and gone, as have the people who have made them possible. Thanks, *emeritus*, to Karen Davis, Vinessa Nevala, Barbara King, and the late David Friedman.

Finally my gratitude to the following people who were actively engaged with me in various ways during the writing process: Scott and

Barbara Ainslie, Lynn Bell, Virginia Bell, Cheryl Benedict, Chris Brennan, Olivier Clerq, Brian Colter, Chip Conley, Sarrah Christiansen, Cui "Chloe" Ying – my intrepid Chinese translator, Rona Elliot and Roger Brossy, Ryan Evans, Michael Faith, Basil Fearrington, Hadley Fitzgerald, the Fuhrmann clan (Marc, Melina and Kalea), Rishi Giovanni Gatti, Robert and Diana Griffin, the Grossenbacher clan (John, Ryan, and Dr. Tracy Gaudet), Pamela Hoback, Susie and Mark Hodge, Kathy Jacobson, Bill Janis, Sherry Jayne, Kelly Ruey Jeng Jean, Mark Jones, Hayley Kaufman, Kathy King, Peter and Ingrid Kondos, Lisa Kostova, Kate, Alex, and Paisley Laird, Monica Lewinski, Laurie Lindgren, Elizabeth Long, Juliana McCarthy, Kym and Scott McNabb, Cristin McVey, Thomas Miller, Dominic Miller, Sol Forrest Miron, Elizabeth Motyka, Jim Mullaney, Rafael Nasser, Brian O'Flynn, Annette O'Neill, Marie O'Neill, Nina Ortega and Miguel Bracho, Carol Peebles, Joey Paynter, Paulina Poriskova, Steven Poster and Susan Williams, Christa Pynn, Aminah Raheem and Fritz Smith, Claire Rauwel, Dusty Recor and "Indian Joe" Stewart, Evelyn Roberts, Teal Rowe, Paige Ruane and Jack McDonald, Allison Simon, Dr. Mamta Singhvi, Fran Slavich, Katie Sloan, Debbie and Scott Steingraber, Sting and Trudie Sumner-Styler, Kay Taylor, Eric and Margie Thaler, Elaine and Mark Thomas, Brad Tolinski, Jaan Uhelszki, Dick and Artemisa Walker, Beverly Welch, Cindy Wyatt, Scotty Young and Diane Colie Swan, and Helen Zou.

FOREWORD

When I first walked into Steven Forrest's office in Borrego Springs, California, I was a little nervous — bedazzled, if I am going to be honest. But first I'd like to make something clear. That's not something that happens to me very often. I've been a music journalist since I was seventeen, one of the founding editors of *Creem*, a publication that had the audacity to call itself "America's Only Rock and Roll Magazine" back in the more innocent 1970s. So I'm used to famous people. Well, famous rock stars. I've been on tour with Led Zeppelin twice, I interviewed Neil Young in a hallway after he got locked out of his Texas hotel room, told off Rod Stewart when he got handsy with a friend of mine, drank tequila for breakfast with John Lydon standing up at his kitchen counter in Malibu, and chided Stephen Stills for writing *Love the One You're With*, turning the idea of true romance on its pointed little head. I even performed onstage with KISS in full makeup at the height of their (platformed-heeled) fame.

In short: I am not easily unnerved.

Borrego Springs itself was a little unsettling: Its name was derived from the Spanish word for lamb, which is a little ominous in a sacrificial, Passover kind of way, bolstered by the town's having been the setting for a few of Dean Koontz's creepy Jane Hawk novels, and that it's a little hard to get to. A little? There's one road in and one road out: a two-lane highway that requires a visitor to travel twenty-seven miles almost straight up from the main highway over the desolate barren moonscape of the Sonora Desert, where you can't get any radio or cell reception.

But it wasn't entirely the end-of-the-world remoteness of this place that made me quake in my pink clogs. It was because among the *cognoscenti* of the astrological community Steven Forrest IS Jimmy Page. I believed that even before I was aware of the similarity between their charts, although with great authority in terms of the real Page, I can say while Forrest has much of the same brilliance and execution in his field, there's very little of the flinty darkness that Zeppelin's Dark Lord possesses.

That's the comparison I made to friends after I read Forrest's second book, *The Changing Sky*, in 1989 – the one with the slightly risqué psychedelic cover that pictured a blue and purple drawing of a beautiful nude hippie goddess-cum-constellation reaching for a rainbow, the orange script beside her assuring readers, "You Already Hold the Key to the Stars." While those lines made me feel strangely empowered about the future of my nascent astrology studies, what really made me buy the book was the spectral, backlit author's photo of Forrest. Wearing a pale suit, a contrasting tie, and a white dress shirt, with shot cuffs, he stared into the camera with an amused stillness and intensity. It made me think he might have a sense of humor about some of life's big questions, the kinds of things that have stumped philosophers, statesmen, seers and wayward dreamers since the beginning of recorded time. It turned out I was right, but even more, that early book answered some of those important questions I had about life, fate and purpose in a more engaging and approachable style than I was used to. This was a guy who took his astrology seriously but not himself.

After I finished *The Changing Sky*, I tucked it into my bulging bookshelf, next to my almost-complete set of Noel Tyl books, along with Marc Edmund Jones, Alan Leo, Grant Lewi, Stephen Arroyo, Dane Rudhyar and Isabell Hickey – astrologers I believed all lived on Mount Olympus. I figured that's where Steven Forrest belonged.

I didn't really think about the book, or even astrology, for a long time. Time had passed and life interceded, the way it does. But twenty-one years later, in 2010, I had a hankering to get back to my studies. I signed up for an astrology class near my then-home in Berkeley, California, and Steven's *The Changing Sky* was on the reading list. It was a small class of mostly serious students. Once a week we sat around the teacher's living room on big lumpy pillows, drank non-caffeinated tea and lavender honey, and talked about houses, planets, aspects and transits. The teacher made some inroads on progressions, but frankly, I just wasn't able to grasp the meanings, or maybe it was the math. But once I picked up *The Changing Sky* and started reading it again, it all started coming back. There was a clarity of vision and an ease in the writing that made a reader feel like it wasn't really written at all. It was a conversation between two friends, one of them a little smarter than the other one. My fellow students talked about Steven Forrest in hushed tones, and either they had had a reading with him or wanted to. My teacher had studied with him and everyone in the class seemed to have some story about him. Everyone but me.

Then everything in my life changed. I had a few life-altering events and a couple of Pluto transits, which resulted in a proper clean sweep of my life, and I found myself living in Palm Desert, California, a place I never had any intention of even visiting. With my life so altered, I thought it might be the time to consult an astrologer, and told my daughter, Hayley, we should get each other readings for that Christmas. Her palmistry teacher had been raving about some astrologer, Hayley told me, and so she had been watching videos of him on YouTube. "We should go see someone like him," she said. "He probably lives in Vermont. Or Lilydale." Then she googled him. "Uh oh, he has a waiting list of three years. Never mind."

"So who is this guy, anyway?" I asked. She told me his name was Steven Forrest. I thought she said Stephen Foster, and I didn't make the connection. I laughed and said, "I guess it doesn't really matter how long his waiting list is; that's the guy who wrote 'Swanee River.' He's been dead for 150 years!"

"No, Forrest! Forrest!" she said, clearly irritated with me. "You know, like 'if a tree fell in the forest and no one was there to hear it, did it really fall at all!'"

Apparently it did. And even more startling was that he lived right down the road from me now, give or take 90 miles. Hayley called to put our names on the waiting list, and it turned out he had two cancellations for the next month. Not only a miracle, but seasonal as well, which was why I found myself two days before Thanksgiving standing outside a long, low stucco building the color of old linen, surrounded by potted geraniums and oleander bushes, when I'd normally be at home thawing a turkey.

We knocked on the heavy wooden door and it was opened slowly not by the serious, suit-wearing gentleman from the back of *The Changing Sky*, but by a tall graceful figure wearing well-worn jeans, a navy crewneck T-shirt, and a red tunic with two patch pockets. His hair was white instead of brown, but the manicured beard was exactly the same, and that impish smile was more impish and warmer. But those eyes – now behind rectangular wire-rimmed glasses – had that same still intensity as on the book cover, making me feel they could bore right into my soul. Which I was certain they did, after that first, of many, readings, though there is much more at work in Steven Forrest than all-seeing eyes. There's a lifetime of scholarship, investigation, and curiosity; well-thought-out theories of human behaviors; and observations that he's gleaned from his deep connections with mentors and students alike. It's the things that he has learned and absorbed from each one of his often-serendipitous encounters, whether with Jungian scholar Robert A. Johnson or Sting and Trudie Styler, with whom he has had a long friendship.

But Forrest is just as much a rock star as Sting, and not because he was a founding member of Dragonship, a band right out of the British traditional folk-rock movement, with a definite prog-rock bend. Think the Strawbs with female singers. Music speaks to him, and it's why he often uses song lyrics by Bono, Bruce Springsteen or Van Morrison (whose *Astral Weeks* makes him cry) to illustrate an astrological point. But also, he is such a maestro of his art – and astrology conducted the way Steven Forrest does it, is an art, not a craft.

He puts a human face on astrology, even more so in *The Endless Sky*, his fifteenth book. Not a textbook or a memoir, it's a collection of articles and newsletters he's written over the past twenty years. Over these three or four hundred pages, the reader gains insight into the inner Steve: his pet peeves, his peak moments, and people and theories that have changed him. If Princess Diana was the People's Princess, Steven Forrest is the people's astrologer. He explains chart rectification by showing us exactly how he and his partner, fine-artist Michelle Kondos, tried to figure out the birthdate and time of their new kitten Benny, so they could construct a chart re-creating the moment they spotted him in a cage with his four brothers, and how his antics helped determine his Ascendant.

You could say *The Endless Sky* is somewhat akin to a cookbook, or an elevated version of *Hints From Heloise*, the astrologer's version, but that still wouldn't come close to how valuable and engaging it is. The Who would call it *Odds and Sods,* Tom Waits might name it *Orphans: Brawlers, Bawlers and Bastards*, the Rolling Stones, *Metamorphosis,* but I just call it genius, and Steven Forrest a wizard without a wand.

—Jaan Uhelszki
August 16, 2021

TABLE OF CONTENTS

SECTION ONE: THE PLANETS AT BIRTH

(Newsletter – September 2020)
Using three Sun-Uranus conjunctions as examples, we see how dependent the actual meaning of a planet is upon the house and sign it occupies, not to mention the level of consciousness of the person embodying it.

(Newsletter – November 2019)
What if instead of thinking that such signs "have a hard time expressing themselves," we trust the universe and say that they aren't *supposed* to express themselves, at least not outwardly? Some pots boil best with the lid on.

(Newsletter – April 2015)
Is it bad to have Mars in Libra? *Is it impossible to fight for peace?* What about the "debility" of having Venus in Aries? *Is anger really the opposite of love – or actually part of it sometimes?*

(Newsletter – February 2021)
Let's take the "high jinx" out of planets in the signs of their falls – and understand how to work consciously with planets in the sign of their exaltations.

(Newsletter – March 2014)
Mars and Saturn are "bad enough," even without them "standing still in the sky" – or so goes the conventional lore. Let's turn that view on its head. Let's make these edgy worlds our friends, even when they are coming at us at a million watts.

(Newsletter – April 2021)
What seems like a picky technical issue might actually move your Moon half a degree away from where you think it is. Doesn't that sound as if it is worth more attention than it gets? It could throw off the timing of your solar arcs by six months.

(Newsletter – June 2021)
Venus picks and chooses people, which means it needs to know how to reject them too. If you want unconditional love, don't ask Venus. That's Neptune's territory.

(Newsletter – April 2013)
The rising sign represents "how you dawn on people" – and how you might find the pathway to your best life. Meet the ways and means of full self-actualization.

(Newsletter – October 2014)
Everyone knows that the planet that rules the Ascendant plays a big role in the chart – but exactly how and why? It may not really be the *strongest* planet you have . . .

SECTION FIVE: PERSONAL REFLECTIONS AND THE ASTROLOGICALLY EXAMINED LIFE

(Newsletter – November 2017)
Looking at a planet in the sky is different from looking at the
glyph of that same planet on a computer screen. Steven blows
the trumpet for what his friend, Jim Mullaney, calls "the photon
connection." That means actually spending some heads-up time
under the night sky.

(Newsletter – January 2019)
We start with some visual astronomy and quickly move into a
consideration of the "Saros cycle" of lunar eclipses and what it
might possibly mean for evolutionary astrology.

(Newsletter – June 2016)
Serious astronomers have offered us ambiguous, controversial,
totally fascinating evidence that a truly huge planet might be
lurking undiscovered out on the far, dark edges of our solar system.
If it's actually there, it will stand astrology on its head. If not . . .
well, never mind.

**SECTION NINE: THE DHARMA OF ASTROLOGICAL
COUNSELING**

(Newsletter – February 2019)
There are many planets, but you have only one head between your
ears. Tying everything together is where astrology goes beyond
memorized key words and becomes a true art. Here are some tips
for how to actually do that.

(Newsletter – October 2021)
People turn to astrologers and psychotherapists when they are
hurting. Many find help. The parallels are obvious – but let's not
underestimate the "perpendiculars" between the two fields. They are
profoundly different, even in the ethics to which they must adhere.

SECTION TEN: EULOGIES

(Newsletter – August 2019)
The beloved founder and editor of the *The Mountain Astrologer*
magazine passed away seemingly long before his time. Here is
Steven's tribute to him.

(Newsletter – May 2021)
They say that when the disciple is ready, the master appears. Steven
says goodbye to his mentor, Jungian writer, Robert A. Johnson.

Steven describes a little personal miracle that opens the door to our
appreciating the huge miracle of synchronicity – the miracle upon
which astrology itself rests.

I gratefully dedicate this book to the students and staff of the Forrest Center for Evolutionary Astrology, and especially to my partners in creating it, Catie Cadge and Jeff Parrett. Together, we will keep this sacred flame burning.

INTRODUCTION

I fancy myself poking around your house and finding this book lying on your bedside table or by your favorite living room chair, perhaps with another book on top of it – the message, in other words, is that sometimes you pick it up and read a few pages at random, while other times weeks pass and you don't give *The Endless Sky* any thought at all.

I picture this book like an astrology friend – someone you met at a class or a conference a year or two ago. Maybe you get together for coffee every few months. Maybe it's mostly about looking at charts and talking about your current transits. You're friends, sincerely enough – but you don't always know exactly what the other one had for dinner last night.

No need to start reading on page one either – just have a look at the table of contents and see what grabs you. I've loaded the material into loosely-defined sections – natal charts, astrological counseling, and so forth – but basically it's all rather random, like a good conversation: you never know exactly where it is going to lead.

There is no pretense of completeness here – for example, you'll learn about Jupiter's transits through Scorpio, but not a peep about its transits through Aries or Taurus. For a more complete soup-to-nuts overview of astrological theory, I would aim you at my four Elements books. There my penchant to start with A and get to Z via a straight and narrow path is in full cry. Not here, not in these pages. This is a mash-up. This is pasta thrown at the wall. This is one of those paintings where you're not sure whether it's worth a million bucks or some kid in kindergarten made it.

You may experience *deja vu* as you read too. Fear not – it's not a prior life that's come back to haunt you. You may very well have read some of this material before over the past twenty years or so. Most of these essays are the monthly newsletters I've been publishing on my website for a couple of decades. A few are articles I've written for other journals. Little is here that has not been seen before somewhere, at least by some of you. It just felt like time to bind it all under one cover for the sake of convenience and easy access. Inevitably reviewing the material meant rewriting and polishing too – nothing is exactly as it was first presented. The grammar is improved, and in many places the thinking is a little deeper.

My books are always full of loose ends and unanswered questions – subjects of real importance that somehow never found a place in those pages, or subjects that were just too weird to fit anywhere. Many such themes are covered here. I focussed special attention on areas that have often been presented in the astrological literature in fearful or shaming ways. What if your poor Venus is "in detriment" in Aries? Are you doomed to endless intimate conflict? What if your beleaguered Mars is in its "fall" in Cancer? Will you always be a wimp unable to stand up for yourself or set any boundaries? What if several planets in your natal chart are retrograde? Are you condemned to discover your shirts are inside-out for the rest of your mortal existence? And – horror – what if you mistakenly put your rent check in the mail even though Mercury was retrograde? Would it have been safer to be two weeks late on paying your rent?

You get the picture. I am writing playfully here, but people have actually been hurt by gloomy, authoritative astrological pronouncements in all of these categories. In the pages that follow, I don't pull my punches about the dark side of things, but you can also read about every one of them in a more uplifting way – and, I promise, in a demonstrably more accurate way too. Everything in astrology has a higher purpose, and, with effort, there is always a way to get there.

With Uranus transiting over the midheaven of his chart, Jim Morrison of The Doors hit a massive, unexpected career peak – *a decade after he had died*. He was gone, but his chart was still working. Ditto for Vincent Van Gogh. The more I think about that, the more absolutely mind-boggling it seems. I'm not sure what to make of it – but it was fun to write about. My monthly newsletter gave me a forum for doing it. You can read about Jim Morrison and Vincent Van Gogh here. It's chapter eleven – and an example of one of those subjects that was just too weird to fit anywhere else.

As you wander through these pages, you'll find yourself reading yesterday's news fairly often. Who cares today about the Uranus–Pluto square of 2012-2015? Who cares about Saturn entering Scorpio back in 2012? What about the total solar eclipse that swept across the United States in the summer of 2017? Anybody want to rehash it?

Fair enough – no need to read those pieces if they don't attract you. But in each one of them, there is still much to learn about how the basic archetypes work and how to think like an evolutionary astrologer. Similarly, Jupiter's past transits through various signs is a subject that takes up quite a few pages. At least with Jupiter's relatively short twelve-year orbit, those transits will be back soon enough.

Bottom line, I only included "past tense" essays here when I felt that they still packed present-tense relevance.

As you read, you will see that while I try to keep the "me, me, me" stuff to a minimum, it definitely plays a part in some of what follows. The last few years have been pivotal ones for me, and to some extent my monthly newsletter has been a bit of a personal blog. I was already reducing my travelling time drastically in order to free up the time I needed to write my four Elements books, along with starting the online Forrest Center for Evolutionary Astrology – two hundred instructional videos later, that school is up and running.

When Covid-19 hit, it basically punched Warp Drive on those changes in my life. I stopped seeing clients in person, which gave me the gift of a lot more unstructured time for these other projects.

Naturally there were astrological correlates for all of those personal events, not to mention for Covid-19. I write about them here, basically trying to walk my own talk as an evolutionary astrologer, letting the planets be my counsellors. Over the years, I have realized that trusting the benevolent guidance of the universe tends to work out more copacetically for me than does offering my ego the steering wheel.

For all of us, our own lives are the ultimate astrological laboratory. That's as true for me as it is for you.

Thank you for reading *The Endless Sky* and for giving me the life you have given me. May the blessings of old Cosmo land gently upon you. I hope you find some smiles and maybe some fresh insights in the pages ahead.

SECTION ONE

THE PLANETS AT BIRTH

The magic we astrologers do . . . even after all these years, it still sometimes just stops me dead in my tracks. We gaze at a map of the sky as it appeared at the moment of someone's birth and from it we divine intimate details, offer illuminating insights, even predict the timing and probable nature of the dramas life will offer down the road. If they are to marry, we can describe their partner — someone who might not yet even have been born. The whole idea seems completely implausible. But it works — and that means that our fundamental "common sense" version of reality is itself implausible. I delight in this radically subversive dimension of our craft — the dominant paradigm doesn't stand a chance against it.

In the following section, I reflect on various specific issues around the way we read the message of the planets themselves in the natal chart — with one addition: there is also a little essay about the deeper nature of the astrological Ascendant. That's not a planet exactly, but it works similarly. Underlying everything you are about to read is a plea to make the astrological symbols into active "verbs" rather than passive "nouns and adjectives." Life is all about change and growth. It has never been my ambition to package anyone in an astrological "personality profile" — to me, that represents an antediluvian system of astrology which reflects the stasis of death rather than the wild, creative unpredictability of life.

1

I open this volume with a toot on my favorite horn: my faith in the sacred idea that planets have virtually no meaning at all unless you place them between somebody's ears. There, they interact, often in unexpected ways, with human imagination and human nobility of spirit, along with human folly, rage, delusion, and selfishness. Naturally, an astrologer can be expected to "define the meaning of a particular planet." Still, he or she must constantly strive to leave some breathing room for human nature and human freedom in those definitions.

WHAT DOES A PLANET MEAN?

(Newsletter – September 2020)

Here's how I am tempted to answer that seemingly legitimate question: *very, very little.* Alone, a planet is really just an abstraction. What does love mean? What does honor mean? Those are similar questions. They are basically meaningless unless you put them in a human context. Mercury, for one quick example, is related to our *curiosity* – and some degree of curiosity exists in more or less everyone. But obviously there are people who are driven by curiosity and people who barely feel it at all. Mercury, in other words, may be strong in one person's chart, and not so centrally placed in another person's chart.

More to the point, what exactly are you curious *about?* Show me an article about human migration patterns as reflected in ancestral genetics or one about 19th century sailing vessels, and I will devour it. Seeing those same articles, you might skip to a piece about how to improve your golf swing – meanwhile I would have to be paid handsomely to even read the first paragraph of that one.

Curiosity is clearly not a question of right or wrong. It's more like different tastes for different people.

We all have Mercury in our charts, and we can make a few general statements about its archetypal nature. But what does Mercury actually mean for an individual? Who knows? . . . or rather, who knows – *unless we give that Mercury a set of distinct motivations and interests by placing it in a specific sign.*

After that, we might give it an *area of characteristic behavior by putting it in a house.*

Then we could further wire it into the larger framework of the birth-chart by studying the aspects that it makes.

A planet in a specific sign and a specific house: for actual human beings, that is the ultimate indivisible *quantum unit of astrological meaning.* A planet alone is only a broad idea, about as "human" as a lecture on taxation algorithms.

- Even once we have a planet planted in such a symbolic triad, there is still much that we cannot know about it. *That is because the consciousness of the individual interacts decisively with the wide field of archetypal possibilities represented by that planet-sign-house combination.*

That last idea is the drum I have been beating all through my astrological career – a drum whose rhythm boils down in many ways to a battle against the astrological determinists. I love astrology, but I really like to keep it in its place – and its location in the food chain of power is always a little bit below that of consciousness itself. My blood pressure goes up when I read some astrologer condemning a configuration as "inherently criminal" or even as "lucky." Astrology is never that rigid. Some idiot on the Internet the other day dismissed my personal tendency toward progressive politics as evidence of my ditzy Sun-Neptune square. Give me a break. Sarah Palin has a Sun-Neptune square. So did Geroge W. Bush.

Astrology is powerful and it always leaves its mark, but it does not run our lives. Instead, we run our own lives in a kind of creative partnership with the planets.

I finally got my box of copies of *The Book of Air*. The shipment had been delayed by the pandemic. Thumbing randomly through the pages, I came upon the opening of chapter seven. I realized it pretty well summarized everything I believe about astrology, and it did that in about a thousand words, using three concrete examples. I'm going to include it here. Before you read, let me spotlight the two main take-away points:

- First, that the planet Uranus – and really *any* planet – has very little meaning in and of itself. It really needs to be placed in an astrological context before it lights up in any truly human way.

- Secondly, as you will see, the wild card of *consciousness* interacts decisively with the planet-sign-house triad. You can build a house with a hammer, or you can bash your thumb with it. Planets work the same way.

Here are the first few paragraphs of chapter seven of *The Book of Air*, "Synthesis I: Putting an Air Planet in a Sign."

We might offer an authoritative, helpful talk at an astrological conference about the significance of the planet Uranus. *But the actual meaning of that planet for individuals is potentially so variable that claiming we know anything at all about it puts us on shaky ground.* The supernaturally brilliant actor, Meryl Streep, for one example, is about as "Uranian" as a person can possibly be – she has the planet only one minute of arc from a perfect conjunction with her natal Sun. But both bodies lie in Cancer, aligned with her twelfth house cusp, underscoring a far more subtle, internalized expression of that normally rather zany planet.

Who is Meryl Streep as a person? I have no idea – and if I were to have dinner with her, I would be "surprised if I weren't surprised" by her. With that twelfth house Sun, ego in the conventional sense simply never fully formed in her. At the risk of a slight over-statement, *Meryl Streep can be anybody she wants to be.* One sees that quality expressed so clearly in her astonishingly fluid acting. Again, ego simply does not automatically define her behavior the same way it does in most of us. That's her twelfth house energy in action.

Add Uranus to the twelfth house, and you thus have a formula that marries two words: *actor* and *genius*.

Add the more retiring energies of Cancer to the mix, and another thing we learn is that she is probably *not all that eager to meet me for dinner.*

After all, I am a total stranger.

Another widely recognized genius – Walt Disney – had a Sun-Uranus conjunction too, but his conjunction fell in groundbreaking, colorful Sagittarius and in the media-oriented third house. Not to rob Walt Disney of his human complexity, but I think it is fair to say that meeting him would be far less of a "discovery mission" than meeting Meryl Streep. Those Sagittarian and third house energies are more straightforward and upfront. Walt Disney would be more like a friendly dog than Meryl's cautious Cancer cat.

This all brings us back to our initial question: *what exactly does Uranus mean?*

Walt and Meryl, taken together, should help us answer that question. After all, they are both highly Uranian. *But they are utterly different human beings.* If Uranus is supposed to correlate with certain specific personality traits, we are standing on shaky ground.

Both of them are widely recognized as *geniuses* – perhaps that's the jackpot. And genius and Uranus are indeed paired in astrological theory.

But here's another Sun-Uranus conjunction for you: Peter Sutcliffe, the infamous Yorkshire Ripper, who murdered at least thirteen women. A genius? There is no way to make that case without bending over backwards. He was a *pathological criminal*, clearly – and "criminal" is another classic Uranian word. With a bow toward modern psychological perspectives, we might add that he was *alienated* and very probably suffering from some kind of *dissociative disorder* – and that too is Uranian language.

Sutcliffe's Sun-Uranus conjunction was in Gemini and in his seventh house. Forgetting his actual story and just reading the symbolism from an evolutionary perspective, we can say that his soul was seeking a *diversity of experiences* (Gemini) in the *relationship category* (seventh house) and that these experiences had to unfold *outside the context of consensual, conventional, socially-approved reality* (Uranus).

Sometimes I get chills writing this stuff.

My point in comparing the very Uranian charts of Meryl Syreep, Walt Disney, and the Yorkshire Ripper is that *claiming that we know very much at all about Uranus seems to verge on pure hubris.* Its meaning is demonstrably quite fluid.

This is one of the reasons, by the way, that a scientifically-convincing "proof of astrology" has been elusive: our variables are simply "too variable." Pinning anything down in a satisfyingly "this means that" kind of way has proven nearly impossible.

Here is the heart of the matter – or really, the twin hearts of the matter.

- The actual meaning of any planet is enormously impacted by the sign and house it occupies, as well as by the larger astrological context in which it finds itself.

- An individual's *level of response* to a planet – the reality of human freedom, in a nutshell – is also pivotal. And that level of response is unpredictable via any internal astrological measurement. You cannot see how a person will use his or her freedom anywhere in the chart itself.

Put Uranus on the Sun in Cancer and the twelfth house, and you get Meryl Streep – or perhaps you might get a *maudlin whiner* with a string of arrests for Driving Under the Influence.

There but for grace goes Meryl . . .

Put Uranus on the Sun in Sagittarius in the third house, and you get Walt Disney – or a *contrarian blowhard* with a windy, self-righteous argument belittling anything you happen to say.

There but for grace goes Walt . . .

Put Uranus on the Sun in Gemini and the seventh house, and you get the Yorkshire Ripper – or a *fascinating, funny lover,* who is an excellent listener and who has boldly made a faithful commitment to someone "born on the wrong side of the tracks."

Uranus, in other words, is only an abstraction. It is these *triads* of planet, sign, and house, flavored by an array of aspects, that are actually the fundamental *quantum units* of astrological reality. That is how we experience the *human* face of the planets.

It is those triads that we must learn to understand if we are to give – or receive – helpful astrological counsel.

And even with exactly the same planet at the center, these triads differ from each other profoundly.

2

Most of us who practice our craft spend a lot of time cleaning up after fear-mongering astrologers. They come in many flavors, but they all share one characteristic delusion: a fervent belief in the existence of "bad" astrological configurations – chart structures which allegedly put an inescapable jinx on anyone unfortunate enough to be born with them. Throughout the years, I've used the bully pulpit of my monthly newsletters to try to counter that kind of dead-end, depressing – and ultimately incorrect – thinking. Here, in this little essay, I address the dark spin such astrologers have often placed on having intercepted signs in the birthchart.

INTERCEPTED SIGNS

(Newsletter – November 2019)

When a sign is completely swallowed up by a house – never touching a house cusp, in other words – it is said to be *intercepted*. I get a lot of questions about that astrological situation so I thought it would be a good topic for a newsletter.

Let me start by saying that in some systems of house division, interception is just not possible. Many astrologers nowadays are drawn to the old ways, using traditional "whole sign houses." No interceptions are possible there since if you have Gemini rising, everything in Gemini is treated as being "in the first house." Houses and signs are conflated in that system, so interception is simply not relevant.

Similarly, in the Equal house system, all houses are thirty degrees wide. The math precludes interception since no house is wide enough to completely swallow a sign.

In all the other systems of house division, the houses vary in width. All circles are of course composed of 360°, so if one house is only 25° wide, another house is always going to have take up the slack. As people's places of birth get further away from the Equator, those differences in house width become more extreme. By the way, that phenomenon is easy to understand if you just reflect for a moment upon "the midnight sun" that happens in midsummer in the arctic or antarctic regions, The Ascendant – also known as the cusp of the first house – is where the sun rises. So what if it never rises? What if it is visible in the sky all "day" long? There is then no Ascendant as we would traditionally understand it. The result is that houses disappear.

Inuit people in the far north who are born in June have birthcharts, of course. There is a mystery here, and I suspect that a close study of our very northern cousins would crack it – and maybe lead to that Holy Grail of astrological theory: a house system which works universally. Until then, we have the Tower of Babel, and perhaps the most serious loose end in modern astrological practice.

By the way, if the sign Taurus is intercepted, so will Scorpio. *Opposite houses are always symmetrical.* No one can have only one intercepted sign. If you have one, you will have two.

I use the Placidus house system myself. I insist on it when I am teaching my serious students, although I know some of them secretly switch everything to Koch or Porphyry when I am not looking. The reason I insist on Placidus in my classes is simple: we all have to speak the same language or confusion reigns. In reality I am not actually so dogmatic. I know and respect many astrologers who use different house systems. I'd never say that "Placidus is the right system" and all the others are wrong. I would only say that Placidus is the one that has always worked most consistently for me. Bottom line, it is the one that explains my own life to me most honestly and clearly, and for all of us, looking into that personal mirror is the acid test.

Whatever house system you choose to use, unless it is Whole sign or Equal, you will soon hit upon the phenomenon of interception: a sign is swallowed up completely by a house; none of its degrees appear on any house cusps.

How can we understand this? When I was a young astrologer, I heard that in such a situation, we would "have a hard time expressing the energy of that intercepted sign."

It wasn't a good thing, in other words.

I don't like that attitude toward interception, and I'll get back to that quibble soon. Right now, I want to use the idea of our "having a hard time" expressing that energy as a jumping off point. There is some truth in the notion; it's just that the wording is loaded with inappropriate and unnecessary negativity. What is fundamentally *right* about saying that intercepted signs have trouble expressing themselves is that *all houses are indeed about some kind of active expression.* They are *behavioral,* in other words – they are about *taking action* in the world.

Another way to say it is that houses are about the sorts of brutally one-dimensional decisions which actually give shape to our lives.

Take the seventh house, the traditional "house of marriage," as an example. To how many people can you be married simultaneously? For most of us, the answer is pretty obvious. Now ask yourself a second question: *how many people have you met with whom, if the stars of circumstance had aligned differently, you might have spent your life?*

But along came the seventh house, saying, "Choose one – and forsake all others."

Ouch – but that's life.

Similarly, at how many careers can you achieve excellence simultaneously? Down that scattered road, at some point you've diluted your energy so much that you become the proverbial "jack of all trades, master of none."

There's the tenth house and the midheaven. Hard choices again. Making our stand in the world. Saying "this, but not that."

All houses are that way; all of them ask us to *choose one possibility out of many and then act on it.* All of them reflect the undeniable fact that life is short. All of them, in the modern phrase, offer you a chance to "live your best life" – and no one in the history of the world has ever accomplished anything even close to "living their best life" by keeping all of his or her options open.

In the words of the song, freedom's just another word for nothing left to lose.

Astrologers who say that intercepted signs "have a hard time expressing themselves" are right about one thing: if house cusps are points of behavioral expression, then a sign that has no connection with a house cusp is indeed a lot less likely to have visible expression in one's life.

There's one glaring exception to that notion, but we will get to that in a moment. First, there is something much more fundamental that needs to be said:

Your chart is perfect.

You yourself probably aren't perfect. Me either. But your chart itself *perfectly reflects your karmic predicament and your optimal path forward from that starting point.* Again, your chart is perfect; your personal imperfections can be best understood as your imperfect response to the challenges and evolutionary opportunities your chart represents. The chart models "your best life." That is the gold standard – and like most gold standards, we can only approach it, never fully achieve it.

To me, all healthy approaches to astrology begin at this same philosophical starting line: there is nothing wrong with anyone's chart, ever. *If you have intercepted signs, then you need them.* Try to understand and appreciate why you have them and in so doing you are aligning yourself with your soul's purpose.

Wish for anything else, and you are a race horse wishing for lead hooves or a painter wishing for blindness.

Intercepted signs "have a hard time expressing themselves" – it is impossible to hear those words and avoid the subliminal message that you would have been better off if neither of those signs were intercepted.

Try turning the idea on its head: if you have intercepted signs in your chart, here's *why* you need to have them. *Any actual behavioral expression of that energy – and the subsequent entanglement of your life in its results – would interfere with your optimal path of evolution in this lifetime.*

There are two major technical caveats in this way of thinking about interception. If we don't grasp them, all that I have said so far will only confuse and mislead you.

First, we are talking about the *biographical expression* of that energy, not the more general *psychic experience* of it. There is a big difference between the two. One of the great strengths of astrology is how it holds a mirror before our inner lives as well as our outer ones. A person might, for example, have Gemini intercepted. Everything else being equal, I might point out to that person that we learn a lot more with our mouths closed than with them open. Deep Geminian *reflection* and *insight* are quite available here – but getting caught up in the role of "expert" or a "talking head" might be counterproductive, at least from the evolutionary point of view.

A second caveat is also critical. There is one simple astrological reality which overrides almost everything that I have been saying about intercepted signs. That is *having planets* in the intercepted sign. Planets are *always behaviorally active*, at least to some degree. Planets represent energy, and in physics, they say that "energy is the capacity to do work." Planets always "work" in some sense of the word. *They are inherently self-expressive.* Some – such as Neptune in the 12th house – might have a very subtle, internal orientation. Like the famous iceberg, 90% of what such quiet planets represent is invisible in one's outer life. But 10% is visibly expressed – and needs to be. For example, with any strong response to Neptune in the 12th house, there will be something that resembles meditation in the behavioral repertoire. The specific *behaviors and experiences* which we associate with a spiritual life are critical triggers to such a person's evolution.

Bottom line, if a sign is intercepted in your chart, it is supposed to be intercepted. Don't frame it as a problem, frame it as your path. It may very well be a big part of your inner life, but in living "your best life," you do not let yourself get too enmeshed in its outward expression. Life is too short for those kinds of entanglements. Practice non-attachment there as best you can.

All that is true unless you have planets in that sign. Planets need worldly experience. We have to honor that fact.

Beyond that point, there is good news and bad news about those intercepted *planets* – planets, not just empty intercepted signs. The bad news is that they may indeed have a tougher time finding meaningful behavioral expression in the world. The good news is that, when they do find it, it comes from a very deep, creative, individuated space inside of you. Their expression is worth waiting for, in other words. Their "births" might be hard – but the baby is likely to be a genius.

3

*Language can be such a minefield. One technical astrologer might
mention to another that "Jupiter is in detriment in Virgo," and the
communication between them can be clear and straightforward. But if I
know nothing about astrology and it is my Jupiter about which they are
talking, hearing the word "detriment" is a bit like hearing your doctor
saying "uh oh" after putting the stethoscope on your chest . . .*

PLANETS IN DETRIMENT

(Newsletter – April 2015)

Personally, I love planets in so-called "detriment." Take Mars, for example. It's not normally viewed as the most cooperative of planets, but just look how nicely Mars is treating me right now. Right on schedule for this April newsletter, on March 31, it leaves Aries and enters Taurus – one of the signs of its alleged detriment – where it will remain until May 11. How convenient! This gives me a chance to write about one of my favorite topics, which is underscoring how unintentionally poisonous to our clients some of our conventional astrological language can be. One out of every twelve of us is born with Mars in Taurus. *How does such a person feel when he or she hears the word, "detriment?"*

Ditto of course for anyone born with Mars in Libra – that is its other sign of alleged "debility," and we encounter another bit of toxic language.

Words such as those can't possibly be good news, can they? Inevitably, this kind of language conveys the notion of a weakness or a flawed condition – some misfortune that is hardwired into one's chart. Talk like that disempowers people. It helps no one. And, to me, thinking darkly about certain planet-and-sign combinations like that simply represents rotten astrological theory.

So what does "detriment" actually signify? In principle, planets always have special affinities with certain signs. We say they "rule" those signs, but what is really going on is only that they simply *like* those signs and feel natural there. Mars, the "god of war," is at ease with the passion and intensity of both Aries and Scorpio. It feels less at ease with the more mellow values of Libra and Taurus. Fair enough – we just have to look a little deeper.

Maybe you are a party animal – loud, exuberant, and direct by nature, with an over-the-top tendency to be theatrical and maybe even risque. *When you are with a crowd of people similar to yourself, you can relax.* Nobody has a problem with you. They like you. They appreciate your spirit. They egg you on. They think that you are fun to be with. As a result, you feel spontaneous and at ease.

That's "rulership." That's the way it feels.

But what if that party animal finds himself spending an evening with a bunch of serious tea-totaling academic introverts? Few smiles, no jokes, and long sober speeches? Our fun-loving hero makes a wisecrack and all he gets in return are uncomprehending looks.

How does he feel now? That's "detriment." Whether you are a planet and or a party animal, you feel as if you are at the wrong party.

Time for a short sermon: *God made all the party animals and God made all the tea-totaling academic introverts.* It's not a question of good or bad. It is only a question of one's nature and its relationship to the social environment. For all of us, some of those environments feel more natural to us than others. It is true of us and it is true of planets too.

Here's where we take the giant step toward really understanding so-called detriment – and thus incidentally our current transit of Mars through Taurus. We have to free ourselves from the conventional style of astrology which has us "blessing this configuration, while cursing that one." Here is how we can do that: inside that party animal there may be a more serious person trying to get out. Inside that tea-totaler, there might be a need to let go and experience some spontaneity and pagan release. The party animal, in other words, *might benefit and grow* from adjusting to the "unnatural" environment created by those more conservative souls. Ditto for the introverted academic, who can perhaps breathe easier once he or she adjusts to a wilder crowd, granting them their humanity.

Each of them is offered the chance to get over himself or herself. Each will be afforded a chance to stretch, to withdraw any negative projections, and to explore new, alien inner possibilities.

That's good, but there's more to it.

Put that party animal at a party full of other party animals, and what happens? Maybe everyone simply has a good time. There's nothing wrong with that. But maybe everyone wakes up with a head-bursting hangover. Maybe people sleep with people they shouldn't have. Maybe a fight breaks out.

Being a party animal is fine, but sometimes a little taste of "allopathic medicine" – an experience of an opposite, and thus *corrective*, environment – can be healing and balancing.

Similarly, those tea-totaling academic introverts can metamorphose into dried-out human prunes unless they get their bodies and their hearts into their lives. To do that, they may need some help from the party-animals.

We don't always like the things that are good for us – that goes not only for people, but for planets too.

- Planets in their own signs – the signs they rule – can become *parodies of themselves*, lacking all perspective, not "getting their own joke," and displaying intolerance and cluelessness when faced with any energy that is different from their own. They are the *natural fanatics* of the world.
- In parallel fashion, planets in "detriment" can embody a *subtlety, tolerance, and wisdom* not often found in the simpler structures of rulership.

My aim here is not to ridicule planets in their rulerships, but only to try to apply some of that "corrective medicine" to the misunderstandings and damage done by words such as "detriment."

In the light of all that, let's look specifically at Mars in Taurus. We will all have front row seats for the show this month and on into mid-May. And the stage is located right between your two ears.

Taurus embodies a kind of earthy, "chicken soup" wisdom. Its symbol is of course the Bull – but the custom of bullfighting has really fouled us all up in thinking about Taurus. We've come to think of a bull as a fire-breathing carnivore, hell-bent on goring anyone in sight. I guess we'd all look that way if someone were sticking lances in us. In thinking about Taurus, it is very helpful to remember that the bull is a *male cow*. And what do you see when you look into the eyes of a cow? There's a kind of calm, earthy intelligence in there, with no overlay of fussy cognition. That's pure Taurus – it represents the *inner animal*: our instinctual side. It symbolizes the sorts of things that we "just know in our bones." We meet some people and they just "smell right" to us, while others don't – Taurus is the astrological name for the perceptual faculty in you that makes that discerning recognition. Taurus is also the part of us all that appreciates peace, good food, familiar faces and familiar places. It is not attracted to fuss or *fru-fru*. It is not interested in your "transformative weekend workshop" about electro-convulsive, cranial-skeletal, deep-dish, locally-grown, chemotherapeutic release-point water-therapy.

Taurus prefers a hug.

Simple answers are not always the right ones, of course. But sometimes they are. *Taurus is the part of us all that is wise enough to know when to be simple.* Are you hungry? *Eat something.* Tired? *Lie down for a while.* Don't like the book? *Close it, you don't have to read it.* Angry? *Get over it.* Feeling poor? *Earn more, spend less, or get used to it.* Want to lose weight? *Eat less.*

You get the idea.

Mars, on the other hand, isn't like any of that! It's not about relaxation or ease at all. There is no calm in it. Mars is competitive. Mars thinks in terms of winning and losing. It gets bored very easily. It perceives *enemies* and *threats* and prepares to deal with them – maybe by fighting, maybe by fleeing, but always responding in a combative *win/lose* fashion.

Despite this scrappy language, there's nothing inherently wrong with having Mars in your chart. Life is indeed competitive sometimes. We've all been attacked. We've all had enemies. We've all been in situations where we needed to defend ourselves or those we love. The trouble with Mars is that it can *so easily read irresolvable combat into situations where peace might be available* through compromise and dialog – or simply by realizing that the stakes are low enough that simply walking away is the biggest victory available.

See how much good the wise simplicity of Taurus can do for fiery Mars? See how healing balance can potentially arise?

- Can't we astrologers think of a better word than "detriment" to describe this helpful tension-of-opposites?

Obviously the world as a whole could use some calming down, forgiveness, and letting go right now – that's the global significance of this Mars transit. But in evolutionary astrology as I practice it, the focus is generally more on the *individual* soul-journey. That's what I am exploring here with you. As ever, much depends on the exact nature of your own chart. Through what house is Mars-in-Taurus passing? What aspects is it making? More deeply, *what are your own issues around Mars* – which is to say, what are your issues around anger, passion, and conflict? What are your resentments?

In thinking about all of that, it is helpful to add one ore item to the list by remembering Sigmund Freud's wise words – d*epression is anger internalized.* Astrologers don't talk about it enough, but that self-destructive state can embody the dark face of Mars too.

What I write here is necessarily of a general nature. The beauty and power of astrology lies in its ability to bring these energies into sharp individual focus through an in-depth consideration of the personal birthchart. Still, between now and mid-May, try looking at your life through these lenses and filters:

- Where am I creating unnecessary drama in my head or in my relationships?
- What battles can I win by walking away?
- What will this conflict look like ten years down the road?
- What does my face in the mirror tell me when I dwell on this resentment?
- Is winning really worth more to me than peace?
- How am I perpetuating pointless conflict? What is my part in that?
- What is my body telling me here?
- Are pride and ego masquerading as an angry god exhorting me to wage *jihad?*
- Where am I trying to teach a pig to sing and *why am I mad at the pig?*

4

Rulership and so-called detriment were the subject of the previous essay. Here I take on their lesser-known cousins – planetary exaltations and falls. The ideas are distinct from rulership and detriment, even though the two are often confused. One point of authentic overlap between them is the sad tendency to view exaltation as good luck and fall as a reason for misery. At first, you'll probably think this essay is a rewrite of the previous one – stick with it for two paragraphs.

PLANETARY EXALTATIONS; PLANETARY FALLS

(Newsletter – February 2021)

Everyone with an interest in astrology soon learns about how particular planets *rule* certain signs. To many astrologers, that makes them automatically "good." To those same astrologers, for a planet to find itself in the *opposite* sign is unfortunate. The term they use there is "detriment" – obviously, not such a good thing. This common notion is simply incorrect, in my experience. The error is easily proven too.

- The infamous Yorkshire Ripper had a really "good" Mercury – in Gemini, conjunct his Gemini Sun. I suspect he excelled at talking his victims into vulnerable positions.

- Meanwhile, Rev. Martin Luther King had a "bad" Neptune – in Virgo, the sign opposite Pisces, the sign it naturally rules. Did that mean he had no spiritual life or that he lacked a visionary imagination?

Instead of calling it "good" when a planet finds itself in the sign it rules, I find it is both equally simple and vastly more accurate to call it *strong*.

But is strong the same as good?

When a planet is in the sign it rules, *they agree with each other.* There is no friction. Their energy flows like a geyser, no questions asked. Conversely, when a planet is in the opposite sign (in detriment), it must deal with *complexity and paradox* – and that is not necessarily such a bad thing.

- *Can we fight for peace?* Ask Mars in Libra.
- *Can questioning, doubting, and correcting ourselves be a path to greatness?* Ask Jupiter in Virgo.
- What about *questioning our own beliefs from time to time?* Any benefits there? Ask Mercury in Sagittarius.

In this newsletter, I want to tackle a subject very similar to rulership and detriment, albeit one that is not as widely known: the notion of planetary *exaltation* and planetary *fall.* It is not quite the same as rulership and detriment, but there are many parallels – including the widespread, unhelpful notion that exaltation is good news and that a planet occupying the sign of its fall automatically spells bad news.

As we just saw, when a planet is in the sign it rules, there is a very straightforward *agreement* between the two energies – Jupiter says "I feel lucky" and Sagittarius chimes in – "You're right! I bet there are no bears in that cave."

With exaltation, the situation is a bit more subtle. In essence, the sign has the effect of *underscoring some specific potential strength in the planet* – or similarly, of *correcting one of its blind spots.* The planet is therefore uplifted – "exalted," if you will.

Before I dive into all of that more deeply, here are the traditional exaltations and falls:

- The Sun is exalted in Aries – and has its fall in Libra
- The Moon is exalted in Taurus – and has its fall in Scorpio

- Mercury is exalted in Virgo – and has its fall in Pisces (Note: this is the same as its rulership/detriment)
- Venus is exalted in Pisces – and has its fall in Virgo
- Mars is exalted in Capricorn – and has its fall in Cancer
- Jupiter is exalted in Cancer – and has its fall in Capricorn
- Saturn is exalted in Libra – and has its fall in Aries

Technically, there are often *specific degrees* given within each of these signs for exaltation and fall – for example, the Sun is said to be exalted (or *particularly* exalted) in the 19th degree of Aries. Make of that what you will. Those traditions go back to the sidereal astrology of the ancient Babylonians, where certain stars were imbued with sweet or sour symbolism. Often in practice, at least in my experience, it is simply the sign position that counts, not the specific degrees.

These are archaic ideas, and I am happy to leave the technical arguments to the traditional astrologers and astrological historians.

Speaking of which, because the roots of exaltation and fall are so old, there is inevitably controversy among the traditionalists over what to do with planets discovered in more recent times – Uranus, Neptune, and Pluto. Some say they are simply *never exalted,* nor are they ever *sign rulers.* Others give Uranus to Scorpio, Neptune to Aquarius – and, from what I have read, they seem to want to let Aquarius, Pisces, Leo, and Virgo fight it out over Pluto.

In this newsletter, I am going to stick to thinking about the traditional planets. Also, just to be clear, my aim is not to squabble with scholars of astrological history, but rather to attempt to modernize our understanding of exaltation and fall, and to place them in an evolutionary context.

- Again, our key concept is that with exaltation, the sign has the effect of *underscoring some specific potential strength in the planet* – or similarly, of *correcting one of its blind spots.*
- Meanwhile, when a planet is in its fall, it is invited to become more conscious and mindful *relative to one of its main potential weaknesses,* and therefore wiser.

Let's go through the classical planets one by one, and contemplate them through this more modern, evolutionary lens.

THE SUN – EXALTED IN ARIES; FALL IN LIBRA

Everything revolves around the Sun – and sometimes you have a right to expect that everything will revolve around *you* too. "Sometimes" is the key word there! But you do have a natural right sometimes to *insist*. You do have a right to *say no*. You have a right to take up some space and to claim some resources. Sun is basically "ego" – and ego, while it presents obvious dangers, is as necessary to your spiritual well being as your lungs are to your physical wellbeing. We all have to *stand up for ourselves* from time to time. *The basic assertiveness of Aries enhances and supports these qualities in the Sun,* while the *empathetic willingness of Libra to prioritize keeping other people happy* can get in the way of doing that. Meanwhile, a little Libran aware-ness of other people's needs and natures can temper the potential for mere egoism that is inherent in the Sun – there's the brighter side of the Sun's so-called "fall" in Libra.

THE MOON – EXALTED IN TAURUS; FALL IN SCORPIO

We normally relate the Moon astrologically to our emotional lives. That's true, but the Moon is also deeply conditioned by our *instincts*. Taurus, meanwhile, of all the signs is the one that lies closest to our "animal na-tures" – the instinctual part of us that *just knows things* without having to think about them too much. Sometimes, for example, "we just have a bad feeling about somebody." Most of us have learned that it is savvy to take such a feeling seriously. Taurus underscores a kind of *wise, reflexive simplic-ity* in the Moon, spontaneously bringing out the best of it, while avoiding Scorpio's tendency to *overthink* and *over-psychologize*. Meanwhile, Scor-pio's willingness to ask the hard questions can counter the lunar tendency to "keep getting on with the past." Maybe the reason you have a bad feel-ing about certain people has nothing to do with them at all. Maybe those people could actually be good for you – but they *remind you of your father,* with whom you have unresolved psychological issues. There's an example of Scorpionic psychology potentially correcting the Taurean need to keep things simple.

MERCURY– EXALTED IN VIRGO; FALL IN PISCES

The situation is messy with Mercury. Astrological tradition is adamant about Mercury being exalted in Virgo – and weirdly, Virgo is one of the signs it rules too. Some traditional astrologers have suggested that Mercury has no sign of exaltation at all. Growing up, I learned from the old British astrologer, "Sepharial," that Mercury was *exalted in Aquarius*. That actually makes more sense to me, but it does cut against the grain of tradition. Virgo brings out a quality of *disciplined precision* in Mercury, correcting its tendency toward scattering its focus. In 'fall," Pisces can indeed blur the Mercury-mind with fantasy and confusion – but it can also *inspire* it with insights that "come out of nowhere." All that is true – but all of it just sounds like rulership to me. Personally, I do prefer assigning Mercury's exaltation to Aquarius in that it "underscores a specific strength" in Mercury, which is its *ability to think for itself*. Another way to say the same thing is that Aquarius "corrects a Mercurial blind spot," which is to forever be "the good student," echoing what it has been taught to echo. Meanwhile, Leo likes the applause that often follows that "echo," and might prefer it over the lonely path of truth. More positively, Leo can add *self-expressive style* to Mercury which helps to get its voice actually *heard*.

VENUS – EXALTED IN PISCES; FALL IN VIRGO

Getting married a second time is often described as "the triumph of hope over experience." Cynics may chortle, but how would human love survive without hope – or *faith*, to use a similarly Piscean word? The romantic drives of Venus are supported by the sheer *soulfulness* of Pisces. Transrational Piscean faith in the idea that "that we were born to be together" has helped many a couple through hard times. Meanwhile, it is easy to see how Virgo's tendency toward *endless fault-finding* can erode Venusian love – hence the idea that Venus has its fall in Virgo. On the other hand, Virgo's *realism, humility*, and *sense of responsibility* can balance the Venusian tendency toward unreachable, unsustainable romanticism.

MARS – EXALTED IN CAPRICORN; FALL IN CANCER

The passionate, even belligerent, do-or-die intensity of Mars derives a lot of benefit from Capricorn's sense of long-term, eye-on-the-prize *strategic direction*. In this planetary exaltation, Capricorn is not so much the brakes on the Martial hotrod as its steering wheel or navigation system – thus correcting the potential Martial blindspot of *blind, passion-driven attack*. Cancer, on the other hand, is self-protective and gentle. Those are two qualities which can potentially stymie any possibility of bold, decisive action – and there's the fall of Mars in Cancer. But let's also remember that *Cancerian mercy* can correct the Martial potential for cruelty, adding a corrective dose of nobility to the "warrior." Going further, at a purely Mars level of warlike thinking, never forget that many battles have been won by a good, patient Cancerian *defence*. Victory is not always about offensive capabilities.

JUPITER – EXALTED IN CANCER; FALL IN CAPRICORN

Jupiter is the king of the gods and historically kings have come in a variety of flavors. We've had despots and tyrants galore, but we've also had good kings – monarchs whose reigns were characterized by generosity, justice, and caring attention toward those who were most vulnerable or disadvantaged. Reflecting on these simple observations, we can see how Jupiter's "drive to reach the top" can be *uplifted* by the nurturing, sensitive qualities of Cancer – and meanwhile how Capricorn's tendencies toward ambition, control, and mechanical efficiency can bring out the worst in the planet, leading it to "a fall." Still, if you want to reach the top in any area of human endeavour, some healthy Capricornian focus, realism and discipline can help to keep your plans grounded and your ambitions in the reachable realm. There's the grace in Jupiter's fall in Capricorn.

SATURN – EXALTED IN LIBRA; FALL IN ARIES

Perhaps above all, Saturn is about *good judgement*. It is the planet that helps us to navigate effectively through the labyrinthine complexities of the real world. Success there calls for reason and caution, along with a fair-minded sense that *every story has two sides*. Libra's *openness to life's ambiguities and paradoxes* helps here in obvious ways, assisting Saturn in being prepared for the unexpected. Going further, many of those "labyrinthine complexities" we face in life are in fact generated by our *interactions with other people* – and there is where Libran *diplomacy* and its ability to size other people up can really underscore Saturn's exaltation in this sign. Meanwhile, Arian "storm the gates" *injudiciousness* can lead Saturn to "a fall." On the positive side, with Saturn in Aries, sometimes to get anything done, you do just have to roll the dice and accept the fact that not everyone will be happy with you . . .

Those are my evolutionary takes on the exaltations and falls of the traditional planets. As you can see, we are miles from labeling anything astrological as inherently lucky or unlucky, but instead, as ever in evolutionary astrology, we are trying to *understand* the energies and determine how they might be employed as consciously as possible.

As usual, these interpretations are different from what one might read in Al Biruni, any of the traditional Jyotish texts, or on cuneiform tablets from Babylon. No apologies there. Test them in your own life, and see if they work for you. As ever, that personal examination, rather than looking for corroboration in historical treatises, is the proof of the pudding.

5

Continuing with our theme of "rehabilitating" some of astrology's allegedly "criminal elements," here we take on the two so-called malefics, Saturn and Mars, in their fiercest modes of expression – when they are making stations. Again, our theme is not that everything is automatically wonderful. Rather it is an affirmation that everything in astrology can potentially serve the evolving soul – everything can potentially be gotten right, in other words. Nothing astrological happens simply to annoy you or make a mess of your life. As you read, you might recall that the "Crimean Crisis" occurred right on schedule – Russia invaded Ukrainian territory and the world was pushed to the brink of war.

STATIONARY "MALEFICS"

(Newsletter – March 2014)

The beginning of March brings us an unusual patch of astrological weather. Both of the so-called "malefic" planets, Mars and Saturn, make stations and turn retrograde pretty much simultaneously. Mars does so on the 1st of the month, near the end of Libra. Saturn follows just about 24 hours later while in the latter part of Scorpio. Mars will remain retrograde in Libra until May 19th. Saturn turns direct a few weeks later, on July 20th, still in Scorpio.

When a planet is stationary, its energy is simply more *pronounced*. Everyone feels it more strongly. A really reliable way to see this effect in action is to observe your own experience with Jupiter. When it is moving fast and it breezes through what might *seem* like an important conjunction in your chart, you might feel like asking your astrologer for your money back. *Where was that promised good luck?* You didn't hit the Powerball after all. But if Jupiter *makes a station* on the same sensitive point, start picking out extra features for your new Lamborghini.

In astrology, slow is powerful. And stopped is as slow as slow can get.

By the way, Jupiter will also make a station during the first week of March – turning Direct on the 6th, about a third of the way into Cancer. If your birthday is near the end of June or early July, head for that car dealership.

Bottom line, for all of us, that first week of March packs a real astrological punch. It is unusual for three planets to make stations within a period of less than a week. (We might add Mercury making a station and turning direct on the 28th of February, but we'll not be concerned with that here.)

All in all, we are looking at a period in which a great many things are coming to a head, both globally and personally. *That's the nature of these planetary stations: the rubber meets the road. Inner energy and outward circumstances connect and ignite.*

Let's start by thinking about Mars and Saturn and their problematic designations as "malefics." There is really nothing inherently unlucky about either planet – or for that matter, any planet. Mars can represent *courage* and *appropriate assertiveness*, while Saturn is about *self-discipline* and *integrity*.

With Mars, if you are brave, the planet is your ally. Is there a situation in your life in which you really need to speak up and make your needs and views felt? If so, you'd better do it near the beginning of the month. *That's because wimpier responses to a Mars station generally leave us victimized and injured.* Just be careful not to get up on your high horse – Mars can bring self-righteousness, excessive passion, and the use of *too much force* into a situation.

In any case, the call to find that Martial middle path will be strong during the first part of the month. The Laws of Synchronicity declare that whatever Mars situations you are facing are reaching critical mass then.

Meanwhile, Saturn calls for strength too, but of a different kind. Sometimes it asks us to simply endure some suffering for the sake of a principle. An example might be when you have a friend who is seriously ill and needs your help and support. You may be tired and over-extended, but you visit her in the hospital anyway. The lazy alternative – blowing her off and staying home – involves such a loss of self-respect and dignity that it is not worth any ease it might bring.

Still, you need to be wary of Saturn! *Whose values are you living out? Your own – or do they come from some bogus sense of right of wrong that originated in someone manipulating you with shame?* Saturn can depress and exhaust us when we are reading our "moral" lines from someone else's script

What about the *combination* of these two planetary stations? The whole, as usual, is not only greater than, but also different from the sum of the parts.

It takes real courage to endure. It takes courage to make a stand. Sometimes it takes great moral strength simply to keep your mouth shut when you are tempted to wreak havoc on the souls of others because you are so angry at them. This is what it feels like when both Saturn and Mars pulse together this way.

At best, Saturn gives moral values and direction to that fiery Martial energy, while Mars charges up Saturn and gives it the ability to blast through a wall of previous limitations. Such a Mars-Saturn period is a time for the use of *measured force*. Reach for *realistic targets* and avoid interpersonal scorched earth policies. But don't be a doormat, unless you want to get accustomed to the role.

Let's add Jupiter to the mix since it will be stationing around the same time. Classically, Jupiter is the Greater Benefic – but during a Jupiter time be careful what you ask for, because you are likely to get it! If Jupiter is stationing near a sensitive spot in your chart, doors are likely to open for you. Your task is to recognize the *right opportunities*, and to avoid all that "which glitters but is not truly gold."

How can you tell the difference? Having Mars and Saturn in play at the same time helps to clarify that question in a specific way. They add a new element to the mix: as we just saw, *they both like challenges.* These two planets actually *enjoy* some difficulty. Jupiter isn't like that, but when it is in partnership with the other two, the total picture becomes a synthesis of all three. I am envisioning the sweetest apple near the top of the tree. *How badly do you want it?* The apple is there, but to get it, you have to do some climbing.

The Laws of Synchronicity declare that such opportunities will be presenting themselves to you in early March, especially if you have sensitivities to the sign and degree positions these three planets currently occupy.

Meanwhile, the Law of Impermanence suggests that these opportunities will not remain available for long. The "stars are aligned" for *ambitious moves requiring effort, moves that take courage, and moves that will give you a sense of pride and dignity as you look back upon them.*

And *looking back* is the spirit of the retrograde periods that begin in early March. As we saw earlier, Mars will remain retrograde until May 19th, while Saturn turns direct later, on July 20th. You will have that period to digest and integrate the fruits of your strong response to those energies – or to reflect upon the price of fear and hesitation.

Meanwhile, Jupiter makes its station and turns direct on the 6th, suggesting expanding horizons – the fruit of the decisiveness, audacity and clarity you mustered at this critical crossroads.

6

As a culture, astrologers create their own consensual reality just as surely as do indigenous people and rocket scientists. I've always been fascinated by what mechanisms drive the contemporary astrological worldview, and by what mechanisms subjects are chosen to be ignored. Why, for example, do we focus on Chiron, but not on Pholus or Nessus? Why Roman planetary mythology, but not Meso-American? In my own mind, the strange case of the parallax Moon earns a spot on the Top Ten list of these riddles. I mean, what if your Moon is not where you think it is? Doesn't that question merit some interest rather than collective avoidance?

THE PARALLAX MOON

(Newsletter – April 2021)

If someone were to ask me about the purpose of my life, I'd say that it was about simply bringing choice-centered, evolutionary astrology to a wider audience. When it comes to accomplishing that goal, the basic problem we all face is that astrology is such a fabulous language, but in order to speak it, *a person needs to take a six-week course in its grammar and vocabulary.* Most people don't have the time or the motivation to do that. That leaves a lot of them thinking only of Sun signs. That's fine, but of course Sun sign astrology is astrology running at 10% of its potential power.

Apart from a stint with *Elle* magazine a couple of decades ago, I've stayed away from that kind of popular astrology. I've tried instead to make my own stand a little higher on the intellectual food chain – but, other than with my serious students and in my books, I've always tried to keep the welcome mat out for beginners. Those of you who have followed this newsletter for a few years know just what I mean. I want to keep the language as inviting as possible. I don't want it to sound like one of those astrology conferences where half the energy seems to go into making other people feel intellectually inadequate.

In this edition of our newsletter, I am going to risk breaking that diplomatic pattern. I want to present a truly advanced subject. It may leave some of you scratching your heads, but I hope it has another effect. I hope it gets you interested in a subject that has been ignored for too long.

The area I want to present, while it's not a new discovery, is a subject which is begging for more attention. *What if the Moon was not quite where you thought it was in your chart?* That sounds important, right?

As ever, it takes the community of astrologers, working over at least a generation, to come to anything like a full understanding of anything new. No one astrologer can do it on his or her own. Going further, Tony Howard tells me that we've had some questions coming in about this subject lately, so maybe it's in the air. In any case, welcome to the curious case of the "Parallax Moon."

What you are about to encounter is taken directly from the second chapter of my *The Book of the Moon,* published in 2010.

WHAT DO WE MEAN BY THE "PARALLAX MOON?"

Parallax is a familiar effect. The classic illustration is to simply hold a finger straight up at arm's length and then look at it first through one eye, then through the other. Of course the finger seems to jump back and forth against the background. But really study it and you will see that there is another, more subtle effect as well. Through your left eye, *you see a little bit more of the left side of your finger.* Through your right eye, the opposite effect happens.

It works the same way with the Moon. People in different parts of the world can be looking at the same Moon at the same moment, but each will have a slightly different angle on it because of the physical distance between them. For example, a person might be looking at the rising Moon from New Zealand, while at the same moment someone in Spain is watching the Moon set. It can happen that way because those two countries are located at each others' antipodes – opposite sides of the Earth. Moonrise for one is approximately Moonset for the other. But each one will see the Moon from a slightly different perspective.

Another way to say it is that Spain and New Zealand have an 8000 mile *baseline* between them, running straight through the center of the Earth. And with the Moon only about 240,000 miles away, that baseline is long enough to produce a noticeable parallax view – we are back to looking at your fingertip through alternate eyes.

Proportionally, it is as if you are looking at a globe that is thirty feet away from you. Then you slide over twelve inches to your left and look at it again. The view of the globe is basically the same, but if you look really carefully, you will notice that you are seeing that globe from a slightly different angle.

Parallax allows us to see approximately another 1% around the Moon on each side. That is not much. You might be wondering why we bother to explain it in these pages. There is a very good reason. Read on.

THE EFFECTS OF THE PARALLAX MOON

Parallax also shifts the Moon's position against the starry background, the same way that the trick with your fingertip makes it seem to jump against the backdrop of your furniture. This is an effect with serious, if little known, astrological consequences. What lunar parallax means is that if you think that your natal Moon lies in 14° Gemini 35'... well, you might need to think again. The actual position depends on your point of view. Were you born in New Zealand or in Spain?

The positions of the Sun, Moon, and planets as they are dished up in most modern astrological computer programs are actually the positions *as they would be seen from the center of the Earth*. The Sun and planets are far enough away that this mathematically-convenient illusion creates no real issues. But the Moon is relatively close to Earth, so parallax generates a noticeable difference.

Here's why:

Maybe you are looking at the Moon rising against the backdrop of the starry sky from the top of the Mauna Kea volcano in Hawaii. Now imagine that you are suddenly shifted to the center of the Earth, looking up through a very long pipe directly at the Moon. The center of the Earth is about *four thousand miles away* from Mauna Kea – enough to make that Moon jump as much as about one degree against the starry background. That is a lot – a degree is twice the Moon's own apparent diameter in the sky.

If this sounds obscure and technical, let me say it more directly. With parallax, we are talking about *where the Moon actually appeared to be in the sky when you were born*. Present day astrological software, with few exceptions, instead defaults to the convenient fiction that we were all born in the center of the Earth.

Which approach makes more intuitive sense? To know where the Moon "really" was when you were born or to believe the computer?

Note that not everyone would see a shift of one degree. That is the extreme. If the Moon were directly overhead in Mauna Kea, being on top of the volcano or four thousand miles straight down beneath it would not move the Moon at all.

Remember how parallax works. If you had only one eye, it would not be an issue. There would be no parallax.

Thinking about parallax with the Moon is cutting-edge astrology. Because the biggest difference it can make – just a degree – does not seem extreme, it can seem like small potatoes. Even at maximum, that probably will not have much impact on a *natal* interpretation of the Moon – although do note that it could potentially shift the Moon into a different sign! Also, if you are using the Sabian degree symbols, the difference would often throw the Moon into the next or previous degree.

But there is more. In the extreme case, that "one degree" does affect the timing of when aspects by transit or progression come into perfect alignment with the Moon.

More critically, *it throws off predictions based on the solar arc Moon by about one year* – enough to be catastrophic.

And it utterly and totally re-frames the lunar return chart – these are charts based on the exact moment the Moon returns (each month) to the place it was when you were born. (I have not personally found the technique of lunar returns to be very helpful. Maybe that is because my lunar returns have all been wrong by about an hour! That is the difference half a degree makes, and in my own chart the parallax happens to be that wide. Other astrologers I know swear by lunar returns. I suspect that, for them, the position of the parallax Moon and the "normal" one are not so far apart.)

Perhaps the ultimate test for the parallax Moon lies in those situations where the Moon changes signs if we apply the parallax method. Say a person is born with the Moon in 0° Virgo 20'. Parallax could potentially shift that position by almost 60'. Forward or backward? You have to answer that question case by case. But if it is backwards, then that individual's Moon is not in Virgo at all—it is in 29° Leo 20'. And that is an entirely different situation.

Should we use the parallax Moon instead of the more conventional one? At this point, in all honesty, I am not convinced one way or the other. The distinction is subtle most of the time. My own personal experience is important to me, but the reality is that astrology advances best when hundreds of astrologers are sharing their collective experience – and it grows stagnant when the field agrees to ignore a question.

If you are interested in learning more about this parallax Moon topic, the best place I know to begin is with the work of Alphee Lavoie, who has really pioneered it. A click on www.Alphee.com will get you going. Hit Education>Astrology Reading Room and look for some articles he wrote based on his research. And, by the way, Alphee's Millennium Star Trax software allows you easily to calculate the parallax Moon, as does the popular Solar Fire program.

That is the end of what I wrote in *The Book of the Moon*, back in 2010. In all honesty, despite my best intentions, I've not followed up on the parallax Moon with the kind of research it deserves. All I can plead is the squeaky wheels getting the grease. I've been busy with other things. Maybe I'll get to it one day.

On the other hand, maybe I won't. Maybe it is up to one of you.

That is how the wheels turn.

7

Familiarity can kill creativity. With repetition, astrologers run the risk of becoming mechanical in their responses. That's one advantage young astrologers have over old ones – they bring fresh ears to the planetary music. Not knowing exactly where the edges of the box are, they tend to think outside of them. Whatever our age, a wise prayer is that we might all retain some of that youthful "rebel mind" – the one that questions everything, including ourselves. In this piece, I try to shock us out of our reflexive feeling that "we know what Venus means." If there's one principle upon which you can always count, it is that with astrology, whatever we know, it is always more than that.

VENUS AND THE FINE ART OF REJECTING PEOPLE

(Newsletter – June 2021)

Once in teaching a class about the planet Venus, I startled my students – and myself too, a little bit. I heard myself say that the main function of Venus lies in *rejecting people.* That of course is far from how we normally think of Venus! We imagine the "goddess of love" greeting us doe-eyed and misty, with open arms, receiving us into her heart without even a smidgeon of criticism, hesitation, or pre-conditions.

People sometimes spend their lives looking for that kind of perfect love. They are humanity's tragic romantics. Most of them die lonely. Pete Townshend of The Who released a song forty years ago that seemed to say it all – *The Sea Refuses No River.* That line, to me, represents one of the high points of rock'n'roll poetry, but it actually has very little to do with Venus. In actuality, his words are purely *Neptunian,* and not just because of the maritime reference. *It is Neptune, not Venus, that loves people unconditionally.* As most of us quickly learn, there is a huge difference between the way we imagine that God loves us and the ways our parents or our partners love us. With parents and partners, while there may be sincere hugs and kisses, the package also includes a few eye-rolls and some disapproving looks, along with "helpful" lists of the myriad ways in which we might improve ourselves.

Venus doesn't "love everybody" – that's Neptune's job. Venus *picks* and *chooses,* and that means some element of rejection must always be part of the process. Venusian love is *personal.* It is "me and you" stuff, not "me and the human race." Sexually Venus tends to be binary, or at least it aspires to that condition.

How often in a lifetime, for example, are you going to say the words, "will you marry me?" Gone are the days when the reflexive answer was "only once" – but most of us who do choose to marry try at least to keep the number down to the fingers on one hand. This observation leads us directly to Forrest's Theorum #376 – *most of us kiss a lot more people than we marry.* And what's a kiss but a preliminary investigation of the possibility of deeper intimacy? Even among the most sincere people in the world, those investigations are far more likely to reveal reasons *not* to be together than reasons to tie a life-long knot.

See? That's rejection! Saying no to people – with wisdom and discernment – is a fundamental Venusian art.

Among those of us who are inclined to form couples, here's the basic script underlying the actual experience of 99% of us: *not you, not you, not you, not you . . . you? Give me a kiss . . . naw, not you either . . . not you, not you . . . you? Kiss me . . . could it really be you? Kiss me again. You! It's you! I've found you!*

All this might sound flippant, but run it through your reality-checker. I would be surprised if it failed the test.

Underlying everything we are considering here is a pivotal point about the planet Venus. What Venus does is to *discern deep, specific comple-*

mentarity between ourselves and another person. Saying that Venus is about "rejecting people" is accurate enough, although in all honesty that catchy phrasing fails to capture the warm spirit of the planet. Maybe we can "love everybody," or at least aspire to do that. But can everybody be "your best friend?" Can everybody be your partner? *Offering anyone that kind of deeply personal intimacy is a rich gift, and one that we cannot give to too many people* – life is simply too short, plus we are all too individuated to find that kind of soul-harmony on every street corner.

Love is a slippery word, one with many different legitimate meanings. That's probably one reason that it is such a popular term with scoundrels. As we have seen, the love you might feel for humanity – the milk of human kindness – is in the boundaryless domain of Neptune. The special, very human, love you feel for a partner or a dear friend is Venusian love. For a person to qualify for receiving it, he or she has to pass a lot of tests – and keep on passing them.

Underlying all of this are six basic truths about the Venusian dimensions of the evolution of the human soul:

- Venus lessons cannot be learned all alone. They are about love and trust, and nobody learns much about those things all by themselves.
- Only *certain specific people* can help you learn the intimate lessons you are here to learn. Tapping random strangers on the back in the local cafe is not a reliable strategy.
- If you truly tune into your heart, you actually have some pretty good instincts about who can help you – and who cannot.
- Those instincts are encoded astrologically in your natal Venus, which is wired to be attracted to the kinds of people who can actually help you grow – and to reject the ones who cannot.
- Failing to reject those who cannot be of positive help to you is the source of oceans of human suffering.
- Recognizing those who can help you and sharing life with them is perhaps the greatest treasure this world can offer.

This month, Venus will spend time in three different signs. June begins with Venus nearing the end of Gemini. It enters Cancer on the 2nd and then Leo on the 26th. Over those four weeks, kids will be born with very different intimate pathways open to them. Each of these children will naturally be in a unique astrological situation – the question is never as simple as what sign Venus occupies. Houses, aspects, nodal karma – many other astrological dimensions are relevant. But signs are important. Let's bring all we've been exploring here down to earth with a quick look at Venus in Gemini, Venus in Cancer, and Venus in Leo. To do that, I'm going to borrow three lightly edited sections from the second volume in my Elements series, *The Book of Earth*. In reading these words, you'll see a message about what people with Venus in each of these signs is learning, who is able to help them with that learning, and what it looks like if they don't master the twin arts of honest self-knowledge and the discerning rejection of those who are not good for them.

VENUS IN GEMINI

Intimate Evolutionary Agenda: Excellent communication is critical to my experience of intimacy. The clear translation of soul-states into vocabulary and syntax is always challenging; I resolve to master that skill, both in terms of my own emotional self-expression and in terms of my ability to listen deeply to another person without being blinded by my own preconceptions. I do not do well in a relationship when I am bored; I resolve to *do my part* to keep all my relationships interesting, growing, and changing.

Essential Qualities in a Natural Partner: Open-mindedness. Curiosity. An eagerness for new experiences and for opportunities to learn. Listening skills. Articulateness – or at least willing verbal self-expression. A natural predilection for conversation. A willingness to discuss anything.

Strategy: I commit to two resolutions: to listen to any partner carefully and to respond clearly and forthrightly from my own heart. I do my part in keeping a relationship interesting: I suggest travel, I read books and talk about what I have learned in them, I dynamite deadening intimate routines for the sheer joy of seeing something different. I ask questions and listen to the answers.

Tools: I like to talk and I like to listen, at least in intimate situations with people I love. I am naturally interested in many things. I am genuinely curious about the perspectives of others, especially those with whom I am sharing my life.

Dealing With The Shadow: there are many interesting and attractive people in the world, but once I am committed to a particular relationship,

I am careful not to be distracted by other people. I will use language as a way of building bridges to people about whom I care; I will zealously monitor myself regarding my tendency to hide my heart behind words and elaborate rationalizations.

VENUS IN CANCER

Intimate Evolutionary Agenda The formation of strong, long-lasting, committed bonds with other human beings. Stability and longevity in relationships are not the only point – the deeper point is that I aim to create an intimate environment for myself in which the most vulnerable parts of my being feel safe enough to be revealed. At the heart level, I am *seeking home,* along with a *feeling of family* in some sense of the word.

Essential Qualities in a Natural Partner: A willingness to be radically committed to me. Faithfulness, reliability, and loyalty. One who is not unduly afraid of a powerful word such as "forever." An urge to nurture – whether that nurturing is of children, pets, a garden, or the relationship itself.

Strategy: I must maintain a creative tension between, on one hand, my natural caution about getting hurt and, on the other hand, volunteering to take the risk of truly opening my heart. I will not be so cautious as to be unreachable.

Tools: A deep and fundamental capacity to love another human being in a spirit of familial devotion and lifelong commitment. A nearly infinite ability simply to *care* for another person. A natural internal marriage of my sexuality with emotions of simple affection.

Dealing With The Shadow: I resolve to be aware of my potential for excessive caution and self protection. I will not hide my true feelings or needs behind the "parental" mask of caregiving.

VENUS IN LEO

Intimate Evolutionary Agenda I resolve not to settle for anything less in my intimate life than the feeling of being *cherished* by someone whom I myself treasure. No one has to be perfect – that is not the point. The agenda here is to be perfectly loving – to celebrate each other, stand up for each other, and to consistently prioritize the wellbeing of the relationship over all other concerns. I need to feel free enough to be vulnerable.

Essential Qualities in a Natural Partner: Expressiveness. An affectionate, demonstrative nature. Supportiveness. The ability to say I love you. Attentiveness and a natural fluency in offering compliments. Self-respect – and respect for me – as demonstrated by a willingness to look and behave his or her best.

Strategy: First and foremost, I resolve never to settle for a partner whom I do not genuinely cherish. I would rather be alone than to abase myself that way. Once having found such a person, I actively commit to an active, lifelong path dedicated to preserving and nurturing the *lasting romance* of our bond.

Tools: I have a certain flair for style and colorful self-expression. An ability to say what I feel in an impactful way, so it is heard deeply. A degree of healthy pride, self-respect, and dignity – all of which support me in not settling for too little in any of my relationships.

Dealing With The Shadow: I remind myself that no one's life needs to revolve around mine. In a healthy relationship, we are like a double star orbiting a common center of gravity which we have created together. It is not "all about me." I express my own needs forthrightly – but I also make space to hear the needs and celebrate the victories of my friends and my partners.

May all the babies born this month find the kind of love that works for them – and may the rest of us find it, preserve it, and treasure it too. May all of us learn to know ourselves and love ourselves enough to walk away from anything less.

8

Years ago, in my first book The Inner Sky, I coined the term Primal Triad as shorthand for the combination of Sun, Moon, and Ascendant. I had come to realize that these three symbols together formed the skeleton of every birthchart. Meanwhile the rest of the planets mostly served to make us all better-looking by adding flesh and hair to that skeleton. As I read the astrology books available at that time, I quickly saw that while there was wide agreement on the meaning of the Sun and Moon, the Ascendant often seemed less well-defined. I began to search for the right language to describe it . . .

A QUICK INTRODUCTION TO THE ASCENDANT

(Newsletter – April 2013)

When I was a kid getting interested in astrology, all the books I was reading agreed that the Ascendant was a big piece of the puzzle. *But what exactly did it mean?* The more I read, the more I heard astrologers rolling the drums and blowing the trumpets for it . . . but I still didn't really get it. What they were saying often made the Ascendant sound pretty much the same as the Sun – I heard "the Ascendant is your identity." It is "your ego." It is all surfaces. "The Ascendant is more important than your Sun Sign" – but the words used to describe it were basically the same.

The more I read, the more confused I became.

I decided I needed to figure it out for myself. I began by thinking about the Ascendant in physical terms. It is of course simply the sign that was rising in the east when you were born. It was, in other words, "dawning" just like the Sun dawns in the morning. And the answer came to me in a flash: *the Ascendant represents how you "dawn on people."* In other words, it is your style, your affect, the way you *present yourself to the social world.*

Pretty soon I found myself in my early thirties and under contract to write a book about a new take on the astrological basics for Bantam Books. In a triumph for poetry, it eventually became *The Inner Sky*... after passing perilously close to being given the corporate name *Astrology 101.* But that is another story! In writing *The Inner Sky*, I spoke of the Ascendant as *The Mask.* I drew the term from Jungian psychology, where Carl Jung described our social personality as the *persona,* which is the Greek word for "mask." Then as now, I prefer plain English, so I stuck with the simple word "mask."

And "mask" is a pretty good term for the Ascendant. We all wear a "mask" in the countless essentially superficial social situations that dominate our lives. Someone asks, "how are you?" And by reflex we say, "fine, thanks. How are you?"

But when was the last time you were ever actually "fine, thanks?"

There's nothing wrong with that – we all have to streamline the expression of our inner lives in order to function in the world. Few people are really interested in the nuances of our emotional lives. That much information would just get in the way of the practical affairs of living. We all learn to avoid people who waste half an hour of our own lives actually answering that "how are you" question in detail. Do we really care to learn about their migraine headaches? Probably only if they are among your near and dear. *You face an entirely different situation when your best friend, whom you have not seen for six months, sits down with you, looks you straight in the eye and asks, "how are you?"*

Then, you need an hour just to hit the headlines. But that conversation is not fundamentally in the domain we are exploring here. Most of our relationships are superficial though, and that is the natural domain of the Ascendant. We'll go deeper into its symbolism before we are done here, but remember: *the dawning sign represents how we dawn on people –* and that's a different perspective than what we see when we've slept with someone for ten years.

Naturally, blessedly, some of our relationships are really deep. Does the Ascendant disappear then? Is it all about social pleasantries and convenient over-simplifications? Not really – and that observation is what led me to my promise of a deeper understanding of how the Ascendant works. I still call it The Mask sometimes – the term works pretty well. But I've come up with a better metaphor. *The Ascendant is like the stained glass through which the rest of the psyche shines into the world.*

Stained glass filters the light that passes through it; it *tints* the light, gives it a *hue*. That's exactly how the Ascendant operates. Its task is to *translate the inner complexity of the psyche into the three-dimensional terms of the social world.*

Say you have red stained glass. You shine yellow light through it. What do you see? Orange light – that's the result of the mixture of red and yellow. But now instead shine blue light through that same red stained glass, and you'll see violet.

One bottom line: *if someone asks you what a Cancer Ascendant means, you had better ask about the rest of the chart!* Cancer rising looks really different on a Leo than it does on a Scorpio. Different light is shining through that Cancerian stained glass.

Visualizing these kinds of blends is the heart of understanding how the Ascendant works.

Even in our most intimate interactions, we cannot help expressing ourselves through the Ascendant.

- Sagittarius rising? You'll probably put a plucky spin on everything you say, even when you are feeling glum.
- Scorpio rising? There will be that characteristic lingering eye contact – that extra dose of Scorpionic intensity, even if you are Libra with a Pisces Moon.
- Virgo Ascendant? You won't spare a detail.

Even in the most intimate moments, we all still have a style. And *tuning it so it serves your real intentions is authentic evolutionary work.* Get it right and the membrane that separates your consciousness from the social world works efficiently.

- Aries rising and you attract *adventures* – and *adventurous people* who open bold doors for you.

- Gemini rising and you attract *information* and *communication*. People want to talk with you.

Picture someone with Cancer rising. She might start out shy, but over the years, *she evolves into being a quiet person.* There is a big difference! Being shy is painful – but being a quiet person who accepts herself as she is and does not feel that there is anything wrong with her just because she doesn't feel like going to your "damned party" . . . well, that is evolutionary progress down the Ascendant road – a road of true *self-actualization* and *self-acceptance.*

With conscious effort, you can *improve the way you dawn on the world.* You can make it serve the higher calling of your soul.

9

The planetary ruler of the sign that was rising when you were born is often called the "ruler of the chart." But what exactly does that mean? That planet certainly doesn't tell the rest of the chart what to do – it doesn't "rule the chart" in any domineering sense. It is often not even the best candidate for being "the most important planet in the chart." So why does it carry such an impressive title? How does the ruler of the Ascendant actually work? Why is it so special and how is it different from the rest of the planets?

THE RULER OF THE CHART

(Newsletter – October 2014)

The mighty Sun just started to blaze over the Anza-Borrego desert where I live. I am writing these words in haste here just after dawn. Speed is of the essence since I need to pack my bags and head for the Palm Springs airport in four hours. From there, I have to make my way up to San Francisco and points north to teach one of my Apprenticeship Programs.

Michelle and I just arrived here at our home in the desert a week ago, so it hurts to leave again so soon. Lately, we live part of the time at her place in New Orleans. We just completed the three-day cross-country drive to get from there to here. When I close my eyes, I'm still hallucinating the white lines of the highway stretching out before me.

When I get back from this teaching trip up to the Bay Area, I'll only have about ten days at home again before I need to leave to teach a pair of seminars in Beijing and Shanghai. When I get back from Asia, I will once more only have about ten days at home before I need to leave yet again to teach the southern California edition of my Apprenticeship Program. That one is easier – it's just a 90 minute drive and a five-day trip.

Does this strike you as an insane way to live?

As I read over my words, that assessment sounds pretty accurate. But I am used to it. I have been living this way for the last three decades. Anyone who looked at my life from outside would see these same behavioral patterns consistently and prominently: *traveling, teaching, and writing.*

And of course doing astrological readings: *talking.*

- *Teaching, writing, and talking*: what astrological house are we spotlighting? Most astrologers would say, correctly, the 3rd house. Some would astutely add the 9th house for its link to education and publishing.
- *Traveling:* what house carries that symbolism? Most astrologers would say the 9th. And some, if they had much practical experience, would mention the 3rd house in connection with travel too.

(Let me clarify that last point. In some of the older books, the 3rd House was related to "short journeys," while the 9th referred to "long journeys." In my experience, it's not the length of the journey that counts, but rather how exotic or familiar it is. The first time I went to China, it felt like a 9th House experience. This month, I'll make my fourth trip. I will see familiar faces and places. I will hug old friends and catch up with their lives. The trip feels a bit more like "commuting." That's the 3rd house travel signature. It doesn't have the "questing" feeling of the 9th house.)

Here's the linch-pin of what I am getting at: *anyone looking at me from the outside would see a vivid 3rd/9th house fingerprint on my daily life.* No surprise, both of those houses are activated in my natal chart. I have Pluto in the 9th house and a Mars/Mercury conjunction on the cusp of the 3rd.

And here for our purposes is the critical link – and the actual point of this essay: I have a Scorpio Ascendant, so *two of those planets, Pluto and Mars, are "the rulers of my chart."*

And that is what I want to explore here.

Go to an astrology conference and ask which planet rules Scorpio and you may start a fistfight. Classically, the answer is Mars. Modern astrologers favor Pluto. People argue vehemently on both sides of the question. To me, the argument is silly – both rulerships are valid. Mars and Pluto each have an affinity with Scorpio, and that is what rulership is about.

As we saw in the first few words of this essay, astrologers have always recognized that the planet which rules the Ascendant plays a dramatically underscored role in a person's life.   That's why it came to be called "the ruler of the chart."

But why exactly?

To answer that, we need to recall some deeper thoughts about the nature of the Ascendant itself. That is a big subject, but one elemental observation is that the Ascendent represents a person's *style of social and behavioral manifestation.* As we saw in the previous chapter, you meet people at a party, they say "how are you?" You say, "Fine thanks, how's about you?" They say, "Fine thanks." *And you instantly like them* –or dislike them! *Something of their core nature shines through that superficial social behavior.* As strange as it sounds, we can – and do – actually learn a lot about people by how they say, "Fine, thanks." An energetic signature comes through every human gesture, in other words. *I always think of the Ascendant as the stained glass through which the light of the psyche is shining.* It translates the deeper layers of the psyche into the world of social behavior. The Ascendant represents how you *act* in the world.

Right there, we hold the key to understanding why the planet that rules the Ascendant is so important. Like the Ascendant itself, the ruler of the Ascendant is *behaviorally activated.* We see the signature of that planet very clearly in the existential and social behavior of a person.
The birthchart holds many clues about profoundly intimate, even hidden, elements of a person's experience and character. While the ruler of the Ascendant carries such deeper meanings as well, it always carries that simple quality of the Ascendant itself: *visible behavior.*

So, off I go to yet another airport, to teach yet another class, to talk my head off about things I've written about. That is what my life *looks like.*

Is that what I *am?* Yes, sure – and I am grateful for it. But I am not that simple. And neither are you.

There is a planet that rules your Ascendant too. It's in a sign and a house and it makes aspects. Take a second look at that planet from the point of view we have explored here. Do that, and you will – to paraphrase the words of the great Scots poet, Robert Burns— "see yourself as others see you." . . . because what they see is *what you do,* not who you are.

And yet those – what you do and what you are – are not *unrelated,* just not exactly the same. Sit with that paradox and you've gone a long, long way toward unraveling the mysteries of the planet that rules your chart.

10

We continue here with a theme close to my heart – taking a second, more encouraging look at astrological configurations which often frighten people. In this case, our subject is retrograde planets, especially in their "permanent" condition – as features in a person's natal chart. Like everything else in astrology, retrograde planets can "break bad." But when they "break good," the possibilities they represent can be quite exciting to contemplate.

RETROGRADE NATAL PLANETS

(Newsletter – March 2021)

Yikes! What if Mercury was retrograde when I was born? Am I doomed? Will the check be lost in the mail *for the rest of my life?* Will my luggage never arrive in the same city that I do?

Retrograde natal planets often scare people, as if something were wrong with planets moving in that "backwards" condition. Yet most of us have at least one of them, and often more. They are far from rare, in other words. And they aren't some kind of high jinx in your chart either. They are just different from planets moving in direct motion.

It's sort of like being left-handed. Not bad, not good. Again: just different.

In understanding retrograde motion, the overriding principle is that, first and foremost, there is nothing "wrong with" *anyone's* chart, ever. The basic laws of the universe preclude that possibility. Your chart is perfect. It fits the needs and conditions of your soul like the proverbial glove. Retrograde planets, squares, oppositions, Mars, Saturn, and Pluto – all the astrological "bad guys" – we need every one of them, and they can all be "good for you."

That's a philosophical point obviously, but understanding it is mission-critical, at least in the context of evolutionary astrology. (If you would prefer an astrologer who would describe you as *doomed* by some configuration in your chart, I can make some referrals.)

Hold your arm out in front of you and point your index finger straight up. Now look at your fingertip through your left eye, then through your right eye, then your left eye again. Naturally, your fingertip seems to jump back and forth against the background scenery.

Look at Pluto against the starry background in March, then look at it again in September. *It's exactly the same situation.* Like your finger, Pluto too has seemingly jumped backwards. *That's because in March, the Earth was on one side of its orbit, while in September it was halfway around, on the other side.* That's as if the distance between your left eye and your right eye were about 186 million miles – and that's far enough to make even distant Pluto seem to jump.

In reality, Pluto has of course continued to plod forward in its orbit. It is only our changing earthly perspective that has made it *appear* to go backwards. That's how retrogradation works. That is why all the planets are subject to it – we are watching all of them from the moving Earth, as if we were on a merry-go-round looking at our mom against the distant background of arcade games and cotton candy stands. As we approached her, we might see her in front of the shooting gallery. As we whipped by, and looked back at her over our shoulder, we'd see her against the backdrop of the roller coaster. She hadn't actually moved at all – it was us that was moving.

Only the Sun and the Moon are immune to this effect. That's because we orbit the Sun and the Moon orbits us. It's a different situation.

Again, there is nothing wrong with a planet going backwards. But when you are born with a planet in that condition, it does have some distinguishing characteristics. Like everything else in astrology, it is possible to get it right and it is possible to get it wrong. Let's focus first on how to get it right, then we will take a peek at the possible dark sides of the equation.

We begin by understanding a core point: *planets act upon the world.* They are the *active ingredients* in astrology, not to mention in life. They *do things.* Their spirit is generally, "forward – *march!*"

All of that hits a simple bull's eye, *so long as a planet is in direct motion.* It is boldly going where it has not gone before – at least not in this particular cycle. It is entering *new degrees,* which is to say, *fresh territory.*

But when a planet is retrograde, it is moving in the opposite direction: revisiting where it has already been, moving *toward the past rather than toward the future.* It is not that it stops "acting on the world," but rather that some of its energy is siphoned off, re-purposed to pay attention to inner worlds and, above all, *to yesterday rather than tomorrow.*

- Instead of action, it is inclined toward reflection.
- Instead of objectivity, it favors subjectivity.
- Instead of looking toward the future, it contemplates the past.
- Instead of going outward, it is going inward.
- Instead of being extroverted, it tends toward introversion.
- Instead of participating in consensual reality, it *thinks for itself –* and keeps its thoughts to itself.

Among astrologers who are inclined toward discouraging thoughts about retrograde planets, the view is often held that they "have a harder time expressing themselves." There is a kernel of truth in that observation – but beware of the implication that this hesitancy must be understood one-dimensionally as some kind of flaw.

Who do you like better, someone who shoots from the hip verbally without forethought or someone who reflects before he or she speaks?

Easy question, right? Retrograde planets are more like that second person. It's not so much that they always have "a harder time expressing themselves" as the fact that they are simply not quite so *eager* to.

Go back in your imagination to the sixth grade. There's a quiet girl in your class, sitting near the back of the room, kind of hiding out behind her thick glasses. When the teacher calls on her, she always knows the answer, but she never volunteers much. The other kids *like* her all right, but they don't really *know* her very well. If they thought about her, they'd decide that she was a little mysterious … but they actually don't think much about her at all. She hasn't given them any reason to.

In her chart, seven planets are retrograde, and she is acting that way.

Years later, there's a big class reunion. The "quiet girl" is now a well-known novelist. Curious, you buy her bestseller. Turns out, it's a tale set in a strangely-familiar grammar school. As you read, you start recognizing the characters. There is a devastatingly insightful portrait of someone you quickly recognize as your pompous history teacher. As you read about him and his improper relationship with a rubber duck, tears of laughter are running down your cheeks. A few pages further on, you pick out the snootiest "pretty girl" in the class, along with the most arrogant "muscle boy."

The novelist has nailed everyone in a brilliant, trenchant way. You are soon praying there's no character who resembles *you* waiting for you in the next chapter.

Back in her school days, our novelist didn't have much to say – *but she didn't miss a thing*. Better late than never, you are now looking at her retrograde planets in action. Like daffodil bulbs planted deeply, they took longer to come up and bloom – but when they did, they were "floriferous."

She actually had many of those funny, piercing insights when she was eleven years old – but she was forty before she was ready to share them.

Retrograde planets tend to withdraw more from the world than the more active planets that are in direct motion. That withdrawn quality gives them a certain freedom from the gravitational field of *consensual reality*.

Here's a way of thinking about how that works. Many of us have heard of "laughing yoga." In a group, someone starts laughing for no apparent reason. Pretty soon everyone else is laughing too. It works the same way in a theater. Someone coughs – and you guessed it, soon someone else coughs too.

Humans are herd creatures.

People with a strong retrograde influences are less likely than most of us to laugh or cough under those circumstances. *With retrograde planets, there is a certain immunity to being herded by the group.*

I am not sure where this idea originated, but I have always heard that retrograde planets frequently appear in the charts of geniuses. I find that notion very plausible, so long as we don't get too one-dimensional about it – obviously, not everyone with retrograde planets is a genius. And there are other astrological correlates of genius that have nothing to do with retrograde planets – strong Uranian or Aquarian influences, for example, or planets Out of Bounds by declination.

Still, the primary characteristic of all true geniuses is that they "think outside the box." They all have, in other words, *a relative immunity to "group think."* That's why they are geniuses. I suspect they are less likely to laugh just because others are laughing or cough just because others are coughing.

And those "genius qualities" are retrograde qualities.

As evolutionary astrologers, we always ask a question that other astrologers tend not to even think about – that's the question of *why* you have the chart that you have? Since you've had your chart since the day you were born, anything that *caused* you to have it needed to have happened before you were born. We mostly use the language of reincarnation to make sense of all of that, although some people might prefer to speak of ancestral themes encoded in our DNA or some other perspective.

In the light of that idea, *why might you have retrograde planets?* In a meaningful, purposeful universe, what *caused* that condition in you?

Those questions quickly get us into deep waters, but basically those "backwards" planets *strongly equip you to get to the karmic roots of any issues you have retained from previous lifetimes.*

- For example, with Mars retrograde in your birthchart, you are equipped to deal with *unresolved hurts and resentments* from prior lifetimes, perhaps even issues linked to *violence.*
- With Venus retrograde in your natal chart, you will be meeting a lot of people who seem "strangely familiar." Together, you are aiming to untangle some kind of karmic knot with them – something rooted in the "retrograde" past, the time before you both were born.

What about the dark side of retrograde planets? As with everything else in astrology, there are ways to make a mess of them. We might, for example, plant those "daffodil bulbs" so deep that they never come up at all. It is in fact fair to say that retrograde planets "have a harder time expressing themselves" – so long as we balance that criticism with a second perspective: planets in direct motion might have a harder time *thinking* for themselves.

- Picture the poet who dies with reams of luminous, *but unpublished,* poetry in a box under her bed. No one ever reads a word of it. Maybe that's the effect of a weak response to Mercury (*the voice*) or Venus (*the arts*) moving retrograde in her natal chart.
- Picture the "armchair adventurer" who never dared to cross an ocean or to climb a mountain. Could that be a retrograde Mars?
- Picture the "astrology fan" who reads avidly for forty years and yet is never bold enough to sit with a friend in need and talk about his transit-tortured chart. Could that be Uranus retrograde?
- Picture the "tragic romantic" who spends her life longing for love, but never takes the risk of actually loving anyone. Are we looking at a retrograde Saturn in the 7th house?
- Picture someone working for minimum wage, but with a dozen "million dollar ideas" for businesses or products, none of which she or he is bold enough to try. Is that a natal 10th house Jupiter in retrograde motion?

Again, our aim here is to recognize that retrograde planets do in fact have their dangers – something that evolutionary astrological theory holds true about *every other possible configuration.* Their particular danger lies in being "planted so deeply" that they settle for being flowers that never open.

But if we strive to get those flowers open, patiently but relentlessly, their perfume can fill a city, a country, or a century. Think of the towering musical genius, Ludwig von Beethoven, for one example. He had four retrograde planets – Mars, Saturn, Uranus, and Neptune.

There are many other illustrations, but I will leave you with the thought of how Beethoven's 9th Symphony is still opening hearts and putting tears in people's eyes so many centuries later. Many of us have heard that stirring music, *but Beethoven heard it first echoing in the dark caverns of his retrograde planets.*

11

This little essay was a lot of fun to write. It's also a bit jaw-dropping – or at least a bit of a metaphysical head-scratcher. It seems that while people die, their charts do not – their transits and progressions continue to work even after the people are gone. I suspect this is true for everyone, but it is easiest to see in the lives of people who were famous during their lifetimes. Often their fame lives on after them, and that means that "career events" might still occur – such as Jim Morrison's record sales going through the roof long after he was laid to rest in Pere Lachaise cemetery in Paris or poor Vincent Van Gogh finally selling a painting or two, even though it happened too late to help him pay his rent or buy any absinthe.

CHARTS NEVER DIE

(Newsletter – May 2020)

On September 17, 1981, sexy Doors' singer Jim Morrison's bedroom eyes gazed out from the cover of *Rolling Stone* magazine. The caption read *"He's hot, he's sexy and he's dead."* That caption might not mark a milestone on the history of good taste, but astrologically, the event has always intrigued me. What was going on in Jim Morrisons's chart when that happened? Or more pressingly, *would his chart still work "even though he was no longer in it?"*

Morrison had died, probably in a bathtub, probably as a result of a heroin overdose, in Paris ten years earlier. That had put an end to The Doors, a band which had formed six riotous years earlier in Los Angeles.

Ten years gone, and yet Jim Morrison's career was suddenly on a roll again.

Looking at 1980, sales of every single Doors' album had doubled or tripled compared to 1979. Joe Smith, the chairman of Elektra Records, said, "No group *that isn't around anymore* has sold that well for us." The Doors' *magnum opus, The End,* had been featured in Francis Ford Coppola's hit film, *Apocalypse Now,* in 1979. The following year, a Morrison biography, *No One Gets Out of Here Alive,* by Jerry Hopkins, sold unexpectedly well.

Jim Morrison was born in Melbourne, Florida at 11:55 AM-EWT on December 8, 1943. Even though he exited that chart in 1971, it seems that it lived on, even without him.

I want to display Morrison's transits, progressions, and solar arcs for his Rolling Stone cover. Personally, I find quad wheels too dense and hard to read, so I'm going to show two charts. The first is his natal chart surrounded by progressions and, in the outer ring, his transits.

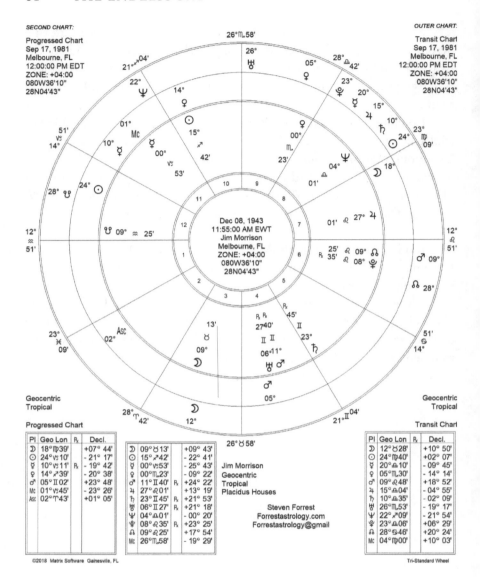

SECOND CHART:

Progressed Chart
Sep 17, 1981
Melbourne, FL
12:00:00 PM EDT
ZONE: +04:00
080W36'10"
28N04'43"

OUTER CHART:

Transit Chart
Sep 17, 1981
Melbourne, FL
12:00:00 PM EDT
ZONE: +04:00
080W36'10"
28N04'43"

Dec 08, 1943
11:55:00 AM EWT
Jim Morrison
Melbourne, FL
ZONE: +04:00
080W36'10"
28N04'43"

Geocentric
Tropical

Progressed Chart

Geocentric
Tropical

Transit Chart

Pl	Geo Lon	Rx	Decl.
☽	18°♍39'		+07° 44'
☉	24°♍10'		- 21° 17'
☿	10°♒11'	Rx	- 19° 42'
♀	14°♐39'		- 20° 38'
♂	05°♊02'		+23° 48'
Mc	01°♑45'		- 23° 26'
Asc	02°♈43'		+01° 05'

☽	09°♉13'		+09° 43'
☉	15°♐42'		- 22° 41'
☿	00°♑53'		- 25° 43'
♀	00°♏23'		- 09° 22'
♂	11°♊40'	Rx	+24° 22'
♃	27°♌01'		+13° 19'
♄	23°♊45'	Rx	+21° 53'
♅	06°♊27'	Rx	+21° 18'
♆	04°♎01'		- 00° 20'
♇	08°♌35'	Rx	+23° 25'
☊	09°♌25'		+17° 54'
Mc	26°♏58'		- 19° 29'

Jim Morrison
Geocentric
Tropical
Placidus Houses

Steven Forrest
Forrestastrology.com
Forrestastrology@gmail

Pl	Geo Lon	Rx	Decl.
☽	12°♉28'		+10° 50'
☉	24°♍40'		+02° 07'
☿	20°♎10'		- 09° 45'
♀	05°♏30'		- 14° 14'
♂	09°♌48'		+18° 52'
♃	15°♎04'		- 04° 55'
♄	10°♏35'		- 02° 09'
♅	26°♏53'		- 19° 17'
♆	22°♐09'		- 21° 54'
♇	23°♎06'		+06° 29'
☊	28°♋46'		+20° 24'
Mc	04°♍00'		+10° 03'

©2018 Matrix Software Gainesville, FL

Tri-Standard Wheel

And here are Jim Morrison's solar arcs displayed around his natal chart:

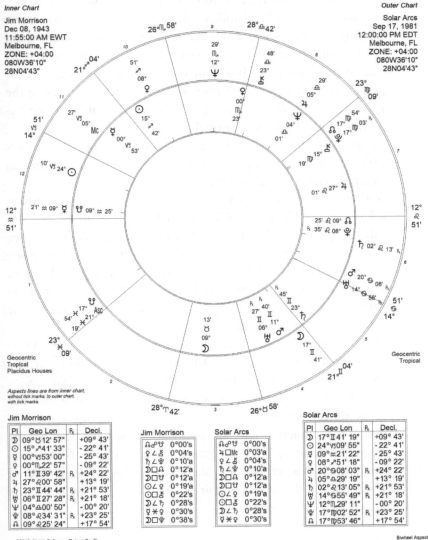

Inner Chart

Jim Morrison
Dec 08, 1943
11:55:00 AM EWT
Melbourne, FL
ZONE: +04:00
080W36'10"
28N04'43"

Outer Chart

Solar Arcs
Sep 17, 1981
12:00:00 PM EDT
Melbourne, FL
ZONE: +04:00
080W36'10"
28N04'43"

Geocentric
Tropical
Placidus Houses

Geocentric
Tropical

Aspects lines are from inner chart,
without tick marks, to outer chart,
with tick marks.

©2018 Matrix Software Gainesville, FL

Biwheel Aspects

Jim Morrison

Pl	Geo Lon	R	Decl.
☽	09° ♉ 12' 57"		+09° 43'
☉	15° ♐ 41' 33"		- 22° 41'
☿	00° ♑ 53' 00"		- 25° 43'
♀	00° ♏ 22' 57"		- 09° 22'
♂	11° ♊ 39' 42"	R	+24° 22'
♃	27° ♌ 00' 58"		+13° 19'
♄	23° ♊ 44' 44"	R	+21° 53'
♅	06° ♊ 27' 28"	R	+21° 18'
♆	04° ♎ 00' 50"		- 00° 20'
♇	08° ♌ 34' 31"	R	+23° 25'
☊	09° ♌ 25' 24"		+17° 54'

Jim Morrison   Solar Arcs

☊☌♅	0°00's	
♀∠♇	0°04's	
♄∠♇	0°10'a	
☽□☊	0°12'a	
☽□♅	0°12'a	
☉∠♀	0°19'a	
☉□♇	0°22's	
☽∠♄	0°28's	
☿☆♀	0°30's	
☽□♇	0°38's	

☊☌♅	0°00's	
♃□Mc	0°03'a	
♀∠♇	0°04's	
♄∠♇	0°10'a	
☽□☊	0°12'a	
☽□♅	0°12'a	
☉∠♀	0°19'a	
☽∠♄	0°28's	
☿☆♀	0°30's	

Solar Arcs

Pl	Geo Lon	R	Decl.
☽	17° ♊ 41' 19"		+09° 43'
☉	24° ♑ 09' 55"		- 22° 41'
☿	09° ♒ 21' 22"		- 25° 43'
♀	08° ♐ 51' 18"		- 09° 22'
♂	20° ♋ 08' 03"	R	+24° 22'
♃	05° ♎ 29' 19"		+13° 19'
♄	02° ♌ 13' 05"	R	+21° 53'
♅	14° ♋ 55' 49"	R	+21° 18'
♆	12° ♏ 29' 11"		- 00° 20'
♇	17° ♍ 02' 52"	R	+23° 25'
☊	17° ♍ 53' 46"		+17° 54'

- When someone's Moon progresses into the seventh house, it's not just about personal relationships. That event typically coincides with increasing public visibility – in fact, the whole period when the progressed Moon is above the horizon has that property, but it is the literal *rising of the progressed Moon* that often represents a dramatic emergence. Jim Morrison experienced such a "Progressed Moonrise" on September 6, 1978 – three years before the infamous *Rolling Stone* cover – but right on schedule with the rising tide of his posthumous popularity.
- On May 19, 1980, as his record sales were exploding, Morrison's solar arc Pluto – also in his seventh house – formed a triggering square to his *tenth house* Sagittarian Sun.
- Transiting Uranus conjuncted Morrison's Midheaven three times: in December 1980, June 1981, and finally on September 19, 1981 – that last date is only *two days* after the pub date of that *Rolling Stone* cover. Seeing Uranus crossing the Midheaven, if I were sitting with a client, I might have said "expect the unexpected in your career." That might be how I would have said to Jim Morrison too – but I would have needed a Ouija Board to do it. He was maybe hot and sexy, but he was dead.
- There's more: Solar Arc Mercury made a conjunction with Morrison's lunar South Node on October 11, 1981, while Solar Arc Venus had just made a trine to his Pluto on June 8, 1981. Note that Pluto ruled Morrison's Scorpio Midheaven, linking that Venus event directly to his career. Meanwhile, by progression, Venus formed a conjunction with his tenth house Sun less than a year later, on August 1, 1982. Progressed Venus hits the Midheaven and an artist's career takes off like a rocket? No astrologer would be surprised at that development – *but what if the artist had died a decade earlier?*

All of this raises some really profound questions about how astrology works, and how a chart might live on under its own steam, even after death. Maybe that's true . . . but a great danger in astrology lies in generalizing too much from a single example. *"I'm a Sagittarian and I hate parakeets. Therefore Sagittarians hate parakeets."*

Could the uncanny relevance of Jim Morrison's posthumous transits, progressions, and solar arcs be some kind of fluke?

I have not made an exhaustive study of all of this. The subject fascinates me, so I wish that I had the time to do that. I think it would make an excellent topic for a book, in fact. Lacking the opportunity to dive into the question in an exhaustive way, I figured I would check out another example – the first one that happened to come into my mind – and simply see if the pattern still held. If it worked a second time, maybe I was onto something. If it failed . . . well, if it failed, I would not be writing this newsletter.

As I cast about for another possibility, I immediately thought of Vincent Van Gogh. Arguably, no painter in the past two centuries has become so instantly recognizable, so widely copied, nor had such an impact upon collective taste. *And yet during his life, Van Gogh was poverty-stricken.* By most reports, he sold only one single painting in his lifetime – and that only seven months before he died. In other words, in my search for people whose lives illustrated a burst of posthumous fame, Van Gogh supplied an even better test than Jim Morrison, at least in terms of contrast. Unlike Van Gogh, Morrison did enjoy enormous fame – perhaps enjoyed it a little too much – during his life.

Van Gogh, on the other hand, was lucky to get a meal.

Vincent Van Gogh was born in Zundert, Holland on March 30, 1853, at 11:00 AM. That birth time, given on the hour, seems potentially shaky, but it has a Rodden rating of AA. Again, as with Jim Morrison, I want to look at his transits, progressions, and solar arcs for a big moment in Van Gogh's . . .*er* . . . life. Once more I'll present this information in two charts. This first one shows his progressions and transits for May 15, 1990 . . .

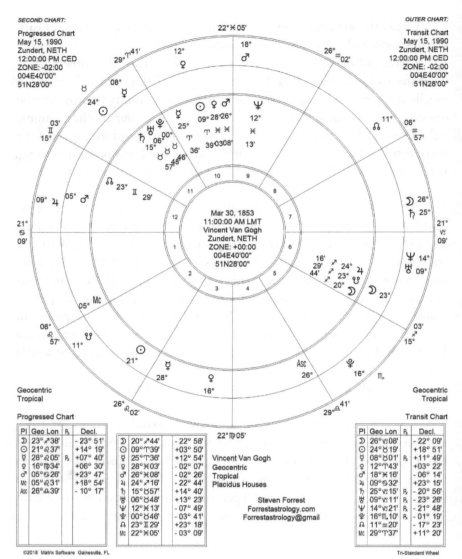

©2018 Matrix Software Gainesville, FL

And here are Vincent Van Gogh's solar arcs for that same date:

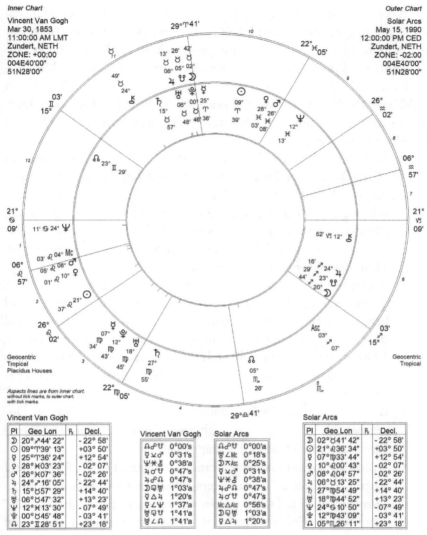

Inner Chart

Vincent Van Gogh
Mar 30, 1853
11:00:00 AM LMT
Zundert, NETH
ZONE: +00:00
004E40'00"
51N28'00"

Outer Chart

Solar Arcs
May 15, 1990
12:00:00 PM CED
Zundert, NETH
ZONE: -02:00
004E40'00"
51N28'00"

Geocentric
Tropical
Placidus Houses

Aspects lines are from inner chart,
without tick marks, to outer chart,
with tick marks.

Geocentric
Tropical

©2018 Matrix Software Gainesville, FL

Biwheel Aspects

Vincent Van Gogh

Pl	Geo Lon	R	Decl.
☽	20°♐44' 22"		- 22° 58'
☉	09°♈39' 13"		+03° 50'
☿	25°♈36' 24"		+12° 54'
♀	28°♓03' 23"		- 02° 07'
♂	26°♓07' 36"		- 02° 26'
♃	24°♐16' 05"		- 22° 44'
♄	15°♉57' 29"		+14° 40'
♅	06°♉47' 32"		+13° 23'
♆	12°♓13' 30"		- 07° 49'
♇	00°♉45' 48"		- 03° 41'
☊	23°♊28' 51"		+23° 18'

Vincent Van Gogh   Solar Arcs

☊♂♅	0°00's	☊♂♅	0°00'a
☿⛢♂	0°31's	♅∠Mc	0°18's
♆⚹♅	0°38'a	☽⊼Asc	0°25's
♃♂♇	0°47's	☿⛢♂	0°31's
♃♂☊	0°47's	♆⚹♅	0°38'a
☽♅♅	1°03'a	♃♂☊	0°47's
☿△♃	1°20's	♃♂♅	0°47's
☿∠♆	1°37'a	Mc△Asc	0°56's
♅♅♀	1°41'a	☽♅♅	1°03's
♅∠☊	1°41'a	☿△♃	1°20's

Solar Arcs

Pl	Geo Lon	R	Decl.
☽	02°♉41' 42"		- 22° 58'
☉	21°♌36' 34"		+03° 50'
☿	07°♍33' 44"		+12° 54'
♀	10°♌00' 43"		- 02° 07'
♂	08°♌04' 57"		- 02° 26'
♃	06°♉13' 25"		- 22° 44'
♄	27°♍54' 49"		+14° 40'
♅	18°♍44' 52"		+13° 23'
♆	24°♋10' 50"		- 07° 49'
♇	12°♍43' 09"		- 03° 41'
☊	05°♏26' 11"		+23° 18'

As of this writing, the highest price, corrected for inflation, ever fetched by any painting in auction was US$82.5 million. That happened (in under three minutes) on May 15, 1990. The painting was *The Portrait of Dr. Gachet,* painted in June 1890, just one month before Van Gogh shot himself.

I cannot help but ponder the sense of irony that Vincent Van Gogh would have felt had he known the price that painting of his would fetch almost exactly one century after his death. That money would have bought him a lot of absinthe.

- In Vincent Van Gogh's natal chart, we see a triple conjunction of the Moon, the lunar south node, and Jupiter, aoo of them in Sagittarius and in the sixth house. When *The Portrait of Dr Gachet* sold for that jackpot price, the progressed Moon was right there aligned with those sensitive points. It had just conjuncted the artist's natal Moon on March 1, 1990. It hit his south node on May 11 and his Jupiter on the 31st – right on schedule.

- Transiting Jupiter made a square to his Sun on October 1, 1989, quickly retrograded over it again on November 24, 1989 . . . and here is my favorite part. Jupiter squared Van Gogh's Sun a final time on the very day his painting broke all the records: May 15, 1990, a hundred years after he was gone. (And anybody who thinks squares are automatically bad news obviously needs a reality-check.)

- By solar arc, Van Gogh's Venus made a trine to his Sun on December 29, 1989. It was, in other words, only half a degree past exactitude when the big sale happened.

- Jupiter conjoined his natal Uranus on December 17, 1990 – and when I see Jupiter-Uranus interactions, I always tell my clients to *enter contests*. (I tell them deeper things too!) Van Gogh "won big" – but was it Vincent Van Gogh or just his chart that won? And what exactly is the difference? Discuss.

Again, extensive research might possibly reveal that these two examples are just weirdly lucky, but I doubt it. I think this phenomenon is real. The questions it raises are about as juicy as astrological questions get. The souls of Jim Morrison and Vincent Van Gogh were no longer bound in any definitive way to their birthcharts. Were those souls sailing in astral realms? Had either of them already reincarnated? Van Gogh had a century to think about returning, Morrison only a decade. Both had tragic deaths – dare I say "dumb deaths?" One died by unintentional overdose and the other one by suicide. I've often heard lamas and metaphysical teachers say that such precipitous exits tend to lead to quick re-entries.

The inescapable fact is that neither of these human beings were "in" their charts anymore, at least not in the ways that we customarily assume. *And yet their charts lived on*, still actively responding to astrological stimulus, as if they were ghosts or machines whose batteries had not yet run down.

And maybe those are the right metaphors, more or less – that your chart lives on after you no longer need it, as if it were a ghost or a machine. Charts seem to still work, at least in a mechanical sort of way, after we pass away. Our two examples demonstrate that principle pretty clearly, I think.

Let me take this one step further – meanwhile hoping that you can handle a little more weirdness.

I knew a little bit about Vincent Van Gogh when I was young, but seeing his museum in Amsterdam when I was twenty-four impacted me so profoundly that I felt compelled to write about it in my second book, *The Changing Sky*. (It's Chapter Thirteen, "Weather Working," if you want to follow up – I still remember having tears in my eyes as I wrote those words so long ago.)

That backpacking, youth-hostelling trip to Europe happened in 1973. Van Gogh had already been dead for over eighty years. If I said that "his art still touched me," no one would bat an eye. *But was what touched me more than his art?* Was his "ghost" still in the air?

That Sagittarian complex in Vincent Van Gogh's chart happens to align with my natal Venus – and, weirdly, *his* progressed Moon was entering *my* seventh house around that time . . .

. . . *but at some point, astrology can drive you crazy, and I think maybe I just put my toe over that line.*

In any case, Jim Morrison and Vincnt Van Gogh got me thinking. I see that my own progressed Sun will trine my Midheaven on September 1, 2058. Four years later, Jupiter will do the same thing by solar arc.

Looks pretty good for my career then, eh?

Of course I'll be a hundred and nine years old when all that gets going, so I am hoping they serve hot buttered popcorn on the other side of the veil.

Until then, please stay well. I'll do my best to do the same.

SECTION TWO

THE ASTROLOGICAL HOUSES

We astrologers can all agree on where Mercury is located in a chart – but the cusp of the third house? Where exactly is that? Voices quickly rise in disagreement and they tend to drown each other out. In the opening chapter of this section, I make my case for Placidus houses – but I hope you'll read between the lines and detect my deeper argument, which is for civility and open-mindedness in this contentious area. Still, trying to do astrology without houses would be like trying to put together a puzzle with a third of the pieces missing. We've all got to choose a system, as flawed as they all are.

Later in this section, you'll also read a long piece about one of my favorite subjects: what's missing from our contemporary understanding of the sixth house – and then another piece wrestling with the complex interdependency of the third and sixth houses, along with their corresponding signs, Gemini and Virgo. How can they be both ruled by the same planet and yet also square to each other? Are they friends or enemies?

Finally, there's a piece about my adventures in China and what they've taught me about how astrology might take a more visceral view of the ninth house.

12

Should you happen to enjoy dirty looks, all you need to do is to find a diverse group of astrologers and mention which system of house division you've found to be the most effective. In my experience, astrologers get more foam-at-the-mouth partisan about this subject than any other. In this next essay, I paint the fateful bull's eye on my own forehead by making my case for Placidus houses. As you will read between the lines in the words that follow, I am reporting my thoughts and experience, along with some often-misunderstood astrological history, rather than seeking converts.

WHY I USE PLACIDUS HOUSES

(Newsletter – July 2021)

There are many different schools of thought in astrology. Strange as it might seem, in the right hands all of them seem to work pretty well, even systems that contradict each other very directly. Western Tropical astrology versus Vedic astrology is perhaps the classic illustration – those two systems can't even agree on where Aries is!

I think of myself as a Capricorn, but in Benares I am transformed into a Sagittarian. It's confusing, but I like to keep the word "versus" out of the discussion as much as possible. Both systems, Western and Vedic, *can help people*. Both can illuminate the mystery we call human life.

Reading an astrological chart is not linear and logical like reading a newspaper or a column of figures. I always despair when someone asks if I can "take a quick glance at their chart." There is no such thing as "a quick glance." Deciphering the message of the planets is a lot more like interpreting a dream or a poem – there's more than one right way to make sense of it, in other words. You have to sit with it for a while.

The last time I had a reading myself, it was actually with a Vedic astrologer. That was intentional. I knew that if I asked an evolutionary astrologer to look at my chart, my ego would get in the way. I'd be too busy "correcting" the person to learn anything. But Vedic – I know almost nothing about it, so I was able to put my ego aside and simply listen. It was helpful, so long as I focussed on the plain English of what the astrologer was saying, and ignored the discordant astrological language.

Me, a Sagittarian? Mister work-all-the-time Capricorn? Forget about it.

Anyway, I am writing all of this because in this newsletter, I am going to jump into one of the bloodiest shark tanks in the whole chaotic, contentious astrological community – the question of which house system to use.

There are at least a dozen different ways of laying out the houses of a chart, maybe more. When I was a young astrologer, I tried as many of them as I could find, naturally always using my own chart – and the realities of my own experience – as the acid test. Very little in astrology is ever totally clear cut – again, a chart is more like a dream than a computer manual. But during those early years, Placidus houses won the battle for my heart and my mind. I've used them ever since, successfully, with thousands upon thousands of clients over the past fifty years. Nowadays, I rarely even consider other systems.

That said, I am miles away from being a "house system fundamentalist." I respect the work of many astrologers who operate in different frameworks. As Robert Hand once quipped, "which is truer, French or German?" Obviously one can lie in either language – or illuminate us all with the nectar of truth.

That said, in my old apprenticeship programs and in my current online school, the Forrest Center for Evolutionary Astrology, I do insist on everyone using the Placidus system. That is mainly so that we are all speaking the same language. In those programs, I am narrowly focussed on teaching my own system rather than giving a cross-cultural overview of the wide world of contemporary astrological practice. It's a trade school, not a university.

I am unclear about the ratio of diplomacy to truth in what I am about to say. I know there's some of both in the mixture. When challenged about my adherence to Placidus houses, I often say that, of all the house systems I have tried, Placidus seems to be the one which *best answers the questions in which I am interested.* And not all astrologers are interested in the same questions! Personally, I am eternally drawn to wondering about how the soul's journey through life casts a shadow on our psychological processes – how soul and psyche mirror each other, in other words. I am interested in helping people grow, both psychologically and spiritually. The Placidus system addresses those kinds of evolutionary issues eloquently and reliably.

On the other hand, I am not drawn to questions about money or when I will get married or which horse will win the race. I don't do anything with medical astrology. I am not interested in the stock market. Maybe other house systems would do better in those areas, I don't know.

Technically, the Placidus system is easy to explain. Most, but not all, systems of house division are founded on the horizon and the *meridian,* which is the line connecting the noon point and the midnight point. These are the familiar *four angles* of the birthchart, and there's nothing controversial about their locations: sunrise, sunset, noon, and midnight. The intervening house cusps are the ones over which astrologers squabble.

Here's how Placidus works. Start your stopwatch at sunrise. Stop it when the Sun reaches the highest point it will reach in the sky that day – that's the Midheaven, and roughly corresponds to high noon.

How long a period of time elapsed?

In average terms, the answer will run about six hours, but that figure varies enormously with the seasons. Let's go ahead and start with the idea of six hours. Where was the Sun after *two* of those hours had passed? That's your 12th house cusp. Two *more* hours? That's the 11th house cusp.

Once you've got houses 12 and 11 nailed down, you already know 6 and 5 – they are always directly opposite 12 and 11 – if your 12th house starts in mid-Cancer, your 6th house starts in mid-Capricorn, in other words.

Now time the passage of the Sun from high noon down to sunset, do the same equal division of time, and you've got the rest of the Placidian house cusps.

That's it, really. The only complication is that, as we mentioned, the sunrise-to-noon figure is not always six hours. In winter, for example, the daylight hours are shorter. Depending on where you live, there may only be sunlight for, say, ten hours. That means it will not take as long for the Sun to reach its highest elevation and go down again. But you still calculate Placidus houses in exactly the same way – you are simply *trisecting the time* it takes for the Sun to pass through each *quadrant* of the chart. Each one-third of that time marks a house cusp.

The math may be tricky, but the basic concept is, as you can see, really simple.

Astrologer Anthony Louis makes the point that Placidus houses represented something really prescient in that the system anticipated the Einsteinian notion of "a spacetime continuum." With Placidus houses, we are talking about the *geometry of spacetime* rather than just the three-dimensional geometry of space alone.

Louis also points out that the origins of the Placidus system are truly ancient. I'll give you the quick version of the history here, but if you want to learn more just Google these four words: *Anthony Louis house systems*. As you'll discover, Louis is a true scholar, but one with the gift of writing clearly and never trying to impress anyone with mere erudite obfuscation – as I just did with those three words. I really appreciate all that Anthony Louis has contributed to the uplifting of modern astrological discourse both in terms of content and attitude.

Anyway, let's get to the quick version of the history behind Placidus houses. We start by going back to the city of Alexandria in Egypt in the second century A.D. There we find Ptolemy, often viewed as the father of western astrology. He wrote his famous *Tetrabiblios* which includes the method of house-calculation which much, much later, after following a winding road, came to be known as the Placidus system. So it goes back at least that far – although it is obscure where Ptolemy himself got the ideas behind it. The Placidus system may be much older.

Skip forward some centuries, add the Dark Ages to the mix, and we come to the work of an astrologer known as Regiomontanus. Born Johannes Müller von Königsberg, he was a mathematician and astronomer living in Germany in the 15th century. According to Anthony Louis, Regiomontanus misread or misunderstood Ptolemy and created a system of house division based on unwitting errors of translation.

"Regiomontanus" houses soon became the dominant system all across Europe.

Meanwhile, back in the 11th century, in Muslim Spain, Jewish scholar, Ibn ben Ezra, had *correctly* understood Ptolemy's work and had written about it – in Hebrew, which few people outside the Jewish community could read.

Finally, enter an Olivetan monk named Placidus de Titus, who was a 17th century professor of mathematics, physics, and astronomy at the University of Pavia in what is now Italy. Unlike Regiomontanus, he got it right. He read Ibn ben Ezra's take on Ptolemy correctly, published his work, and thus the so-called "Placidus" house system burst upon the western world, *under a misleading name, and about a millennium and a half after Ptolemy had first written about it.*

Bad astrological theory can thrive in discussion groups, but it fails miserably and painfully in the counseling room. Sitting with clients, talking about their charts, if you say something they know simply does not fit their reality, it is painfully awkward for both them and yourself. And of course if you say something that moves them or ignites the lightbulb of insight over their heads, it's an uplifting experience for the astrologer as well as for the client. That was presumably just as true in the 17th century as it is today.

Bottom line, Placidus worked better than Regiomontanus and so it soon took over.

There are many other systems of house division – Koch, Morinus, Porphyry, Alcabitious. Again, I am not a fundamentalist about any of this. I just know that Placidus houses have served my clients and myself very well for a long while. More importantly, they have been around for a couple thousand years and they have stood the test of time.

Are Placidus houses the final answer? *Is there a final answer?* I have no idea.

One problem is that, in common with many systems, Placidus houses break down at extreme northerly or southerly latitudes. Just think of the "Land of the Midnight Sun." *Where there is no sunset, how can there be a Descendant? Where the Sun never rises, as in the arctic winter, how can there be a Midheaven?*

Perhaps some astrological genius not yet born will answer these questions and come up with a better system. Studying the lives of Finns, Laplanders, and Inuit people might provide a path to the answer. Too cold there for me, but it puts a sparkle in my eye to think there might be some young astrologer reading these words and thinking of booking a flight to Reykjavik, Thule, or Helsinki.

Some astrologers use Equal houses. Again, bless us one and all. But personally, I just don't like that floating Midheaven. Why have a little island of 10th house energy sometimes floating around in the 9th house. That's just too sloppy for me.

Then there are *whole sign houses,* where if you have Gemini rising, anything in Gemini is in your 1st house, anything in Cancer is in your 2nd house, and so on. This is the heart of the Hellenistic system, which has experienced a rebirth in popularity over the past twenty years or so. My friend Chris Brennan has done brilliant and popular work spearheading that resurgence.

As I have already emphasized, I think that many distinct forms of astrology can all contradict each other and still all produce helpful results, just as there might be several helpful interpretations of the same dream. But personally, give me a *timed* Ascendant, and I am a lot happier. I see a lot of difference between a planet in the 12th house and one in the 1st house, even if they are both in Gemini.

Saying this will get me in trouble, but I think that whole sign houses were a brilliant work-around regarding a serious practical problem the astrologers of antiquity faced: they didn't know what time it was. They had no clocks.

So that's my story and I'm sticking to it. I speak Placidus. That's the system I use and that's what I teach. It has never failed me, except with births at extreme latitudes. I happily encourage newcomers to astrology to give it a try and see if it speaks to them. Ultimately though the true test is always your own heart and your own experience.

13

*I've always been a big fan of the Mountain Astrologer magazine. I
appreciate its welcoming, "big tent" approach to our field. Over the years,
I've written several articles which appeared in its pages. Some of them
appear again in this volume, and next up is one of my favorites. It's
a rambling piece about something I figured out about the sixth house
– something which I felt particularly eager to share with the larger
astrological community since I had found it so helpful and relevant myself.*

THE CASE OF THE
DISAPPEARING SIXTH
HOUSE

(The Mountain Astrologer magazine, 6/2002, issue #103)

Who killed the sixth house? I am about to explore its symbolism with
you and I am extremely excited about the material I'm about to
present.

Excited? *About the sixth house?* This may be the first time in four or
five hundred years that any astrologer who wasn't a Virgo could make that
kind of statement.

Right away, we have our first clue . . .

CLUE NUMBER ONE

In the astrological houses, we take life in all its enormity and we divide it into twelve boxes. *Can you imagine leaving one of the boxes boring and flat?* What's wrong with this picture? But let's face it: in most astrological literature, the sixth house is generally represented as the House of Pocket Protectors. When we're studying Astrology 101, we dutifully learn the requisite key words: *routines, habits, service, work, maybe health.* And then we quickly move on to the juicier terrain of the seventh house and perhaps the even juicier terrain of the eighth house.

What's missing here? Doesn't it feel as if there might be a great big hole where the human richness of sixth house symbolism should go?

So far this doesn't tell us much – only that something might be missing. No house should be boring, not with only twelve boxes to hold all of life.

That is our first clue.

CLUE NUMBER TWO

Speaking of holes, let's talk about another one. Consider the wheel of houses. As most of us know, the seventh house is traditionally associated with *marriage and intimacy,* with the seventh cusp being the quintessential astrological symbol of relationship – the person sitting on the other side of the table from you, a person with whom you are connecting romantically, or maybe a person onto whom you are projecting your own unresolved psychological issues.

If we stand back and see the whole western side of the chart coming to a focus at that seventh cusp, representing "The Other," a lot of things fall into place. Most of the houses on the western (right!) side of the chart are about relationships. Why not the sixth? As we've already seen, the seventh is the classic "House of Marriage." Most of us doing psychologically sophisticated astrology recognize that *the eighth house is about sexual mating and bonding,* among other things. *The fifth is the "House of Love Affairs"* and of course it's the House of Children too – another form of human connectedness. The fourth house with its "home and hearth" symbolism, should be included here too.

So in terms of astrology's relationship-oriented houses, the count goes: *four, five . . . hmmm . . . seven, eight.*

That's our second clue: *there is a gaping hole where the intimate symbolism of the sixth house should be*. But it is not normally seen as a relationship house – except perhaps in the dreary sense of it referring to our responsibilities toward others.

I believe that the sixth house is a vibrant symbol of certain kinds of relationships as well. We're going to discover that just like the other four western-side houses that I've just mentioned, the sixth house refers to a very particular and unique kind of human relationship – one that has tended to be eclipsed from our understanding in modern Western culture.

The cycle of these five houses – four, five, six, seven, and eight – I would incidentally call the *Arc of Intimacy*. This is a term my ex-wife, Jodie, and I introduced in our synastry book, *Skymates*, many years ago.

Summarizing what we've learned so far:

- Our first clue is that there is a great big vacuum of energetic, compelling meaning where sixth house symbolism should go.
- Our second clue is that this lost piece must have something to do with relationships – and perhaps some aspect of human relationship about which we are currently in a culturally foggy state. Otherwise we wouldn't have misplaced it.

CLUE NUMBER THREE

What's the house of work? Probably the first answer off the top of your head is the tenth house, which is of course the classic "House of Career." But the sixth house usually gets added to the pile too. I would guess that the majority of modern astrologers, in the realities of the counseling room, do not make a particularly stark distinction between sixth house symbolism and tenth house symbolism when a client is asking career-related questions. We simply use both of those houses, and see them both as pertinent to the issue of work, each in its own way. The tenth house has more to do with status, while the sixth is more "Monday morning."

I do believe that practice is valid, but it does suggest some fuzziness in our theories. Why should we have two houses that are so nearly interchangeable? To me, that suggests that we're making some kind of systematic error in our thinking.

There's our third clue: is there *something about work in relation to the sixth house which we are missing?* Something that makes it fundamentally different from the tenth house rather than just a watered-down, also-ran version of the same thing?

CLUE NUMBER FOUR

Our fourth hint comes from horary astrology, and it's basically about counting houses.

Let's say your cat has lost her bell and you want to find it with an horary chart. Here's how it would work: we know that possessions are represented by the second house. Meanwhile, pets are represented by the sixth house. "Where is my cat's bell?" In this case, according to the laws of horary astrology, the eighth house would give the answer. Why? *Because it's the second house from the sixth house.* It's your *pet's* possession for which you are searching.

Here's how that leads us to our fourth clue.

The fourth house refers to your parents – and I'll just say both of them, and avoid the whole mess about whether the fourth house is your father or your mother. Meanwhile, the third house refers to brothers and sisters. So, *the third house counted from the fourth would then represent your parents' brothers or sisters.*

That of course would be the sixth house.

We have a formal term for your father's or mother's sister in relation to you: your *aunt.* And their brother is of course your *uncle.* So, in this form of traditional astrology, the sixth house refers to your aunts and your uncles. You still sometimes find that reference when you open up some of the older books.

That's our fourth clue: *the sixth house is about aunts and uncles.*

Relations between aunts and uncles and their nieces and nephews, in traditional cultures, are rich and important, with very specific functions. We've lost much of that connection nowadays. Most of us no longer have very intimate relationships with our aunts and uncles.

Maybe we're now beginning to perceive some of that "cultural fogginess" I mentioned a few paragraphs back? Maybe we are zero-ing in on our fourth clue about the missing pieces of the sixth house.

Here's how all of this came alive for me. I have a nephew named Tim. He's graduating from college now, but this story goes back to when he was pubescent. There was a big Fourth of July gathering down on the Carolina coast where my parents live. The whole family was there. I found myself away from the other adults, hanging out with Tim and some of the other boys. Their average age was probably about eleven. We were lighting bottle rockets and firecrackers and having a good time.

One of the kids – the "wild" one – decides to test my edges a bit. He tells a dirty joke. (I believe the complete text of the joke boiled down to "penis, penis, penis.") Of course, all the other pubescent boys get a big laugh. This kid had strutted a bir, showing some style and daring: he had ventured out on thin ice in front of one of the grown-ups. Maybe I would yell at him or rat him out to his mother – but he was betting I wouldn't.

Poor Tim was suddenly in a very tough political situation. He really wanted to save face with his friends, and in order to do that, he had to laugh knowingly at the joke. But, he also feared that I might be a pipeline back to his mom – I'm her brother after all. He sensed his mom's bad attitude toward dirty jokes.

You could just about watch Tim looking at the other kids, and then looking at me, trying to figure out which risk was the lesser of two evils. If he had been a cat, his tail would have been nervously twitching.

Welcome to the wonderful world of adult neurosis, Tim.

Fortunately, as synchronicity would have it, I'd begun to do a little thinking about the sixth house. I'm Tim's uncle. *So, what's my role?* I had to laugh at the joke! I laughed as if "penis, penis, penis" were the funniest thing I'd ever heard.

Naturally, making the adult laugh was worth some points to these young guys too. So another kid gets brave and tells a joke. I think that one was "vagina, vagina, vagina."

After a cycle of these jokes, little Tim finally got around to telling one of his own. You could tell he was really taking a big risk. But, with my approval implicit in my laughter, I'd made it safe.

Tim, in common with a lot of young people today, doesn't live with his "bio" dad anymore. He's been through that emotional meat-grinder. He's toughened up a lot because of it, and I suspect, silenced a lot in himself because of it.

Two days after the joke-fest, Tim and I went for a walk, and without any prompting on my part, he opened up to me about some of his real feelings about his family. We could call that "chance," but I don't think so. By laughing at those jokes and implicitly creating a bond of confidentiality between us, I had filled the archetypal role of the uncle for him. Tim sensed that too. He was a young kid at the time and he probably didn't think philosophically about such matters. He didn't need to. Like everyone else, he has a sixth house, which is to say that he has an instinctual place in his psyche where this uncle/nephew relationship fits – or more broadly, where his relationship with an adult *mentor* or *initiator* fits.

- This mentoring, initiating relationship, to me, is the lost soul of sixth house symbolism.

Tim was a boy facing puberty – may God help him, right?

How much good can mom and dad do for Tim as he faces puberty? Some, maybe! They have a role to play there, but there are limits on what they can do. The natural instinct of a healthy mother or father towards children is to protect them no matter what, to make the world safe for them. Of all the things that are likely to hurt us in life, sex is near the top of the list – and here I mean the word "sex" broadly, including all the complex and sometimes heartbreaking realities that unfold between people who are involved with each other, body, heart, and soul.

Is there any way a parent could protect a child from those hard realities? Of course not. And yet, the parent still has that protective instinct. One result is that parents, generally speaking, tend to be a little too suppressive of a child's sexuality as he or she hits puberty.

I love my nephew, *but I don't love him the way his mother does.* This small degree of emotional distance gives me one tremendous advantage over her: *I am vastly more at peace with the idea that Tim is going to have to face adult life than any decent parent ever could be.* One result was that I could stand there joking about sexuality with this twelve-year-old boy, and thus *help initiate him into the world of maleness.*

Sexuality is a lot more complicated than dirty jokes. But it was developmentally significant for my nephew and me, out of the earshot of women, to broach this taboo subject. The interaction announced loudly and clearly that speaking of this powerful, strange energy is no longer forbidden between us – that "as men" our sexuality, and its joys, fascinations, and dilemmas, is something that we share. While we are of different ages, we're both in that same boat. Implicit in the interaction was an assurance that while I can't make sexual realities safe for him, I can maybe give some advice or at least respond to questions.

It said *I can be your mentor.* "Uncle" – and "aunt" – are just other words for the same thing.

CLUE NUMBER FIVE

In traditional astrology, we find the sixth house described as the "House of Servants." Because servants are scarcer than they used to be, "servant" has devolved in practice into "service." Thus, in learning about the sixth house, we hear about *helpfulness* and our sense of *duty towards others.*

Let's not throw out the baby with the bathwater. There is another clue hidden in there.

A servant serves a master. We're looking at a relationship that's *inherently unequal.* Just like the bond between an uncle and a nephew or an aunt and a niece, the servant and the master are on different planes in terms of power. I was "Uncle Steve," while Tim was just Tim. I had a title – one that he was expected to use – while he lacked one. Obviously none of this "went to my head" – I didn't walk around feeling superior to my nephew. But the *underlying hierarchical social structure* was implicit in the language. I knew it and he knew it. If I had wanted to, I could have "turned him in" for telling a dirty joke.

Go way back into the esoteric astrological traditions and you find the sixth house emerging as the "House of Discipleship." That's another part of our fifth clue: there's a very fine line between a servant and a disciple. In both cases, *the servant or the disciple derives identity from a relationship with one whom he or she calls a "master"* – although the word "master" obviously takes on a very different connotation in each of those relationships.

With one short step, we can add another layer: the relationship of an *apprentice* to a master. The master electrician takes on an apprentice whom he mentors, The same can be said for the piano teacher and her student.

Once when we get right down to the *underlying unequal power structure* of the interaction, it's exactly the same kind of relationship in all of these cases – and by introducing the word *apprentice*, we've hit pay dirt – we've linked sixth house symbolism back to *work*, via the master-apprentice relationship.

THE DARK SIDE

Let's take a quick glance in the direction of the devil and introduce a darker sixth house word: *slave*. A slave also serves a master. The hierarchical master/servant logic is the same, but now we see it expressed in a twisted, evil version.

This should not surprise us. In common with all astrological symbols, the sixth house has a horrific side, as well as a beautiful, dharmic side. Slavery is sixth house garbage. And not all slaves wear chains: *when an aunt, uncle, master or mentor assumes inappropriate levels of dominion over a younger person, or abuses that younger person, we are looking at sixth house slavery.*

BACK TO THE LIGHT

The critical point is that throughout history in traditional societies all over the earth – *with the possible exception of western civilization for the last hundred years or so* – we've institutionalized this kind of healthy, mutually-satisfying relationship between people who were not on an equal footing. It is fundamental to human sanity, and it takes many healthy forms.

- The spiritual master and the disciple.
- The craft-master and the apprentice.
- The uncle or aunt and the niece or nephew.
- The mentor, hero, or role-model and those who model themselves on that person or draw inspiration there.

Today, many of us are mothers and fathers, which is hard enough – *but we're also asked to fill the shoes of aunt and uncle.* That's one of the reasons for the pervasive sense that there's something inherently wrong with the idea of a "nuclear" family. To develop normally, every child needs a variety of mentors and adult role models. The sixth house refers to every one of them – *except for mother and father!*

We've created various surrogates in an attempt to fill this vacuum. *"Meet my Aunt Sue – she's not really my aunt, but . . . "* In our culture, that syntax is commonplace, demonstrating how we've even managed to transfer the literal words, "aunt and uncle," by solid sixth house instinct, into relationships that are not actually based on kinship, but which fill the same psychological and developmental purpose.

Nowadays, school teachers are often expected to mentor children – then they're constrained and sometimes punished legally when they try.

There's television, which can be a dark mentor. How many kids nowadays are raised by TV? How many find their heroes and role models there? Or on Youtube? That's the one wound that my Pluto-in-Leo generation has failed to mythologize – that we were the first generation in history to be raised by television sets instead of by human beings. I got my sense of what was expected of me as a man by watching *The Lone Ranger* and *Superman*.

Meanwhile, my dad was at work.

How strange that the Industrial Revolution created that twisted reality – for a man to be a good husband and father, he had to abandon the company of his family before dawn every morning and not see them again until he was exhausted and the sun had gone down!

How can a son learn anything from his father that way?

Uncles, even devoted ones, are even more absent. Mothers and aunts have been swept down the same torrent only in the past half century, but now they're gone as well.

They're often at work too.

LINEAGE

In my imagination, I see a line of human beings. They're all dressed in white robes. Tracing it back, we see the line disappearing into a bank of fog. We don't know how far back the line goes. Everyone in this long line is holding a candle. None of the candles are burning except for the one belonging to the first person. She stares at the flame for a moment, then she slowly turns and looks up, making eye contact with the next person in the line. She lights that person's candle.

Then she then withdraws her own candle, blows it out, and lowers her chin.

That's her death.

The next person now holds the sacred flame. The process repeats. Thus, one single flame is passed on, person to person, down the line of the centuries.

What is this flame? It is a *quality of consciousness* – something that can only be passed along one-to-one, eye-to-eye, from elder to younger, from master to apprentice. Every step happens in the context of precious, intimate sixth house relationships.

Does it matter if we get seven people down the line and number seven forgets the name of number one? Not at all, not really – although some traditions make a ritual of remembering all the names. Think of the lineages of Tibetan Buddhist gurus tracing their teachers back to Buddha, or the lineage of the Roman Catholic Popes going back to Saint Peter and Jesus.

Still, remembering names doesn't really matter. What matters is the *flame itself,* present tense, along with the delicate process of passing it on.

Some of these flames go back so far that we could fairly say that they predate the human species. That's an extreme statement perhaps – but some lineages are so elemental that they existed in the animal traditions from which we descended: *parents nurturing children who thus learn to nurture their own children* is the most obvious example.

Others are johnny-come-latelies, such as the astrological lineage in which we are all participating. Or Buddhism or Christianity.

There are a few total newcomers among the lineages: talk to a young "grunge" guitar player from Seattle about Neil Young . . . but then talk to Neil Young about John Lee Hooker. Does that grunge guitar player know about the African origins of the beat he is playing? Does he know where the pentatonic scale he is using and which sounds so natural to his ears originated? Probably not – and does it matter? The music still sounds good, and the music has been playing for 20,000 years or more . . . all because of our "aunts and uncles."

What exactly is passed down that battered sixth house chain of lineage, from master to disciple? Almost invariably, it includes simple information: the master luthier teaches his student how to make a fine mandolin. The guru teaches a meditation practice. But something else flows down that line of candles – something that passes directly through the eyes, through the cells of the body, person to person, by-passing intellect.

Hindus, for example, value having the *darshan* of a spiritual teacher— which may mean simply sitting with that person while talking about the weather . . . and it is valued beyond diamonds and emeralds.

What is this mysterious energy that passes between people on different levels of consciousness when they're in physical proximity with each other? What really happens in eye contact? What is this thing that we cannot name, but we hold precious enough that we are willing, for example, to come to an astrology conference a thousand miles away just to hear a teacher speak? We could buy her or his books for a fraction of the cost of attending the event.

That is sixth house magic. That is the flame passed down from lama to lama, from Christ to the disciples, from shaman to apprentice, from aunt to niece.

- *Central to these observations about the lost dimensions of the sixth house is the notion that nobody can be fully human, fully activated, fully potentiated, without proper mentoring.*

We simply need it. If we are not properly mentored, if we are not properly initiated, then something is missing in us, *and we feel terrible grief.* Furthermore, because no one *taught us how to be huma*n, we tend to make a lot more mistakes. And the mistakes deepen our grief and breed shame in us.

- Thus, it shames us to have not been mentored – we can't help but wonder why – and then we further shame ourselves through our resulting blunders.

In conclusion, I believe that we've all been born into an Age in which one of humanity's great works lies in the *re-creation of these lines of mentoring.* If you have a strong sixth house, this is part of what you've signed up to do. Especially as you move into the second half of your life, you'll begin to find younger people coming to your door, asking to "borrow a cup of sugar." They're really just making a pretext to sit with you. They want to hang with you; they want to pull something out of your cells.

They don't know what it is, but they know you have it.

You don't know what it is either, but you'd better admit it's there!

It's your dharma to be with them and to quietly help *initiate them into humanness.* That's how we can reestablish these lineages. That's how we can breathe life back into the lost sixth house.

That's how we can re-ignite this holy line of candles that we blew out when we invented the automobile, the work week, the television, and the Internet.

14

In my teaching, a question I hear over and over again is, "I get it about Mercury ruling Gemini – that's obvious – but why does it also rule Virgo?" The confusion is understandable given the gaps in our understanding of the sixth house, with its natural resonance with Virgo – a subject I just explored in the previous article. Thirteen years after that piece came out in The Mountain Astrologer, its editor – late, lamented Tem Tarriktar – invited me to write a second piece wrestling with the strange, Mercury-tinged relationship between those two houses and their corresponding signs.

THE AWKWARD, FRUITFUL MARRIAGE OF HOUSES THREE AND SIX

(Mountain Astrologer magazine, 12/2015, #184)

We astrologers take the universe and all the possibilities that have ever existed in it or ever will exist in it, then we divide that huge pie into twelve slices. Each house of the horoscope represents an archetypal field of such epic proportions that it would require an infinite number of astrologers writing an infinite number of articles in an infinite number of *Mountain Astrologer* magazines to thoroughly explore any single one of them. When Tem Tarriktar invited me to write an article about houses three and six, I breathed a sigh of relief – ah, only *1/6th* of all infinity!

My aim here in this brief article is not to offer the impossible – an exhaustive analysis of these two vast subjects. Instead it is to explore the curious, awkward linkages between the two of them. Underlying everything I am about to say is the fundamental paradox that both merges and divides houses three and six:

- These two houses are forever joined at the hip by their common Mercury rulership while they are simultaneously forever at loggerheads via the fact that they square each other.

George Bernard Shaw described England and America as "two nations divided by a common language." We might say the same for these two houses.

Let's take it step by step. We start our exploration by thinking some deep thoughts about the exact process represented by the square aspect.

IF YOU ARE A VIRGO, DON'T MARRY A GEMINI

When a person first encounters astrology, he or she is very likely to hear about "bad aspects" which are alleged to have the power to doom a relationship. Among the major aspects, the opposition and the square are the Prince and Princess of Darkness, respectively – at least as far as that limited view of astrology goes. It is not a very helpful view, nor ultimately a very accurate one, in my opinion. A line my students hear over and over again is that *all aspects are about integration*. In plain English, here is what that means: always, the aim is to bring "the voices in your head" into some kind of unity or shared purpose. With the so-called "bad" aspects, that integrative process is simply more difficult. They are *hard*, not "bad," and there is a big difference.

- In a human partnership, a "scattered, distracted" Gemini person can drive an "orderly, reasonable" Virgo person crazy.
- Meanwhile, a "picky, critical, negative, narrow-minded" Virgo can frustrate the pants off the "soaring, visionary, experimental mind" of a good Gemini.

The tensions can be very real. But so can the higher, integrative possibilities. Gemini can trigger some potential for "thinking outside the box" in Virgo . . . *if Virgo listens*. Meanwhile, Virgo can correct, systematize, and improve Geminian thinking . . . so long as Gemini can accept constructive criticism and the scrutiny of rigorous analysis.

And therein lies the whole point with squares. Leavened with humility and openness, the tensions they represent, once integrated, can be evolutionary rocket fuel.

As we proceed with our exploration of the friction between houses three and six, keep all this in mind. Their natural square could be called a "disharmonious link" between them – and we will indeed see how they can undercut and undermine each other. We will also see how they can make each other shine.

But first we need to think about the more harmonious dimension of the link between these two houses – an inescapable archetypal fact that has joined them in an eternal cosmic marriage. They share a common ruler: Mercury.

THE MESSENGER OF THE GODS

"Data in and data out." That's a modern phrase, but it's an old idea. And it is very much the essence of Mercury. Just five words, but they actually provide a good working definition of some elusive, hard-to-define concepts, such as life and consciousness themselves. How? Start with this: *anything alive and aware responds to its environment.* The triggering mechanism of that response always happens via the *senses,* at least in some understanding of the word. In that, we see "data in" – and thus one half of the Mercury equation.

"Data out" arises as those senses, having fed awareness of the environment into consciousness, then trigger some sort of behavior in the organism. *We respond to what we have sensed about the world around us.* That resultant behavior is always the outgoing signal. The unicellular amoeba propels itself away from a too-hot electric wire. *Data out*: "I don't like you," says the amoeba.

- In this manner, Mercury *links consciousness to cosmos.* It does so via the senses which feed cosmos into consciousness, triggering thought and reaction, which is then fed back into the cosmos via behavior.

Among humans, one major form of this expressive, reactive behavior is *speech*. And as all astrologers know, in practical terms, speech is absolutely central to our understanding and experience of Mercury.

What about the idea of rulership? What does it mean that Mercury is the natural "ruler" of the third and the sixth houses and their corresponding signs, Gemini and Virgo? In essence, rulership is simply about *connection* – there is a natural resonance between the energies represented by the planet and the corresponding sign or house. Trigger one and you trigger the other, even when there are no aspects joining them.

If, for example, I say, "money rules politics," everyone knows what I mean: you can't talk long about politics before you find yourself talking about money. They are not exactly the same, but they are forever linked. Similarly, you can't talk for long about *teaching and learning* (Mercury) without talking about a person's third house. Both symbols refer to the same subject. Specifically, do you want an astrological insight into someone's natural style of speech or learning? By all means, look at the condition of his or her Mercury – but don't forget to merge that information with the message of any planet in the third house. That *linkage via resonance* is the underlying concept in rulership.

Bottom line, the core language and logic of astrology suggests to us that these two squared houses – three and six – must share a major strand of symbolic DNA via their common Mercury rulership. The "messenger of the gods" has his finger in both pies.

Meanwhile, the square implies that there is *also some tension in the process*, along with an integrative opportunity, albeit a challenging one. These two houses may somehow be at "crossed purposes" with each other – but there is also momentous potential for vitality and energy deriving from that creative tension.

Who or what can bridge them, bringing them into alliance and fusion? None other than our hero, Mercury, the gods' own messenger, the planet that drives us to know the cosmos and to communicate our knowledge of it.

Let's proceed by looking at each of these houses individually, focusing on those particular dimensions of each one of them that illuminate the Mercurial connection.

THE THIRD HOUSE: THE HERESY OF PERCEPTION

Conventionally, we think of the third house as the symbol of *speaking and listening, reading and writing, teaching and learning.* We might also encounter the idea of "short journeys" and all methods of *transportation.* We learn that it represents *siblings.* These interpretations are all valid and supported by our collective astrological experience. They provide a solid practical starting point for our deeper explorations.

You have no doubt met someone who "looks at the world through rose-colored glasses." We all know what that expression means. It refers to an individual who sees only positive possibilities in any situation – with the implication that a certain blindness to life's darker side often renders this person naive, vulnerable, and somewhat clueless.

The underlying point here is that all of us behold the world through *some kind* of "glasses." We see the world according to our natures, in other words. As people in India say, "When the pickpocket meets the saint, he sees pockets."

Here's the key: *the energy of the signs and planets involved with your third house constitute your glasses.* You are looking at the world through those lenses. To take this thought beyond merely descriptive forms of astrology, let's add an active ingredient: *it is your job to keep those lenses polished and clear.* The planets and signs involved in your third house will tell you how to do that. They will also tell you what kind of perceptual distortions you will be experiencing if you fail in that lens-polishing.

Several years ago, I was doing readings in Manhattan. A very Martial gentleman came to sit with me. I instantly had the impression that rather than actually wanting a reading, he was there at the behest of his girlfriend. He had Pluto in the third house, so I knew he would behold the world through a Plutonian lens – looking deeply, suspiciously, and penetratingly into everyone and everything. This fellow sure appeared that way when he looked at me – he was sitting there in his skin-tight muscle shirt, arms akimbo, wearing reflective sunglasses, studying me as if I were a bug in his soup.

Normally, seeing Pluto in his third house, I might have said, "you have the mind of a psychoanalyst." But calling him a "psychoanalyst" would have been ludicrous. He looked more like a bouncer at a nightclub in a sketchy neighborhood. So I improvised. I said, *"you have the mind of a pri-*

vate detective" – which was basically the same Plutonian idea, modified to reflect his muscle shirt and his reflective sunglasses.

His jaw dropped, off came those sunglasses, and out came his wallet. He showed me his license. He actually *was* a private detective.

Of course I couldn't "see that in his chart." What I saw was an archetypal field, of which being a private detective was one possible manifestation.

I got lucky, in other words. Naturally he was very attentive throughout the rest of the session.

The sign-and-planet energies in the third house *correlate with perception*. That is the root insight. That is the first layer of meaning in this symbolism. The rest follows easily: *upon the foundation of perception rests thought*. Without perception we would have nothing to think about, no dots to connect. And *upon the foundation of thought rests speech*.

And it cycles around again – if I speak, you perceive my speech, you think about what I said and you form your own views and opinions of it. Then it is your turn to speak. I in turn perceive what you have said, react to it . . . and so forth.

Thus, upon this three-layered system – *perception leading to thought, thought leading to speech* – rests the delightful human phenomenon of a good, long talk. And we encounter yet another commonplace third house key word: *conversation*.

I heard Robert Hand speaking at a conference once. He was teaching in the cultural framework of Europe a few hundred years ago. He made the familiar reference to the ninth house as the classical "House of Religion." He pointed out that back then religion often meant "The One True Faith" – the Roman Catholic Church, in other words. Then he pointed out that *the third house opposes the ninth house*, and he asked the obvious corollary question: so what *opposes* the One True Faith?

The answer was *heresy*. Back then, the third house was the House of Heresy.

Nowadays, of course, heresy is hardly an issue, but five or six hundred years ago, it could get you burned at the stake. The point is that, if you think about the *meaning of the word heresy*, you can learn something really elemental about the third house. Heretics always *question orthodoxy*. That's what makes them heretics. *There is nothing more heretical than questions.* And the third house is the House of Questions – questions that usually lead to more questions.

- What happens to the little Catholic girl who asks the mean nun about the fate of little Hindu girls who die having never heard of Jesus?
- What happened to you when you "came out" as someone who believed in astrology?

One drive that underlies the third house is a hunger for *fresh questions*. It is a hunger for perception. This hunger has a familiar name: *curiosity*. In working with a client with a strong third house, a line I often use is, "*By the time you are old, you will know all sorts of things that don't make you any money.*" When they stop laughing, I point out that my comment was a compliment. I was underscoring the fact that they would always be eager to *learn for the sake of learning*, and not only for "practical" reasons.

Speaking of heresy, our thoughts might immediately turn to the chart of the most successful heretic in Western history: Martin Luther himself. There's some controversy about his time of birth, but the chart offered in AstroDataBank has a Rodden AA rating. I like it; it shows Luther with three planets in his third house: Pluto and Jupiter in Libra and Mars in Scorpio. As most of us know, Luther *questioned the Church*, named its corruption, and was excommunicated for it – and unwittingly triggered the Protestant Reformation.

Note Luther's strong parallel with my "private detective" – Luther too had Pluto in the third house, aided by Mars in Scorpio. He looked *suspiciously and penetratingly* (Pluto and Scorpio) at the culture of his time, saw "enemies" and spoke combatively (Mars) about them, and by all appearances felt positive and righteous (Jupiter) about his views and his right to express them.

Another one of my favorite illustrations of third house functioning is Albert Einstein. He had Uranus in Virgo in the third. Through what color glasses did Einstein see the world? They were distinctly Uranian – he questioned the "received wisdom" of his era. He doubted the very foundations of all he had been taught about science and reason. Specifically, he dared to wonder if space and time were *not* actually constants. That an inch was an inch and a minute was a minute everywhere in the universe was quite literally the foundation of Aristotelian and Newtonian thought. "Everyone knew that;" it was "obvious." And Einstein proved that it was incorrect.

Albert Einstein's name became synonymous with that classic Uranian word: *genius.* Why? Because "his I.Q. was in the genius range?" There's a really dumb idea! Lots of profoundly intelligent people are not geniuses. It is not intelligence we are talking about, but rather another quality, and a wilder, edgier one by far. From the astrological perspective, Albert Einstein was a genius because he was doubly a heretic – first, just for having a planet in the House of Questions, and secondly for the planet being Uranus, with its natural suspicion of authority. He looked at the world through Uranian glasses.

And of course much later in his life, Einstein's mouth continued to get him into Uranian trouble as he opposed the proliferation of nuclear armaments and espoused other "liberal" causes.

Adolph Hitler can usually be counted upon to serve splendidly as a bad example, and he does not fail us here. Hitler had a conjunction of the Moon and Jupiter in the third house in the sign Capricorn. As he perceived the world, what did he see? Here are some hints: the Moon can mean *home, land, roots, and family.* Capricorn is ruled by Saturn, which is so often related to the *Father* archetype. Hitler viewed Germany as "the Fatherland" and spoke passionately and emotionally in what he perceived to be its defense. With Moon as Mother and Capricorn as Father, we can easily see how Hitler looked at his nation and its people through the "glasses" of a protective parent, "knowing what was best" and "taking responsibility for those who depended upon him."

We have to be careful here. It is a helpful astrological exercise as we learn about the third house to remember that it is about *what people perceive.* Their perceptions may be wildly wrong or even immoral – an easy case to make with Adolph Hitler – but those perceptions *establish their sense of reality.* Once we understand them, the craziest behaviors often have a kind of twisted logic about them. I speak no German, but just listening to old newsreels of Hitler addressing the crowds, I can feel his Jupiterian charisma pouring out of his third house mouth. He spoke with the *emotional* (Moon), *authoritative* (Capricorn) *voice of the King* (Jupiter). And yet underlying his eloquence, one can easily detect that classic dark Capricornian signature: *the need for total control.*

I did a deeper analysis of Hitler's chart in my book *Yesterday's Sky,* if you are interested. At the risk of putting it too mildly, suffice to say that Hitler failed to clean the lenses of his perceptions, freeing them from their emotional and grandiose baggage. This failure distorted his thinking. And what came out of his mouth, while still carrying the theatrical energy of his chart, was lies of the worst and most persuasive kind – lies that he himself believed.

What is our bottom line here?

- That the third house is about the developmental trinity of perception > thought > speech.
- That each of us carries inside us a "holy heretic" – which is to say that each of us can potentially see the world according to our own true and best natures, rather than through the lens of how we have been taught to think and understand.
- And finally that, if we get that right, we *find our own voice* and that voice is incredibly powerful, original, and authoritative.

THE SIXTH HOUSE: SERVICE, HUMILITY, SKILL

The sixth house is on my personal short list for the most misunderstood of the twelve. Essentially it seems to have become the astrological repository for everything left over after the other eleven houses have claimed the interesting stuff. We hear the usual litany of sixth house words: duties, responsibilities, and routines. Visiting your boring relatives. Monday morning, paying your electric bill. Brushing your teeth.

On a more interesting note, health – and illness – are often mentioned. But the sixth house of contemporary astrological literature is mostly dull fare.

All that is true and worth knowing. All those boring things are part of life and must have astrological symbolism connected with them. But as I mentioned in the opening of this article, and in the previous one, we astrologers take the universe and divide it into twelve pie-slices. What are the chances that one of them would simply be boring? And, more to the point, *why is there so little evidence in any of those familiar sixth house keywords of Mercury's fingerprints?*

The evidence points in one direction: we astrologers seem to have lost something essential in our interpretation of the sixth house. Further, it seems that the conspicuously *missing Mercury elements* in the sixth house might well provide the clue that solves the mystery.

Much of what follows is based on the previous article, The Case of the Disappearing Sixth House. I'll summarize it again here.

The key lies in what is probably the most common old name for the sixth house: "The House of Servants." A servant serves a master, which brings us to the heart of the matter: in this house, we encounter the idea of *relationships based upon inequality*. To modern ears, the term "inequality" has a negative ring. We prefer the notion that "all men are created equal." Meanwhile, "inequality" implies an endorsement of hierarchical social structures: snootiness and snobbery, or outright oppression, tyranny, even slave-holding.

Of course there is no shortage of those realities in the modern world. And the sixth house can refer to such holier-than-thou dictatorships, whether they are on the national scale or around the dinner table.

But let's not throw the baby out with the bath water. Not all situations based on inequality are so dark. Our current discomfort with these sixth house realities has created a vacuum in contemporary astrological thought. That led me to search in older astrological literature for the right clues. We don't have to go back very far in time to find them. Of the sixth house, Marc Edmund Jones in his *Horary Astrology*, first published in 1943, page 88 in my edition, writes, *"it identifies the deference that must be paid to others because they occupy a better position in the world, together with the same deferring to self that may be compelled from whoever occupies an inferior position."*

Astrologers have always adapted to the social world in which they find themselves. That's how we relate to our clients. I am sure this hierarchical, class-conscious language worked fine for Marc Edmund Jones back in the days in which he practiced astrology. Nowadays his words sound off-key. How many of us go around looking at people as "our betters" or as "our inferiors" in the present time? Or at least how many of us admit it? That which was simply assumed in 1943 is now very much out of style.

The literature is not all so grim and off-putting. Going further, let's look at *The Technique of Prediction*, by the great Ronald C. Davison, published in 1955. Regarding the sixth house, on page 34, we read, *"... his work as a subordinate or an apprentice – whether learning the essentials of a trade or whether training himself for physical or spiritual conquests (perfection can only be achieved after long and diligent practice in a subordinate role, understudying those who are more skilled and experienced) ..."*

Davison's words ring truer today than those of Jones, and I believe they bring us very close to the forgotten heart of the sixth house. In this part of the birthchart, we see the symbolism of those who might guide us. We look to our *role models, heroes* and our *teachers* – those who, due to age, accomplishment, or spiritual advancement, are simply further along on the same road that we aspire to travel ourselves.

One mysterious feature of this house lies in the inexplicable and trans-logical quality of *transmission* that arises when teacher and student come together in close relationship. That word might sound exotic, but as we will see, it represents a common, even universal, experience. Here's an illustration: once I shook hands with the great British guitarist, Eric Clapton. We had a friend in common and Mr. Clapton and I had a conversation that probably lasted five minutes. I was star-struck, of course. All my life I've noodled on the guitar and often played in bands, so Eric Clapton has always been an Olympian figure for me. After that brief contact with him, I immediately felt a great need to go home and strum my Telecaster. I also felt that I played better. I joked about "not wanting to wash my hand."

Crazy? How could merely shaking Eric Clapton's hand make me a better guitarist? It sounds suspiciously like, "Oops, I forgot to study . . . I think I'll sleep with the Algebra textbook under my pillow."

But in this case, it actually seemed to work for me.

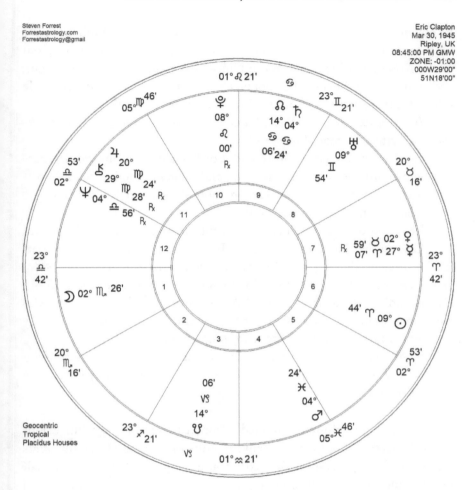

Steven Forrest
Forrestastrology.com
Forrestastrology@gmail

Eric Clapton
Mar 30, 1945
Ripley, UK
08:45:00 PM GMW
ZONE: -01:00
000W29'00"
51N18'00"

Geocentric
Tropical
Placidus Houses

©2018 Matrix Software Gainesville, FL

Standard Wheel

Have a look at Eric Clapton's chart. This is based on Dirty Data – a Rodden rating of DD, so we've got to be careful. There's a strand of evidence that suggests an early *morning* birth, as well as this particular 8:45 pm in the *evening* version. Having met him and having been aware of the patterns of his public life for many years, I find this evening chart more convincing. I direct your attention to one feature: Clapton's Aries Sun lies in the sixth. Is he anyone's "servant?" No, he's a rock star. But Eric Clapton inherited the blues tradition from the Afro-American musical geniuses who came up out of the Mississippi Delta, moved to Chicago, bought their electric guitars, and transformed the sound of popular music, and *he understands that.* He celebrates these artists and often admits his great debt to them.

In classic sixth house fashion, Eric Clapton subordinated himself to a tradition. He "sat at the feet of masters."

Think of Eric Clapton in the light of Ronald Davison's words, "Perfection can only be achieved after long and diligent practice in a subordinate role, understudying those who are more skilled and experienced."

Clapton embodies those words.

Let's add one more critical link to the chain: as I write these words, Eric Clapton has just turned seventy. How many generations of guitarists has he influenced? *He gratefully and humbly received a tradition and he has generously passed it on.* That two-sided coin is an essential element in our understanding of the sixth house. We apprentice ourselves to those who are more advanced; we receive a gift from them; we complete the circle by passing the gift onward to those who come after us.

- You can't tell the chart of a caterpillar from that of a butterfly – and if you want to be a guru, you must first humble yourself as a disciple.

Our present culture has tended to forget these *initiatory* dimensions of life. Correspondingly, our present literature of astrology generally offers a watered-down version of the sixth house, stripped of its soul and half its meaning. Since mentoring, apprenticeship, and initiation are pivotal to human development, it profoundly enriches our astrological practice to recognize their symbolic corollaries here in this "disappeared" part of the sixth house.

On my bookshelf, I have a yellowing 1962 edition of "Sepharial's" *Manual of Astrology.* An English Theosophist, he actually lived from 1864 to 1929 and his real name was Walter Gorn Old. On page 29 of my more recent edition of his book, under the sixth house, I read: *"the father's brothers and sisters in a female horoscope; the mother's brothers and sisters in a male horoscope."* Aunts and Uncles, in other words. This is a nearly-forgotten piece of sixth house symbolism – and actually it was forgotten for a good, practical reason: nowadays, most of us are not really very close to our aunts and uncles – or, by the same token, to our nieces and nephews. The world has changed. The extended kinship systems that defined the word "family" though much of human history are largely fragmented now. People move around; divorce is common. But historically, to be someone's aunt or uncle implied an active relationship, one of both mentorship and confidential counsel, almost always beyond the purview of one's parents. It was not unusual in the past for a child literally to go live with an aunt or uncle and perhaps learn a trade, but more importantly, experience a kind of initiation into adulthood.

"*You've got to meet my Aunt Betty . . . she's not really my Aunt, but . . .*" How often have you heard that phrase? Funny how we still often use the terms "aunt" and "uncle" to refer to this kind of mentoring relationship between a beloved, trusted adult and a younger person. The historic kinship systems may have fragmented, but the basic circuit-board of the sixth house remains intact, and it will do so for eternity. It is an archetype. Archetypes change in form, but they are ultimately indestructible.

In the following imaginary dialog, the "niece" opens with a familiar ritual phrase:

Niece: Promise you won't tell my mom . . . ?

Aunt: (She actually does not even need to reply. Eye contact and a nod alone are enough. Confidentiality is part of the sixth house archetype, and everyone understands that.)

Niece: Jason and I did it.

- So a young woman has launched her boat upon the stormy seas of human sexuality. *Is it not comforting to know that she has a caring adult with whom she can speak and seek counsel?*
- Isn't it natural that this adult is not her mother, who would probably tend to be over-protective?
- And isn't it primordially righteous that the aunt keeps her niece's secret, even from the mother?

Being truly human is difficult, but our species has been doing it for a long time. There are stored up treasures of earthy wisdom, often hard-won, and passed down the generations. "Want respect? *Learn a skill.*" "Want to get married? *Stop sleeping with other people.*" Need money? *Get a job.* Want other people to like you? *Try shutting up and listening to them.* These insights are not instinctual; they need to be taught and learned. None of us can grow up right without such mentoring and guidance. We often hear the African proverb, "it takes a village to raise a child." That's worth saying. But in the sixth house, we are not talking about the village. We are talking about a small number of adults, not the child's parents, who at one time or another take a special interest in the child, spend time with him or her, and just *vibrate* together.

Funny how "vibrate" seems like a flaky word there. But it isn't flaky – it refers to a fundamental method for the transmission of integrated body-mind-spirit information between human beings who are in a loving relationship, but on an unequal footing. It is something we feel – and it always involves more than transmitting rote knowledge.

You sit in an audience listening to your favorite author give a lecture. Amidst the stream of words, in a hall with two hundred people, the author makes eye-contact with you for five seconds from the podium. Something passes from her into you. You feel it; it is real. Probably the author feels it too. You were thirty feet from the stage, in a crowd. But soul-lightning shot between you. If you talk about it, you will sound as if you are babbling. But the phenomenon is real, and ancient. That's the sixth house in action – in a mild form, but real.

It's not just about kids and their "aunts" and "uncles." It is available to all of us.

Maybe you are reading this magazine because you aspire to become a professional astrologer. Maybe you sign up for a personal reading with an astrologer whom you admire. The reading goes well; you learn from it. But you have learned something else. By sitting in engaged rapport with that master, something of his or her skill and energy has passed into you. Welcome to the sixth house.

Few of us practicing psychological or archetypal forms of astrology today could do it without having stood on the shoulders of the late, great Carl Gustav Jung. His chart is given a Rodden C rating. According to AstroDataBank, he reported that he was born when "the last rays of the setting sun lit the room." That would clearly place his Sun in the seventh house – which leaves his Venus/Mercury conjunction in Cancer solidly in the sixth house. He famously apprenticed himself to Sigmund Freud and when that mentor-student relationship collapsed, Jung went on to become the "uncle" of just about everyone practicing the deeper, modern forms of astrology, not to mention his being the inspiration for generations of Jungian analysts. (I explore his chart a lot more fully in *Yesterday's Sky* if you're interested.)

The point is that once again, in Carl Jung, we see that same lost signature of the sixth house: *the receiving and the giving of initiation.*

HOUSES THREE AND SIX: SQUARED, BUT FOREVER MARRIED

We began our inquiries with a dilemma: how can two symbols be caught in an "irreconcilable" square aspect and still share a common ruler? As we investigated the question, we encountered an intriguing clue: something seems to be missing from our current astrological view of the sixth house, and that "something" seems to have a connection with Mercury. Specifically, even though we say "Mercury rules the sixth house and Virgo," we actually don't detect much evidence for that notion in our current literature and practice. Mercury's signature in the third house is readily apparent: communication, learning, teaching, curiosity, the media. But in the sixth? Duty, service and servants, routines, responsibilities, health? Brushing your teeth? Where is Mercury in all that?

Then we picked up another clue: we realized that there is a long-lost dimension to the sixth house, still described in the old books but not so evident in modern astrological practice: *lines of mentorship and initiation* – the older, more experienced ones passing on what they have learned to the younger, less experienced ones. The elders are grateful to those who have gone before them, and the younger ones are grateful to receive the precious gifts that will help them be more productive, effective, and sane. Remember: these are *personal* relationships. There is usually love, or something like it, in them.

Exploring further, we realized that the sixth house is not just about elders helping the young, but that it also extends to many other kinds of relationships throughout the life-cycle. We could be taking piano lessons in our geriatric years from a youthful prodigy – we may know more about life, but she knows more about the piano. And in that case, the prodigy may be learning something about life from us while we are learning our musical scales from her. From this perspective, the sixth house is a rich, complex part of life, cradle to grave.

- Bingo: this dimension of the sixth house is about teaching and learning.

There's our missing Mercury signature: teaching and learning. There's the connection between the third and sixth houses. There's the common strand of DNA we've been missing.

What about the other horn of our dilemma? What about the square aspect between houses three and six? Let me first give it to you in telegraphic form:

- In the sixth house we surrender our egos and learn from others, while in the third house, we learn by doubting everything we have ever been taught.

To learn in sixth house fashion requires tremendous *humility*. We have to accept that another person is smarter, wiser or more advanced than ourselves. And we have to be willing to accept discipline and guidance. We must swallow our pride. We must surrender.

But in the third house, we are practicing the *heresy of perception* – that is to say, we are learning to see through our own eyes, according to our own instincts. We are sorting out what is actually real for us from what we have been taught to see, to expect and to believe. These authentic perceptions become the foundation for original thought, which in turn becomes the foundation for the fabled Holy Grail of the third house – *finding our own voice*. To accomplish that, we must be *wary* of teachers and their teachings. We must listen critically. We must, like Albert Einstein, *doubt what we have been told*.

From a third house point of view, all those sixth house hierarchies, with all their blue ribbons, booby prizes, grading systems, and name dropping can be stultifying. Give somebody a badge and a uniform, and what happens? How often have the famous letters "PhD" gone straight to somebody's head? How often do members of the clergy start believing they speak for God? And is that the fault of the clergy or the fault of the congregation – the potentially poisonous alchemy of the sixth house works in both directions. And that last point reminds us that . . .

- *The sixth house needs the chaos and creativity unleashed in the third.*

Faith needs doubt. Science needs bold, new questions. As Peter Gabriel said in his tune, *That Voice Again*, "It is only in uncertainty that we are naked and alive."

But without the guidance of those who have gone before us, we may waste a lot of time *re-inventing the wheel*. We may also come up with a wheel that's a pentangle, promising a bruising ride. There has never been a shortage of stupid things said spontaneously, nor dumb decisions based on erroneous perceptions. And that tells us that . . .

- *The third house needs the discipline, structure, tradition, criticism, and guidance offered in the sixth.*

The third house and the sixth house are in a square aspect to each other – the way cougars and deer are square. The relationship looks bloody, but they balance and correct each other. Without deer, cougars would starve – and without cougars, deer would proliferate to the point of starvation. In all squares, if you look hard enough, you can always find the potential for this kind of fierce, interdependent *symbiosis*. Remember, all aspects are about integration. In this essay, we are simply considering the specific nature of the integration represented by the square between houses three and six.

So: seek your true teachers, humbly learn from them – and never cease questioning them.

Sounds true, doesn't it? You know it and I know it. And that instinctual certainty is the resolution of our dilemma. That is the essence of the awkward, fruitful, interdependent marriage of houses three and six.

15

Over the years, I've made many teaching trips to China. Visiting the country has gone from feeling like an "interplanetary" experience to feeling almost like returning to a second home. This rather personal piece dates to one of my early trips there, back when I was still trying to digest and integrate the experience of being offered a plate of boiled frogs to eat, seeing people walking down the street dressed in their pajamas, and receiving generous offers to have little fish nibble the dried skin off my feet . . .

NINTH HOUSE CULTURAL CROSSOVER

(Newsletter – November 2012)

The very day the progressed Moon hit my ninth house cusp, I flew back to China – perfect timing considering that the Moon takes over twenty-seven years to get around the chart. That was October 13. As the symbolism suggested, I was ready for a big cross-cultural adventure. This time, I was not offered any frogs to eat – a mercy! But I certainly felt stretched, both in terms of my mythic horizons and my waistline. I taught two big weekend classes in Beijing under the able guidance of Felicia Jiang and David Railey of No Door Productions. My translator, Xinxin, was profoundly able, and everything went swimmingly.

There are cultural differences between America and China, for sure. But mostly what strikes me is our common humanity. When I began traveling there, I was concerned that my work might be incomprehensible to Chinese people simply because our societies are so different. No worry – they, just like us, are baffled by their relationships, laugh easily, hug each other a lot, and complain about the government. I went there expecting fear, control, and a certain rigidity, and found that I was completely wrong on all counts. I found warmth, humor, and humanity.

In those senses, being in China was no more a ninth house experience for me than being in Peoria, Illinois. Human beings are human beings.

But there were some eye-opening moments too.

First, here's a silly one – but one that is emblematic of all those startling leaps over cultural divides that are so characteristic of the ninth house. *I would approach a closed door while walking with a woman. As a card-carrying member of Western civilization, I had an instinct to slow down and gallantly allow the woman to pass through the door ahead of me.*

Trouble is, Chinese women have the opposite reflex: they insist that I pass through the door ahead of them. I'm not sure, but I think it is not about my being male, but rather about my being older.

This led to many awkward moments of, *"No, no, please, you first"*. . *"No, you* . . . *"No, I insist* . . . *"*

My Chinese friends soon caught on to the joke. Every time we approached a door, it became a hilarious mock battle. Sometimes I "won," and sometimes I "lost." I adjusted to losing – but my stomach still clenched a little every time I "arrogantly" walked ahead of a female. I felt as if I had been caught picking my nose or observed with a critical zipper open.

Cultural assumptions sink deep into your bones. You stop thinking about them, take them for granted. And they can blind you.

And that's why God made the ninth house.

Underlying all that playful door-drama was another cultural divide, and one whose implications I am still digesting: in China, I had a heck of a time getting used to being treated as an elder. I am 63, but like most Americans, I am not preoccupied with role-expectations based on that number. I guess I would say that most of the time I feel as if I am just being myself and not thinking about my age. "Life has a long middle" is one of my favorite expressions.

And yet in China, I was seen as . . . well, what I actually am: *an old guy.*

One woman wouldn't even let me walk down a staircase without shep-herding me by the elbow, as if I were some pretzel-boned octogenarian. I caught myself feeling annoyed with her – once I childishly (and stupidly) scrambled ahead of her over broken stone steps at The Great Wall just to get away from her and "prove myself."

I was lucky I didn't fall down and break my leg – and thus totally vindicate her view of me!

Being "perceived as an elder" this way was another manifestation of the progressed Moon crossing my ninth house cusp. *I was getting "my myth of the world stretched."* I didn't believe I had issues around ageing. I felt comfortable in my skin. But being *seen as what I actually am through Chinese eyes* really got me thinking outside my reflexive comfort zone. It delivered a bracing shock to my existing system of beliefs

Just like feeling that I "naturally should" pass through a door *after* a woman, there is much else that I just simply assume to be true and natural without thinking about it – *until someone from another world invites me to stand outside it and re-consider it.*

Not wanting to be seen through the lens of my actual chronological age is a fine example of that. *Why shouldn't I be seen that way?* Might there be a collective agreement in my own country to avoid thinking about age-ing? How would you feel if the first thing out of the mouth of a friend whom you had not seen for a year or two was, *"Wow, you've aged a lot?"*

In China, all of that "elder" stuff undoubtedly became conflated with my being a teacher, especially one teaching about spiritual matters. The "guru-projection" is an occupational hazard in what all spiritually-oriented astrologers do, even here in the United States. It feels stronger in China, and it interacts vigorously with the elder-projections. They have a long tradition of spiritual teachers who are of course often *older males*. So why was I surprised that I was treated like a lama? I am not one! But these were Chinese people looking at me through their own ninth house eyes. What did they see? I am "an old man" sitting on a high chair in front of a group of mostly younger people, all the while teaching dharma in astrological language. Why should I have been surprised at their guru-inflected inter-pretation of me? In a sense, I had asked for it – or, better said, I unwittingly triggered it.

In America, where we are relatively unburdened by any such formal tradition of spiritual teachers, I can sit easily in the role of the "old hippie who's into astrology," poking fun at myself as I teach. But in China, I might as well have had "Call Me Mister Guru" pasted on my forehead.

While wrestling with this projection there Beijing I remembered another ninth house experience I had many years ago. I was visiting a place in Michigan where a Tibetan lama was scheduled to teach two days later. A tall throne had been erected for him, complete with gold brocade coverings. I remember thinking, *"Who does this guy think he is?"* As an American, I was resistant to the pomp and circumstance. I imagined the lama to be some kind of egomaniac.

When he arrived, he was utterly humble, unpretentious and human. But when he ascended that throne, he was transformed. He was not an egomaniac, but he was indeed an embodiment of spiritual authority.

I realized that the throne was not for him; it was a way of honoring the ancient teachings for which he was a transitory vessel.

There, sitting on my own "throne" in China, while experiencing the evolutionary pressure of my ninth house progressed Moon, I found myself feeling sort of *elastic.* I was fitting myself to an irresistible force – the shape of another cultural projection. *I found myself trying hard to be worthy of it.* Honoring myself was not the point. Rather, China helped me better to honor the sacred teachings for which I too, like that lama in Michigan, am a transitory, imperfect vessel.

China also helped me realize that while I may not feel like a "worthy elder," I sure am older than most people I meet, so it looks like I am elected! People *need* elders. I needed them myself when I was younger, and I still appreciate them now.

All I can do is to try to do my best. To rise to the expectations. To carry the teachings with dignity and respect. The opportunity to learn all of this is a gift of my ninth house progressed Moon – a gift that my Chinese students and friends have given me. I am grateful for it.

I can think of no single geopolitical question more pivotal to the human future than there being friendship between China and America. I am happy to play a little role in building the necessary bridges. I will return for my third visit there next October. My Moon will still be in the ninth house, and all I can anticipate . . . is the unanticipated. May I be sufficiently free of my "inner expert" to see it. May I also be as free as possible of my own "Americanness" – not that being American is anything shameful, it's just too narrow to contain the wide world.

We may all understand that notion *in principle*. But the best way I know to really get it into your bones is to immerse yourself in the sheer strangeness of other cultures.

The most fundamental ninth house yoga I know involves a passport.

SECTION THREE

THE LUNAR NODES AND REINCARNATION

Ask anyone in the astrological community about what distinguishes evolution-
ary astrology from the other forms of our craft and you will almost certainly hear,
"those people believe in past lives." And it's true: the belief that there is some-
thing immortal inside us all, something that is learning lessons from lifetime to
lifetime, is absolutely central to the philosophy behind what we evolutionary as-
trologers do. Lost in the shuffle however is another factor: while we do generally
believe in reincarnation, we also believe in personal evolution from moment to
moment — that most of us are observably and undeniably learning and growing
in this present lifetime. One line that quickly gets us to the heart of the matter is
"just think how dumb you were ten years ago." That's evolution!

Still, the royal road to understanding the big evolutionary picture lies in
the way the nodes of the Moon open the door to grasping a person's unresolved
prior-lifetime riddles. You'll find that perspective peppered throughout a lot of
what I've written in this entire volume, but in this section, you'll see these ideas
presented in starker technical detail. The second piece is a very human case study
of a young boy recalling a lifetime as a World War Two fighter pilot. Beyond that
chapter, most of what you will read is about how the lunar nodes reveal karma
operating at the collective level — we'll see, in other words, the "karmic chickens"
of humanity coming home to roost as it is reflected in transiting nodal activity.

16

An acceptance of the notion of past lives is pretty fundamental
to how evolutionary astrology actually works. For many people,
that acceptance requires an uncomfortably long leap of faith.
This rational hesitancy is probably the biggest hurdle that we
evolutionary astrologers face in our endless campaign for hearts and
minds. We seem to be winning it too – at least among astrologers.

ASTROLOGY, ASTROLOGERS, AND REINCARNATION

(Newsletter – June 2019)

The August 2018 edition of Ed Snow's wonderful Astrology News Service (http://astrologynewsservice.com) revealed the results of a survey he had conducted among members of various astrology organizations. It turns out that 68.5% of the five hundred astrologers he surveyed accepted the idea of reincarnation, while only a relatively tiny 12% disagreed with the idea.

That so many of us practicing this craft believe in prior lifetimes actually came as a big surprise to me. The idea of reincarnation is of course fundamental to evolutionary astrology. But, while evolutionary astrology is increasingly popular, it is still a minority voice in the larger context of our profession. I would have imagined that far fewer astrologers were concerned with who they or their clients had been in their past lives. But more than two-thirds of us do apparently feel that way.

I'll put my obvious cards on the table here first.

Yippee! This is good news!

I sincerely believe in reincarnation myself. At the risk of sounding arrogant, I'll even go so far as to say that I feel like "I know it." I also love astrology – and the more the practice of astrology is aligned with the truth of life, the happier I will be. It's a delicate area though. Astrologers aren't supposed to be preachers.

Here are my less-obvious cards: in my opinion, astrologers have no business pushing their metaphysical beliefs on anyone. It is in the very DNA of our craft that we celebrate human individuality, diversity and freedom. As most of you know, my own work is very much rooted in the idea of how our present birthchart develops logically out of unresolved issues from prior lifetimes. Still, unless a client has been very clear with me about personally accepting reincarnation, I always try to frame the "past life" parts of my readings in more flexible, less preachy, terms. I make a little speech about "ancestral past-lives" living on within us via genetics – and I actually do believe that ancestral themes are at least part of what we see in the chart. I usually also add a line about how "maybe that's just the way God made you."

- The underlying point is that, however we look at it, *all of us were born with intrinsic natures.* Unless the universe is completely pointless and random, there must be a *reason* behind our having those natures. *And since effects follow causes, the "reason" had to come before you had your present chart.*

None of that "proves" reincarnation by any means. But these two ideas – "past lives" and the idea that "there is a reason that you have the chart you have" – get along like peanut butter and jelly.

Here are a few lines from the first chapter of my 2008 book, *Yesterday's Sky: Astrology and Reincarnation.*

Two points, however, are objectively certain. A third one flows naturally from the first two:

1. All who accept reincarnation agree that our present personalities and circumstances are rooted in our previous lives.

2. All astrologers agree that our personalities and circumstances are reflected somehow in our birthcharts.

Logic draws us to a third point:

3. If we accept both astrology and reincarnation, we are compelled to recognize that our present chart must reflect prior-life dynamics – that hidden in our natal configurations are clues, however subtle, about who we were and what we were doing in previous lifetimes.

If we accept both astrology and reincarnation, no other position is logically defensible.

Again, I would never claim that any of this "proves reincarnation." But with nearly seven out of every ten astrologers "believing in past lives," it seems like it's time for evolutionary astrology to rule the profession.

I hate talking that way though! I don't need people to think the way I do; I want them to think for themselves.

Still, based on Ed Snow's survey, it looks as if astrologers "have some thinking to do." Anyone who accepts both astrology and reincarnation cannot long sustain the logic of putting a wall between those two beliefs.

One more point before I move on: when I speak of "evolutionary astrology," what I am referring to is simply the marriage of three disciplines: *modern psychology, ancient reincarnational metaphysics, and astrology.* I do not intend to refer narrowly to people who work in the exact technical style that I've been teaching all these years, nor in the Jeffrey Wolf Green style (which is solid, but substantial different technically from mine). I can easily embrace the idea of Vedic "evolutionary astrologers," Hellenistic "evolutionary astrologers," Uranian, Cosmobiological, or Renaissance "evolutionary astrologers."

In my mind, it's a big tent.

There is much that is appealing about the idea of reincarnation. Simply "not really dying" has a friendly ring to it, for starters. And then there's the happy idea that, despite worldly appearances, there is a kind of ultimately unerring justice in the world. That moron who cut you off in traffic or that scoundrel who stole your true love are going to have their days of reckoning.

Lovely! Of course that means that you will have your own day of reckoning too . . .

So reincarnation is generally an appealing idea. So is the idea of the dawning of an age of world peace. Or astrologers being lauded and paid what they are worth. Or artists not starving.

The point is that much that is appealing is still not true. What about reincarnation? Are there any compelling objective reasons to believe in it? Obviously, it is a difficult thing to prove, one way or the other.

Ten years ago, when I was writing *Yesterday's Sky*, I realized that I was asking my readers to take a prodigious leap of faith. That did not seem fair to them. So I began "researching the research" about the evidence for reincarnation, and found there was quite a lot of rational support for the idea.

With Ed Snow's striking survey results still fresh, it seems like a good time to reach out to anyone who is interested in astrology, but who has logical doubts about reincarnation. My aim is not to harangue anyone here – only to speak rationally and respectfully to questioning minds.

To that end, and at the grave risk of sounding like an infomercial, allow me to recommend the second chapter of *Yesterday's Sky*, entitled "Why Believe in Reincarnation?" The evidence for the idea of consciousness experiencing multiple lifetimes, and evolving through them, is compelling. But of course the notion of "past lives" seems exotic to many of us, and that source of doubt can create a serious hurdle for anyone drawn tentatively to evolutionary astrology. That is why I wrote that chapter, even though it is not really about astrology in any narrow sense. I never want anyone to take anything I say on faith. I want them to compare what I say with their own experience and intuition, and maybe to absorb a few facts that lie outside the mainstream of consensual reality.

No one needs to check logic and reason at the door when they enter the house of astrology, even evolutionary astrology.

17

Reincarnation – so central to evolutionary astrology – is admittedly
difficult to prove. In writing the following essay about the eminently
verifiable past life memories of young James Leininger, I had two
agendas. The first was simply to recount a knock-your-socks off anecdotal
argument for believing that human beings evolve from lifetime
to lifetime. The second was to rigorously demonstrate evolutionary
astrology's formal procedures of nodal analysis, and to give them a chance
to show their mettle in the rare situation where we actually know
someone's past life story, enabling us to compare the two perspectives.

A CASE STUDY IN
REINCARNATION

(Newsletter – September 2021)

Past lives are a slippery subject. An unscrupulous astrologer could tell you that you were once Christopher Columbus's red-headed Scorpio girl-friend, and what can you say? It can't really be proven one way or the other.

Reality itself is the ultimate test for any theory. Much of the theory behind evolutionary astrology rests upon an acceptance of reincarnation, but how can we actually test any of it, let alone prove it? Our critics often make that exact argument and it is difficult to refute. Probably the best response we can put forth rests in the words of the Tibetan saint, Padma

Sambhava, who once simply said, "if you want to know your past lives, consider your present circumstances." The evidence of your prior lifetimes is, in other words, visible in your *present* life. The stories we tell based on our analysis of the Moon's south node and the planets connected with it *echo in our daily lives today.* That's really the heart of the matter and our best response to our critics – but it doesn't get even close to really *proving* the idea of reincarnation.

And that circles us back around to our initial dilemma: *our whole system rests on something that people have to take on faith – or not.*

Compelling, objective evidence for the reality of prior lifetimes is actually fairly abundant. As I mentioned in the previous essay, I covered a lot of that ground in an early chapter of my book, *Yesterday's Sky: Astrology and Reincarnation,* but that is not what this newsletter is about. It is about what is perhaps the most convincing evidence for reincarnation to emerge in a generation.

In June 2009, a bombshell book was published: *Soul Survivor: The Reincarnation of a World War II Fighter Pilot,* by Andrea and Bruce Leininger. From his earliest days, their son James was obsessed with aviation, but at the age of two, he began having terrible nightmares about being caught inside a burning, crashing airplane. Tellingly, his knowledge of World War Two fighter planes was eerily specific. For example, he knew that a type of fighter plane called the Corsair tended to get flat tires. For another, at the age of three, his mother bought him a toy plane, and she pointed to something that appeared to be a bomb attached to its underbelly. She tells us that James immediately corrected her, informing her that it was actually a *drop tank* – an extra tank of fuel that could be used then dumped in mid-air – and not a bomb at all. "I'd never heard of a drop tank," she said. "I didn't know what a drop tank was."

Remember: when this conversation happened, James was only three years old.

As the wheels turned, young James brought forth more and more information, culminating in him *naming the ship from which he had taken off* – he called it "the *Natoma.*" He also recalled the name of his best friend aboard that ship, Jack Larson. *Both of these highly specific facts were verified.* Jack Larson turned out to be real – he was old, but still alive and well and living in Arkansas. And he had flown from the *Natoma Bay*, which was a small aircraft carrier serving near Iwo Jima in World War Two. *Young James had told his father that he had been shot down in the fierce battle for that same island.*

There's more. According to a January 2006 story posted by ABC news, through some research, James' dad, Bruce Leininger, learned that only one pilot from the *Natoma Bay* had actually been killed in the battle for Iwo Jima. His name was *James* M. Huston, Jr. Further research revealed that Ralph Clarbourne, a rear gunner on a U.S. airplane that also flew off the *Natoma Bay*, said his own plane was right next to one flown by James M. Huston Jr. during a raid near Iwo Jima on March 3, 1945. He added that, "he saw Huston's plane struck by anti-aircraft fire. "I would say he was hit head on, right in the middle of the engine."

This of course echoed young James' nightmarish memory of going down in a burning airplane.

I've only scratched the surface of James Leininger's story here. If you'd like to learn more, go ahead and read *Soul Survivor*. Leslie Kean's fascinating 2017 book, *Surviving Death*, also covers the tale with a journalist's eye. If you prefer video, there's a 2021 six-part docu-series, also called *Surviving Death*, based on her book. It contains compelling footage of the Leiningers speaking for themselves as well as a lot of other mind-boggling material.

Proof of reincarnation? Stories such as James Leininger's are as close as we are likely ever to get to winning that grand prize. Disbelievers like to dismiss such tales with words like "coincidence" – or, worse, hoax. In this case, "coincidence" obviously strains credulity. Hoax is always possible – but see that chapter in *Yesterday's Sky* if you'd like a source for another *1700* similarly-documented cases.

I was delighted to find A-rated birth data for James Leininger in AstroDataBank. Here's his birthchart:

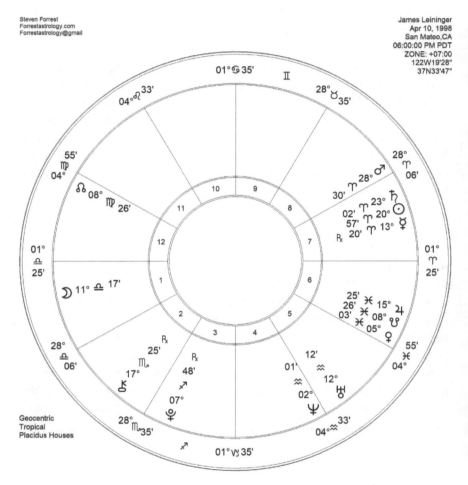

For those of you who are new to evolutionary astrology, let me provide a quick summary of our technique for scrying the outlines of a past life story from a present-day birthchart – or at least for getting to the karmic essence of it. I want to emphasize that these are stable, standard analytic techniques which I've taught to thousands of people, written about extensively, and used for many years with my private clients. I am not in any way adjusting the methodology to make it better fit Leininger's story.

Let's put the techniques to the test.

The process starts by discerning *who the person was* in the prior lifetime. There are three steps to accomplishing that:
- Look to the lunar south node in terms of its sign and house.
- See if any planets are conjunct the south node
- Look at the sign and house position of the planetary ruler(s) of the south node, and any planets conjunct them.

Next we discern the *circumstances* the person faced by adding two more steps to the analysis.
- What aspects (other than the conjunction) are formed by the south node?
- What aspects (other than the conjunction) are formed by the south node's ruler (or rulers?)

Let's go through these steps methodically one-by-one as we analyze James Leininger's chart, seeing how well they resonate with the story he tells . . .

SOUTH NODE SIGN AND HOUSE

James Leininger's south node lies in Pisces and in the 6th house. When we think of war, Pisces is not the first sign to come to mind. But remember: the south node refers to *unresolved karma carried forward into the present life*. If that is true, then we should see it quite visibly today.

Bull's eye – exactly *why* are you now reading about James Leininger? *Because he demonstrated the spectacularly Piscean mystical and psychic feat of recalling the details of a previous lifetime* – details that were precise and verifiable.

That salient, defining fact of Leininger's present life reflects Pisces perfectly – and hints at prior-life psychic development.

Take it a step further. Over the years ahead, how many times is James Leininger going to hear the words, *"Oh, you're the guy that book was about . . .?"*

Karma haunts us in the present life, and it is far from always being a welcome or pleasant thing.

What about the south node being in the 6th house? That spells *duty, required behaviors, servants* – and of course he was "under orders" in his prior life as an aviator. He was, after all, a soldier. How many truly Piscean souls have ever *felt like* going to war? Mostly, they did so only because they were required to. In this prior lifetime, James' soul was conditioned by that classic 6th house parameter: *obeying orders.*

We might further tie house and sign together, and speculate that he had been some kind of *spiritual disciple* in a lifetime prior to his experiences as a World War Two fighter pilot – perhaps he was once a monk under vows of obedience and service, and perhaps that's where he developed his psychic sensitivities.

Monks and nuns, by the way, "wear uniforms" in order to minimize individual differences. So do soldiers.

PLANETS CONJUNCT THE SOUTH NODE

In James Leininger's chart we see two such planets, Jupiter and Venus, with the south node squeezed in between them. At a deep level, we are again seeing evidence of a person with a *benign, loving nature.*

Do we have a problem here? Initially, we are quick to recognize that so far none of this seems to have the slightest connection with James Leininger's horrific past-life memories. But remember where we are in our procedural outline: *we are still looking at his nature rather than at his circumstances.* How many "benign, loving" humans have been caught up in war against their wills and their natures simply because they were "under orders?" Is that the story we are seeing emerge?

So far though, we've still not encountered any evidence of Japanese anti-aircraft fire – read on for that. We will soon get there.

Jupiter and Venus in conjunction with the south node can be read in a more superficial way too, and still tell us something that might be useful to know. Whatever its fearful realities, from a social perspective being a fighter pilot is a *dashing, romantic role* – at least that is the public perception. Jupiter and Venus reflect those "star" qualities.

If you doubt what I am saying, watch that old Tom Cruise film, *Top Gun.*

THE PLANETARY RULERS OF THE SOUTH NODE

In this case, we have two such rulers: Neptune, the modern ruler of Pisces, and Jupiter, its classical ruler. I always advocate using both of them, with the classical ruler often more focused on the person's *objective* past life situation and the modern ruler typically giving us more psychological information – what it *felt like* at the time more than what it *looked like*, in other words.

We've already explored Jupiter since it is conjunct the south node. All that we add by knowing that it is also the ruler of the south node is a little more emphasis on the "star quality" Jupiter dimensions of his previous identity, while fading the Venusian elements a bit simply by comparison.

Neptune has the nature of Pisces, and so the planet itself doesn't add much that we have not already seen. However, Neptune lies in early Aquarius late in the 4th house, and that's valuable new information. Neptune being in Aquarius adds a *rebel note* to the mix – that James *felt like an outsider*. The term "felt like" is echoed in Neptune's placement in the very hidden and feeling-oriented 4th house.

Note how we are once again seeing the theme of a person under orders to be in a situation antithetical to his actual nature.

Remember though: our attention is still focused on learning about James' prior-life *identity*. Figuring out the *circumstances* he faced still lies ahead in our analysis.

Superficial does not always mean unimportant, and astrology can often supply us with interesting superficial information as well as deeper psychological perspectives. Here's an example of that. In the astrology books of the first half of the 20th century, Aquarius was often connected with *aviation*. That's faded a bit lately. Nowadays we often see Aquarius connected instead with the *digital revolution*. Those are two entirely different subjects, but they both have the same archetypal Aquarian DNA – *modernism*, however it happens to be defined in the moment. Put yourself back in 1945 – airplanes, especially cutting edge fighting airplanes, were the essence of modernism, and James was piloting one of them. There's an example of a very literal expression of the Aquarian dimension of his node-ruling Neptune.

Going deeper, let's note that the 4th house is always connected with *home* and *family*. Let's further add that Japan was a fearsome enemy, and that there were serious concerns that the Japanese war machine could defeat and subjugate the United States and rule it with cruelty. How many soldiers who fought in World War Two felt very sincerely – and quite rationally – that they were *fighting to defend their land and the people they loved?* There's yet another 4th house dimension of our analysis – one that is particularly resonant with the *self-sacrificial* elements of Pisces and Neptune. "To be willing to die for your country" – how do we translate that sentiment into astrological language? Neptune in the 4th house is one obvious possibility.

So that's who James Leininger *was* in the prior lifetime. That's what his present chart reveals about his nature back then.

Let's turn to the next question: *what actually happened to him?*

WHAT ASPECTS ARE FORMED BY THE SOUTH NODE?

The matrix of aspects (other than conjunctions) that impact the south lunar node, along with its planetary rulers, carry us directly to the next level of our analysis. With all that we have considered so far, we have been exploring James Leininger's past life *character.* Now it's time to add some *plot* to the story. What – and perhaps who – *impacted* him in this previous incarnation? What did he *face?* And what did he leave *unresolved*, to be faced again in this present lifetime?

In practice, I am particularly drawn to squares and oppositions at this stage of karmic analysis. They represent *what we are up against.* Trine and sextiles are evocative too, symbolizing *supportive circumstances* – or perhaps *temptations not resisted.* If the hard aspects tell a rich enough story, I find I often leave out the softer ones.

Immediately the eye is drawn to that all-powerful Pluto – it lies in Sagittarius in the 3rd house, *almost dead-on square to that Piscean south node,* only 38 minutes of arc away from exactitude. In everything we have explored so far, we have been looking at a person under 6th house orders to function in a situation that was counter to his nature. With this dramatic, frightening Pluto placement, everything now becomes vividly specific – *sensitive, Piscean James Leininger was under orders, both practical and moral, to look down the barrel of Japanese anti-aircraft weaponry on Iwo Jima.*

That interpretation is at least perfectly consistent with hellish Pluto "squaring him." As ever, the astrological symbols indicate the outlines of the karmic story, not the specific facts. Pluto could have other meanings too, all of them nightmarish. Getting hit head-on by an artillery shell while flying at 350 mph over ice cold water is at the very least an excellent illustration. In Leininger's case, we have compelling reasons to consider taking it literally.

I never like the term "bad aspects" or "afflictions" while talking about someone's chart in the present tense. With prior lifetimes – with the water already under the bridge, in other words – I'm fine thinking of squares and oppositions in negative terms. In this case, we can surely see that the planet Pluto – a.k.a., "the god hell" – *afflicted* James Leininger in a prior life, and did so with particular intensity because the square aspect was so precise. Further specific resonances of that symbolism are abundant. For one example, Sagittarius gives Pluto a *foreign* flavor – and of course the Japanese were viewed as an "exotic" enemy, as well as a viciously Plutonian one. *And they did actually kill him* – there's that harsh square in action.

In *The Inner Sky*, I made the point that, instead of thinking of Sagittarius as the centaur-archer, it can be understood simply and purely as *the arrow flying through the air* – and that symbolism is quite literal and telegraphic in James Leininger's case. That arrow can represent his fighter plane, but it can also refer to the artillery shell that crashed into his engine, literally "afflicting" him in an awful, fatal way.

Meanwhile, the 3rd house is often linked to speech, which has no clear connection here – but it's also related to *transportation* and *vehicles*, so there again we have some solid possible airplane symbolism.

It's time to insert an important note: normally in this kind of karmic analysis, astrologers are in the position of using the symbols to create a past-life story which we assume to run parallel to the actual reincarnational reality. The story is taken to be *symbolic* – true in some larger sense of the word "true," but not necessarily factual. As evolutionary astrologers, we never make the indefensible claim of literalism; instead we claim *evocative, even cathartic, emotional relevance*. In this newsletter, we are in an entirely different situation: we are in the rare position, for starters, of actually *knowing* the past-life story. We are testing our methodology against known facts. That is not our usual situation – but it offers us a unique and precious chance for evolutionary astrology to face a reality check.

What have we learned so far?

Thinking integratively here, *we have seen evidence of a fundamentally gentle, benign Piscean soul being attacked and shattered by the nightmarish "god of hell."* The symbolism is brutal – and so is James Leininger's story. It was in fact so brutal and had such a profound impact upon him that *the memories of it survived the mind-erasing trauma of death and rebirth almost completely intact.* That is rare! Almost sixty years later, in a new body, he still remembered the name of the ship from which he took off for the last time, along with the name of his best friend. He still remembered being trapped in a burning, crashing, out of control, airplane. For that kind of karmic memory to make it through the between-life mysteries requires two things in abundance:

- One is an extremely psychic, extremely sensitive, extremely impressionable "Piscean" soul.
- The other is an experience whose impact is so fiercely intense that it is practically *branded* onto the mindstream as if it had been applied with a red-hot iron.

WHAT ASPECTS ARE FORMED BY THE SOUTH NODE'S RULERS?

Jupiter – one of his south node rulers – is also squared by that same dramatic, traumatic Pluto, but that aspect only echoes what we have already seen. There is no need to repeat any of those points, although it's worth mentioning that those same harsh themes are further underscored by this square aspect to the nodal ruler.

Neptune – the other south node ruler – is where we can take our story a step further. As we have seen, it lies in early Aquarius near the end of Leininger's 4th house. Neptune is also in a wide conjunction with a powerful 5th house Uranus, also in Aquarius. That aspect is worth a few words. The "aviation" angle – modernism – is echoed yet again here. Going further, Uranus – lord of earthquakes and lightning bolts – has resonances with suddenness, shock, and trauma, and they are also obviously relevant.

Still, the Neptune-Uranus conjunction is very wide – just over that ten-degree mark I suggested earlier as a guideline, so I only want to mention it while not overplaying its role.

Where Neptune quickly becomes a lot more interesting is when we pair it with James Leininger's Mars. The red planet is in an extremely powerful position, placed in both a sign (Aries) and a house (the 8th) that it rules. Even though Mars is in Aries and Neptune is in Aquarius, it is absolutely mission-critical that we do not neglect the fact that the two planets form a solid square, just three and a half degrees away from exactitude. We're accustomed to thinking of Taurus and Scorpio as the signs that square Aquarius, so this pivotal aspect would be easy to miss. Making that error would leave us without a final, and extremely definitive, clue. It would also be a classic amateur's mistake.

James is represented by that Neptune – that's the meaning of it being the ruler of his south node. As such, he is personally "afflicted by" that hot Mars through the difficult square aspect.

At the most elemental level, Mars is of course the god of war, and it is especially virulent in that regard when it lies in Aries. The symbolism could hardly be more transparent there: in a prior lifetime, *James Leininger was afflicted by war.*

But we can take it a big step further. The 8th house was traditionally known as the *house of death.* What clearer symbolism could astrologers possibly invent for *death by violence* than to have an Arian Mars squaring the south node ruler from that 8th house? The theme of death by violence is even further emphasized when we add an astrological technicality – the 8th house has two *natural* rulers, which means planets which rule that house universally for everyone. They are Mars and Pluto. Tying that broad principle in with James Leininger specifically, note that Mars squares one of the south node rulers, while Pluto squares the other one, along with squaring the south node itself.

Death is a pressing issue here.

In prior lifetimes, naturally 100% of us have experienced death. But the death symbolism is utterly electrified in James' chart – and don't forget: the south node story specifically reveals our *unresolved* karma. His *death itself* is part of that irresolution, and not everyone's death works that way. If for example you slip quietly away in the night at the tender age of 97, that's not likely to be unresolved karma.

James Leininger's nightmarish, sudden, violent exit from the flesh impacted him profoundly – so profoundly that he woke up in this present lifetime with the memory of it still haunting him, still giving him screaming nightmares . . . and *fascinating* him too. His soul knew that he had to heal from it, and to do that, he had to face it squarely.

How?

The precious, healing answer to that question would lie with his *north node* in Virgo and the 12th house, which is ruled by his Mercury in the house of love. But that part of the story is beyond the scope of this newsletter. Here our aim is just to give our karmic theories a reality check.

Judge for yourself: is there a resonance between the story told in *Soul Survivor* and the story that James Leininger's chart reveals? In this situation, we have a rare chance to compare theory and reality. Is evolutionary astrology proving that it can stand up to rigorous scrutiny?

To me, the theory looks quite robust. All I would add is that, not only does the nodal analysis resonate well with the remembered facts, it actually goes further. Over and over again, we encounter the notion of a person *bound by duty to play a role that did not reflect his actual nature.* That statement is purely astrological – it does not come through in any of the published material about Leininger's prior lifetime. An astrological counselor would warn him of the dangers of *repeating that pattern* in his present lifetime. That's how karma works.

If I were counseling James today, I might bring up the subject of how he feels about "the fates" having appointed him to be the "poster boy" for reincarnation.

I imagine that question would prompt the beginning of a fruitful conversation.

Again, we find ourselves in the highly unusual situation of knowing concretely "who James Leininger was" in the prior lifetime that his nodal analysis reveals. There is compelling evidence that the answer is that he once took birth as James McCready Huston, Jr., who died off Iwo Jima on March 3, 1945 at the age of twenty-one. A quick Internet search reveals that Huston was born on October 22, 1923 in Montgomery County, Pennsylvania. No birth time is available. Norristown is the county seat, so I used that for his birth place and set up a simple noon chart.

We always have to be cautious with such charts. Naturally, we don't know the Ascendant, plus all the house positions are wrong. If the person were actually born early or late in the day, the Moon's position would be off by several degrees. The rest of the planets and points are pretty accurate by sign, however. I wondered what kinds of connections, if any, there would be between James Leininger's chart and what we know of James Huston's?

This is an area that hasn't been studied much since the basic data is so hard to come by.

Here's a biwheel with Leininger's chart in the middle and Huston's planets and nodes in the outer wheel:

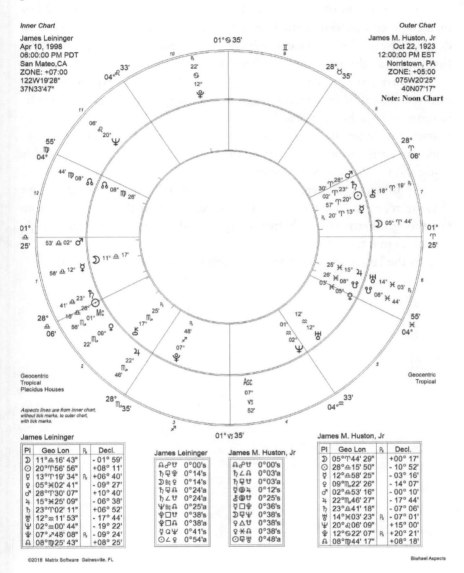

Inner Chart

James Leininger
Apr 10, 1998
06:00:00 PM PDT
San Mateo,CA
ZONE: +07:00
122W19'28"
37N33'47"

Outer Chart

James M. Huston, Jr
Oct 22, 1923
12:00:00 PM EST
Norristown, PA
ZONE: +05:00
075W20'25"
40N07'17"

Note: Noon Chart

Geocentric
Tropical
Placidus Houses

Aspects lines are from inner chart,
without tick marks, to outer chart,
with tick marks.

Geocentric
Tropical

©2018 Matrix Software Gainesville, FL

James Leininger

Pl	Geo Lon	Ŗ	Decl.
☽	11°♎16' 43"		- 01° 59'
☉	20°♈56' 56"		+08° 11'
☿	13°♈19' 34"	Ŗ	+06° 40'
♀	05°♓02' 41"		- 09° 27'
♂	28°♈30' 07"		+10° 40'
♃	15°♓25' 09"		- 06° 38'
♄	23°♈02' 11"		+06° 52'
♅	12°♒11' 53"		- 17° 44'
♆	02°♒00' 44"		- 19° 22'
♇	07°♐48' 08"	Ŗ	- 09° 24'
☊	08°♍25' 43"		+08° 25'

James Leininger

☊♂♅	0°00's	
♄♇♆	0°14's	
☽ßq♀	0°14's	
♄♇☊	0°24'a	
♄∠♅	0°24'a	
♆ßq☊	0°25'a	
♀□♅	0°38's	
♀□☊	0°38'a	
☿Q♀	0°41's	
☉∠♀	0°54'a	

James M. Huston, Jr

☊♂♅	0°00's	
♄∠☊	0°03'a	
♄♇♅	0°03'a	
☿☉♅	0°12's	
♄☉♅	0°25's	
☿□♆	0°36's	
☽♇♆	0°38's	
♀△♅	0°38's	
♀✶☊	0°38's	
☉♇♅	0°48'a	

James M. Huston, Jr

Pl	Geo Lon	Ŗ	Decl.
☽	05°♈44' 29"		+00° 17'
☉	28°♎15' 50"		- 10° 52'
☿	12°♏58' 25"		- 03° 16'
♀	09°♏22' 26"		- 14° 07'
♂	02°♎53' 16"		- 00° 10'
♃	22°♏46' 27"		- 17° 44'
♄	23°♎41' 18"		- 07° 06'
♅	14°♓03' 23"	Ŗ	- 07° 01'
♆	20°♌06' 09"		+15° 00'
♇	12°♋22' 07"	Ŗ	+20° 21'
☊	08°♍44' 17"		+08° 18'

Biwheel Aspects

Should we be shocked or not? James M. Huston's lunar south node lies in Pisces only 18' – about a quarter of a degree – away from a perfect conjunction with Leininger's own south node. Meanwhile, Huston's Uranus (remember "aviation?") echoes Leininger's Jupiter placement, near the node.

Mars plays an obvious role in their story, and there is Huston's Mars in a tight conjunction with Leininger's Ascendant. At the moment of death, Huston's Mars was undoubtedly supercharged. Leininger took his first breath as almost that same degree was rising.

Mostly I am drawn to think about that duplicated nodal axis. What can we make of it? It certainly suggests some degree of "singing in unison" in terms of their basic karma. That shouldn't be much of a surprise since, in a sense, they were the same person. Huston died at a tragically young age – we can easily understand that he didn't have time to "finish his earthly work." So the universe set it up again.

An imperfect metaphor here is that if we "fail the seventh grade," we "have to repeat it." Under the circumstances, saying it that way is far from fair though. Perhaps it is better to say that the same great work simply continues in a fresh body.

In the larger scheme of things, death is only a minor interruption.

18

This newsletter is connected with many sweet memories for me. Often I write about the current astrological weather as it affects us all. This time I wrote instead about the kids who were about to be born – and who would carry a little hologram of November 2016 inside them for the rest of their lives. As you will see, they promise to be an amazing group. I was touched by the many appreciative messages I received from newly-minted moms and dads around the time this piece came out. Readers tended to share it with friends, even with "pregnant people" who were open-minded, but not particularly drawn to astrology. But who is not interested in their own kids? I pray my words here helped them to receive and welcome these sensitive, promising souls into this beleaguered world.

WHEN THE SAINTS COME MARCHING IN

(Newsletter – November 2016)

Know anyone getting close to having a baby? Anyone due in November? She might be carrying a saint in her womb. That's my prediction: that we've got a good crop of fresh saints about to appear on the earth, right when we desperately need a few of them.

Saints are like that. They always appear on schedule.

"Saint" is, I admit, a dramatic word to use. It conjures up images of ethereal beings gazing up into heaven, with never an impure or unworthy thought in their haloed heads. But I am not using the word that way. I am talking about flesh and blood saints, with attitudes, genitals, and personalities. That's who I see coming.

You very likely know a few of them – but obviously not the ones in this group I am talking about. They're not here yet. You just know some of the ones who are here already. How do you recognize them? They probably don't walk on water. They don't glow in the dark. *You recognize them by their acts of kindness and their expressions of wisdom.* They are the people who are always there when you need them. They give of themselves. They don't hit you over the head with their piety or with supernatural powers. They probably don't have "Highly Evolved Psychic Shaman Healer Astrologer" emblazoned on their business cards – their egos aren't that hungry. Instead, their saintliness sneaks up on you.

They are the school teachers who buy notebooks for the kids who can't afford them.

They are the psychotherapists who go the extra mile.

They visit sick people.

They suffer fools with grace.

Why do I think that more of these saints are on the way? It's really very simple: November 2016 is an extremely *Neptunian* month and Neptune is the planet of saints. Kids born with this energy in their charts have the signature of the Mystic deep in their core.

There will be some *drunks* among them too, but we'll get to that.

Two astrological factors come together to support this happy prediction. The first is that Neptune makes a station this month. The second is that it conjuncts the Moon's south node.

The former is common, happening twice a year. The second is somewhat more unusual, hooked to the 18.6 year cycle of the lunar nodes. Neptune's conjunction with the south node is therefore not truly rare either.

What strikes me is that these two events are happening *just a couple of weeks apart* and thus reinforcing each other like crazy. That's the "rare" part. Another way to say it is that Neptune's position at its station and the position of its conjunction with the south lunar node are nearly the same, separated by only five minutes of arc – just one-twelfth of a degree.

Let's first look at these events separately, then let's add them up. In this case, the whole is definitely greater than the sum of the parts.

Planetary stations are not uncommon. With the slow-moving outer planets, every half a year or so a planet slows down and turns retrograde – that, or it reverses its motion and goes direct. It's simple to understand why. We are looking at, say, Neptune from one side of our orbit around the Sun. Six months later we are 186 million miles away, on the other side of our orbit. Neptune jumps back and forth just like your index finger jumps back and forth when you blink from one eye to the other.

That's the astronomy behind planetary stations. The astrological part is pretty simple too. When a planet is stationary, its effects are amplified. It gets more focused. It is as if the "amperage" of the planet has increased. (The significance of a planet being retrograde or direct is another topic, and not the one we need to understand here.)

Neptune made a Station at 12° 02' of Pisces and turned retrograde on June 13, just a few months ago. On November 19, its retrograde cycle ends. Neptune makes its station at 9° 14' of Pisces and begins to advance once more. Like a train reversing direction, the process takes time to decelerate and accelerate again. Therefore, Neptune is moving very slowly throughout the whole month, starting out retrograde at 9° 20', backing up until the 19th when it stops at 9° 14', then only getting as far as 9° 16' by November 30th.

The numbers are not important. What is important is that Neptune is basically "stopped" all month.

And that makes it very powerful.

The conjunction with the Moon's south node is our second factor – the one that makes all of this so compelling. That's why I've predicted the births of saints, but I am still a little ahead of myself.

Let's start with a look at the nodal configuration itself. On November 3, 2016, Neptune and the south node form an exact conjunction at 9° 19' Pisces. As any of you who've studied with me or read *Yesterday's Sky* would know, the south node reflects a person's karma. Pisces is ruled by Neptune in modern astrology, so *having Neptune conjunct the south node in Pisces is about as "Neptunian" as anyone's karma can possibly get.*

The nodes move slowly too. By month's end, the south node will have only retrograded (it's always retrograde!) back to 7° 52', so even children born on the last day of the month will have a tight 1° 24' Neptune/south node alignment If fact, without stretching our theories too much, we can speak of this highly Neptunian vibration extending pretty through the last quarter of the year – not all the incoming saints will have November birthdays.

All of this is further amplified by Neptune actually being in Pisces now. With its 165 year orbit, you don't hold your breath waiting for that to happen! It was there starting in 2011 and will not be completely done until 2026. That's a long time – but this month marks a real crescendo in the energy.

What does that tell us about these children?

Among them there will be many who in prior lifetimes have experienced *deep spiritual initiations* and profound *mind-training*. There will be *far-seeing psychics, energy workers,* and *meditation masters.* There will be *visionaries*, both spiritual and those who are simply imaginative in an inspired way.

Even better, with their north lunar nodes in Virgo, they have come here to be of service. All that training and wisdom have ripened. They now feel the need to become a gift to others.

That means us!

With the south node, we always need to be aware of limiting karma too, even dark karma. Inner work such as some of these kids have experienced can be addictive. It can create a quality of *self-absorption.* If you want to meet true egomaniacs, join a spiritual group, in other words. One of the reasons these children have a service-oriented Virgo north node is that there is no better remedy for spiritual self-importance than making other people's needs more important to us than our own, at least for a while.

Some of them will have simply "spent so long in a Tibetan cave" that emerging into the social world of human interaction is going to be a challenge for them. They will require our patience, and maybe some good role-modeling about how to function in the social world.

All symbols in astrology represent a spectrum of possibilities. Moving down the evolutionary food chain, we encounter some darker pathways. Mixed in with the crop of saints, we will also see some *scoundrels, natural-born liars and deceivers,* and people who are *simply crazy.* These are some of the bleaker faces of Neptune. Going further, among them, we will see "drunks" of various persuasions – and "drunk" doesn't only mean a penchant for booze. There are countless other ways of escaping reality. Your Uncle Harry who died of an overdose in 1982 may be returning.

We've been talking about "saints marching in," and that is a reliable prediction. With these more distressing references, we are also in Neptunian territory, and those predictions are certain to come true as well.

Among these children, there will also be some who are sitting on the fence between getting it right and getting it wrong. They can't quite handle their own psychic sensitivity – but with a little help, *maybe they can learn.* If they do, then they blossom into treasures.

More about that in a minute.

First, how can we distinguish among these different Neptunian types? It will be easy enough to simply see the distinction in their actual behavior as they reveal their true natures over the coming decades. I cannot emphasize strongly enough that there is *no technical astrological method for distinguishing among them!* Every chart contains beautiful, high possibilities – and low ones too.

One thing is virtually certain: by the very nature of the south node, almost all of these kids, even the best of them, will have some *unresolved issues* around Neptune and Pisces. That's what the south node means. *They can benefit us all enormously, but we need to receive them into our world and our families very consciously.* The irony is that, while humanity sorely needs them, they also need us.

Among them there will be a few truly lofty beings – "saints" so close to enlightenment that none of us could possibly assist them except by listening and receiving their precious gifts. They will take care of themselves. Here, I am thinking more about how we can support the ones in "the middle of the pack." By that I mean the children who, while very gifted and evolved, might be *overwhelmed by their own Piscean qualities.* How can we help them? Each one is individual, but here are some general guidelines:

- First and foremost, these children are extraordinarily sensitive at every level. Noise is going to be hard on them. Their sleep may be fitful and easily disturbed. An out-gassing carpet or a Wi Fi router might trigger hard-to-trace symptoms in them. They will pick up on subtle vibrations too – if for example you are silently angry at your partner, the child will feel that energy. Obviously, none of these realities can be eliminated from life or totally controlled. Being mindful is a help, though – any reduction in those kinds of tensions really helps to welcome the child into the world. We want them to feel safe. The last thing we need to do is frighten them.

- Secondly, pay attention and be open when the little Neptunian seems to be operating in "another world." Even an infant might suddenly turn and stare at a corner of the room. Even if "nothing is there," go ahead and look that way too and behave reassuringly. When speech arrives in a few years, listen openly and supportively to stories about "imaginary friends," past lives, and angels. Nothing alienates and silences such a child so effectively as mockery, shaming, or flat-out pig-ignorance in such matters.

- Thirdly, your own example is a huge and potentially helpful element here. I can think of no gift so supportive to such a child as being born into a family with genuine spirituality and some kind of active practice. Quiet prayer, yoga, meditation – any of those behaviors can create a supportive, welcoming vibration. A little statue of the Buddha, a cross on the wall, even a plastic angel from Walmart – they all signal support to the child.

What about the rest of us? Say you are not pregnant and no kid is on the immediate horizon of your life, then what does this Neptunian month mean to you?

Broadly, in such times the "veil between the worlds" grows thinner for all of us. This November is an auspicious month for any kind of spiritual practice. You'll naturally feel drawn in that direction. You can further focus that notion by seeing where the tenth degree of Pisces falls in your chart.

- Conjunct your Saturn? Maybe you would benefit from some solitary meditation.
- In your 11th House? Maybe you need some kind of fellowship, so take a yoga class, do some public, shared religious or spiritual practice.
- In your 6th house while triggering a Virgo planet? Service is a powerful practice for you now.

Often in these newsletters, we look at the "astrology of the moment" and talk about how best to navigate it. But there is always this second level, which may in the long run be the more important one. *The kids born under these energies embody them for a lifetime.* Among these newborns are a few who will be precious to all humanity. The birth of a saint is a quiet thing. There may be subtle omens, but angels blowing trumpets only appear in the sky in Renaissance paintings, not in reality. Yet a seed is planted. Give it a few decades and the world is changed.

Is a Messiah or an Avatar about to be born? Is that what this Neptunian month portends? I would not rule that out, but I would stake my life on the birth of spiritual teachers, yogis, and loving crusaders for generous causes.

Remember: saints come along when they are needed. That is eternal law. The need is great in the world now. That need is always there, but it is peaking here in November 2016.

Ask yourself in the light of today's headlines, does it look like we need some saints on the earth now?

Hold that welcome mat in your heart. That is this month's spiritual practice for every conscious person in the world.

And if you are involved with a birth any time soon, count that experience as a blessing beyond easy reckoning.

19

In this newsletter, the previous one, and in the next three, I follow the cycle of the lunar nodes moving through various signs and interacting with various planets. In each one of them, we see collective karma ripening. More importantly, in each one by concentrating on the north node we are presented with a rational, skillful basis for becoming the architects of our own salvation. Some of the events about which I write here might seem like yesterday's news, but if you are an astrologer, I hope that my words will be relevant to your practice as you encounter clients with these nodal placements in their natal charts. And of course, the same energies come around again every eighteen years – we really never have that long to wait before we see essentially these same energies repeating . . . or reincarnating.

THE SOUTH LUNAR NODE EXITS PISCES, ENTERS AQUARIUS: THE KARMIC WINDS ARE SHIFTING

(Newsletter – June 2017)

We are running a little late on this one, but don't worry – we haven't missed the show! On April 28, 2017, the axis of the Mean lunar nodes changed signs. The south node left Pisces, where it had been since

October 9, 2015, and simultaneously entered Aquarius. (Remember that the Mean nodes are always retrograde.) That of course tells us that the other end of the axis – the north node – also changed signs. It left Virgo and crossed into Leo.

As usual, the nodes will remain in their new signs for about a year and a half. On November 15, 2018, they will cross over into Capricorn/Cancer.

The lunar nodes are the royal road into understanding anyone's karmic predicament, so this says a lot about the karma of the children currently being born. As we saw in the previous chapter, we've just birthed a crop of very Piscean kids, regardless of their actual Sun signs. Now we welcome a crop of Aquarian ones. Just like the rest of us, each one of them will all be dealing with these underlying karmic issues in their own way for the rest of their lives, hopefully working their way out of their south node sink-holes into north node epiphanies and liberations.

The nodal shift also tells us something beyond the natures of the kids being born: it says a lot about the underlying karma of the present times. That "weather" affects everyone regardless of where the nodes were when they were born.

That big picture is what I want to explore in this newsletter.

Just a quick review for those of you who are new to this kind of astrology. The south node always has a troublesome dimension to it. It is not utterly "negative" across the board, but the central point with the south node is that it reflects unresolved issues, damage, and tragedy from prior lifetimes – karma that has "ripened" in this lifetime and is thus surely going to manifest somehow. Meanwhile, the north node is always "the remedy" – that is, it represents the most efficient pathway toward the resolution of the karmic tangle.

That's a lot of astrological theory in a few words. If you want to delve into it more deeply, have a look at my book, *Yesterday's Sky: The Astrology of Reincarnation.*

Before we reflect on the times we are entering, let's take a peek in the rearview mirror. The south node entered Pisces in Fall 2015. We would expect the world's karma to reflect the dark side of Pisces during this recent period. For starters, one of the classic "bad words" for Pisces is "drunkenness." We can corroborate this straightforward piece of the puzzle very objectively. *Fortune* magazine for February 7, 2017 has a story headlined, "3 Signs the U.S. Liquor Business Had a Great 2016."

Liquor sales were up a hefty 4.5%.

And of course it is a short step from "drunkenness" to thinking about drugs and the terrible Opioid crisis sweeping America and much of the world.

Going deeper, why do people turn to alcohol and drugs? The answer is often that they are hurting or feeling stressed. *But how much does something hurt?* First you have to know about the person's level of sensitivity. And, with all this Piscean karma ripening for the past year and a half, everyone's sensitivities have been exaggerated. No wonder booze, and heavier medicines, have been in high demand.

Many of you have undoubtedly already thought about the current political situation, which I am sure has driven many people to have a second drink – or a third.

I don't want to sound prim about alcohol or drugs. That would be hypocritical, at least about the alcohol. I'd not begrudge anyone the comfort of an evening cocktail, for example. But, as we all know, some people seem to think that if one cocktail helps a little . . . you know the rest: how's about a second or a third?

There is simple creature-comfort and there is flat-out escapism. With the south node in Pisces, there has been a demonstrable epidemic of that escapism.

Escapism is not just about drink and drugs. People can escape from their pain by diving into work, into exercise, into pornography, into their cell phones and digital devices. The list of ways *we can numb ourselves* is long. People can also escape into fantasies – and they can mistake fantasies for reality. Hence the age-old correlation of dark Piscean energy with madness and delusion in all its myriad forms.

Pisces is "mystical." That word that leads quickly to "religion" – and, being attentive here to the dark side, let's think of *bad* religion. *"I used to be screwed up on drugs. Now I am screwed up on . . ."*

. . . let's stay safe and say, *"Zoroastrianism."*

Judge for yourself, and take the word "religion" broadly: over the past couple of years, have you seen a pattern of people escaping from their pain by fleeing into delusional belief-systems? Remember that those delusional belief-systems are not just "religions" in the narrow sense of the word. They also include all "interpretations of reality," including social, mythic, and political ones.

And what about this? Has any evidence of actual *madness and delusion at the level of leadership in society* recently crossed your desk? And I am not only talking about the United States of America.

All of this confusion, delusion, and drunken escapism reflects the south node in Pisces. We have all been impacted by it.

Why?

What has there been in it for us to learn? That question brings us to the Virgo *north* node, whose reign only ended a few weeks ago, on April 28.

In interpreting the north node, we always accentuate the positive. That's where the "good medicine" lies. It is the inverse of why we need to pay attention to Shadow issues with the south node.

Perhaps the highest positive quality in Virgo is simply *humility*. None of us has all the answers. We are all works-in-progress and it behooves us to accept that reality. Paradoxically, even though there is a positive spiritual side to Pisces, it is important to remember that the dark side of the sign can unrealistically inflate the ego – we get variations on the theme of people "thinking they are Jesus."

A little Virgoan humility can be a big help there!

Still thinking of the good north node medicine ... Virgo, as an Earth sign, is also *oriented to detail,* to analyzing reality *as it actually is* – in a nutshell, Virgo likes *fact-checking*. I almost laugh at the clear light astrology casts on the headlines sometimes! *Could the world have benefitted from some more scrupulous Virgoan fact-checking over the past couple of years?* "Fake news" has become a hot issue, and it is a totally Piscean concept – an example of a delusional view of reality. Our escapist attachment to deluded belief systems can only be cured by a daily dose of 2+2=4.

There's Virgo.

What's the right medicine here in practical terms? *Look it up before you post it to Facebook!* Have we all done that? No, obviously. I've failed a lot too myself – I don't want to sound preachy here. *But can you feel the gravitational tug of that fantasy world?* Of being "drunk" on "alternate facts?" It has swept society over the past year and a half.

Virgo is the only medicine that can cure "Pisces-osis."

The underlying point is that between October 2015 and April 2017, all of humanity has been experiencing the dangerous, "soul-cage" dimension of Piscean energy – and at the same time we have all been afforded the evolutionary opportunity to correct it and even heal it with a healthy dose of Virgoan groundedness, humility, and an open-minded *willingness to learn*.

As ever, some of us have learned the lesson. Some of us have not.

So what about now? The cosmic weather changed a few weeks ago. On April 28, our collective south node "dilemma" crossed into Aquarius, while the north node "cure" moved into Leo. We will be swimming in that fresh nodal energy until November 2018.

Let's unpack it, starting with the south node.

Aquarius, like the other eleven signs, is a Divine Principle – a glorious, luminous evolutionary path, leading eventually to full Enlightenment. But anything so bright casts a dark shadow, and that is what we need to consider here. High Aquarius represents *pure individuality* – genuinely knowing one's self and being true to one's self, no matter what anyone says.

But its dark side is cold. Take the phrase, "I don't give a damn what you think," and savor it for both its nobility and its horror. Is it about true freedom or just a hardened heart? Reflect on that question for a moment and you've got the full spectrum of Aquarius in your bones.

Here are some good archetypal words and phrases for Aquarius. As you read through them, try to let them have both "fronts" and "backs" – that is, high, positive meanings, and dark ones too. *The Outsider. The Rebel. The Alien. The Genius. The Revolutionary. The Troublemaker. The Voice Crying in the Wilderness. The Doubter.*

Let me make the same point in a totally different way.

Personally, I would be an absolutely terrible Emergency Medical Technician. I am too empathetic. I'd see somebody's guts hanging out on the highway and I would be totally identified with their pain and horror. If they need to talk about it, I'm their man! *But they don't need to talk about it.* What they need is a cool, calm, efficient, *dissociated* EMT who can pack their guts back where they belong and get the poor soul to the hospital. I just don't have enough Aquarius in me to do that. I'm not clear enough in the face of such strong emotional stimuli. My heart gets in the way.

In that, you can see the high and low ends of the Aquarian spectrum. By definition though, with the south node transiting through Aquarius until near the end of 2018, we will be dealing with its darker manifestations. *In a word, there is now a chill in the air.*

Cutting to the chase, watch out for the following phenomenon in your own consciousness:

Not giving a damn as the rest of the world goes to hell.

Coldness. Detachment. Dissociation. And a feeling of being "apart from it all." Of not caring. Of taking refuge in abstractions and rationalizations – and remember Aquarius is an Air sign. It lives in a mental world. That's not inherently a bad thing, but, like everything else, it has a negative dimension. Life is not an idea. Humans have hearts as well as minds. And nerve-endings.

Going deeper, Aquarius is related to *trauma and shock.* If someone receives a bad existential blow or some unthinkably nightmarish news, you know how he or she might typically react. *"No! I can't believe it. It can't be true. You are wrong."*

Detachment. Distance. Denial. The mind defends itself against un-thinkable realities. In World War One, they called it "shell shock." In World War Two, they called it "the thousand-yard stare." More recently, it has become known as Post Traumatic Stress Disorder.

There has been no shortage of nightmares in human history. In prior lives, we have all experienced dreadful things. *With the south node transiting through Aquarius, that collective shock-karma is ripening.* Depending on our individual soul histories, some of us will be more reactive than others to this hard, cold energy. If your natal south node looks very traumatized, then the time between now and late 2018 is going to bring a lot of that deep ancient woundedness to the surface.

But all of us will feel it to some degree.

This insight adds a note of *compassion* to the mix. Here's how: Imagine that you tell someone you are upset because you just lost your job. He just sits there, unreactive and not seeming to care at all. Naturally you feel hurt and angry at his "insensitivity." Then someone tells you that this man *just learned ten minutes ago that his son had been killed in a motorcycle accident.*

See how that information completely transforms your attitude?

That's what I mean by adding compassion to the mix. *Compassion arises naturally when we understand that unresolved trauma is the true source of the perceived "coldness."* It is comforting, and also spiritually helpful, to remember this. I am trying to remind myself of it as well, to be honest. I see so many terrible things happening in the world. I see monsters and scoundrels running amuck, triumphing. And I see people sitting back, letting it happen. I want to shout at them. Wake up! Resist! Protest! Turn off your television! Get out on the streets and scream your head off!

And that's like me standing in judgment of the man who just lost his son. He is shell-shocked, that's all. We all are now to some extent.

Karmically, *the present world-horror is triggering collective memories of unresolved previous horrors.* Some people are so wounded that they can only stand back and stare as the fires burn and the wounds bleed out.

What is the cure?

The north node is in Leo and that is where the evolutionary magic lies. In response to what I've just written here, I want to explore "the Leo cure" on two levels.

LEO CURE NUMBER ONE

First, as we have just seen, there are souls who will experience a flux of dissociative energy as the south node passes through Aquarius. How can they heal and thus create the conditions in themselves which might eventually allow them to participate lovingly and openly again in the human race? Here's a core Leo answer: *tell them to have some fun.* I know how shallow that sounds. *But joy is one cure for pain.* Finding joy after Aquarian trauma is fundamental to the deeper meaning of the Leo path. It is an honorable, necessary step.

So is creativity in the broadest sense. Any kind of self-expression is an efficient Leonine healing vector for Aquarian PTSD. Call it "art therapy" if you want, although I would want to define "art" as broadly as possible. Gardening is art. Painting the walls of your house is art. Getting dressed up and going out to dinner at a fancy restaurant has, at least, a certain "art" to it. Everything is about taking the risk of self-expression and about trusting life enough to risk being vulnerable.

LEO CURE NUMBER TWO

Secondly, remember that Leo is the Lion. With the north node in Leo, *it is time to roar.* It is time to *feel your power* and to express it. In the famous words of Marianne Williamson, *"Our deepest fear is not that we are inadequate. Our deepest fear is that we are powerful beyond measure."* In this case, I will quibble with Marianne a bit. As we have seen, with the south node passing through Aquarius, old traumas that led to cold distance and dissociation are surfacing in the collective. Those traumas did in fact infect us with *a sense of defeat and powerlessness*. We probably came to those wounds via *genuine tragedy*, in other words. And just as with the man who lost his son, we must honor the pain. We must honor the wound.

But we must also resolve collectively not to be *defined* by that wound forever. From this day forward, we will not be cowed into distance and silence.

Again, it is time to roar like lions. To celebrate life.

And to never, never, never give up.

20

Watching the lunar nodes transit from sign to sign every year and a half speaks to us all at a deeply personal level – but it also telegraphs to us the nature of the archetypal dilemmas that will inevitably lie behind the upcoming news cycle. The south node gives us an advance peek at the tone of the new headlines in all their madness and horror, while the north node offers us something we don't seem to ever get in the conventional media – as if wise angels were writing the editorials, making us aware of what hurts, why we hurt, and how we might heal it.

THE LUNAR NODES ENTER CANCER/CAPRICORN

(Newsletter – November 2018)

As we enter November, the big news looming on the astrological front is that the Mean lunar nodes are about to change signs. That is always a crucial development even though it happens every year and a half.

What does it signify?

- First, that the nature of the collective "karmic chickens coming home to roost" is about to shift dramatically.
- Second, that we will soon see the births of children who are members of a very different soul-tribe than the babies who've been born since early 2017.

That latter point is because south node energy is what you see in a newborn baby's eyes – at least once you have stripped away all the cooing. Babies are as human as you or me – they come packaged with "warts and all," in other words.

As the south node switches signs, the nature of the warts switches too.

Here are the details of the timing:

On November 15, the lunar north node – always retrograde – backs out of Leo and enters Cancer, where it will remain until June 4, 2020.

It is customary astrologically to give the position of the north node, and to just assume that everyone automatically understands that the south node is always directly opposite it. Most computer programs default to not even *showing* the south node. Fair enough – except that in many ways the south node is the more pressingly obvious of the two nodes in its effects. There is much subliminal folly in not displaying it.

This focus on the north node derives, I suspect, from the same font of colonial "wisdom" that defines north as "up" and laments a relationship or a business "heading south." It's just a hemispheric expression of something analogous to racism or sexism.

In any case, the translation that we now contemplate is that on November 15, as the north node is entering Cancer, the south lunar node crosses out of Aquarius and enters Capricorn, where it will also remain until June 4, 2020.

While for the past eighteen months we've been seeing Aquarian chickens coming home to roost, now we are going to see some Capricornian ones. And the "warts" on those very human babies? You guessed it – the ones born since April 28, 2017 have had Aquarian warts. This new bunch will have Goat-warts instead. And maybe some Goat-wisdom as well.

By the way, the dates I am quoting here are for the Mean nodes, not the so-called "True" ones. The two are always in almost the same position, but the test comes at "cuspy" times such as these. By the standards of the True nodes, the axis should switch into Cancer/Capricorn about a week earlier. The kids born between November 6 and 15, are the test case – I'd say their south nodes are in Aquarius, while many astrologers would say, no, they're already in Capricorn.

With the nodes changing signs only every eighteen months, there are obviously not a lot of people in this ambiguous situation. Over the years, I've encountered a few – and in almost every case, the south node story fit the reality of their lives a lot better if I stuck with the Mean node. So that's what I do.

If you would like a fuller discussion of the complexities underlying this whole question, just go to www.forrestastrology.com and enter "Mean vs True Nodes" in the search function up at the top of the opening page.

So, onward to the big question: *what does it mean in human terms for the north node to shift into Cancer and the south node into Capricorn?*

Always, with the nodes, regardless of the signs involved, the underlying idea is as follows: the south node represents unresolved karma – dead-end patterns that get us nowhere and yet tend to keep repeating. "There are lessons I have learned hundreds of times" – get that joke and you get the south node. Meanwhile, the north node seems very foreign and unnatural – but if we make a little effort to break our bad habits and instead try on the north node attitudes and behaviors, they work wonders and miracles. They leave us astonished – sort of like a doctor's medicine that actually cures us.

Personally, I think the origin of the south node attachments, illusions, and self-defeating behaviors is karmic – *i.e.* originating in past lives. You can think of it anyway you want, from bad ancestral DNA, to family patterns – even to just plain "shit happens," if you prefer. I don't want to say that "philosophy doesn't matter." I think it does. But, with the nodes, we do not need to be philosophical. They work at a practical level even if the extent of your philosophy goes no further than a Gallic shrug of the shoulders.

- Think of the south node as a bad habit and the north node as its remedy.
- Think of the south node as an erroneous assumption, gumming up all your perspectives and interpretations, while the north node is the light bulb lighting over your head.

If you know anything about 12-Step programs, astrologer Michael Lutin said it best: "the south node is the bottle and the north node is the meeting."

There's nothing inherently wrong with Capricorn or any other sign, but all twelve of them have dark sides. That dark side is what the south node brings out. In the simplest terms, it is something *that you got wrong in a past life.* Just as easily, it might be a place where you got hurt.

As the south node swings through Capricorn, the harmful energies will play out on two levels, one of them is noisy, while the other one is far more important.

Level One is the daily headlines – and the general condition of the zeitgeist – between now and June 2020.

Level Two is the soul-condition of all the babies born between now and then.

As we just saw, unresolved karma – always the essence of the south node's message – can sometimes have its origin simply in bad behavior in a past life. Somebody annoyed you, so you koshed them on the head.

It can arise from your virtues too. Sometimes "doing the right thing" leaves a scar on us, like staying in a rotten marriage for the sake of the kids.

Then there are areas of simple tragedy or of "the evil men do" to each other.

Capricorn represents one-twelfth of all the stories in the universe. That's a lot of stories. But they have certain common denominators. Above all, Capricorn represents *endurance*. Imagine facing the winter in Duluth, Minnesota, or Tromsø, Norway. The steel that would have to arise in you as you face those long, dark, cold months is the essence of this sign. You put your pain aside and you do what you have to do.

Many of the kids who are about to take birth *have already endured enormous suffering*. They are tough – and *toughened*. The majority of them developed a certain *stoicism* in the face of these difficulties. Many were responsible not only for themselves, but for others as well. Crushing responsibilities arise sometimes – responsibilities that we simply cannot shirk no matter what the cost.

For all of these kids, drying the tears – or not crying them in the first place – then simply *doing what had to be done* has been their signature karmic pattern. Many of them will seem like adults right from their first breath. When you look them straight in the eye, some of them, fresh from the womb, will feel strangely like old men and old women, wise – but weary.

Virtue and strength can come at a high price.

If your kids are starving, would you steal a loaf of bread in order to feed them? Most of us have the same answer.

What if you yourself were starving?

What if the person from whom you contemplated stealing that bread was also starving? It's you or him – *what are you going to do then?*

Necessity creates complex moral territory and it does not always bring out the best in people. Life can be very hard. Anyone born with a Capricorn south node knows exactly what I mean by all that.

This is a tough group of souls. They've been hardened in the fires. Some of them are heroic paragons of moral strength – with scars to prove it. Some have been corrupted by life's sheer enormity, broken on the rack of grim necessity.

All of them carry another Capricorn mark: *a karma of loneliness.* There is loneliness that comes from literal isolation, physically or emotionally. Ask the lighthouse keeper. Ask anyone who has endured an empty marriage that lasted for decades. There is also a kind of "loneliness at the top" – something all leaders know. At a simple level, in thinking about "loneliness at the top," you might think of the loneliness of the single mother with three children. In terms of responsibility, she's "at the top" as surely as a president or a CEO. She might never get a moment to herself, but she is lonely anyway. Even though the kids love her, they cannot really understand her. And feeling seen and known is the cure for loneliness, not just "nearby flesh."

Translate any of these metaphors and images into past-life stories, and you've got it: this new crop of babies is populated with a lot of *strong, tired souls.*

By the way, all of this is particularly intensified, both in terms of the kids born and probably the daily headlines, when the nodes contact Pluto and Saturn, which are also resident in Capricorn throughout this period. Pluto aligns with the south node on March 28, 2019. With Saturn, there are three conjunctions, all in 2019: May 20, June 23, and September 25.

Why are these souls returning to the earth? *As with all of us, the reason is that their work is not yet done.* How can they go forward? The answer is pretty obvious based on all that we have just seen. *They have come to the earth for healing.* They need a hug. They need a rest. They need some gentleness. They need someone else to share their burdens – or even to carry them for a mile a two. They need a laugh. They need a long, hot bath. They need a

drink. They need to eat too much, and to give themselves a break about it
– remember: some of these souls have had experiences of literal starvation.
Above all, they need a good cry.

Crying. There's a mystery! We humans face dreadful losses sometimes.
How do we recover? *We let water come out of our eyes.* Try explaining that to
some alien debarking from a UFO in Roswell, New Mexico!

But crying works. Bottling up our feelings only puts us in a kind of
emotional deep freeze.

Some of these incoming souls have been frozen for a thousand years –
just remember that some of that "freeze" comes from them doing the right
thing and being strong in face of unimaginable difficulty.

The remedy of crying that I have just described in plain human terms
is part of what astrologers call the sign Cancer – at least Cancer at its best.
These souls have reincarnated with their north nodes "in the sign of the
Great Mother." They just need to sit in Her lap for a while. If you find
yourself in the role of being a parent to one of them, please try to let your
see-saw balance in the direction of kindness, forgiveness, and gentleness
rather than discipline

Again, they have come to the earth for healing.

What about the collective karma symbolized by the south node shifting into Capricorn? What does the north node entering Cancer mean for
the big world?

First some broad hints that apply to this "mundane" perspective on
the nodes in a general way . . .

"The soul of the human race" *(The oversoul? The collective unconscious?
Gaia? God?)* has a long, complicated history – it too has karma, in other
words. When it ripens, that karma manifests in the headlines, just as it
does in the life of an individual.

Think of all the famines and pestilence humanity has endured. Think
of all the mad kings who have created nothing but misery. Think of refu-
gees. Think of persecutions.

That is the kind of karma that ripens when the south node passes
through Capricorn.

Now think in more immediate terms – that is what really brings all this home. Consider for a moment the emotional wear-and-tear you have endured in this present lifetime of yours. Not to "cry in your beer," but rather just to think honestly and objectively about all difficulties that you have faced, particularly those you faced "with a stiff upper lip."

Even when exercising that kind of strength and maturity is right and morally laudable, the simple point is that *you paid a price for it.*

That karma has now ripened. You need a hug too!

Here's the bull's eye: *are you tired enough yet?* Reflect on what we have faced as a species over just the past few years. Are you happy with our political leadership, feeling like the world is in good hands? How is the 24/7/365 economy treating you?

No worries, right?

No worry about global climate disruption, the looming failure of antibiotics, genetically modified crops, idiots with nuclear bombs, terrorists, psychotic shooters with guns that Patton and Rommel would have envied, rage and discourtesy on Facebook, kids watching porno on their cell phones instead of flirting with each other, kids in cages on the border, skyrocketing medical costs, overdose deaths in the heartland, the ebola virus, *e-coli* in the lettuce, and a Russian operative in every voting booth across the free world . . .

I repeat: *are you tired enough yet?*

That is Capricorn karma ripening. If you *can't* feel it . . . well, then you are a living, breathing illustration of that overly-stoic Capricorn karma.

The cure?

The Cancer north node. We all need some gentleness now. We all need some healing. We all need a rest.

It starts with being kinder to ourselves.

From there, it spreads out towards others.

From there, it can heal this tired, battered world.

21

Astrologically there is really no such thing as a simple situation. Cycles interact with cycles in kaleidoscopic fashion. The true artists in our field are the ones who can pull many multicolored threads together and convey the big, integrated tapestry. I attempt to "juggle the balls" that way in this short piece about how the transiting lunar nodes interact with the rest of the contemporary astrological weather. As you'll see, in this case that weather report was particularly stormy. Just for reference, Googling the month of October 2019 yields the following headlines: Hong Kong protests worsen, four people stabbed in Paris, violent protests in Ecuador, shooting near German synagogue, ground offensive launched in Syria, state of emergency in Chile, Bangladesh riot over Facebook post, mass shooting at Siberian military base, ISIS leader dead, and deadly protests in Ethiopia.

HEALING THE COLLECTIVE HURT

(Newsletter – October 2019)

The month of October brings us a hot combination of Scorpionic energies and quite a lot of nodal stimulus as well. This promises a bouncy ride, but one which might do us all a lot of good. We will see it reflected in our own lives and hearts, and it will certainly leave its signature on the headlines.

One quick take-away is that this panel of astrological energies is guaranteed to bring out the best in the best of us, while simultaneously accentuating the worst in the worst of us. All in all, I expect that this prophecy bodes well for the kinds of people who are motivated to read this newsletter.

The headlines, however, are likely to be a different story.

The Scorpionic energies begin with a bang. Pluto, the modern ruler of Scorpio, stations on October 2 at 20 degrees 38' of Capricorn. When a planet is stationary, its amperage hits the ceiling. That heightened Pluto effect should last dramatically for a week or so on either side of the actual date of the station. Naturally, people with sensitivity to that part of Capricorn will experience those energies most vividly.

Then comes the parade: Mercury enters Scorpio on October 3. Venus enters Scorpio on October 8. Finally, the Sun enters Scorpio on October 23. All of them remain there through the end of the month, carrying Pluto's "opening statements" forward.

Meanwhile, the nodes of the Moon remain in Cancer and Capricorn, as they have been since November 15, 2018 and will be until June 4, 2020, when the north node retrogrades into Gemini. That's a big subject. I'll say a few words about it in this newsletter, but for deeper background, have a look at the previous chapter. Regarding the lunar nodes, what I want to talk about this month is the fact that four major aspects will be made to them before Halloween: the Sun squares both nodes on October 6. Mercury trines the north node on October 12. Venus trines the north node on October 18. Mars squares the nodes on October 22.

How does all of that tie in with the intensified Scorpionic themes, and with the current sign positions of the lunar nodes themselves?

Here's the big picture, starting with the evolutionary drama of the nodes in the background. As we saw in the previous chapter, the *pain* and *longsuffering* symbolized by the Capricorn south node are trying to open hearts to a kind of healing that is eminently available – but only if we recognize it. The questions are simple: are you tired enough yet? How much longer can you go on putting one foot in front of the other in the face of the endless, hopeless hurt of this crazy world?

Added to that underlying dynamic, we have this powerful pulse of Scorpionic energy. Inevitably, *Scorpio brings buried energies to the surface,* where they either can be healed and released, or where they grab the steering wheel and start mowing down pedestrians.

The third and final ingredient is the fact that the Sun, Mercury, Venus, and Mars all take turns triggering the nodes. Those aspects are guaranteed to precipitate events that reflect the whole spectrum of possibilities we have just cataloged. They open doors for healing – and they might provide opportunities or stimulus for people *acting out frustrations, angers, and resentments.*

Let me start with an analogy. Imagine a good, strong woman locked in an unsatisfying marriage. Maybe kids are involved. Maybe the family owns a house. Maybe her husband never hits her or treats her abusively. Maybe he is just cold and distant. Maybe the last meaningful conversation they had occurred five years ago. They are "keeping on keeping on," for practical reasons and for the sake of the children.

She is like the famous frog in the bucket of slowly heating water.

I initially described this woman as "good and strong." Those are Capricorn qualities, and obviously most people would think of them as virtues. But in reflecting on this woman's situation, we see the dark side of Capricorn. In a spirit of self-discipline and self-denial, she is enduring enormous emotional privations – *even ones that she does not necessarily need to endure.*

Ask this woman how she is doing, and she is likely to respond that *she is okay.* But she is not okay. *Her strength has blinded her to her pain.* That is the Capricorn dilemma.

Now imagine that this woman has a wise friend – someone with lots of Cancer energy, obviously symbolizing the healing path of the north node. One day, the friend – who understands the realities of this woman's marriage – hears our hero say that she is "doing all right." The friend sees through it. She does not argue. Instead she simply holds this woman in her arms. She does not let go. At first there is resistance, then there is surrender. Tears soon follow.

And simply crying is a miracle sometimes. Who knows why, but it helps. That is one of the mysteries of the sign Cancer.

The whole world is carrying an epochal backlog of pent up pain – for everyone on the planet, in other words, the south node is now transiting through Capricorn. *That is the collective karma that is currently ripening.*

That is one reason we see such an epidemic of negative projection about the human future. So much looks impossible, depressing, or hopeless in the world. Not to belittle the daunting realities the human race is actually facing today – they are real enough. *But we are also wrestling with the distorting effects of shared pain rooted in prior lifetimes – the hurt implicit in all of the dispiriting events of human history,* in other words. That karma is now manifesting.

Nodal theory also dictates that we are re-creating some of those ancient realities.

- *With all the Scorpionic energy in the mix this month, our ability to hold those energies out of consciousness is diminished.*

The good news there is that, for some of us, the emergence of that hurt leads us to put aside our stoicism and simply ask for a hug. The bad news is that, for some of us, as the pain surfaces, our feelings of resentment and anger increase proportionately. The next thing that happens is that *we want everyone else to hurt the same way that we do.*

We will surely see both of these phenomena. My hope in writing these words is that I can encourage a few of us to be mindful of the fact that it is time to attend to the needs of our own hearts. And if we do that – and *only* if we do that – we can offer some comfort to some of our fellow travelers in this passion play.

Meanwhile, October brings those four transiting aspects to the nodes. Each event will last for a few days; each one offers specific possibilities for getting this healing process right.

Let's look at them in order, one at a time.

The Sun squares both nodes on October 6. This aspect overlaps with the Pluto station on October 2, and the Sun is always a mighty force in its own right. Basically, everything we have explored so far should be utterly obvious right from the beginning. For better or for worse, the process starts with a very loud bang.

Mercury trines the north node – and sextiles the south – on October 12. This is a time for conversation. Putting feelings into words has always helped people. "Psychotherapy" is the template here, although let's include a long talk with a dear friend as well. Synchronicities will abound – books you need to read will fall off the shelf and land on your toe.

Venus trines the north node – and sextiles the south node – on October 18. The words "I love you" are an enormous comfort. Be brave; say them. Hugs have figured in all we've been considering. Now is the time to ask for them and offer them. The arts can be a balm to the soul. I picture you listening to your favorite musical recording a little too loudly, with tears pouring down your cheeks. Van Morrison does that for me; you know who does it for you.

Mars squares both nodes on October 22. This aspect is something of the "final exam" on what you have potentially been healing for the past three weeks. If you have not done the work, then there is likely to be some kind of outburst now – anger, an accident, or words you wish you could take back. If you have done well, you ice the cake of your own healing with an explosion of exuberance – you dance the night away, you lose yourself in Dionysian rhythms and pagan delights, you make love as if you were still twenty-one.

22

Once again, we reflect on the manifestation of collective karma as Pluto interacts with the nodal axis. Fundamental to the practice of evolutionary astrology is the principle that one can never fully understand a Pluto transit without making reference to the lunar nodes, and vice versa. That is because both Pluto and the nodes deal with the wounds we all carry in our souls, the price we pay for carrying them, and how we might eventually put that heavy burden down.

PLUTO DANCES WITH THE SOUTH NODE

(Newsletter – April 2019)

On March 28, Pluto and the lunar south node formed a conjunction. Since they both move slowly, the date itself is not terribly important. Back at the beginning of March, the two points were already separated by less than 2°. And on the last day of April, their separation will only be 1° 55'. The Pluto-node interaction is ongoing, in other words, and we are all very much in the stew.

There's more: we can expect an intensification of these complicated energies around the middle of this month. The all-powerful Sun squares the nodes on the 12th and quickly goes on to square Pluto the next day.

That promises to be a colorful week.

Another date to circle on your calendar: April 30. When a planet turns from going retrograde to direct motion, or *vice versa,* there is also a great focusing of its energies – a turning of the tide, so to speak. On April 30, Pluto makes such a "station," so that will mark yet another crossroads. As we mentioned a few lines ago, when that station happens, the separation between Pluto and the south node will be less than two degrees – and that is still a very solid conjunction.

All of this is happening in the sign Capricorn, where the Pluto-node alignment is aided and abetted by the planet Saturn, also passing through that sign. Saturn's presence further intensifies and complicates the situation. Its fingerprints play an exaggerated role since Saturn is the ruler of Capricorn – thus it is extra strong, and its energy pervades that south node situation.

In Saturn times, *reality always faces us squarely* – and invites us to do the same.

If you have any planets or sensitive points between 20° and 25° of Capricorn, these transits have your name on them. Almost the same level of relevance would apply if you have any astrological sensitivities in the same degree zones of the signs Cancer, Libra, or Aries.

The presence of the south node on a sensitive point always suggests karma ripening. My November 2018 newsletter, "The Lunar Nodes Change to Cancer - Capricorn," covers the fundamentals. I won't repeat all of that here.

Pluto always brings truth to the surface, especially the kinds of realizations that we tend not to welcome.

Saturn, as we saw, can also be confrontive: bills come due, hard choices must be made, push comes to shove.

It is impossible, in other words, to look at this Spring astrologically without recognizing that both individually and collectively, the karmic chickens are coming home to roost. The personal meaning of all of this can only be determined via a full astrological analysis – exactly what are your individual sensitivities to those degrees of Capricorn, and what is the specific nature of your own karmic predicament. Any competent evolutionary astrologer can help you with all that, or maybe you can figure it out for yourself. To do that would require some degree of astrological skill – not to mention emotional and spiritual courage.

Massive astrological events such as this one also make themselves felt in the collective. Humanity itself is impacted. They leave their marks on history. You read about them in the headlines.

Before I go any further, I fear I must afflict you with a brief sermon. I will try to keep it as short as possible, but it is important to underscore an ethical point. I am about to tread out onto the notoriously thin ice of politics and cultural commentary. Just like you, I have opinions, some of them passionate. I think that is a healthy trait; democracy is a vigorous process and if any of us are worthy of its best manifestations, it is only because we think and participate in the collective conversation. As astrologers, however, we must celebrate human diversity above all. I find it absolutely toxic when an astrologer – even one with whom I agree politically – pronounces *ex cathedra* that the heavens themselves insist that you must vote for a specific candidate.

Your politics, just like the rest of your life, are your own business.

In what follows, I am going to strive to be as non-partisan as I can possibly be. Within the limits imposed by the nature of my own individuality, I want to look as clearly and neutrally as I can into the mirror of the heavens. I want to bring our astrological attention to bear upon the current dance of Pluto, Capricorn, Saturn, and the lunar south node.

Pluto, as Lord of the underworld, always brings shadow material to the surface. As it passes through a sign, the darker dimensions of that sign loom large in the collective experience. This is a vast subject, worthy of book length treatment. But let me prove it to you in just a few words.

- When Pluto was in *Libra*, the sign of marriage, from 1971 to 1983, the divorce rates went through the roof. The stultifying, shadow side of marriage was revealed. Collectively, we became much more honest about the soul-misery inflicted on us all by traditional marital values. A necessary healing? Fair enough. An uncomfortable process? For sure. Some of you older readers lived though it – and some of you younger ones – children of those times – bear the deeper scars of it.

- When Pluto was in *Scorpio* (1983-1995), the AIDS crisis struck. Suddenly, being honest about human sexuality became a matter of life and death. And we vividly saw the dark side of unbridled sexual freedom.

- When Pluto was in *Sagittarius* (1995-2008), the bleak side of big religion pressed upon us from all directions. Religiously-inspired terrorism horrified the world, while the plague of priestly pedophilia dominated the headlines.

As you can see, the "Pluto Equals Shadow Work" principle is reliable; it does not fail. Underlying it is a broader astrological law: *that every front has a back*. Every symbol in astrology has a divine purpose – and every one of them can be misused and trick us down a dark road. The evolutionary purpose of Pluto is to support our being honest about those soul-cages.

So what about Pluto entering Capricorn? It crossed that line in 2008 and will not enter Aquarius until 2023. Here we enter the delicate territory which I mentioned a few paragraphs back.

Capricorn is an innately *conservative* sign. The word "conservative" has of course become very charged lately. Initially here, to keep perspective, let us honor this "conservative" dimension of Capricorn. *It is about healthy conservative values such as integrity, loyalty, self-sacrifice, and maturity*. It is about *taking responsibility* for one's self and for the results of one's own actions. It is about *hard work* and stepping up to the plate as a man or a woman in full. Capricorn represents the *polar opposite of childishness*. If Capricorn energy disappeared and suddenly there were only eleven signs in the zodiac, human consciousness would be radically diminished.

Still, once again, every front has a back: *there is a dark side to conservatism*. On schedule, that dark side is being revealed. Who can look at the current headlines and have any doubt about that? Traditional conservative values such as integrity and personal responsibility are worth conserving. But what about "traditional values" such as racism, sexism, homophobia, and the right to endlessly exploit the earth? Are we seeing their dark side lately?

Dark Capricorn can be frightening. It invokes the image of the controlling tyrant suppressing truth and murdering enemies, real or perceived. Ultimately, it is not even really about a political ideology. Ultimately it is about *fear* – the fear of losing control or power, the fear of change, the fear of anything or anyone perceived as alien, and fear of the unknowable future.

The south node of the Moon, like Pluto, brings wounded material to the surface. The combination of the two symbols last month and this month suggests that *the "boil" of the fear-driven side of conservatism is cur-*

rently bursting. Everything truly terrifying about it is being laid on the table of collective consciousness.

Here in America, the long-awaited Mueller report was delivered just one week before the exact Pluto-south node alignment.

So where is it?

What taboo Plutonian information does the report contain? Only our Trump-appointed Attorney General, William Barr, knows. And as I write these words, he refuses to tell us. Two weeks before the alignment, the U.S. House of Representatives voted 420-0 to release the report – lots of political conservatives did the right thing that day.

And yet all that we have seen so far is a scant four pages of white-washed summary.

I doubt that this situation of futile, desperate control will prove stable for very long. I want to be an astrologer here, not a political commentator, so I am not going to say anything more about that.

The deeper question is, do you sense in all of this any evidence of "karmic chickens" coming home to roost? Do you sense fear – and the resultant dark Capricornian obsession with control – behind it? That is the fingerprint of the Pluto alignment with the south node. With that aspect exact on March 28, the timing could hardly be more perfect.

Once again, if you are politically conservative, I respect your right to your own thoughts and your own values. I feel that if those were not my sentiments, I would have no business being in the field of astrology. You have a right to be different from me; I not only respect that, I celebrate it. What I am attempting to do here is astrological commentary, not strictly political analysis.

I suspect that starting in 2023, as Pluto enters Aquarius, we will begin to see the shadow side of the progressive movement. That is a long story, and not the one we are exploring today. Simply said, the pendulum will swing. Some things are truly eternal.

More immediately, I expect colorful headlines about this collective crisis around the middle of the month when the transiting Sun triggers Pluto and the nodes.

And then, of course, we have mighty Pluto standing still in its tracks at the end of the month, staring us all right in the eye, inviting us to stare back courageously into the fierce mirror of truth.

We all have front row seats for whatever they might mean. May old Cosmo have mercy upon us.

SECTION FOUR

THE POWER – AND PERILS – OF SEEING THE FUTURE

As seductive as the voodoo practice might be, there is nothing in my opinion that presents a greater obstacle to the wider public acceptance of astrology than the false notion that "astrologers can see the future." We cannot see the future! *Worse, many astrologers themselves continue to advertise this damaging, misleading idea, promising something that we actually cannot reliably deliver – and paying the inevitable public relations price for lying about it.*

We who practice this craft are not powerless! Astrologers can predict the questions *we will be facing and the* timing *of those questions. Within the limits of our wisdom, we can also suggest better answers to those questions – and warn people of tempting, dumb answers. That's a lot! That's helpful! But seeing in advance what will actually happen? Well, all I can really say is that sometimes we get lucky.*

The actual uncertainty which is eternally implicit in the future is naturally frightening – bad things always could happen, of course. This understandable anxiety creates an unhealthy symbiosis between certain kinds of astrologers and fearful clients, as those astrologers unwittingly collude with their clients' compulsive need to have some false sense of control over the future simply by foreseeing it. Meanwhile, that same fearful mood unconsciously warps the astrologers' view of things, creating an unfortunate bias toward making a splash with dark, scary, overly-dramatic predictions, especially with certain planets which they view as particularly demonic.

I've obviously mounted the pulpit here! That's because, to me, these are not simply technical issues. These are issues of astrological morality and ethics. That's because we can't have true human freedom — or the possibility of personal responsibility — without having some degree of uncertainty as one of the main vegetables in our philosophical stew. We are not puppets and the planets do not have us by the strings. For good or for Ill, it is the choices we make that shape our futures, not Saturn or Jupiter.

The essays which follow cover many bases, all of them in the "predictive" realm. In each one of them, you will see one principle pervading every word I write: that there is no astrological configuration that cannot be gotten right, and that in getting it right, we can not only learn and grow — we can also circumvent unnecessary hurt and pain.

23

Astrology has no shortage of antagonists, but I lament the fact that we astrologers are often our own worst enemies. We hurt ourselves in many ways, but perhaps in no way that is more balefully effective than succumbing to the siren call of "making predictions." We have created that expectation of us in the media, but it is a promise that we cannot reliably keep. That's not because of any weakness in astrology. Instead it is because of a great strength in human consciousness: our imaginations, our moral fiber, and our free will. As I wrote in The Changing Sky many years ago: Our job is not to predict the future. It is to create it.

THE PERILS OF PREDICTION

(Newsletter – February 2017)

At the big International Society for Astrological Research (ISAR) conference in California this past October, a panel of astrologers predicted who would win the U.S. presidential election. None of them picked Donald Trump. Their calculations suggested a Clinton victory, just as the majority of pollsters had predicted.

As they say, "the rest is history." The astrologers obviously got it wrong. This was not a glorious day for our craft. One vitriolic Internet article trumpeted, *"Astrologers Were Wrong About the 2016 Election, Casting Serious*

Doubt on Their Predictive Abilities." The piece opened with the lines, "Astrology is bullshit. But for some reason, many Americans still believe that astrologists have the ability to predict the future."

You can imagine the rest.

I posted the nasty article to Facebook with the following comment:

> *I think the idea that 'astrologers can see the future' has done our field nothing but harm. We cannot see the future! Probabilities . . . yes — that's why our predictions are often correct. Questions and issues, certainly — there is the heart of our craft. ISAR made a mistake simply with the PREMISE of this panel. It is time for a major paradigm shift in astrological thinking.*

God bless ISAR for all the good work it does in bringing astrologers together to learn from each other. I proudly served on its Ethics Committee for about five years. I am not writing to attack the organization. I'd have been speaking at the conference myself except that I had a previous commitment to teach in China. I write these words out of loyalty to the astrological community, along with a desire to try to take some personal responsibility for improving the place of astrology in modern society.

In voicing this criticism, I think that it is also obvious that winning any ISAR-sponsored popularity contests is not my main aim in life. Much closer to my heart is seeing healthy forms of astrology enhancing the mental health and general well-being of far vaster numbers of human beings than it does now. That worthy goal confronts many obstacles: fear-based, control-freak religion and dogmatic science are our most obvious antagonists. But I think that we astrologers ourselves are half the problem. *We make promises we cannot keep. Every time we break one, we lose public credibility.*

And false promise *numero uno* is that we can see the future.

That incorrect belief has done more to discredit and misrepresent astrology than every silly semi-annual announcement that "The Zodiac Is Wrong." Worse, it is we astrologers who perpetuate the lie.

Symbolism is not literalism. And astrology is a symbolic language. If we could truly accept that elemental principle, we would all be better astrologers. Symbols are more like dreams than newspapers.

What do we actually see when we gaze into the crystal ball of astrology? One good answer might be *probabilities.* I think there is a better answer though – one that we will get to soon. But let's stay with the idea of just "seeing probabilities" for a moment.

Say you are planning a picnic for ten days from now. You check the long-range weather forecast. They predict rain. Do you believe it? Do you cancel your picnic? Of course not. You understand that meteorologists are often wrong about tomorrow, let alone the weather over a week into the future.

Literal, back-and-white astrological prediction has a similar level of reliability and for similar reasons. Meteorologists work with statistical models. Astrologers don't do that . . . not exactly. Better said, the traditions of predictive astrology are essentially "folk-statistics," ideas gradually accumulated through centuries of observation, with one eye on the sky and the other eye on human affairs. As such, they often work – and of course realistically that bad weather forecast probably does mean that there is a fair chance it will rain on your picnic. *But you don't count on it.* In parallel fashion, if Uranus transits into your House of Marriage, there is an excellent chance there will be significant changes in your primary relationships. But any astrologer who says unequivocally that "you will get a divorce" is abusing astrology.

And abusing you too.

A moment ago I asked, "What do we actually see when we gaze into the crystal ball of astrology?" I said that one good answer was "probabilities." What are some better answers?

Questions. Possibilities. Potentials. Warnings.

The best answers, in my opinion: *Your Path. The Dharma. The Great Tao. The Will of God.*

In my Facebook post, I suggested that astrology badly needed a paradigm shift. Like most true paradigm shifts, it is not terribly difficult to reduce its pivotal premise to a few words. Still, those few words can change everything.

Examples: Earth is not flat, but round. Planets orbit the Sun. Gayness is not a disease. Time and Space are not constants. Women are the equals of men.

The astrological equivalent? *Your chart predicts questions, not answers.*

Prior to the 20th Century, science described a universe governed by laws and logic. Then along came relativity and quantum mechanics. As Sir

James Jeans famously put it, *"The universe begins to look more like a great thought than like a great machine."* Fundamental to quantum mechanics is the notion of worlds governed, not by immutable mechanical laws, but by probabilities. A ripened apple is highly likely to fall to the ground – but there is a slight statistical possibility that it will "fall" up. Furthermore, in quantum theory, *the consciousness of the observer interacts with every experiment.* Consciousness itself cannot be separated from our understanding of any physical process.

That, to me, is astrology's bridge to the future. We humans are the "unpredictable quanta" in the astrological equation. *It is our fate to face certain questions and certain possibilities at certain times.* How we respond to them is governed by human consciousness, not by the planets. Quantum mechanics, as Gary Zukav wrote in *The Dancing Wu Li Masters,* "has explained everything from subatomic particles to transistors to stellar energy. It has never failed. It has no competition."

Astrologers simply must cast off the push-and-pull shackles of thinking like 19th century physicists and enter the quantum age if our craft is going to avoid the looming trap of being finally and utterly dismissed as an outdated mythology.

So, we assemble a panel of experienced astrologers and ask them the straightforward question, "Who will win the US presidential election?" And, unanimously and authoritatively, they all get it wrong. Afterwards, naturally, there is an unseemly scramble to save face. The lack of a reliable, verified time of birth for Clinton was a grievous technical problem. It was trotted out as an explanation for the failure. At least one astrologer on the panel came closest to the truth by predicting that Clinton would win the election, but not be inaugurated. And, OK, Clinton did win the popular vote by three million and of course she will not be inaugurated. I still think it is fair to say, "close, but no banana." There is some resemblance between the prediction and what actually happened, but there is also the looming bottom line: *every astrologer on the panel answered the straightforward predictive question incorrectly.*

And that made astrology look bad.

My point here is not to disparage anyone. I'm intentionally not even naming names. My point is that the very existence of the panel did not do any favors for our profession. Stand back from the technical world of astrology and think like "the person on the street" – or, better said, think like the kind of person we astrologers would like to reach and help. The headline screams, "Astrologers Predict Clinton Victory." And Trump wins.

There is no way to frame that as a good day for astrology.

In my opinion, the fiasco arose, not from a "wrong prediction," but from prediction itself. We made a promise we could not keep, and the parts of the media that cared about astrology at all savaged us for it.

Victoria Naumann Smoot, an editor with the ISAR technical journal, had submitted a talk for the conference which warned of the "perils of prediction," but it was not chosen for the conference's roster. Generously, she writes, "The warnings against the pitfalls of forecasting with astrology were covered or alluded to . . . in more gently titled talks, so no harm and no foul. I know I received some votes, but I did not make the cut with enough to be chosen." Victoria goes on to add, "But then, the panels on the presidential elections bore out an instinctive feeling I had when I was writing an editorial introduction to the ISAR journal, *The International Astrologer*. . . In the latest issue of our journal, I wrote, "Our 2016 Symposium could have been just as aptly named 'The Power of Choice Meets the Consequence of Forecasting.'"

With those last words, Ms. Smoot hits the nail on the head as far as I am concerned. We simply cannot do accurate astrology and simultaneously ignore the power of the human will. And, as this panel demonstrated, "forecasting" has "consequences" – often grave ones.

What is the alternative? What positive proposal can we make for getting this right? Let's not simply cry over spilled milk, point fingers, and then try to let bygones be bygones. Let's think of how we might do better and present our sacred craft in a better light. What if the panel had instead been tasked with "predicting questions" rather than predicting which horse would win the race? What if half a dozen intelligent, informed astrologers had been invited to "ask the planets" questions such as these:

- What is the present soul-path for the entity we call the United States of America?
- What does the nation need to learn – and what is the price for not learning it?
- What is the direction of maximum well-being for this entity?
- What "shadows" and darkness is it now facing?

- What sage guidance might you offer?
- What kinds of synchronistic phenomena are likely to arise in concert with these planetary energies?
- Which candidate's birthchart seems most positively aligned with these ideals?
- And finally – any guesses about who is likely to win?

I can almost see the shaking heads and heavenward, hopeless gazes of any conventional astrologers reading these words! *That Steven Forrest is such an airhead . . . there he goes again.* But here is my response: these are questions that astrology *can* actually answer, and answer wisely and helpfully. Clearly we failed to answer the "practical question" of who would win the election. I also believe that, with the right astrologers on the panel, such an approach would have produced an elegant, intelligent result, full of "quotable quotes" and sharp, telling insights – in short, something that would have done astrology proud rather than our walking into a public relations catastrophe that will keep our critics salivating for at least a few more years.

My hope is that the community of astrologers as a whole learns from this failure rather than compartmentalizing it, rationalizing, and ultimately forgetting about the whole embarrassing mess and the public damage it did to us.

A fine astrologer, now gone, named Jayj Jacobs once hilariously quipped, "Having Mars in Pisces is like trying to hammer a nail with a fish." I am not so pessimistic about Mars in Pisces, but I loved the line and will merrily steal it here. Using astrology to see the future is . . . well, you guessed it.

So why does predictive astrology work as well as it often does? In terms of the point I am making here, that question is the "elephant in the living room." Astrology's long history of successful predictions might seem to undercut my entire tirade.

Actually it does not. A line from my Facebook post: *"We cannot see the future. Probabilities . . . yes – that's why our predictions are often correct."*

An experienced astrologer blessed with some common sense can often make an educated guess about the most likely kinds of developments based on current planetary configurations. That system works well a lot of the time. But remember: *the hardest errors to detect are the ones that you can usually get away with.* Try diagnosing an *intermittent* bug in a computer program. Or think about this line: *"I've been driving for fifteen years without a seatbelt and it hasn't done me any harm."*

Prediction is like that. You may often be right. And being "right" is addictive, especially when spiced with feedback along the lines of "you are so amazing . . ."

Furthermore, people are hungry to feel that they have some control over the future. "Prediction" satisfies some of that drive, or at least promises to do so.

Robert Hand famously predicted something that very much resembled the 9/11 attacks. Hats off to him. Almost forty years ago in the pages of a magazine called *The Sun,* I myself even anticipated the break-up of the Soviet Union.

Prediction does work sometimes.

After the ISAR fiasco, Facebook was festooned with astrologers hooting, "I predicted Trump, I predicted Trump!" And I am sure they were telling the truth. But all of that success is beside the point.

To remain within the bounds of integrity, we must also admit that our predictions are wrong a lot too.

When we are right, it is emphatically not that way "by chance," as our critics often claim. We astrologers are correct way too often for "lucky chance" to be the explanation. But when we are right, it is not because the universe is mechanical and we are puppets in it – it is because *we placed our bet on the high probability outcome.* With experience, an astrologer can get pretty good at doing that. But so much is lost.

Astrologers getting hooked on "being right" in this way reminds me of those experiments where rats die of starvation because they choose cocaine over food.

My own first spiritual teacher, Marian Starnes, once taught me, *"The ambition of any true prophet is to be proven wrong."* Her words have never left me, strange as they sound at first. As astrologers, we can sometimes see difficulty looming ahead. Get to the heart of the matter and you can always find that there is a path forward through it – one that typically avoids a pointless crisis and an empty drama, even though traveling to reach that higher ground might not be easy. With a client, I will often lay out a traditional prediction, then I say, "prove me wrong."

The lazier the client, the more likely the conventional prediction will turn out to be true.

Earlier I mentioned Uranus transiting into the seventh house. I can't remember how many times I have cleaned up after an astrologer who predicted divorce based on that transit! And it *can* mean divorce, for sure, as well as intimate renewal and other possibilities. This is a big subject and the entirety of a person's chart must be taken into account, but boiling it down to a *question* we can reliably predict, here it is:

* *When Uranus transits into your seventh house, how can you reframe your primary relationships in such a way that they do not block the expression of your emerging individuality?*

That is the essence of it. See how such a question can trigger creative, clear thought? It is vastly more helpful than a grim prognosis for anyone's marriage, as if the "planets were going to trash your happy home." Without stretching our imaginations too far, it is not hard to think of a scenario where *planting that seed in someone's mind* might actually save a marriage that was heading for the rocks.

So often just coming up with the right question is the first step toward an effective answer, not to mention effective counsel. Astrology can do that, in spades – and thus be of genuine help.

During that ISAR conference, Saturn was squaring Neptune. The universe was asking all of us everywhere to do a Saturnian reality-check on our fantasies and delusions – in the light of the election results, we might say the same for the United States in general. My prayer is that we, the community of astrologers, can rise to this opportunity, re-frame our craft in a way that honors the power of consciousness, and let go of our addiction to the predictive delusion that keeps us increasingly isolated in a fading, self-congratulatory intellectual ghetto.

24

This is one of my favorite newsletters. It's about a specific technical area of astrology that is actually quite powerful and meaningful, as I am confident you will soon see – and yet relatively unknown and unexplored. As I wrote this piece, I was speculating about the meaning of an astrological – or more properly, astronomical – event that was unfolding at the time. Now, as I write these introductory words a decade down the road, we are all in a position to judge the accuracy of my 2012 speculations. By the way, I am hoping that some young astrologers might take the ideas I introduce here and run with them, taking them beyond the horizons of my own imagination.

THIS IS NOT YOUR GRANDMOTHER'S VENUS RETROGRADE . . . OR MAYBE IT IS!

(Newsletter – May 2012)

Venus turns retrograde on May 15. It forms a station on June 27 and after that it will be in direct motion until the end of 2013. None of this is earth-shaking news. Venus moves fast. Unless you are in diapers and weigh about the same as a Thanksgiving turkey, you've been through this kind of Venus event before. Venus's *synodic* cycle – the length of time between two successive Earth-Venus-Sun alignments – runs about 584 days. It spends about forty of those days in retrograde condition. In other words, Venus is retrograde for a little over a month out of every year and a half or so – an interesting subject, but again, it's really no big deal.

This upcoming retrograde period is an entirely different beast though, so hold onto your hats. This retrogradation of Venus might even change the world.

On June 5, Venus will *transit* the Sun – and that word "transit" is where we need to start. I am using the term as an astronomer would use it, which is totally different from the way an astrologer employs it.

Astronomically, when a planet "transits" the Sun, that means it *actually crosses the Sun's disk.* The simplest illustration of an *astronomical* transit is a total solar eclipse. Every month, there is a New Moon – a Sun/Moon conjunction. *But only rarely are the two bodies actually directly lined up so perfectly that the Moon covers the Sun's face.* That's a transit, as an astronomer would use the word. And that's what Venus does on June 5th – although of course the disk of Venus is tiny so it can't really fully "eclipse" the Sun. It just passes across it, a tiny little black dot, taking about six hours to make it across the Sun's fiery surface.

Don't look at it! It will blind you. Use #14 welder's goggles or something similar. With care, it's a naked eye event.

The astronomical geometry behind a Venus transit such as this one is complex. As with a solar eclipse, a lot of things have to fall just right for it to happen. First, it has to be an "inferior conjunction" of Venus. A superior one will not do. Not familiar with those terms? No surprise – astrologers don't normally use them. Again, they're in astronomy's lexicon, not ours.

If you think about it, there are two ways Venus can be aligned with the Sun in your chart. One is when Venus passes *between the Earth and the Sun* – that's the *inferior conjunction.* The other is when *the Sun is between Venus and the Earth,* with Venus of course far away on the other side of the solar system. There's no way it can cross the Sun's face then – instead, the Sun is crossing it. In normal astrological practice, these two kinds of conjunctions look the same – *almost.* The difference is that in the inferior conjunction, Venus is always retrograde. (In the superior conjunction, it is always direct.)

Again: no big deal – these inferior conjunctions occur every 583.92 days, like clockwork. In fact, before the age of atomic clocks, this Venus cycle was the solar system's premier time-keeper.

For a solar eclipse to occur, the Sun/Moon conjunction must occur close to the lunar nodes. It's the same with Venus – it has nodes too and if the inferior Sun-Venus conjunction falls too far away from them, then Venus will be a little too high or low actually to cross the Sun's face. Those Venusian nodes are now in Sagittarius-Gemini, so this time we are in luck.

Some of you probably know about the eight-year pentagonal cycle of Venus. A full discussion of it is beyond our space limitations here. Suffice to say that during an eight year cycle of five inferior conjunctions, Venus traces out a nearly perfect pentagon – a five-pointed star. After 7.977 years, it starts the cycle over again at a point two or three degrees earlier in the zodiac. *So these Venus transits across the Sun's face occur in pairs just about exactly eight years apart.* The one June 5 is actually the second one of the pair. The first one occurred on June 8, 2004.

Don't hold your breath for the next one. It occurs in 2117.

- *The bottom line is that we get matched pairs of these supercharged Venus transits separated by eight years every century or so.*

Even trickier, the actual rhythm is that these pairs of events oscillate between happening every 105.5 years and every 121.5 years. The last pair occurred a long time ago – on December 8, 1874 and December 6, 1882. That's why the title of this essay mentioned your grandmother – although obviously for you younger people we might need to put the word "great" ahead of grandma once or twice.

What do such transits signify? In practical astrology, the big themes of life are defined by the slow-moving outer plants, while the quick motions of Mercury, Venus, and Mars serve more as triggers for specific events. As we have seen, Venus forms an inferior conjunction with the Sun about every nineteen months – too often for its meaning to rival, for example, the life-changing power of a Pluto transit over your natal Sun. Obviously, to say that your "life is completely changed" every nineteen months is hyperbolic.

- *But here, with our current transit-pair, we have a major Venus cycle that has over a century to develop depth and complexity of meaning.*

We are looking at something that hasn't happened in the last four or five generations.

Our working premise is that all humanity began a new relationship with Venus between 1874 and 1882, and that we are doing the same thing again now. Plainly we need to stand back and take in the big picture to comprehend such a glacial event. To get a taste of it, let's focus on three classic Venusian categories: *art, "the Feminine,"* and *"human relationships."*

ART

With Art, we hit paydirt right away. The period between 1874 and 1882 was extraordinarily fertile artistically. In painting, artists such as Cezanne, Pissaro, Whistler, Manet, Renoir, Monet, Homer, and Rodin were in full flower. Musically, we had peak expressions from Rimsky-Korzakov, Tchaikovsky, Brahms, Moussorgsky, Verdi, Bizet, Wagner, Saint-Saens, Gilbert and Sullivan, and Bartok. That list is a *Who's Who,* of course. For our purposes, its significance lies in the fact that human art *renewed its vision* during this period.

Has something similar been occurring over the past eight years? Would we even know? It is a classic question of what the fish knows of the sea – we are in the midst of this present period, and we cannot yet see it clearly. Not all of these luminaries were recognized and celebrated during their lifetimes. Bottom line, we can assume that the foundations of a new vision have been laid and we will watch the structures rise over the next century. I am not sure what it is, but I am sure it runs deeper than better digital delivery systems and 3-D glasses.

Could it be video games? My younger friends tell me that there are worlds to be explored there, worlds that run much deeper than "first person shooter" silliness. What new novelists, poets, film makers, and graphic artists have arisen to be the big "Last Names" of a century from now?

THE FEMININE

Feminism has a long, complex history and this is meant to be a short article! Let me cite one single, hugely symbolic event dating back to that last pair of Venus transits – the passing of The Married Women's Property Act in The United Kingdom in 1882. Essentially, this major legal event was the culmination of a long feminist struggle, and it reflected the changing nature of the relationship between men and women during this previous seminal Venusian period. *Essentially, for the first time, it allowed married women to control and own their own property.*

It is interesting and concerning to me that we are currently experiencing so much backlash relative to the equality of women – the so-called "War on Women" is raging, and even issues such as equal pay and access to birth control are being debated. Will we step backwards and reverse the gains made by the brave women of the last Venus transits? I doubt it, but it is telling that these issues are "up" in the collective consciousness again. We are "reconsidering the Feminine."

Here of course I write as an American. In other parts of the world, for better and for worse, the roles of women are being re-framed as well. The pivotal female role in the Arab Spring movement is one emblematic expression of all this.

Relating Venus strictly to females is, in my view, ultimately a dead-end. Men have Venus in their charts too! I believe that the obvious and practical associations between Venus and women in conventional astrological practice reflects cultural, rather than archetypal, realities. It ain't permanent, in other words.

In this larger view, I would contemplate a wider perspective on various cultural changes cemented over the past eight years. High on the list is the fact that it is now OK to be gay – at least compared to the rampant prejudices of the past. There are still homophobes everywhere of course, but their ranks are thinning. To see this, simply contemplate the normalization of gayness on television shows, in film, and in popular music.

RELATIONSHIPS

Perhaps even more deeply, I suggest that the past eight years have marked the beginning of *a new cultural paradigm of human intimacy in general.*

As the old cliche goes, each generation imagines that it has invented sex. The joke is obvious, but the line also reflects an underlying reality. Each generation does indeed re-create the *customs* and *assumptions* that shape the ever-shifting meaning of "normal" sexual behavior. For example, some people think that marriage is fading as an institution. Certainly in many circles it is seen as increasing "optional," and maybe even a little quaint. And that is a major change. Has this attitude taken root in the mainstream during the past eight years? Today divorce and remarriage tend to be at least halfway *assumed to be the norm* rather than as an aberration or a personal failure.

The age of the commitedly, happily *non-celibate single person* is emerging – and today such a person represents a far more welcome dinner guest than he or she would have been in 1882! Sexually confident, even sexually assertive, young *women* are everywhere – as are young men capable of saying, "thanks, but I don't know you well enough yet." Compare either of those with the norms of the 1950s.

This all reflects one of the beauties of astrology. These are changes we can only see and appreciate clearly if we sit on the astrological mountaintop. Without that century-wide perspective, we are too close to the action to see the turning of the wheels.

So perhaps we can recognize that the upcoming retrograde cycle of Venus is a special one, even though it's not common to hear astrologers speaking of "transits" in this particular fashion. With these two passages of Venus over the face of the Sun, we complete something – or more accurately, we complete the *foundation* of something. And, going back to the title of this article, perhaps it does have a connection with something your grandmother or your great-grandmother triggered in her own brave way – and perhaps we must look through her eyes to fully appreciate its magnitude.

25

Spring 2014 looked pretty frightening, planet-wise. Astrological doomsayers were outdoing each other in their ominous prophecies. Faced with that kind of situation, I am always of two minds. On one hand, I know that hard things do often tend to happen under difficult astrological configurations – that's basic astrology. On the other hand, I love it when fatalistic astrologers are proven wrong – that helps keep us honest about the "uncertainty principle" which is always introduced into the equations by the power of human will, imagination, and creativity. What actually happened that Spring? Ebola, the loss of those two Malaysian airliners, mayhem as usual in the usual hotspots – but the world did not end. In this piece, I aimed to look at the big world – but also at the little world we all inhabit, offering the best guidance I could about how individuals could make the right responses to these harsh energies. I can't prove this, but here is what I believe actually happened back then in Spring 2014 – I think that enough conscious people all over the planet made spiritually healthy choices during this time and thus lifted us above the hell-worlds that some of our more gloomy colleagues had prophesied. If evolutionary astrology teaches us anything at all, it is that we are not powerless, but rather that we have powers we have barely imagined.

HELL IN THE HEAVENS?

(Newsletter – April 2014)

Hellfire and brimstone? Economic collapse? Nuclear explosions? Or is it the arrival of Elvis and a Sasquatch in a UFO to change our DNA and lead us all in chanting in a drum circle for world peace?

April 2014 promises all of it . . . depending on which astrologer you read.

Astrologers tend to be a rather hysterical crowd. I'm 65 and I have lost count of the number of demi-apocalypses I have survived – how many times I have heard that the sky was falling.

The reality, as I have come to understand it, is that the future is not fixed, and that therefore it cannot be reliably predicted. Consciousness interacts with vast archetypal fields of possibility and probability. What actually happens is the result of the collision of both forces. Consciousness and intention are too powerful to discount, and our duty as astrologers is, I believe, to fan the flames of mindfulness and kindness rather than to feed fear and to spread feelings of helpless fatalism.

That's my sermon.

But April 2014 looms, and it does truly look incendiary. All month long we have a grand cross in the sky. Pluto and Uranus are square, as most of us know, from 2012 through 2015. But during April, Mars opposes Uranus, while Jupiter opposes Pluto. The four-pointed configuration reaches its most precise geometry around April 22, but it is very strong all through the month.

Four squares or two oppositions – these are the so-called "bad aspects," indicative of conflict. And who's fighting? Well . . . that's not very encouraging either. Uranus, the Lord of Earthquakes and Lightning Bolts is squared off against Pluto, the Lord of the Underworld. Meanwhile, Mars, the god of War, opposes Uranus and squares Pluto.

Jupiter is often viewed as a bright spot – but in this kind of neighborhood, even "the Greater Benefic" has its work cut out.

Is there any hope for us?

I think so. But I don't want to whitewash this fearsome configuration. Astrologically, it looks about as comforting as sighting a great funnel of dark cloud outside your window while wondering why you suddenly hear something like an approaching railroad train.

With squares and oppositions, things tend to come to a head. Push comes to shove. Breaking points are reached. Crisis reigns. Squares and oppositions are exactly like the sound your engine eventually makes when you've decided to ignore the little red oil light on your dashboard. And the reasons are exactly the same: *at squares and oppositions, bad behavior catches up with us.* The law of consequences reigns.

How has humanity been doing lately? I think we will see something like our "report card" this month. I don't want to overreact, but I doubt it will be smooth sailing. There is a high probability of drama – and trauma. That's a statement about the planet Earth – a statement about the 6 o'clock news, in other words. Political and social frustrations will boil over. Some systemic breakdowns will occur. I wouldn't be surprised if the Earth itself offers up some complaints in the form of earthquakes, storms, plague, volcanic activity, and so on.

If you have astrological sensitivities to the middle of the Cardinal signs – Aries, Cancer, Libra, and Capricorn – issues will come to a boil in your own personal life too. What issues? Much there depends on the specific houses of your chart that are being affected and the aspects those four planets are making to it by transit.

The heart of this Grand Cross is the ongoing square of Pluto and Uranus. The basic issue with that big, long-lasting square is summarized in the words, "breakthrough or breakdown." Seemingly irresolvable tensions reach critical mass. Something has to give, something has to evolve and change. The longer we wait, the more explosive the tensions become.

Jupiter, in Cancer, entered the equations last summer, so it's not exactly a new player. We've been living with a T-square among it, plus Pluto and Uranus since then. Mars is the new element, and of course what itchier trigger-finger is there than the god of war? But do keep perspective: the same Grand Cross, although not quite as precise in its geometry, was in effect in late December 2013. We survived that one.

Mars advanced through Libra nearly to the end of the sign – and thus out of the orbs of the grand cross – until March 1, when it turned retrograde. Now it is heading right back into the cross-hairs. The full four-sided configuration reaches its height of precision – and presumably of intensity – on April 22, with Mars still retrograde.

Mars turns around again on May 19 at about 9 degrees of Libra. That's a day to mark too. *Mars stations can bring things to a head just as surely as any exact aspect.* With Mars advancing, the grand cross grows tighter again, but by the time Mars is back into its exact hard aspects with Uranus and Pluto, Jupiter has begun to move onward through Cancer, and the structure is breaking up.

That's a long-winded paragraph! But the take-away is that it is misleading to think of this Grand Cross as something "happening on April 22." The reality is that it *peaks* then, but it is "happening" from December 2013 through the end of this May. It is a period of *months*, not a single day-long event. Too long a time to spend hiding under the bed!

How can we get it right?

One piece of the puzzle is that your "inner liberal" and your "inner conservative" need to do a better job of shaking hands so we can stop compartmentalizing ourselves and projecting so mercilessly onto each other. I've explored that idea elsewhere, looking more narrowly at the Uranus-Pluto square. In this short article, I want to focus more on Mars and Jupiter. They are what make this present situation unique. *They turn the simple square into the complex, four-planet structure we call the Grand Cross.* They also represent fresh, new energetic vectors in a very *stuck* situation, just like when someone whose voice has not been heard enters an argument that is going nowhere and brings some genuine new insights.

Maybe we listen to that person, and maybe we don't, but there is at least a fresh avenue of possibility.

Jupiter in Cancer – here we have an expansive, optimistic vibration connected with Cancerian concerns: *home, family, land, the inner life.* The subject is vast, but here's one thread in the tapestry: I drive and fly around America quite a lot, and I've got to say the place is falling apart. The highways, the bridges, even the tray-tables on the big jets. Why? Why don't people notice? What would it do for our economy and our relationships with each other as citizens if we acknowledged this and started re-building the place? *Where is our pride (Jupiter) in our home (Cancer)?* Because of synchronicity, we may well see evidence of this issue – a tragic bridge collapse, for example.

This is just one meaning of Jupiter in Cancer, but it suggests a way of thinking that can add new dimensions to the current impasses, socially, culturally and politically.

While we've been fighting with each other, the place has been falling apart.

Cancer is about *nutrition* too. *What's happened to the food supply?* Don't we deserve better? Are we poisoning ourselves with pesticides and GMOs? Why are so many people suddenly "gluten intolerant?" Maybe it's not the gluten at all. Maybe it's what Monsanto, et al, have done to the wheat. Will the laws of synchronicity lead to some kind of miserable event that demonstrates all of this to us? A plague of diarrhea? Do we need that, or can we get the message in a healthier way?

At a more personal level, what about your own home? Does it need some paint? A garden? What about your "home" in a more intimate sense of the word? *Have I told you lately that I love you?* Have you heard those words coming back at you lately? We all have families in one sense or another – and here I want to count *families of choice* as well as the old shared-DNA or marriage models.

Our roots require attention now. That's Jupiter in Cancer! Get that kind of healing going, and many log-jam dilemmas are shattered. I spoke as an American a moment ago when I mentioned the infrastructure falling apart, but this applies to Damascus and Aleppo and Kiev and probably everywhere else too.

Mars is a big *trigger* in the mix. It is in Libra, the traditional sign of its "detriment." As we saw earlier in this volume, I've never liked that word. Such a configuration just means that a planet is in a complex, paradoxical situation – sort of like being over sixteen years old. *Can we fight (Mars) for peace (Libra)?* Of course we can – and that is an excellent idea right now. There is obvious irony in the phrase, "fighting for peace," but achieving peace takes effort and courage. Think of the courage it takes to disarm, for example.

How can you help? Try disarming at home. Try dropping defenses. Try "fighting for peace" in your own little world. Try making your community (Jupiter in Cancer) into a place of reconciliation (Uranus integrated with Pluto).

Be nice to somebody with a bad bumper sticker. Let them get ahead of you in traffic, and smile at them.

This is how astrology – and the universe – actually works. As above, so below – and as below, so above. *That means that your own consciousness is a force in the larger pattern of things.*

What will happen this month? Crisis leading to breakthrough, with spiritual heroes making their voices heard? Or crisis making the rubble bounce some more?

The answer is not entirely out of your hands.

26

Pluto is the Roman lord of the underworld – which, loosely translated, becomes "the god of hell." As dinner guests go, when Pluto knocks on the door, most astrologers are not too eager to put out their best china. Should we cringe before Pluto transits? Not . . . exactly. They can indeed be frightening, and it is unrealistic to ignore that dimension of them. But it is worse – in fact, tragic, wasteful, and stupid – to ignore the higher ground they promise. In this rather personal piece, I try to cover all the scary bases humbly and honestly, but without losing sight of Pluto's loftier possibilities and how to get to them.

THE DREADED
TRANSITS OF PLUTO

(June 2015 – Newsletter)

Transiting Pluto is currently sitting right smack on my Sun – the "god of hell," in other words, is right up my nose, and yet, despite all the gleefully horrific prognostications of the doomsayers, I am still alive. When I was a young astrologer, still conditioned by the books I was reading, I might have seen that transit coming and bet anyone five dollars that it would kill me. Such was my training.

It is truly spooky to reflect on how deeply a culture of fear can sneak into our blood as we learn astrology.

Many of my private clients come to me knowing at least a little bit about astrology – often "just enough to be dangerous." I mention one word about an upcoming transit of Pluto or Saturn and they grow pale, as if iI were about to pronounce some kind of death sentence.

As most of you know, I constantly preach against that kind of astrology. But am I myself immune to the fear? Not entirely. I've got a student who adds a cool little colophon to her emails – "Start listening to your own lectures." That's a good reminder . . . for me, as much as for the rest of us.

Not to be a Pollyanna here – transits of Pluto can definitely bring us face to face with real darkness. They often offer us a chance to face our deepest fears – although "a chance" makes it sound too much like an option we might choose not to exercise. It is of course never quite as simple as telling Lord Pluto "no, thank you." The reality is that Plutonian times very often do correlate with our seeing the things that we most fear standing right there before our eyes, complete with sulfurous breath, horns and a tail, and fire coming out of their noses.

- Ask any experienced astrologer and you'll get the same response: in Plutonian times, there is a real pattern of people being confronted with death, disease, betrayal, divorce, or grievous loss.
- But then there are also the people who seemingly "get lucky," and nothing of that unpleasant nature happens at all. They appear to have "dodged the bullet."

What can we make of these two phenomena? Is astrology imperfect? I actually doubt that – but I think astrologers themselves are a different story. We astrologers are all imperfect. And the task of each generation of us is to become a little less imperfect. We must try constantly to allow reality to speak to us more clearly through the fog of error in our books and our traditions.

Pluto sometimes brings nightmares to life – we simply cannot dismiss that statement. But, as we have seen, rigid predictions of Plutonian doom are never completely reliable either. As I mentioned, Pluto is sitting on my Sun now and I'm fine – *so far.*

(See how the fear creeps in?)

(But, Steve: take heart! As you might have noticed, there are still a few live Sagittarians over the age of fifteen walking around. Every one of them survived Pluto conjuncting his or her Sun between 1995 and 2008.)

A few lines ago, I wrote that Pluto transits offer us "a chance to face our deepest fears." So what do you fear? Death, disease, betrayal, malice, accident, bereavement, violence, divorce, or grievous loss? Of course – *everyone fears those things*. They are the "nine horsemen of the Apocalypse."

But what about *success?* Do you fear that? What about *prosperity?* What about *your own power?*

Those kinds of fears are not nearly so widely discussed, but they too are very real. Failure can feel very safe and secure – you're off the hook. "Not having enough money" can be a fabulous excuse for not claiming a life. Avoiding our power can get us out of our larger responsibilities to the human community.

Let's start putting two and two together and see if we can come up with a "unified field theory" of Plutonian energy.

When nothing bad happens during a Pluto transit, never think that you just "got lucky." That's not how the universe actually works. The reliable Plutonian principle here is not a gloomy prediction about awful things happening; *the reliable prediction is that you will have a chance to face your fears, whatever they are*. You have now grown strong enough to integrate some previously unconscious material. In other words, to your conscious mind, that material is "PG-13" – *and you are now fourteen*. You are ready. Maybe you weren't ready a year before, but now you are. Something that previously would have simply scared you to no good purpose can now make you stronger. That's the deeper meaning – and the higher purpose – of a Pluto event.

So, once again, what are your fears?

Your chart will tell you. Answering that question gets into the technical side of astrological analysis. To learn the details, you might read my *The Book of Pluto*. In what house and sign is your natal Pluto? What aspects does it make? Where is transiting Pluto currently located? What issues is it triggering?

Answer those questions and your chart will define the basic DNA of the fear you are ready to face.

Going further, in evolutionary astrology, one bedrock principle in Plutonian times is *always to have a look at the Moon's south node*. That symbol reveals our deepest underlying blindness, which we assume to have its origins in a prior lifetime. In some way, it is always connected with a primordial fear.

- Pluto transits always trigger our deepest issues and the south node always defines those issues, so the two are forever linked.

That's true even if Pluto is not making any aspect to the nodes themselves or to their rulers. And remember: always, every transit you experience has a high potential meaning – something connected to your evolution as a soul. *A good rule of thumb is that ultimately the easiest possible path for you lies in embracing that soul lesson rather than in fighting it.*

In my apprenticeship programs, I have often taught a class entitled, "Intentional Transits." The idea is that instead of looking at the chart not as a tool for making predictions, we see it as a guide to what we are learning and how to best navigate those questions. *We can set conscious intentions about how to use any transit.* Instead of seeing astrology as a crystal ball, we have a kind of wise counselor who can aim us "intentionally" toward the right – and thus ultimately the most painless – expressions of whatever astrological energies we are currently experiencing, even frightening ones such as Pluto.

Each planet holds different teachings. With Pluto, as we have seen, a good way to frame the question is to ask yourself, "what do I fear?" *Then think about how you might overcome that fear.* Again, always remember you might fear good things even more than you fear bad ones. The wounds of shame can do that to you.

My aim in these newsletters is to share big ideas and thoughts about evolutionary astrology. It is not exactly a personal blog – at least not in the sense of my making sure that you all know about my current mood, hair emergencies, or choice of breakfast cereals. But in this edition of the newsletter, I'm using myself as an example. I am not immune to the hard side of Pluto, of course. No one is. When Pluto squared my Moon, my marriage of nearly thirty years ended. I lost my home, my cats, and half my money. When it first contacted my Sun, I lost a young family member under tragic circumstances – that hurt me badly and I'm still shaken by it.

Grief arises. You go through it. Eventually it fades, even though it never leaves entirely.

My natal Sun is in the second house, so it relates to *money* and *possessions*, among other things. With Pluto transiting there, I recently experienced two minor material losses. As you will see, these are totally trivial stories, but once we unpack them, they will carry us into deeper waters.

Both events were weird. First, I lost a case of telescope eyepieces. They just disappeared. I'd had them since I was a kid peering at planets through my 6" reflector on the roof of my apartment building in New York City. I was emotionally attached to them. And they just went poof. Gone. No idea why or how.

Ditto for a light backpack to which I'd also grown very attached – I hike a lot and that pack and I had leapt merrily across many a gully and many a rattlesnake out here in the Anza-Borrego desert where I live.

I missed that backpack as much as I missed the eyepieces.

Pluto hits my second house (the house of possessions), and I experience two material losses – neither one of them really a big deal – but clearly astrology in action. Against the backdrop of all human suffering, the loss of my eyepieces and my backpack are small potatoes – but rich in meaning. *At the simplest level, I was invited to face the fear of material loss.* But always with the second house, it is helpful to consider that there might be issues of *self-worth* and *confidence* involved as well.

Money and dignity: what strange bedfellows – but you often find them in bed together.

I grew up very much in a working class culture. My home was a three-room walk-up apartment on the fourth floor in a semi-rough neighborhood a mile or so outside the Bronx in New York. Like most of us "who started out as kids," I internalized that somewhat "disadvantaged" reality.

I am not poor anymore – and Pluto signaled that I was ready spiritually to face any second house "poverty wounds" left over from my childhood that I was still carrying. And . . . this sounds really dumb . . . *I realized that I could buy new eyepieces and new hiking equipment.*

Duh.

But for me, the realization was actually rather profound. It was empowering to realize that I could face my fear of material loss and my historic *adaptation to lack.* The *events* of those two losses were nothing – but they afforded me a chance to *face a fear* and to *claim a power* I did not realize I had. Instead of reflexively "accepting a loss" in stoic fashion, I could do something about it.

It got weirder for me – and it will get weirder for you too. Here's the next synchronistic link in the chain. So much has been written about the unpleasant side of Pluto. What about its positive power? *What's the prize for getting it right?*

Right after all the events I just recounted, a philanthropist appeared on the scene, eager to support my work. Out of kindness and generosity, he has funded me to write a new book. I'll be starting on it this summer. Right now, I don't want to yack about the specifics. Suffice to say that it will be another one to put on the shelf next to *The Inner Sky* or any of the others.

More to the point, I do not believe that this generous gift – *(there's a high, bright face of Pluto hitting a second house Sun)* – would have come to me if I had not *primed the pump* by realizing that I could be *generous with myself* and buy myself new eyepieces and a new backpack.

I believe that is how the universe actually works. You can see it – and harness that sweet energy yourself – when you stop practicing the astrology of fearful prediction and begin practicing the astrology of magic, evolution, and positive, conscious intention.

These archetypal fields are vast, and there is no escaping them.

That is your fate.

Your freedom lies in making choices that trigger the higher purposes and potentials of these energy fields. That is intentional astrology.

It worked for me and it can work for you too.

27

There's a moment I always treasure with my students. That's when I see one of them move beyond reciting memorized phrases about individual astrological symbols and begin instead to pull them together, surfing integratively over a complex, multi-dimensional configuration of planets, and speaking about them in plain English. It's that "pulling everything together" that is the heart of our craft. In this newsletter, I attempt to demonstrate that skill, starting with a big Saturn-Neptune square in the 2016 sky, then watching how it might interact with an unusually dense environment of Piscean energies – energies which favor Neptune, but which (we hope!) do not entirely eclipse Saturn's voice.

ON BALANCE . . .

(Newsletter – March 2016)

Acouple of months ago, I wrote about the ongoing square of two very different planets: Neptune and Saturn. We explored how our rational minds and our intuitive ones are currently engaged in a long, creative talk.

All aspects are about integration, even when the planetary energies involved seem very different from each other. Currently and collectively we are invited to aim for the integration of *our capacity for reason* (Saturn) and our *capacity for spiritual experience* (Neptune).

We need to allow each of these modalities of thought and perception to have equal time, and to encourage them to support each other as truly good friends do – that is, with *hard questions, helpful criticism, and unexpected insights.*

Those edgier words are where the square aspect comes into play.

- We observe that under this Saturn-Neptune aspect any cherished, but ungrounded beliefs we hold will be challenged by pressing Saturnian reality. We could deny that challenge – and choose to live in a spiritual fairyland. Or we can accept it and become far wiser.

- Equally – and a lot more fun to say – we recognize that our attachment to "grounded reason" would likely be humbled by inexplicable experiences: *miracles, acts of grace, and visionary moments.*

This integrative process continues until the Saturn-Neptune square fades out over the last two or three months of this year. But this month, the argument loses all semblance of fairness. *Neptune utterly swamps Saturn, bringing in massive reinforcements in the form of a battalion of Piscean energies.*

As the month opens, we find Chiron and the Moon's south node in Pisces, along with a close-but-separating conjunction of Neptune and the Sun. That alone is a formidable array of "Neptunian" energy – remembering of course that Neptune is the modern ruler of Pisces and so there is a lot of shared DNA between Neptune and anything that happens to be passing through Pisces.

That combo platter of energies in Pisces right there already on March 1 is only the beginning. On the 5th day of the month, Mercury joins them. On the 12th, so does Venus. The party begins to break up on the 20th when the Sun crosses into Aries. The following day, Mercury does the same.

But for an amazing eight solid days, we have a total of six Piscean energies all working together: the Sun, Mercury, Venus, Chiron, Neptune, and the Moon's south node.

Poor Saturn doesn't stand a chance! *Who needs reason when you have that much Piscean energy available?* Before you cheer, let's remember that while Saturn may not be much fun, he is not our enemy here. The whole point of the Saturn-Neptune square is the realization that *reason is not antagonistic to spirituality* – it is only antagonistic to bad religion and comforting metaphysical fantasies. Ultimately, the ongoing square of Saturn and Neptune is about *spiritual maturity* – and none of us are opposed to that, at least not in principle.

So what does this cosmic traffic jam in Pisces portend? An excellent rule of thumb in astrology is that every configuration has a high meaning and high evolutionary purpose, along with lower possible manifestations. It is our own choices and effort that determines whether the coin lands heads up – or butt up.

We will surely see that principle active here.

With all this Piscean energy in the air, I really do think that if you keep your eyes open, you will see some *actual miracles*. By "miracles," I don't necessarily mean anything drastic – I only mean events that you cannot explain. They may not be dramatic – but if you think about them, they will raise enormous questions about the actual nature of reality. I am talking about simple happenings such as dreaming of someone you haven't seen for a few years and then getting an email from that person the next day. I am talking about playing Parcheesi with your friends and just knowing that you are about to roll double sixes – and, boom: you roll a twelve.

If you babble out loud about such events, you'll sound like you are delusional. *I just knew that! I knew it was going to be box cars!*

The part of you that knows better than to babble that way is good old Saturn talking, running his tapes about "staying grounded." But these miracles will actually be there, right before your eyes. They come in through the Piscean doorway that separates everyday reality from other planes of existence – and that magical door is wide open during this period.

Close your eyes and things will get even more miraculous. With six bodies in Pisces, the veil between this world and the next grows very transparent. Your meditations during this month – and particularly during those magical eight days – can be quite profound. Your third eye is opening. Maybe you will feel the presence of God or angels or higher beings. Maybe you will see a ghost. Maybe you will take a walk in a forest and find yourself sitting on a holy rock. You'll feel its holiness too – and what you won't know is that a thousand years ago, a shaman used to sit there. That's why that rock is holy. You don't need to know the facts to make that true. All you have to do is to *suspend your Saturnian disbelief* and you will feel it in your bones.

Because your spiritual power is so enhanced, especially during that time between March 12th and 20th, please visualize some peace in this crazy world – and, meanwhile, *remember that people who feel that war is the answer will be visualizing in their own way too.* We're all going to be a bit empowered that way, even people whom I wish were not.

- In the larger scheme of things, the Neptunian side of the current Saturn-Neptune square is simply gathering a lot of momentum this month.

Meanwhile, Saturn's job is a quiet one. It only involves standing back and letting the Piscean mind and senses engage with a wider reality than your high school math teacher probably ever glimpsed.

Your soul is gathering data.

What about the dark side of it? Anything this powerful has one. We already mentioned that people who believe that wars can help will be visualizing too. Everyone's magic is enhanced. Closer to the heart of the matter, during this month be careful of the parts of yourself that *want to believe.*

- Desires – and fears too – can easily be conflated with reality during times of Piscean emphasis.

The *spiritual ego* can sneak into your radar-room. Want to "believe that you are very psychic?" When you roll those Parcheesi dice, you'll *just know* that some number between 2 and 12 is coming up – and, lo and behold, you are right!

Proof!

Be wary of these beguiling "spiritual" ego-traps. The Virgin Mary's face in the clouds and Jesus in the rust stains – they'll be here too, if you have a *psychological need* to see them.

With Venus in the picture from March 12 until April 5, be particularly wary of "seeing what you want to believe" in romantic or intimate situations. Those areas of life are famously fraught with illusion anyway, and the hormonal fog is likely to be particularly thick during this period.

All of these cautions are timely – but let's not throw the baby out with the bath water. As we have seen, this Piscean cluster is all part of the ongoing negotiations between Saturn and Neptune. During this month, Neptune is bringing forth some very strong arguments on his side of the discussion – *arguments that support the ultimate truth that we are ancient, luminous beings in a multi-dimensional universe,* and that Saturn's great lies about death, taxes, and reason as the boundaries of our existence are miles away from the mark.

Collectively, we *need* to see some miracles.

They are on their way.

28

In this newsletter, I beat a drum I've beaten a few times before – I take a seemingly-frightening current astrological event and I talk about its higher meaning and how to get there. This time, at the risk of sounding preachy, I delve more deeply into an idea I introduced in chapter twenty-five – my understanding of how one person's willingness to face daunting inner work can ripple out into the collective and make a difference in the wider world. To some people, this notion might seem fanciful – but really it is cut from the same cloth from which astrology itself is cut: the idea that the distinction between "the inner sky" and "the outer sky" is not nearly as cut-and-dried as many people believe. "As above, so below" – those four words are the essence of astrological theory. But they are also a magical formula. What happens if we actively, intentionally change things here "below . . . ?"

TWO SCARY PLANETS . . .

(Newsletter – April 2016)

There is a divine, evolutionary purpose behind everything that happens in the sky. For me, that is the foundational principle of our craft. Aiming ourselves towards the higher ground is ultimately what it is all about – and there is *always* higher ground, no matter how grim the configuration might appear to be.

I believe in that principle fervently. It is elemental to everything I teach, write and practice with my clients.

But I've got to say, my knees got weak when I looked at this month's planetary patterns. On the 17th, Mars makes a Station, turning retrograde, at 8° 54' Sagittarius. The next day, Pluto does the same at 17° 29' Capricorn. That's two very scary planets, both getting very intense at the same time, reinforcing each other.

I will stick to the best truths I know here: *this combination of energies represents an open evolutionary avenue for us all.* There is a higher purpose in it.

Astrology is the mirror in the sky. Everything that arises there among the planets reflects something arising inside of us, and it is always about our evolution. Sometimes certain conditions need to coalesce in order to create necessary *evolutionary opportunities.* Sometimes those conditions are frightening ones. Whatever they might look like, everything reflects *evolutionary necessity*, and there is always a way to get it right.

Of course there is always a way to get it wrong too, and that is often a popular choice. That's what makes this Plutonian and Martial one-two punch look so edgy.

Getting it wrong could take a merciless turn.

A little background in case you are new to astrology. You pass a slower car on the highway. For a moment as you pull abreast of it, the optical illusion is that the other car is going backwards. It isn't, of course. We know that. But it looks that way.

Similar effects happen in the solar system as Earth "passes" other planets. Our moving point-of-view generates the appearance of the planet stopping and turning backward for a while. That's why planets go retrograde. Retrogradation is a complex subject interpretively, but for our purposes one point is central.

- The more slowly a planet is moving, the more powerful it becomes. That's why Pluto transits are more momentous than Mercury transits – they simply have more time to interact with your mind, your attitude and your life.

And a planet cannot get slower than flat-out stopped. Therefore, a stationary planet is at maximum power. *To have Pluto and Mars both reach peak amperage within one day of each other is a rare and daunting prospect.*

Both of these planets make better friends than enemies. Mars is the god of war. And Pluto – Lord of the Underworld to the Romans – could be called "the god of hell." So *war and hell* are in cahoots with each other, both in their raging, pedal-to-the-metal, bloody-minded full cry.

Stand back, in other words.

Soon, as promised, we will explore the higher meaning of this striking configuration. That higher meaning is there, and alive and powerful, I promise. But we do need to consider the dark side too.

Because of our unabashedly spiritual orientation, I've occasionally heard ignorant people describe evolutionary astrology as rose-colored glasses for bliss ninnies, as if our system embodied all of the silly wishful thinking we associate with the dumber divisions of "New Age" beliefs. Nothing could be further from the truth. In evolutionary astrology, *every front has a back* – everything has a dark side as well as a light one. It is consciousness that makes the choices. We evolutionary astrologers do not pull punches about the Shadow. And with Mars and Pluto both stationary at the same time, there is plenty of Shadow to talk about.

Dark Pluto can be insane, literally – the kind of insanity that arises when we don't deal with our issues and instead project them onto other people or onto the universe. We mistake our inner demons for outer ones, and either hide under the bed or start throwing punches.

Dark Mars loves a fight. It can be furious and destructive.

Put two and two together, and with Mars and Pluto both making stations, you've got the potential for *berserk violence driven by madness*, and the whole process reaching a crescendo.

Will there be some horrendous terrorist event around mid-month? Will another theater or nursery school be riddled with gunfire?

What about something even worse? Your imagination can do as good a job of painting nightmares as my own, so I will leave it to you. I hate writing words such as these, but I have to be honest.

That dark, mad energy – which is not lacking in the world lately – reaches some kind of boiling point in the middle of April 2016.

Do we act it out or do we figure it out?

A wise spiritual teacher of mine back in my twenties, Marian Starnes, once told me, *"The purpose of every true prophet is to be proven wrong."* When while using astrology, we see a looming danger, maybe we can describe it – *and describe how to evade it.* And the path to evading it always boils down to the same strategy: *getting the energy right.* Understanding its true purpose. The spiritual disasters only arise when we misuse the energy and miss its higher potential and meaning.

So how can we aim this Martial and Plutonian crescendo toward the greater good?

Let's remember that beyond the global headlines, the configuration has personal, private meaning for you too – something we can clarify by considering the aspects these planets are making in your own birthchart. And of course the event also has *collective meaning.* My sense is that if enough individuals get it right at the personal level, much of the venom goes out of the worldly manifestation. If nothing happens, it's not just that the human race "got lucky" or that "astrology isn't perfect."

It means that enough of us got it right to defuse the bomb.

Everything retrograde is about reflection. It is about *re-thinking the past,* as a planet goes back into degrees it has already covered. Pluto at its best is always about asking ourselves hard, uncomfortable questions – facing our own Shadow, withdrawing our projections. *It is about seeing our personal history more clearly now, today, than when we first experienced it.*

Mars is always about our passions and desires, not to mention our angers, fears, and resentments – and when it is retrograde, we need to think about their nature and origin. That means that this month, we are collectively invited to *reflect upon our rage and our resentments,* to purify them of any elements of madness, and perhaps to get on with our lives – especially once these two planets turn direct again.

That's June 29th for Mars and September 26th for Pluto.

I heard a Native American speak once about forgiving the white man for what he had done. He made a simple, eloquent, goose-bumper of a point: *the white man did not deserve his forgiveness* – what the white man had done was unforgivable. But the Native American realized that holding onto his righteous rage was slowly killing him. So, *for his own sake,* he realized he needed to forgive the white man. It had nothing to do with any virtue or merit in the white man at all.

That pretty well summarizes the higher ground, with uber-honest Pluto interacting with bloody-minded Mars.

Even at their best, these are edgy, fierce energies.

The Dalai Lama, long ago, said "the world is drunk on anger." Those words have never been more true than they are today. You feel it everywhere. God knows, you hear it in many political speeches lately.

In writing that last line, I was tempted to name the name of a presidential candidate (or two) in the current US election race. I decided not to. I decided to walk my talk. If I had named a name, what good would it have done? Well, I would have felt good personally for a moment, giving "some son-of-a-bitch what he deserves" right here standing on my own bully pulpit.

But maybe out there among my readers is someone who plans to vote for him. I could have acted out my anger, "gotten some revenge" – and made an enemy of a reader, thus adding in a minor way to sum total of bitter, futile rage in the world.

And the whole point of everything I write here is that the world's quotient of bitter, futile rage is approaching critical mass.

How can each one of us avoid adding more to it?

A better use of my time is to reflect on the actual origins of my passion – in this case, a political passion. As I've mentioned before, I grew up working class. I grew up always hearing about "those selfish rich people." I grew up excluded from the culture of prosperity. When I was young, nobody taught me the right social moves. Nobody opened any doors. Because of the success of my astrological work, my life has moved in more prosperous directions since then. I live in a style I could not have imagined as a child. But some of the old conditioning remains. My heart is not pure when it comes to thinking of people in privileged social and economic positions.

Am I "psychologizing away" my political attitudes? No, not at all. I know my values and I know how I am going to vote – *take care of the earth, give worthy young people a chance, and blessed are the peacemakers.*

But I am also trying to separate the genuine "meditations of my heart" from a lot of angry working class crap I grew up with. That's me trying to do my Pluto work on a Mars issue – that's me, in other words, going back into the past, trying to understand the origins of a passion in me that is so strong that it could lead me to dehumanize certain people simply because I disagree with them politically or resent their unearned wealth.

- How many of us can engage in some parallel inner alchemy, especially around the middle of this month? I think that if enough of us do that inner work, the healing effects of it will not be limited to the space between your ears. I think we can use this energy to uplift the world – or at least to blunt some of the more extreme expressions of its madness.

Fatalism beckons here – *hey, it doesn't take many crazy people to detonate a bomb somewhere, so what does it matter if a more conscious minority does some inner evolutionary work?*

Well, yes: bombs might indeed go off regardless of your personal efforts. You can't stop other people from being crazy. But I do believe that a few people making conscious steps toward the higher ground can have a disproportionate effect upon the collective reality.

Moods in a society shift as if by whimsy or magic – you've seen it. Look what's happening to homophobia, for one example – it's not gone, but it's a lot less pervasive nowadays than it was even just a few years ago. Look what happened to the idea that sex outside of wedlock was a sin. What happened to the idea that a woman's place was in the home? Or that we should always obey our parents?

The strings that wiggle this world are not entirely visible. You are holding one of them in your hands. It is time to do some *brave* (Mars) *psychological* (Pluto) spelunking, looking for the true origins of some of that acid in your tummy.

The holy grail towards which we are feeling our way in the dark is called *forgiveness.*

29

*Some astrologers have only a few clients, but they work with them
intensively, seeing them often, almost as a psychotherapist would.
My own practice has been different, built around many thousands of
clients, which has naturally necessitated my seeing them individually
far less frequently. That in turn has led me to focus on slow-moving,
theme-building "big picture" forms of astrology, while not paying much
attention to the "little triggers," such as fast-moving Mercury or the
transiting Sun. Still, understanding those "fireflies" can be helpful. They
often nail down the timing of specific events connected with those more
"glacial" evolutionary lessons. In this newsletter, my aim is to model how
to look at quick transits in a flowing, integrative way, seeing how one
little trigger leads to the next, and the next . . .*

THE LITTLE TRIGGERS

(Newsletter – August 2016)

The devil is in the details. So are the angels sometimes. In my transits and progressions work with clients, the focus is always on the
"big picture." That grand evolutionary perspective emerges most clearly
when we reflect on the slow-moving, theme-building planets – basically
the transits of everything out beyond Mars, plus the progressions and solar
arcs. In the counseling room, it is usually practical to ignore the little "fire-
fly" transits of Mercury and Venus, or the Sun and the Moon. They go by

so quickly that they don't have much time to develop depth and complexity of meaning.

But they sure "work!" Let Mercury transit over your Sun one Tuesday, for example, and your phone is ringing like crazy and your email Inbox looks like the president's. By Friday, it's all over.

- The difference between a Mercury transit and Pluto transit isn't that "Pluto is more powerful." It's just that Pluto has a lot more time to work on you, that's all.

This month, looking at the planetary dance, what caught my eye was one of these quick transiting configurations: in mid-month, as Mercury and Venus leap over the Cancer-to-Leo frontier, they are practically holding hands. Venus goes first, entering Leo on the 12th. Mercury does the same a little after midnight (PDT) on the 13th – and check your own time zone if you are not on the west coast of the USA.

Wherever you are located, there is only a gap of about nineteen hours between the two crossings. By transiting standards, it is almost a simultaneous event. We will experience a shock-wave of Leo energy, especially against the contrasting background of Cancer.

A few more techie details, then we will look into the interpretive crystal ball: both Mercury and Venus are in Cancer as the month begins. After crossing into Leo on the 12th and 13th, they form a conjunction on July 16th at 5° Leo 45'. Venus spends the rest of the month in Leo, only crossing into Virgo on August 5th. Mercury exits Leo on July 30th.

Many astrologers like to "make predictions" based on these kinds of configurations. I always try to avoid that temptation. For one thing, I've never found that kind of "crystal ball" astrology to be very reliable. I also think it misses the point. I think the planets function more like *suggestions*. They certainly don't control us. Instead, they try to guide us . . . that is, if we are willing to listen.

So what kind of guidance is implicit in this moment of Venus and Mercury "holding hands" as they leap into Leo together?

Let's start by putting our clues on the table: Mercury is about *communication*. Venus is about *intimacy and aesthetics*, among other things. So when they come together, we are talking about the idea of *intimate, graceful communication*.

Leo is my first pick for the most misunderstood sign of the Zodiac. That noisy, self-important Leo you read about in the shopping mall astrology books is not really such a common creature. But Leo does represent the part of you that *thrives on attention.*

Let's respect that need, and, even better, try to understand it. Think of a kid swinging higher and higher on a swing-set, yelling *"Mommy! Daddy! Look at me! Look at me!"* There's nothing wrong with that. The child wants simply to be *witnessed.* He or she wants *validation.* And everyone of us is, ultimately, *nothing but a child who survived.* We all sometimes need that same kind of validation, no matter our age. *We all need to be seen and to be appreciated.* That's Leo expressed as an evolutionary pathway.

Asking for that kind of support is risky. It takes courage to do it. Maybe you write a poem, straight from your heart. Think how shaky you feel inside when you announce to a friend – or even to your partner – what you have done. Suddenly all eyes are on you. You have put yourself out there in a vulnerable way. Revealing your soul like that is scary for everyone. If your partner reads that poem and flippantly suggests that you should "stick with cooking," how do you feel? *And how long will it be before you show him or her another poem?* It is devastating, even if your poem is awful . . . hey, it's your heart and soul laid on the table!

And what if instead your friend or partner gets teary and says, "That's so beautiful?" Feel how much closer you have become? Why? *Because you took that Leo risk of self-expression. Because you took that Leo risk of vulnerability.*

That is what Leo is all about.

I am pretty sure that the world's output of poetry will go up by 37.2% during the final three weeks of July. I'm smiling as I write that line, but impressionistically, I suspect it is pretty close to the truth. That's one effect of the conjunction of Mercury and Venus in Leo. But having more poetry in the world is not the point – the point is about *boldly expressing* (Leo) *in words* (Mercury) *what you really need or want in your most important relationships* (Venus.)

Probably the most straightforward illustration of what it looks like to get this right is an old standby that never really grows old – just simply looking someone in the eye and saying, "I love you." That might not technically be "asking for what you want," but everybody knows the rest: *you will be disappointed if you don't hear those same words coming back at you.* The phrase, "I love you," contains an implicit request for reciprocation – and therefore it bears the classic Leo signature: *a willingness to endure the terrible risk of not hearing that sentiment reflected back again.*

Doubt it? Ask anyone who has ever said those momentous words and been greeted by a blank stare or an awkward silence.

Sometimes knowing what we truly want or need is not so obvious. This leads to another critical point – *before we can be vulnerable to another person, we need to be vulnerable to ourselves.* We must dare to feel. That is another critical link in our chain. This is where we begin to look at astrological symbolism integratively. *What sign of the Zodiac represents pure emotion and pure need?* Cancer, of course. When planetary energies focus in Cancer – as they do earlier this month – they resonate directly with the emotional body. We often simply *feel quieter* at such times. We want time alone – some "down time." We want high walls between us and all the noise and pressures of the world. Left to our own devices, we simply tend to *sleep* more. We thereby invite *dreaming* – that royal road into direct communion with the emotional body. We are like the crab inside the shell.

As July opens, Mercury and Venus are already in Cancer. So is the Sun. Until the 12th and 13th, the guidance the cosmos offers us is that we need to *reflect quietly on what we need.* As you do that, don't be afraid to think about what is missing in your friendships or partnerships. Go ahead and even whine a little, if you want – just do it internally. Don't be afraid of tears. Just feel.

And try to keep your mouth shut about what you are feeling!

I know that last line sounds contrarian, even wrong. But it isn't. In divine order, you are *getting ready* to make an important speech – but only after the 12th. Right now, you are *writing the speech in your head and in your heart.* Take your time and get it right. Give yourself space and time to feel. No limits, no reality checks.

Your commitment to temporary silence buys you absolute emotional freedom. Remember that feelings are a bottomless, murky well, not always easy to understand at first glance.

This inner Cancerian process *of preparing for the active Leo self-expression* that comes in the second half of July is critical. First you've got to get it right inside your own head or your Leo speech runs the risk of not being rooted in the best truth you know.

It would still be loud though! That's Leo. And that combination can make a mess.

The foundational process of getting grounded authentically in your own interior reality reaches a dramatic crescendo at the month's New Moon, which is exact around 4 o'clock in the morning (PDT) on the 4th of July. A New Moon in Cancer is arguably the "mooniest" Moon of the year – and this year that Sun-Moon conjunction in the thirteenth degree of the sign is flanked on one side by Mercury at 9° 37' and by Venus on the other side at 20° 26'.

This is a Cancer New Moon on steroids. It promises to be particularly emotional.

And that is a good thing, assuming that you surf those interior waves with grace and honesty. Open your heart to it all – *and then sit on it for a week or so*. When Mercury and Venus cross into Leo, you will be not only ready to roar, but ready to roar with wisdom, authenticity, and authority.

And when Truth roars, people listen.

30

Declination – and the possibility of a planet being Out of Bounds –
are subjects that I feel deserve more widespread astrological attention.
In this piece, I take the opportunity to introduce them briefly, using
a Mars transit into OOB territory as my launching pad. Mostly this
essay uses astrological principles as a gateway into an exploration of
the controversial realms of changing gender roles – and specifically, the
plight of the beleaguered male psyche in a confusing, changing world.

MARS OUT OF BOUNDS
IN CAPRICORN

(Newsletter – March 2018)

Mars, currently in Sagittarius, enters Capricorn on March 17th, joining Saturn and Pluto there. Interestingly, around the same time, it
also goes "Out of Bounds," which means that it crosses *south of the Sun's*
most southerly possible declination. Mars remains in that strange, volatile
"OOB" condition until early April. On April 1, it forms a conjunction with
Saturn. Finally, after returning within bounds, it catches up with Pluto on
April 26th.

All of that promises a colorful few weeks.

Before I attempt to unravel the symbolism, first let's have a quick word
about what it means when a planet goes Out of Bounds just so everyone is

up to speed. It's an important concept and not really hard to understand, but one that is not as well known as it should be in astrological practice.

Imagine Earth's equator projected onto the heavens. Planets are usually above it or below it, just as New York lies at a more northerly latitude than Miami, or as Tierra del Fuego is at a more southerly latitude than Buenos Aires.

- What we call "latitude" here on Earth is called "declination" when it is translated into the sky.

When the Sun reaches its maximum northerly declination, it is as high as it can get in the sky, at least up here in the northern hemisphere. That's the Summer Solstice, marking the start of our summer. After that, it's all "downhill" for the Sun – until six months later, when it reaches "the bottom" and our northern winter begins. Meanwhile, our Aussie friends are firing up their barbies. It's the beginning of summer down there.

- The Moon and most of the planets can get a little further north or south than the farthest points that the Sun can ever reach. *When they do that, they are said to be Out of Bounds.*
- When that happens, they get a little weird, as if they have been unleashed from the repressive, controlling grip of the Sun.

That's what Mars will do around the 17th, right as it passes into Capricorn.

The Sun's gravity is what *tethers* the solar system. *As above, so below* – so the Sun is what *tethers your head* too, or tries to. The Sun represents your *core values* and the basis of your *psychological identity* – that to which you must be true if you are going to be sane, whole, and authentic.

What would happen to you if, for example, your Venus grabbed the steering wheel and made all your decisions? Or your Neptune?

Dangerous, right?

Those simple statements offer a hint about what an Out of Bounds planet is like – it is *highly independent, profoundly creative and self-expressive, and a bit unhinged.* When the Moon or a planet moves Out of Bounds, that planet has "gone to the wilderness in order to re-invent itself." The part of you it represents has been too stifled by customs and other people's expectations. It is sick to death of "the rules." As a result, it will look a little crazy for a while, but there is a good chance that when it returns in bounds, it will be refreshed, liberated, and renewed – and significantly *re-oriented*. One simple way of thinking about an OOB planet is that it takes on a rather *Uranian* tone, as if it were in a conjunction with Uranus.

Progressions are personal. Transits are collective, even though they have personal meaning too. That means that this month, everyone on earth will experience Mars going Out of Bounds, right as it crosses into Capricorn. The fact that Capricorn is already supercharged by the presence of two slow-moving "heavies" – Saturn and Pluto – really puts this upcoming Mars event in the spotlight.

Bottom line, for about three weeks the epochal cultural processes symbolized by having Saturn and Pluto in Capricorn will be served with some additional hot sauce.

(Let me add that Mars will again go Out of Bounds this summer starting in early July and running into late September. Apart from a brief return to Capricorn from August 13 through September 10, much of that passage will happen with Mars in Aquarius. So apart from those three weeks, that is a different ball game than the one I am discussing here.)

So what does it all signify?

I wrote quite a lot about what it means when the Moon is Out of Bounds in *The Book of the Moon*. Tony Howard has really begun to make his mark as a pioneer researcher, writer, and lecturer about the Out of Bounds expressions of Mercury, Venus, and Mars. You can check out his work or read my book for some solid grounding in the broader principles of declination.

The subject is a broad one. Before we get specifically to Mars, let's quickly set the stage by thinking of the slower, theme-building planets that are already waiting in Capricorn. This extra-edgy Mars will definitely trigger a fierce and perhaps highly creative expression of something – but of what?

Pluto brings shadows to light. Secrets are revealed. Lines of taboo – or control – are crossed. Truth surfaces.

Meanwhile, Saturn deals with justice – the eternal law that *all actions have consequences.*

Underlying both planets right now is the archetypal field we call Capricorn. Among other things, Capricorn represents the *existing order of things*. With Pluto in Capricorn (2008 -2023), one pattern we are seeing revealed is the dark side of *conservatism* and *traditional values* – and I don't just mean a political philosophy. I mean the existing, underlying "conservative" structure of society. We are talking about social class, national boundaries, the patriarchy, the current economic systems, gender definitions . . . and it gets darker . . . sexism, racism, homophobia, and so forth – the whole enchilada of society's "givens."

Not all "traditional values" are worth keeping, in other words. With Pluto in Capricorn, that is showing now, at least for those with eyes to see it.

Saturn in Capricorn (now through 2020) is another big deal. Justice – plus a re-definition of integrity – is the heart of it.

Now add Mars to the mix, and *passion, anger,* and *intensity* enter the equations. Throw in the fact that Mars is Out of Bounds and we simultaneously *throw out the rule book* regarding the expression of that passion, anger, and intensity.

Positively, it is time for some *bold creativity* relative to all those old dinosaurs.

Negatively, pent-up destructive forces of rage and resentment are freed from any moral boundaries or scruples that might previously have constrained them.

The subject, again, is vast. The definitive textbook will be this month's headlines. Here, in this limited essay, I want to focus on one critical contemporary aspect of the configuration, paying particular attention to its Martial ingredients. Specifically I want to think about *gender.* And I want to start with Mars – which astrologers have often defined uncritically as a "masculine" planet.

Astrologically, the idea that Mars is male is ancient, but that notion must be scrutinized carefully as human cultures transition into their future forms. Not to over-simplify, but a good opening "Tweet" here is that "I've seen a lot of women's charts and I've never seen one without a Mars."

Ditto, naturally, the same is true for men and Venus. Obviously, we've all got the full complement of planets regardless of our plumbing.

A generation ago, psychologist John Gray made a ton of money with his popular book, *Men Are From Mars, Women Are From Venus.* Some people, myself included, were annoyed by its black-and-white dichotomizing of male and female psychology, but the book spoke to a lot of people – I'll admit, myself included again.

So, *are males more Martial than females by nature* – and females more naturally Venusian than males? Or is that just social conditioning?

Damned if I know.

And I'd rather not be subjected to a long, boring dinner with anyone "who has it all figured out." The gender revolution is both unfathomably profound and still in progress. Personally,I bet it has another century to go before anything is really clear.

One effect of this momentous shift is that it has put men – and Mars energy – in very tricky territory. That is the issue that I want to explore here. These gender tensions are boiling over anyway as Saturn and Pluto challenge the old Capricornian hierarchies and assumptions. *"Traditional values" include a lot of heavy expectations regarding each gender.* With Mars about to enter the fray – and Out of Bounds, to boot – we can anticipate some pyrotechnics. And, hopefully, we will see some creative thinking too.

An absolutely reliable principle in astrology is that planetary energy – just like any energy in physics – *will always manifest somehow*. But the *form* in which it manifests is subject to the influence of human consciousness. In a nutshell, if we don't get a planet right, we will surely get it wrong. Add some shades of gray in between and you have the theoretical foundation of evolutionary astrology.

Running with this idea of "the conservation of energy," we recognize that Mars is the war-god. Immediately that frames Mars energy in violent terms. There is far more to the planet than violence, but let's not be so prim as to avoid the tiger in the living room. *Mars kills.* If you are a guy, Mars is what punched you in the nose when you were in high school. If you are a woman, Mars is what wolf-whistled and made "improper suggestions" as you walked by the construction site.

All that aggression is truly part of the nature of Mars – but none of it reflects the higher Martial ground. Mars also *protects. It is the part of every woman – and every man – that would attack a rabid dog with our bare hands if that beast were attacking our child.* That is violent behavior too, but let's not throw the baby out with the water. That face of Mars is the *heroic* part of your nature.

Let's get really primal here. For almost the entirety of human history, a lot of that specifically *protective* Mars work has fallen to men. The reasons are straightforward – a man's part in making a baby is generally not terribly burdensome to him, nor very time-consuming. A pregnant woman results

– and she may be as tough as Ayla in *Clan of the Cave Bear*, but she is still pregnant and therefore significantly incapacitated for a few months. Then she is *nursing* and recovering from (the very Martial) ordeal of childbirth – and, given prehistoric reality, she is probably pregnant again before long.

Meanwhile, traditionally a male – *in order to be considered honorable and "a man in full"* – needed to protect her and their child. This wasn't because the woman was weak or helpless – far from it. It was because she needed him and she trusted him *because* she was in that vulnerable state.

- There was thus, historically, a natural symbiosis between men's Mars energy and women's Venus energy. That symbiosis allowed our species to survive. It is probably a big part of why we are here today.

All this was simply the biological truth of life for something like 99% of human history.

Then the world changed.

Modern society emerged. Survival became less dicey. People had fewer babies, and more of them survived. Life got longer. Cities rose up. Efficient birth control entered the picture. The "Tiger Problem" faded as a daily concern. Women had multidimensional lives. So did men.

And suddenly women no longer really needed men to protect them.

Cards on the table: in my opinion (and feel free to have a different one) *feminism is the single most fundamental revolution of the past century or more.* It has rocked the world, and will continue to rock it. That said, I hope that the poisonously misleading word "feminism" quickly fades away – not because I have any problems with its principle values, but rather because the word "feminism" implies that the whole thing is a female issue. That is as blindly wrong-headed as believing that prostitution is caused by women. This revolution is rocking men's consciousness every bit as much as it is rocking the world of women.

- A closer scrutiny of the exclusionary effect of the word "feminism" gives us another critical clue: in general, since they lack social and mythic support, men are dealing with this whole evolutionary explosion in a far more unconscious way than are the women.

One takeaway is simply that it is a lonely and confusing time to be a man – and if that thought doesn't trigger a little trill of compassion in your heart, then you are part of the problem, not part of the solution.

Not to be sidetracked here, but the current #metoo movement was triggered like clockwork astrologically by Jupiter's entry into Scorpio – which crystallized some of the deeper rumblings of Pluto's passage through Capricorn. Remember: with Pluto in the mix, the Shadow dimension of old social structures – in this case, the dark side of *patriarchy* – is being revealed. Male sexual aggression can no longer hide behind the cloak of denial.

- As we saw a moment ago, throughout almost the entirety of human history, an honorable man "defended the women and children." *This social reality provided men with a positive and necessary expression of pure Mars energy.* Men rightfully drew dignity, identity, and self-respect from their protective, providing role.
- Then the world changed. Women were not so dependent upon men any longer.
- What became of the male avenue for healthy Mars expression? Poof. Suddenly it was gone.

A few paragraphs ago, we said, "an absolutely reliable principle in astrology is that planetary energy will always manifest somehow. If we don't get a planet right, we will surely get it wrong."

Sometimes putting two and two together is frightening business . . .

With far fewer positive avenues available for male expression of Mars energy, it is not difficult to see what had to happen. These eternal astrological principles work with a high degree of reliability. *Lacking positive avenues of Mars expression, men would inevitably be drawn to less positive ones, and eventually pulled into truly negative ones* . . .

. . . unless paradigms shift. Unless radical creativity creates new answers. More about all that in a minute . . .

So, historically it was a man's job to "protect the women and children." *Have you detected what appears to be an epidemic of the exact opposite?* Instead of high Mars energy, a plague of low Mars energy is passing like a virus through the male population. Specifically, we see men attacking women. Rape is the most obvious illustration. But what about men attacking children? Or, only slightly different, men *abandoning* their own children – which may not be intended as an "attack," but certainly functions as one?

This quickly bleeds out into the whole sorry world of exploitive or degrading pornography. What about "revenge porn?"

All of these evolutionary dramas have made the headlines recently as #metoo exposes male abuse toward females in the professional world – meet Harvey Weinstein, and all that he represents.

Going further, *why are there so many films and novels nowadays in which "something terrible happens to a woman?"* – and then of course male violence and male vengeance ride in on their white horse, masquerading as justice.

Misguided, misqualified Mars energy is everywhere. It is an epidemic. There is no way to overestimate its horror. Without exaggeration, we recognize that this disease could actually destroy the world.

On a milder level, male obsession with *televised violent sports* is a sublimation of this Mars energy too – and with sports, let's be careful to make a distinction between "enjoying a football game" and the compulsive, life-and-death *addiction* to watching sports.

It is a short, disheartening, step from here to seeing how this same dark "us vs. them" Mars energy has infected politics, where a sports-like "fan" relationship to a political party leads to a nation's real needs going down the drain – all in the sacred name of "my team winning."

Are men to blame for all of this?

Some people try to make a case for that gender finger-pointing, but I'm not convinced of it – and that's for the same reason that I don't like the word "feminism." This is a *human* problem, not a male one.

Men will not fix it. Humanity will fix it.

Mars' current entry into Capricorn and its brief tour Out of Bounds are not likely to provide any quick answers. But I believe we have come to a significant moment in this evolutionary process. That statement brings us back to the big astrological picture – I am referring to the effects of Pluto and Saturn in Capricorn, while Jupiter passes through Scorpio. Mars OOB will probably trigger some headlines that reflect these underlying tensions, for good or for ill.

My deepest hope – and I address this to you, my readers, knowing that you are not simply representatives of the status quo, but rather active ingredients in cultural evolution – is that these words catalyze mindfulness and creative reflection in you, and that you can thus add to the collective treasury of hope and insight. Men need help now. The situation is growing desperate – and not just for men.

To surf the wave of this Mars-on-steroids energy, you will have to avoid being seduced by passion and rage. That's the dark side of the "Mars OOB" territory, and it exerts a powerful suction. When we are feeling "righteously indignant," it is difficult not to appoint ourselves judge and jury.

Knowing that the fish's knowledge of the sea is limited, here briefly are my own tentative thoughts:

- I believe the time is ending when men are naturally identified with Mars and women with Venus. That gender-labeling was necessary, perhaps even healthy, for a long while. But no longer. Burn any of your astrology books that promote that heresy – or at least read them critically.
- You astrologers, please stop speaking of "masculine" and "feminine" planets. We are all made of the same star-stuff. Women are from Mars – and from Venus too. Ditto for men. Using the old language only further entrenches the problem.
- Let's recognize and actively appreciate the creative role that the LGBTQ communities are providing. They are very literally reflecting the blurring of these archaic gender-boundaries. They are on the front lines, and that's a place where there are always a lot of casualties. We all have a lot to learn from their stories.
- Men, try to actively claim your Venusian energy. Buy flowers for the sheer joy of it. Cook candle-lit meals. Ask for help. Write a poem. Consult other people for their opinions. Cry. Tell your friends you love them. Be brave enough to be dependent on someone else. And change your underpants.
- Women, you can help by actively claiming your Mars energies. Take some physical risks. Get sweaty. Go out on the streets looking like what you really look like. Tell us exactly what you want. Be brave enough to cherish your independence even if someone wants to take care of you. Initiate sex.
- All of us – try to have some compassion for the suffering of good men as they struggle to hold back the negative expressions of their Mars energy without any clear, positive sense of where they might redirect it.
- Listen carefully, deeply, and with an open mind to anyone who makes startling statements about gender. Most of them will be wrong! But a few of them carry the seeds of the future – and remember: the future always surprises us.

As we equilibrate the division of Martial and Venusian energy in our own lives, we are addressing these problems right at the core archetypal level of their origin. Never forget that all humanity can benefit from your own inner work.

Creatively, jointly, with both genders holding hands in a spirit of mutual respect, let's harness the full power of our visionary imaginations and wrestle with this question: *how can we devise more positive outlets for men and their Martial force?* . . . (because we know that if men do not find a positive release for that red-hot energy, it will continue to manifest in harmful ways.)

In parallel fashion, how can we support women in exactly the same areas?

I am aware that I am treading on thin ice – and probably some toes – as I write all of this. I am wide-open to the idea that I am wrong about some of it – and I am 100% certain that I've missed 99% of it. But it is through this kind of thinking and shared public dialog that we create a human future worth living. And I think that between March 17 and early April, some significant seeds are going to be planted. May they soon sprout!

One more point – even if those seeds do not sprout in any obvious, immediate way, don't despair. Little boys and little girls will soon be joining us, being born all around the world. Each one of them will have this paradigm-shattering archetypal structure hardwired into his or her consciousness, and a lifetime ahead in which to explore it.

I wish we could see now what they will have learned fifty years from today.

31

Mercury retrograde – lately, the very words generally strike mortal fear into the heart of anyone who can correctly name more than six of the twelve astrological signs. Having transiting Mercury in that "backwards" condition is actually a rather minor piece of astrological theory, but for some reason it has captured the public imagination in a big way. There are simple things to know about Mercury retrograde, starting with being careful not to exaggerate its effects. But there are deeper waters to fathom with it too – ways to use it consciously and skillfully by understanding its purpose. Those skills are mostly what I explore in this newsletter.

MERCURY GOES RETROGRADE

(Newsletter – July 2019)

Beware! Beware! Mercury will be retrograde from July 7 through the last day of the month! Sign nothing! Buy nothing! Don't expect your check to arrive!

I've found that Mercury doesn't even have to be retrograde for it to be blamed for every minor misfortune, miscalculation, and misunderstanding that might arise. Say "Venus retrograde" or "Jupiter retrograde," and in most places all you get is a blank look. But utter the fearful words, "Mercury is retrograde" and the blood drains from people's faces.

For some reason, this little piece of technical astrology has lately entered the popular imagination in a deep way. It is just as common as knowing that you are a Gemini or a Taurus. And to people who only know a little bit about astrology, Mercury retrograde always spells trouble.

Ask any experienced astrologer – at least one who has no need for mood stabilizers – and you are likely to hear a more nuanced attitude: "Mercury retrograde is a real phenomenon – but don't sell your earthly possessions and join a doomsday cult because of it."

Keep some perspective, in other words.

Cutting to the chase, that softer, more nuanced attitude reflects the realities of my own experience with Mercury retrograde. And I've had a lot of experience with it too – *and so have you.* It is not a rare event. Mercury goes through a retrograde period about three times each year, remaining retrograde for an average of a little over three weeks each time. At any given moment, in other words, there is about a 1-in-5 chance that Mercury is going backwards.

The rest of the time, you have to blame yourself for forgetting to mail the check, missing the anniversary, misplacing your cell phone, or spilling olive oil on your laptop.

Mercury rules over *communication* in general, so quite fundamental to the "standard model" of Mercury retrograde is the idea that *misunderstandings* – that is, *errors of communication* – abound. "Let's eat, grandma!" gets heard as "Let's eat grandma" – and you wonder why everyone is giving you a hard look.

Still in the communication-miscues category, we hear about letters being lost in the mail or inexplicably delayed. Sent emails fail to arrive. Epic spellcheck fails abound.

Anything electronic seems particularly susceptible to Mercury's baleful influence. It is best not to buy a new computer or a new cell phone at such a time, if you can possibly avoid it – although it's a bit of a *Catch-22* in that the reason that your old computer or cell phone just crashed can be laid at Mercury's doorstep as well.

Never book an airline flight under Mercury retrograde, unless your luggage has expressed a desire to put Timbuktu on its bucket list.

The list of warnings goes on.

You probably sense a certain underlying dismissiveness in my attitude here. That does not entirely reflect my experience – only maybe half-reflects it. The described effects of Mercury retrograde in all those categories are real and demonstrable – it's just that its influence is so often hyped; there is nothing *reliably* negative about it on a case-by-case basis.

A March 14, 2019, article in *The New York Times* was titled, *"Mercury Is in Retrograde. Don't Be Alarmed."* As such reporting goes, the piece was mildly sympathetic to astrologers – although the term "pseudoscience" made its presence felt. It also contained the patently untrue line, "In fact, studies have shown no correlation between the behavior of planets and of people."

But that's not my story here. I only reference the article to demonstrate what a big deal Mercury retrograde has become. The editors at *The New York Times* felt there was enough interest in it that it warranted a story.

About my "patently untrue" remark a moment ago . . . once again, back to the venerable *New York Times*, this time looking at an article from November 2006 entitled *Yes, Mercury is in Retrograde, So What?* Despite its snarkiness, I've used the article for years to assuage the fears of clients who were cornered into having to make some big move during a Mercury retrograde period. As is often the case with this kind of journalism, there's a kind of schizophrenic quality to it. On one hand, it actually cites evidence for astrology, while on the other hand, it continues to quote the party lines about "no evidence" and "pseudoscience."

According to figures from the federal Bureau of Transportation Statistics, the percentage of late flights into and out of La Guardia Airport during the past three summers rose to 24.6 during retrograde periods from 22.8 during non-retrograde periods. What's more, during the past three years, claims of mishandled domestic baggage rose to 5.44 per 1,000 passengers during months when Mercury spent more than half the time in retrograde from 5.38 per 1,000 in months when the planet was not in retrograde. That works out to one extra lost bag per 15,000 passengers.

Two comments:

- First – so much for the erroneous idea that "studies have shown no correlation between the behavior of planets and of people." Somebody mishandled those bags!

- Second, if you do wind up having to fly during a Mercury retrograde period, it does not mean that you should kiss your checked luggage goodbye. Unless you are the one unfortunate soul out of 15,000 passengers, you will be teeth-brushed and decked out in fresh undies just fine the morning after your arrival.

Here is a vexation the angels in heaven face every day: astrology works, and more and more humans are beginning to see and accept that fact. But humans always seem to want to use astrology for the wrong purposes. Astrology can indeed pull off a few party tricks. But what it really does – and what its true purpose is – connects far more deeply with our soul's journey than it does with our prospects for lost luggage, crashing digital devices, or anyone misunderstanding us and putting poor grandma on the barbecue.

- When any planet is in retrograde motion, *it is going back over places it has already been.*
- Mercury correlates with information in general. Information which you already have is called *memory.*
- 1+1+1 = 3: so one term for the *purpose* of Mercury retrograde periods is going back and *reviewing your memories.*

A nostalgic trip down memory lane? It could only be just that, and no harm done. But imagine a man in mid-life. His father was always distant, while the son felt unloved and unwanted. Dad died seven years ago. During a Mercury retrograde period, the planet passes over the man's fourth house Saturn – a planet that often represents the father. Something prompts him to get out an old family photo album. He finds himself gazing at a picture of his father – *but seeing him for the first time through his adult eyes.* Previously, his memories reflected the perceptions of the boy who felt so unloved. Now what he senses in his father's eyes – even though they are just the images of eyes in a photograph – is a lost soul, afflicted with depression, and probably feeling very unloved himself.

- This hypothetical man's response to Mercury retrograde has been perfect. *He has just gone back into the stored memories of an earlier time, and reviewed and revised them in the light of his present-tense wisdom.*

A woman has fought a losing battle against her tendency toward alcoholism. Meanwhile, her psychotherapist happens to ask her about any happy memories she might recall about growing up. The first image to enter her mind is one of her mother convially pouring both of them glasses of wine. The girl was ten years old at the time. She longed for her mother's love and camaraderie. She can now almost hear her mother saying, *"Take, drink. This is my love for you."* Therapist's eyes and client's eyes meet. Their unspoken *Oh my God* hangs in the air. Suddenly everything is as clear as a bell – *even though it was not clear at all to the child who just thought that she was having a special moment with her dysfunctional mother.*

Meanwhile, Mercury is retrograding over the client's Moon – which of course represents her mother, among other things.

We all live out our lives in the context of the flow of time. Memories are constantly being laid down, but they are almost never really objectively true. Always, inevitably, embedded in our memories are various distortions: our *interpretations, opinions, defenses, rationalizations,* and simple *misunderstandings* about what was happening at the time.

And then those memories sit there in your head, gathering dust, unchallenged, just like books on a library shelf that haven't been checked out since 1977 – *books which might seem patently sexist or racist today,* but which were unremarked in those long-gone days.

Meanwhile, with each passing year, most of us are in the process of getting a little bit wiser, step by step. *What would those old memories look like to us today were we to consider them in the light of what we now know?* That is the question that Mercury retrograde always invites us to ask.

The man in our first story now feels a kind of enlightened compassion toward his poor broken father. He no longer feels the weight of a burden he has carried since his childhood: that he was somehow unworthy of his father's love. He knows that he was trying to get blood from a stone. And that insight liberates him.

The woman with the drinking problem comes to understand that she has been "thirsty" for a sense of genuine relationship with her crazy, dramatic, dysfunctional mother – something that alcohol came to symbolize for her back when she was ten years old.

These are dramatic, life-changing stories. Common sense tells us that equivalently powerful experiences probably will not happen to each one of us three times each year. For Mercury retrograde to have this kind of major existential significance, two other astrological conditions must be present.

- The first one is that Mercury is retrograding over a particularly sensitive part of your chart.
- The second condition is that there is something else of a major nature unfolding for you astrologically – likely something of a Plutonian nature, dredging up material from the psychic depths. *That Mercury retrograde needs something bigger to trigger*, in other words. Think of it as a lit match. The results are more spectacular if you drop it in a dynamite factory.

Barring those more epochal conditions, what can a Mercury retrograde period mean for you? It will certainly not be nearly as earth-shaking, but it can still be important.

- The accountant decides to act on an uneasy feeling that has been niggling at him. He goes over some work he did on the company books a few weeks ago – and discovers a misplaced decimal point.
- The musician plays back a recording just before it goes into production; the bass guitar is too loud and it's sucking the life out of the vocal. Time for a re-mix.
- The chef notices that the cream has passed its expiry date. There was a nagging sense that something was not quite right with that *crème brûlée*.
- The lawyer notices that the contract is missing one signature. She's lucky – that could have undone the deal.

Mercury retrograde is all about sending our present-tense mind back into the dizzy, distorted world of memory – one that we all tend to *mistake for reality* until we take a second look at it from the mindful perspective of where we actually are sitting right now, in the present moment, full of the famous "Power of Now."

Lost bags? Computer crashes? Garbled communication?

Sure – they all can and do happen under Mercury retrograde. Many of those problems can be avoided with just a little patience – *if you don't really have to do it right now, why not wait a week or two until Mercury straightens itself out?* There is a good chance that you would be fine anyway even if you ignored Mercury retrograde, but why walk out on thin ice just because it is "probably" thick enough to support your weight?

Going further, during Mercury retrograde times, *it is imperative that you cultivate an attitude of trust and openness toward any uneasy intuitive feelings you might have.* Go back and check things if they are bothering you even slightly.

If you think that it is possible that you said something to a friend that just might have been misunderstood, *ask about it.* There is no harm in being sure. For example, maybe everyone decided – even though you did very clearly suggest that we *eat poor grandma* – that, all in all, your virtues outweigh your quirks so we will just forget about this little lapse of judgment on your part . . .

Going further yet, there are *whimsies you need to heed* when Mercury is retrograde. That is just the way your soul – or your unconscious mind – sometimes speaks to you. Any whimsy that draws back into the past should be taken especially seriously. Something back there is calling you; there is something you need to learn about what *really* happened, some memory that requires updating, something that requires re-alignment with present-tense truths. Re-read old letters. Watch films you have always loved, but which you haven't seen for many years. Visit places that were significant scenes in your earlier life.

Old photographs can be incredibly evocative during such Mercury retrograde times. We are fortunate to live in the age of photography. Who were your parents *really* when they were 29 years old and you were calling them "mommy and daddy?" Look into their eyes – they're staring at you right there in that old family album.

What about your ex-? *Who was that person actually?* (Probably not exactly who you thought . . .)

The great southern novelist, William Faulkner, said it best. *"The past is not dead. It's not even past."* What we have been and seen and done lives with us forever. Everything that ever happened is still happening right now. Even your *past lives* are in the mix, taking the form of present-tense attitudes, fears, and areas of overreaction and exaggerated sensitivity. These memories make you what you are today. You are their summation.

But what if some of those memories are false? What if, today, you would not read a situation as you once did? That situation, when you stop and think about it, is almost certainly the case. You are wiser now than you once were. Of course you would see things differently today.

By paying attention to Mercury's retrograde periods, you might very well avoid a lost bag or a mis-directed check. There is nothing wrong with using astrology that way.

But what if you could also use it to help you know the true story of your own life?

It would truly be a "miscommunication" with yourself to miss that opportunity.

Let's eat grandma, indeed.

32

Retrograde planets in general – and not just Mercury – are literally delving into the past. They are all going back for a second look at degrees that they have recently covered. Right away in that simple observation, we have the key to understanding their broad evolutionary significance. We may not be able to undo the past, but we can undo our mistaken understanding of it, adding to our memories a perspective that we were not wise enough to possess at the time the memories were laid down. In this essay, I use a specific cluster of retrograde planets in summer 2020 to illustrate the point – as ever, specific transits come and go, but the principles which animate them are eternal.

RETROGRADE JAMBOREE

(Newsletter – July 2020)

On July 1, Saturn retrogrades back into Capricorn, where it joins Pluto and Jupiter. Both of them are already retrograde too, and tightly conjunct each other. Meanwhile, Neptune is also retrograde, as is Mercury. Mercury stations and turns direct on the 12th – but one day before that happens, Chiron turns retrograde. On top of all that, Eris – so often under-estimated and ignored – makes its own station on the 19th, and turns retrograde too.

If you like retrograde planets, then July is the month for you, in other words. It's as if the whole cosmic carousel has reversed polarity.

What I want to do in this newsletter is to have a look at what it means to see all of this retrograde energy happening at once. All of the planets from Jupiter on out, with the sole exception of Uranus, are going backwards at the same time, with Chiron trading off a retrograde condition with Mercury toward the middle of the month. The situation is not unprecedented, but it does catch the eye – and as ever, at least from the philosophical perspective of evolutionary astrology, the planetary gods and goddesses are giving us a few tips about where to put our feet next.

A retrograde planet is always going back over ground that it has already covered – that is quite literal. It has seen those degrees before, but now it wants a second look at them. Right there we see the essence of what retrogradation means. It is always ultimately about a *review of the past* – or at the very least it is an indication that a review of the past would be timely and helpful. With Mercury, that review might be a relatively trivial thing. Did you really send that email – or just *think* that you sent it?

It is easy enough to find out. Just have a peek at your Sent box and make sure.

Add one more scene: let's imagine that you *only thought that you had sent it*. In the version where you review the past, the problem is easily solved. You actually send the email this time, maybe a day or two late, with your apologies.

By contrast, in the version where you did not check your Sent box, chaos ensues – chaos which might have been averted had you only been willing to *second-guess yourself.*

An awful lot of Mercury retrograde horror stories could have been avoided by simply taking the planetary cue and "reviewing the past." This little anecdote illustrates how we can let the planets be our *guides* and *counselors*, realizing that we are free to exist in harmony with them. They advise us. They do not control us nor do they bombard us with "fate."

If you stop and reflect for a moment, this attitude of forming an actual *partnership* toward the planets is in radical contrast with a common strain of astrological thinking where they are "favorable" or "unfavorable," and in which they are always "doing things to you."

Beware Mercury retrograde! Your emails will be devoured by the Mercury monster!

Hey, just check your Sent box. You'll be OK.

You might have made a mistake. Maybe you can fix it – *but only if you are willing to learn about it*. And that *learning from the past* is ultimately what *all* retrograde periods are about, not just Mercury.

Mercury is only retrograde until the 12th, and from the larger point of view, it is not such a big deal anyway as we saw in the previous chapter. After all, it happens three times every year. But to have Eris and Neptune retrograde, and Chiron soon to join them, and then to have a retrograde triple conjunction of Jupiter, Saturn, and Pluto on top of it – that is a major astrological event. It seems that the intelligence of the universe is giving all of us a big dose of the same advice: *it is time for us all to review the past*. How did we get to where we are now, both collectively and as individuals?

By the way, that triple conjunction of Jupiter, Saturn, and Pluto will never be exact in the sense of having all three planets lined up in precisely the same degree. But it will be close enough to count, and it is surely fair to call it a triple conjunction. That's because from the time Saturn backs into Capricorn on July 1 until Jupiter and Saturn cross into Aquarius around the third week of December, these three bodies are never more than about eight degrees apart. By most standards, that "orb" is tight enough to qualify as a conjunction. As we get into November they are a lot closer than that.

Don't forget: that entire structure is in turn squared by Eris, a planet whose dark side is connected with cut-throat competitiveness.

The pattern of those four bodies, all moving in lockstep and thus maintaining this massive *en echelon* square, while they are all retrograde, dominates July and August. During the three weeks between September 12 and October 4, Jupiter, Saturn and Pluto all turn direct – while Eris remains retrograde until January.

Let's focus on the next ten weeks or so. *Collectively, all the ghosts of the past are catching up with us.* Let's also add that this has been going on for a while. Pluto turned retrograde in late April, while Jupiter and Saturn did so in mid-May. Eris turning retrograde this month definitely adds another log to the fire. We have been in this haunted-by-the-past period for a while, in other words, but it is coming to a crescendo over the next few weeks.

Both Pluto and Eris relate strongly to unconscious, repressed material. Such wounds always take a terrible bite out of us, but the weird thing is that *since they are unconscious, we are typically not even aware of the price we are paying.* We are just *diminished,* and we don't even know why.

The good news is that, when they are retrograde, maybe we can *review the past,* and find the clues that lead us to the difficult truths – and the corresponding empowerment which comes from facing them.

Meanwhile, Jupiter and Saturn are building toward their liberating conjunction in rebel Aquarius on December 21. But first they must dance a few steps with Lord Pluto before they leave Capricorn. When Jupiter meets Saturn, I always think of *a pot of gold* (Jupiter) *on top of a very tall mountain* (Saturn). The climb is ten times harder than we can imagine – and there is a hundred times more gold in the pot than we anticipated.

It's hard, but it is worth it, in other words.

Add Pluto to the mix, and we realize that *determining exactly which mountain holds the gold* requires some honest inner work – some confrontation with unconscious material locked in the dark vaults of Pluto and Eris.

Now add the fact that all of this is happening in Capricorn, a sign oriented to *tradition.* Tradition can be a beautiful thing, but with Pluto in the mix, we are always called to face the challenge of shadow-work. *What price do we pay for continuing to get on with the past?* What is the dark side of reflexive social and mythic conservatism? And with Pluto retrograde, we add that in order to succeed at this shadow work, we must look honestly at what has brought us to this crossroads.

All of this has enormous personal, private meaning for every one of us. It is a good summer for personal reflection – and a good winter for it if you are in the southern hemisphere. The exact nature of what you need to *remember differently* depends on the specifics of your chart, and where these planets are currently falling in it. But collectively we see the handwriting on the wall. To see all of this enacted on the stage of the world, all you have to do is watch the nightly news. Black Lives Matter has exploded, and there is a pervasive feeling that everything is different this time. Racism seems to have reached some kind of critical mass. Have we come collectively to a place where we can confront the reality of racist history, not to mention its fingerprints on the present structure of society? Are we brave enough to look at that? Do we have the stomach to look squarely at the past and reflect on what we have done – and what we have done in response to what was done to us?

What about Covid-19? That issue is not the moral kindergarten of thinking of cold-hearted murder caught on eight minutes and forty-six seconds of video in the George Floyd tragedy. The moral issues around illness, vaccination, and our collective responsibilities toward each other are more subtle. But how did our prisons turn into overpopulated death camps? *How is it that we can say almost exactly the same thing about how we "store" our elderly population?* How did we create a society where an economic downturn is more frightening to some people than a half a million deaths? How did we wind up with leaders who seem to feel that way themselves? And tying this back into the larger issues of racism, think for a moment about the overtones of the term "the Chinese virus."

These are all pressing issues. These are the present headlines. But just today, I read that the thermometers hit 100 degrees Fahrenheit inside the Arctic circle for the first time in history. The climate crisis didn't come out of nowhere. It was a long time coming. As we review the past with all of these retrograde planets, we see the errors and distorted values that have brought us to this turning point. *What price have we paid for comfort and material prosperity?*

Not to be preachy here – I think of the thousands upon thousands of gallons of jet fuel I personally have conspired to burn in the stratosphere as I flew from place to place to teach astrology. *What have I done?* Do I have any right to point a finger at someone who drives a Hummer? No, I do not – but I think we all need to point a finger at the Hummer itself.

That is just the truth, and it is truth time. Shame, guilt, and despair are not the point. Finger-pointing and blame are certainly not the point. The point, underscored by all these retrograde planets, is *an honest, massive review of the past.* Truth needs to be served up, raw and cold and clear, whether it is about racism or the dark side of modern economics or the environment or any of another host of issues. And this is not only "a helpful suggestion." Due to the laws of synchronicity, this is a *command* from the universe.

The truth is saying, "Ready or not, I'm coming."

There may be many ample reasons for despair, but let's not lose faith or hope. Where does all of this lead? Is there a path forward? Astrology can answer that question too. Remember our tall Saturn mountain with our pot of Jupiter gold on its peak? In December, those two massive planets pull away from Pluto. With their conjunction, we enter a new chapter of human history. They cross the line into Aquarius, a sign which correlates with *breaking tradition and shattering old patterns*. They actually come fully together, finally, just a half a degree into that sign. Their time in Capricorn – and their dance with Pluto – was just the prelude.

If enough of us do our inner work, if we honestly review what has actually happened in our lives, with no excuses and no glossy rationalizations, humanity is scheduled for a fresh new beginning starting around December 21. That Jupiter-Saturn conjunction in groundbreaking Aquarius is the pot of gold.

Please believe in it. Your belief itself has power.

The past may be catching up with us now – but at the next Solstice, doors open to some kind of unprecedented and unforeseen future. *It is as if we have been marching butt-first into the land of tomorrow.* That is an awkward way to walk. The good news is that it gives a great view of where you have been.

On December 21, we turn around and face where we are going.

SECTION FIVE

PERSONAL REFLECTIONS
AND THE ASTROLOGICALLY
EXAMINED LIFE

Only to myself am I the world's most fascinating subject. In writing these news-letters over the years, I've realized that people's interest in my favorite color is limited, so I've tried to focus on broader astrological topics rather than on my own story. Still, from time to time I have risked making exceptions to that good guide-line and written about my personal experience from an astrological perspective. As you've seen already in some of the earlier chapters, the last few years have been a good time for me to do that – much has been changing in my life as I move on from basically being an astrological "country doctor," spending most of my profes-sional ime working directly with clients, to focusing on legacy work. Naturally all of those personal changes have been reflected in the heavens – and the heart of the matter in most of the more autobiographical chapters that follow is how those celestial reflections have helped to guide me in practical ways here on the earth.

I anticipate that when the day arrives that astrology has entered a golden age of public acceptance, the "astrological autobiography" will become a common literary form. All lives are fascinating provided that they are examined – and there is no method more true for putting one's life under an objective, honest microscope than seeing its patterns reflected against the background of the endlessly changing sky.

33

*If I hear the words "in my own chart" too many times during an
astrological lecture, I find it offputting. On the other hand, there is no
escaping the fact – and no shame in the fact – that our own lives are the
laboratory in which we develop our deepest intuitive relationship with the
planets. In this piece, I start with an event in my own life, and hopefully, I
move quickly enough beyond "me, me, me" to offer some real guidance about
a pivotal astrological experience we will all see happen, usually more than
once, in our own lives – specifically, Saturn transiting through the twelfth
house and then hitting the Ascendant. With its twenty-nine year orbit,
there's an excellent chance you will experience it yourself, or already have
and may very well live to see it again. I hope that what I learned from it
can help you navigate the same event when it's your turn.*

SATURN TRANSITING OUT
OF THE 12TH HOUSE

(Newsletter – December 2013)

On Saturday, February 1, I am going to do something I had pretty
much decided that I would never do – a webinar. Instead of a crowd
of faces in a lecture hall, I will be talking intimately to my laptop computer.
I will cling to the belief that somewhere out there in the vague world of
ones and zeros flying through space, there are some actual human beings

who are listening, watching, and hopefully getting something out of the whole enterprise.

I will also moan to myself about the absence of what I have always found to be critical elements in my teaching: eye contact, body language, and that whole mission-critical territory we call "vibes."

While I am doing all that, transiting Saturn will be standing just one-quarter of a degree from my Ascendant.

To the kinds of gloomy astrologers who still think of Saturn as a "malefic," this would seem like a dumb time for me to take any kind of risk at all. They would assume that Saturn would bring some misfortune down on my head. While I am realistic enough to be prepared for some screw-ups and glitches, all in all I think that this is a fine time to launch something new. *After all, the Ascendant is the cusp of the first house – the "beginning of the beginning," so to speak.*

- When anything major hits your Ascendant, there is an excellent chance that you are warp-driving headlong into the kind of fork-in-the-road choice-point whose consequences will echo for a long time.

Good news or bad? That depends on the wisdom of your choice.

Or, in this case, my choice.

As usual with these things, this Saturn alignment "just happened to coincide" with the timing of our first webinar. We didn't plan it that way. Astrology works pretty well, even when we are not looking! A number of practical factors directed my webmaster, Tony Howard, and myself to February 1. Only later did I put two and two together and realize that this would be my initiation into a whole new 29 year Saturn cycle.

In writing this edition of our newsletter, I have a few aims all at once. As you might have detected, I am not adverse to touting our first webinar. Please "attend" (if that is the word.) The class will be about natal planets square to the nodal axis, and attendance will be limited to one hundred people.

Beyond the obvious advertisement, I also want to take this opportunity to talk about how to live peaceably with Saturn transits, despite their doleful reputation. I also want to say a few things about the deeper meaning of the twelfth house and how it blossoms into the first – and how success in the first house depends on success in the twelfth as surely as a flower depends on the soil in which it is planted.

Saturn is, among other things, about the basic processes that keep our feet on the ground – paying the electric bill, showing up for work, doing the wash, making sure your undies are fresh and your socks don't have any holes in them. It is the planetary function that *gives us the ability to do what we don't feel like doing*. Saturn covers the base of everything that we find boring and necessary in life – all the things that are dull, but Lord help us if we ignore them.

Ask anyone who has ever run out of gas on a dark night ten miles from a gas station.

Meanwhile, the twelfth house represents the *end of a cycle*. In it, deaths, resolutions, and endings naturally arise. Wisdom lies in timely recognition of these finalities and in an open-hearted acceptance of them. When bad things come to an end, we are happy. But what about when good things end? In some ways, I wish I had seen a *Tyrannosaurus Rex* with my own eyes. But, really, I am just as happy those beasties Exited Stage Left before I poked my nose around the corner, Stage Right.

Some things *need* to die. That's the only way to make room for the next act.

- When Saturn transits into your twelfth house, what needs to die? The answer is Saturn stuff: *your routines, your definitions of your responsibilities, your methods and your tactics.*

You can reflect on that reality and draw encouragement and faith from it. Or you can let the universe club you upside the head with the evidence for that necessity until it finally gets through to you. That's your choice.

It is also helpful to remember that the twelfth house is a *visionary* one. Angels talk to you there – or, if you prefer purely psychological language, *ideas are constellating in your unconscious mind,* not having quite broken through into consciousness yet. *You don't know what you are doing,* in other words. But an answer is forming anyway. Trust the process! Your primary job in the twelfth house is to *let go of things*. And to make some time for inward listening.

As Saturn crosses into the first house, you begin a period in which the *new definitions of your Saturnian methods and your duties* will actually come into manifestation, based on the good foundation you have laid in the previous house. And that good foundation is, above all, a willingness to let go of the old patterns – a recognition that they have played out and that you are not that person anymore.

With Saturn in my own twelfth house, I was hit over the head with collapsing practical systems. I was living out of a suitcase – and living in my laptop most of the time. I went from Beijing to Florence, Italy, teaching. In one two-day period, I woke up in Maine, flew to Los Angeles, bought a house three hours away here in Borrego Springs, was driven back to Los Angeles International Airport, waited eight hours, caught a night-flight from there to Fiji, spent four hours in Fiji, then flew to Sydney, Australia.

Even writing that sentence was exhausting! What about living it?

Meanwhile, I had fallen way behind on my over-extended schedule of recorded consultations, partly because I was so run down I got sick and was coughing too much to record anything for a while. And Tony Howard and I were struggling to keep the business afloat in the face of the ever-shifting realities of the publishing industry.

It was beyond nuts. Who could keep up that pace? *My old definitions of my duties and my methods were unraveling.* Remember: Saturn symbolizes them and the twelfth house marks the natural ending of things.

Maybe now you see where I got this sentence from a few paragraphs ago – "or you can let the universe club you upside the head with the evidence for that necessity until it finally gets through to you." As usual, there was much that I learned the hard way.

I don't have all the answers yet. I shouldn't! I am still living in the past, and that is OK. What I mean is that, as I write these words, Saturn is still technically in my twelfth house, barely. It is not yet time for me to crystallize the new answers. If I tried I would be faking it out of desperation – which is a classic way to turn the twelfth house into the fabled "House of Troubles."

I am home now for four months, working of course, but also hiking and meditating in my beautiful desert – finally taking the time to listen a bit more attentively to my inner voice.

Astrology comforts me in that it holds the mirror not only before my folly, but also before my wisdom – and in this case, some of my wisdom lies in knowing that *I am not yet the person who will have the answers.* If I play my cards right, they will come in 2014.

I am not sure what this upcoming webinar will mean. If it goes well, we will do more of them. If not, we won't. But I see Saturn sitting there exactly on my Ascendant on that very day, marking "the beginning of the new beginning." That gives me faith in what we are doing. And it also makes me feel thankful for astrology and how it offers all of us that extra dose of *spiritual encouragement.* We might speak glibly about being on "the right path." But how do you know when you are on it or not? Astrology, if we read the symbols honestly, can give you that reality check – and 95% of the time, that information will pass the heart-check as well.

Above all, I feel grateful to have such concrete evidence that the universe is meaningful, not random. It is a school for evolving consciousness – and always right on time.

34

This may be nothing but an urban legend, but I've often heard that among Native American people, turning age fifty meant that you were now an elder and had achieved the right to speak in council. That idea would have annoyed me when I was thirty, but when I turned fifty myself, it began to make a lot of sense. I started to feel some of that classic "elder" archetype – and along with it, a responsibility to try to pass along some of what life had taught me. One result was that I began my Astrological Apprenticeship Program – translated, that meant hundreds of days of teaching that eventually brought me to four continents and a tribe of about two thousand students over the years. Even though I already had several books in print by that time, I can honestly say that the AP is where I truly found my voice, my vision, and my full confidence. I owe so much to it, to the people who attended the classes, and especially to the long-suffering souls who administered it. In this piece, I celebrate a major turning point: the nodal return of the "first breath" of those programs. Little did I know then that the end of this cycle marked the outset of a deeper set of changes – shifts that would eventually morph the AP into the Forrest Center for Evolutionary Astrology. But that's another story . . .

A MILESTONE FOR THE APPRENTICESHIP PROGRAMS

(Newsletter – January 2017)

Happy 2017, one and all! For my teaching programs, 2017 brings a "new year" of a different sort too. This month, on January 10, my Apprenticeship Program completes exactly one cycle of the lunar nodes. On that day, the Moon's north node returns to 5° 35' Virgo – exactly where it was when the whole thing got started.

If I stood on a corner shouting, "a nodal return, a nodal return," reasonable people would give me blank looks and cross the street. But for anyone who has studied the basic methodology of evolutionary astrology, we understand that the lunar nodes are about as central to the system as your third lumbar vertebra is to your back. We could not do evolutionary astrology without them.

So, for the Apprenticeship Program, this is a very big event. *In a nutshell, it is time to affirm our fundamental evolutionary intentions and to renew, review, and update our commitment to them.*

And of course the same thing applies to you every eighteen years or so.

The first official meeting of the "AP" happened in the living room of my old friend, Karen Davis, in Leawood, Kansas, on June 3, 1998. There were eight people in attendance. We were scheduled to begin at 5:00 PM. I suspect that, as is usually the case with informal classes, the "first breath" actually occurred a few minutes later. Here's the chart, set for 5:05 pm.

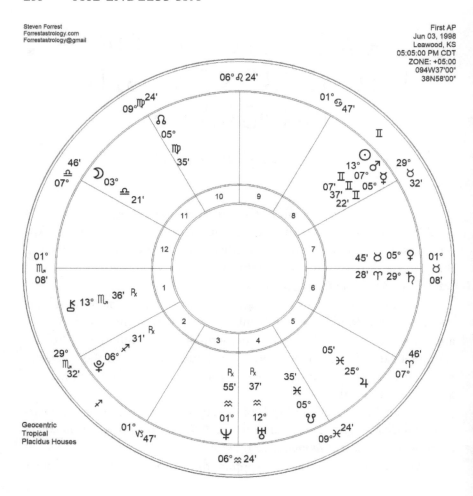

Steven Forrest
Forrestastrology.com
Forrestastrology@gmail

First AP
Jun 03, 1998
Leawood, KS
05:05:00 PM CDT
ZONE: +05:00
094W37'00"
38N58'00"

Geocentric
Tropical
Placidus Houses

©2018 Matrix Software Gainesville, FL

Standard Wheel

I want to talk about the symbolism, but first I'd like to say a few words about the Apprenticeship Program itself. When it all began, I was turning fifty. I wanted to take my teaching to a deeper place than was possible with an endless parade of weekend workshops scattered around North America. As an improvement on that format, I envisioned intimate groups that would meet for six very structured four-day intensives over a three-year period.

It actually worked that way in Kansas – that was before the "AP" metastasized into the international *Godzilla* it is today.

I blame that metastasis on California. I was living in North Carolina at the time, but I had been doing some ongoing teaching out west (which gradually morphed into the second AP.) When that early program in Laguna Beach came to the end of its sixth session, nobody wanted to stop, myself included. It continues today, although we meet near San Diego nowadays.

That "inability to die" set the tone for the rest of the programs. They became ongoing revolving doors – "little red schoolhouses" of astrology with relative beginners sitting alongside very advanced students, and people returning as much for the tribal experience as for the learning.

As of today, there are two "AP tribes" in California, one in North Carolina, one in Beijing, one that floats around Italy, and one in Nelson Bay, Australia. That's a total of six. The California programs meet twice a year; the others once, for a total of eight of these four-or-five day intensives each year.

Attendance ranges from a typical low of about 35 people in Europe to a high that can reach 80 in southern California or well over 100 in China. Most of the programs have waiting lists. Even though no one would call eighty people "an intimate group," we've felt the need to cap it there for practical reasons.

I cannot resist quoting Dorothy in The Wizard of Oz. "Toto, I've a feeling we're not in Kansas anymore."

All together, over two thousand people have attended these seminars, making the program as a whole approximately the same size as ISAR or NCGR – the big international astrology organizations. Many people who have attended have established successful private astrological practices. Several have written books or spoken at conferences. And of course many attend the programs for reasons of personal growth or interest. We've got young folks and old folks, gay folks and straight folks, white people, black people and Asian people. We've got Christians, Jews, Buddhists, Taoists, shamans, and Muslims.

They are all equally welcome. If the whole world were composed of these kinds of open-hearted people, it would be paradise.

Now let's look at the chart, and especially at the nodal axis. This is a classic "event chart." Just like a human birth, it contains the spiritual DNA of the entity that was born at that time and place. The "natal" south node of the Moon falls in Pisces, suggesting something quite obvious – *that the roots of the evolutionary astrology we are learning lie in the spiritual or metaphysical realm*. The reference to the "psychic depths" is echoed in the "psychological" 4th house placement of the south node.

- I've often defined evolutionary astrology simply as "the marriage of ancient metaphysics and modern psychology." One could hardly find better astrological shorthand for that synthesis than "Pisces in the 4th house."

Correspondingly, the north node lies in Virgo and the 10th house, reflecting the evolutionary intention to "go public," to bring a craft rooted in metaphysical tradition (Pisces/4) into the wider human community (Virgo/10).

Mystical Neptune – modern ruler of that Pisces south node – lies in the 3rd House. There's the direct astrological reference to teaching – and specifically to *spiritual* teaching. Neptune lies in Aquarius, which supports the astrological content – Aquarius and astrology have an age-old association, mostly because astrology is ultimately about human individuation, the same as Aquarius.

Aquarius also suggests some tradition of being "exiled" or at least of being an outsider. Read on: that will emerge as a pivotal piece of the puzzle.

I often find that the modern rulers of the nodes take us right to the heart of the matter, but I like to pay attention to classical rulers as well. We have Jupiter, the traditional ruler of Pisces, strongly placed in Pisces and the 5th House. That is certainly a signature of some *playful* karma – and that signature is alive and well in most of the AP groups, where the parties tend to be legendary. The one in northern California even featured a bi-annual talent show, which was always hilarious.

More deeply, I relate both Jupiter and the 5th House to life-affirming "pagan" traditions – and our shared karma as "pagans" in some sense of the word casts further light on the Aquarian themes of *alienation* or *outsider* status. For the past few thousand years, "pagans" have tended to exist in tension with mainstream religions and social structures. That's another hint.

Always with the south node, we have to look for "things we got wrong" in the past or which otherwise damaged us. *What is the "unresolved karma" behind the "entity" we call the Apprenticeship Program?* With both Pisces and the 4th house involved, this nodal structure suggests a feeling of something that was "hidden" or "buried," like a flower that did open.

Putting two and two together, let's add that maybe being "hidden and buried" was a smart move – *a survival adaptation to social reality in which we were "aliens" or "outsiders."*

That notion comes through vividly when we consider the plethora of troublesome hard aspects to the south node. For starters, Pluto squares it from Sagittarius and the 2nd house. Meanwhile, the triple 8th House conjunction of Sun, Mars, and Mercury – all in Gemini – squares the node from the other side.

Clearly, as a karmic "tribe," we needed to hide! We were probably being persecuted, perhaps very successfully. Or even lethally – the 8th House is the traditional House of Death. Four bodies squaring the nodes is a lot! With three of them in the 8th House and the other one Pluto itself, we are in the category of nightmares.

There is clearly a karma of tragedy in the ancient group-soul of the AP. Awful things happen in the world, and the ties that bind the Apprenticeship groups together are the ties of a *clan* (remember that 4th House south node) *that has been through the fire together.*

Want some proof of that? Obviously proof is hard to come by past lives, but here's a piece of the puzzle that supports what we've seen so far.

One of the delights of the Apprenticeship Program is that we rarely look at the charts of famous people. Instead we pull the names of class members out of the "Sorting Hat" – the *Harry Potter* reference was of course inevitable. That way, once we have looked at the chart, we can hear the real story from the horse's mouth and thus learn from each other. In working "at random" that way, statistically, one would expect about an even chance of drawing an "easy" south node as a hard one. That's because softer planets and softer aspects are about as common as the more challenging ones.

It is almost never like that in the AP. It seems like almost everyone's nodal structures reflect some karma of trauma or persecution.

Let's repeat that the 4th House south node suggests a "family" feeling. That's why I've been using the words "tribe" or "tribes" to describe the various Apprenticeship Programs. They actually feel that way – warm, intimate, and bonded. Reflecting that "family karma," we have had deaths, births, romances, life-long friendships, and even a few marriages in these groups. And like a good family, people take care of each other.

Putting all these existential and astrological clues together is not difficult. *The Apprenticeship Program is primarily composed of spiritual (Pisces) soul-families (4th House.) We are people who have often been associated with each other in prior lifetimes and who have carried on metaphysical and spiritual traditions – traditions which ran counter to the culturally dominant ones. And we were therefore persecuted.*

History is sadly abundant with possible illustrations. Just think of "witch-burning" for starters. Or the fate of the Cathars or the medieval Brethren of the Free Spirit. Or really the story of almost any indigenous shamanic tradition as it encountered "big religion" or so-called "progress." Think of banned books and the punishments people endured for reading them. Think of what secrets are buried in the fabled occult libraries of the Vatican and elsewhere. Think of what was lost when they burned the library at Alexandria.

Because of those tribulations, as a group it is a short step to realizing that we got *scared.* So we *hid* – sometimes successfully, sometimes not.

And that is exactly where we encounter the dark, damaged side of our south node.

- As a soul-group *our karmic attachment is that we tend to stay buried. We isolate ourselves. We equate that secrecy with survival.*

To reach our north node, we need to overcome that fearful reflex. It is time for this ancient soul-tribe of spiritual teachers and seekers to be *out in the world* – there's the meaning of the 10th house north node. It also lies in Virgo, suggesting the evolutionary goal of *competent service.* And Virgo is ruled by Mercury, which "hangs in the balance," exactly square the nodal axis, in Gemini. Thus, it is time for this entity to find its *public voice.* That has been the underlying case all along since the birth of the programs – but it is especially important to reaffirm that intention now, with the nodal return.

I celebrate all of you who have been part of the program over the past eighteen years. But I especially applaud all of you who are now helping us do our dharma at this critical juncture in our soul-history – writing your books, teaching your classes, and "quitting your day jobs" to be professional astrological counselors. I appreciate those of you who can relate to the big astrological organizations, making our voice heard there no matter what kind of resistance you encounter. You have chosen the right moment for any of those sacred activities.

Let me also celebrate what we have already accomplished. Evolutionary astrology is now a major movement in the wide world of astrology. *We are now visible.* Books, lectures, and websites abound. We have at last begun to claim our voice.

It is fitting to toot those horns as the nodes complete their circle. We have come a long way from eight people sitting in a living room in Kansas.

No surprise: my own chart mirrors this nodal structure. Natally, I have an exact Saturn-Midheaven conjunction which lies only about *one-quarter degree away from the AP's north node.* That's a very striking signature. The AP is "my baby," for sure.

The personal timing of its birth was interesting too – at that first meeting in Kansas, my progressed Sun was almost exactly opposite that Saturn/Midheaven structure. That was intentional – I was turning fifty and it was time to accept an "elder's" role.

By the way, earlier I mentioned that for practical reasons I suspect the class started a few minutes after 5:00 o'clock – that is of course the eternal way of the world. With the chart set for a reasonable guess of 5:05 pm, my own natal south node is *exactly* conjunct the ascendant. That rings true too. Again, that was not planned. Astrology works just fine even when we aren't looking. As is so often the case, the actual moment of the AP's "first breath" was not something we could easily elect. Practical concerns dictated that we begin with a "bad" chart – the Moon's last aspect before leaving Libra being an opposition to Saturn. Obviously that opposition has not proven fatal – take that, you gloomy fortune-tellers! But the Saturnian signature of hard work and isolation, even from the larger astrological community, has been evident all along.

I am not the only one connected to this chart. I have been struck by an uncannily reliable pattern of people involved with the Apprenticeship Program showing close, specific aspects between their natal charts and this 5° 35' Virgo/Pisces nodal axis. Sensitivity to these particular degrees is so pronounced in people who are drawn to the AP that I have come to regard it as a tell-tale strand of astrological DNA.

I am grateful to all of these individuals for their help and support. I want to honor them by name here. For most of you, the names won't mean anything. What I hope does have meaning for you is that "uncannily reliable pattern" of synastric connections to that AP nodal axis.

First, there's nobody like Tony Howard, who runs Seven Paws Press, my website, and Astrology University. His natal Sun at 6° 55' Virgo conjuncts that AP north node. As my life and work have become more complicated over the years, I simply could not cope without Tony's effective support.

As I've mentioned, a couple thousand people have attended AP's. Over and over again, I have seen their charts closely connected to this Virgo-Pisces axis, usually by conjunctions or squares. Let me name one of them here – Dan Keusal, with his MC/Pluto conjunction at 8° Virgo. I single out Dan for starters in large part because he manifested his Virgoan mastery by supplying me with the exact date and time of that first AP meeting. Thanks, Dan! He was there in Kansas at "our first breath," and he now successfully practices a Jungian style of astrology in Seattle, Washington.

Karen Davis, in whose living room the first meeting occurred has Saturn at 2° Virgo.

Vinessa Nevala ran the northern California program singlehandedly for many years, in Napa. Her south node is in 2° Gemini, squaring our critical axis. Joyce Van Horn took over from Vinessa, again showing the square pattern. Her Sun is in 8° Sagittarius and her Mercury in 7°.

Ingrid Coffin runs the southern California program. Her Geminian Uranus, which rules her south node, is just one degree away from the square to the AP nodal axis.

My European and Australian programs are both run by the able "Mercurial Connections" team of Lisa Jones (Uranus in 10° Virgo) and Christine Murfitt (Venus in 4° Virgo).

In North Carolina, the program is run by Kathy Hallen, with Mars in 9° Virgo, along with Carol McLaurin, whose Ascendant is 5° Sagittarius.

The pattern continues in my Chinese program, administered by the NoDoor.com team of Felicia Jiang and David Railey. Her Neptune is conjunct David's Moon in the fifth degree of Sagittarius, almost exactly square the AP nodal axis.

Finally, the seeds of the southern California program were planted when David Friedman invited me to offer a weekend class in Laguna Beach. After a series of return visits, that group officially became the second true AP. David ran it until Ingrid Coffin took over. David's meridian axis was the same as mine almost exactly, only reversed, with Pisces up top – and thus it lined up with the AP nodal axis almost perfectly.

Sadly, David passed away a few years ago. I thank him too, wherever his soul is sailing.

It is rare to see anything so concrete and "predictive" that works with 100% accuracy in astrology, but here we see it. Virtually everyone who has had a hand in running an AP has a fourth-harmonic aspect to this critical 5°35' Virgo/Pisces nodal axis, almost always within an orb of 3.5°, and often much tighter.

But the larger magic is that we have all found each other again across the wild seas of birth and death, to continue this great work together.

35

Death is the necessary salad course for rebirth, and death is in the domain of Lord Pluto. It takes about two and a half centuries for Pluto to complete a single circuit of the zodiac, so most of us never experience its passage over our natal Suns. Lucky me, I did – and it was transformative in many ways. Death indeed loomed; I lost my mother and a nephew, both beloved. But the specter of my own death pressed at me too, not as a horror nor as a disease, but rather as a stern teacher. I knew I needed to reorient my life. To do that, I knew that some things that I loved would have to die. That is how the space is made for something new. Still, that necessary Plutonian work is never easy.

STEVE'S LITTLE DANCE WITH LORD PLUTO

(Newsletter – April 2017)

Everyone seems to know the myth of Persephone, at least the part where Pluto drags her down to the Underworld "to be his bride." Her mother, Demeter, expresses her grief at her daughter's abduction by putting the world into the deep freeze of an endless winter.

In the end, the Olympian gods and goddesses broker a deal, both to keep humanity from starving and also to keep the worshipful observances coming. From then on, Persephone spends six months of the year with her mother. The other six months of the year, she is ensconced with Pluto in the Underworld.

Demeter is bereft during the months spent without her daughter, and so winter and cold reign over the planet until the two are reunited.

And thus does Spring return every year.

It amazes me how literally astrology expresses itself sometimes. For the past three years or so, Pluto has been transiting through a conjunction with my natal Sun. I've lived the myth. During that time, for about half the year I have been working with clients peacefully at home among the flowers of my desert garden. Pity me – for the other half of the year, I've mostly been in the hell-world of modern airline travel.

When I am standing in an endless TSA line or dealing with a cancelled flight or a lost bag, I can whine like Demeter. My stress levels rise. In China last year I had some kind of mysterious, stress-related Plutonian health crisis. A Tibetan lama warned me of a stroke. Scary! When I got back home, it turned out that I was just dehydrated. A few gallons of water, and my blood pressure was normal. But it was a Plutonian wake-up call.

I may be a Capricorn, but I am learning that I am not bulletproof.

One thing this Pluto transit has meant for me is *learning about my limits*. But, being a Goat, I have an exaggerated sense of responsibility – I always try to keep my promises. And I am very committed to my teaching around the world.

Bottom line, here is the "winter-summer" deal I've brokered with those Olympian gods and goddesses: in a couple of years as I approach my 70th birthday, I will cut back my travel commitments. By then, Pluto will be clear of my Sun.

Until then, for me, The Road Goes Ever Onward – at least during my "Plutonian" months.

I still love to teach! And reflecting how Pluto rules my chart from the 9th House of "Long Journeys," I have been on the road teaching for most of my adult life. Home is where the heart is, and the heart is where the loved ones are – *and now I've got loved ones all over the planet*. Over the years, I have developed a weird sense of having a home "in the world" rather than in a specific place.

And, to be clear: I have no thoughts of retirement and I anticipate that I will continue to do at least some traveling to teach until they are wiping the drool from my wrinkled mouth.

But right now, Pluto has been teaching me that the travel commitments have simply become too much. There are books I want to write that I do not have time to write under the present regimen. Webinars and videos pull at me – and not only because I don't have to travel in order to do them – one reason those media appeal is because they will still exist when those drool-issues eventually sideline me.

Tony Howard and I have also been talking about how to move toward organizing our vast array of existing teaching materials into a more cogent, organized format – one where people who cannot travel to my various classes around the world can at least get a structured education in my style of evolutionary astrology. Most of the material is already there. We just need to arrange it all into a coherent whole, fill in a few blanks, and figure out how to administer the project.

Time is the issue, once again.

(Note: in these words, reading them years later, I see the seeds of the idea that eventually blossomed into the online Forrest Center for Evolutionary Astrology.)

In a nutshell, *Pluto has been having a long, hard talk with me.* The essence of the message has been a reminder that we all get older and eventually we pass from this world. The question of what we leave behind naturally arises. Pluto's message was that I need to start thinking in terms of my legacy – and, by the way, he was also graceless enough to mention that I am not going to remain 35 years old, even in my own mind, for very many more decades.

I'd like to add that my proudest legacy at this point is not my books or even the thousands of readings I have done. It is my students. They are the ones who will carry this bright torch into the future.

Transiting Pluto currently remains in that slow-moving conjunction with my natal Sun, and so again I am called to six months in the "under-world" of the airlines, rental cars, and the tender mercies of the Transporta-tion Security Administration. Pluto's *mordida* looms – once more, I will be living out of my suitcase. But not for much longer – some kind of new Spring lies just around the corner. For something to be born, something must die.

36

No surprise – having transiting Saturn, Pluto, and later Jupiter, all passing over my Sun around the same time was transformative. As I read these words that I wrote in the midst of that fateful period, seeing them from my present perspective just three years further down the road, I am reminded of John Lennon's famous line – that "life is what happens while we are busy making other plans." What I hope you might take away from this next little essay is a sense of the conscious process of integrating a major Saturn transit. One thing I always say about Saturn is that it signals the need to move on to "the next developmental stage" of your life. That line is reliably correct and helpful with pretty much everyone – but of course actually figuring out how to make it real is a complex process. Inevitably a fully-baked idea must start out as a half-baked one. You'll see plenty of that "half-baked" quality in the words that follow. By the way, please forgive a bit of initial redundancy with the previous essay as I set the stage for some deeper reflections.

SATURN AND MY NEXT DEVELOPMENTAL STAGE

(Newsletter – May 2018)

Call me old-fashioned, but in this age of digital relationships, I like to ring the bells for the magic of good old face-to-face, eye-to-eye, human contact. That is especially true when I am teaching astrology. Something beyond easy rational explanation happens between my students and myself in my classes – something beyond what is available in any other way. My favorite way to say it is that, unlike the digital world, human life is composed of more than an audio and a video track.

I think of a treasure: my friendship with Robert A. Johnson, the great Jungian writer and thinker. I had read all his work avidly. It had sunk into my own thinking and had made a real impact on the way I practiced astrology. But when the fates brought us together as neighbors a few years ago, *I felt that I understood his work in a much more multidimensional way.* Jungian psychology had already entered my mind, but after getting to know Robert, it sunk into my heart

How could that happen? Something simply *radiated* from him – something that set up resonances between his soul and my mind. It sounds vague, or even a little flaky. For me, it was as real as heat or cold.

Still, what passed between us could not have been recorded on any digital device.

Humans have been teaching and learning from each other in this mysterious way since the beginning of our time on Earth. For all the wonders of electronic communication, there is something about "skin" that just goes deeper.

I am proud of the webinars that Tony Howard and I have done together. They are a helpful, practical teaching tool. I also understand how they extend the reach of the work. I grew up working-class, so I'm sensitive to financial limitations – I appreciate that there are many people who are drawn to evolutionary astrology and who can afford twenty-five dollars for a webinar, but who could not afford to fly across an ocean or a continent to attend one of my four-day apprenticeship programs.

Tony and I will keep on doing the webinars. In fact, I suspect that starting next year we will do more of them. That is because, despite all the feelings I have just expressed, the time has come for me to do less traveling. Saturn has been talking with me.

As you read these words, I will have just returned, God willing, from a teaching trip to Italy. That will be my last annual trip there.

In mid-August, I make my final annual trip to Australia.

I announced these decisions a couple of years ago, but I wanted to make sure that people who had started those programs could achieve their

Level I certifications. That requires three years, and so I felt the need to follow through and not let them down.

With Saturn heading for my Capricorn Sun and me heading for my seventieth birthday this coming January, I am aware of feeling older. Mostly that is a good thing – I am still pretty strong and healthy. Even better, I can honestly say that I feel I am just now hitting my stride as an astrologer. That is one of the most wonderful things about this craft – you can just keep on getting better and better at it the longer you practice. Looking back over the years from this end of life, I am glad that I wasn't a rock star or a baseball player – fields where the rules of the game are not as generous to those of us with wrinkles on their faces.

Still, in all honesty, blasting from California to Italy, teaching for five days, then blasting back home again the next day, is putting strains on my physical body that are beginning to verge on stupid. I have had some travel related blood pressure scares. "Runner" connections, lost luggage, and the tender mercies of security personnel – all these joys of the modern transportation industry take their toll on one's equilibrium. I love my students and I love the two women who sponsor both my European and Australian programs: Lisa Jones and Christine Murfitt. My feelings about ending those classes are bittersweet, but not really ambiguous: I know it is the right choice.

I try to "walk my talk" as an astrologer, and I know what I would say to people when they are experiencing major Saturn transits: I exhort them to be *mindful of where they are in the life-cycle.* I tell them that old habits are holding them back from becoming what they need to become. I press them to move on to the next developmental stage. To say that Saturn is about "aging gracefully" is accurate enough, but also perhaps a bit of a cliché. I prefer to think of it as aging *mindfully*, recognizing and accepting any emerging limitations – but also claiming our freshly emerging powers.

My intention regarding my international work at this point is to continue my annual trips to China; my work there feels particularly important, given the larger meta-political framework of the world.

Similarly, I have every intention of continuing my two Apprenticeship programs here in California. Those are short trips. They take far less of my precious time, and are much easier on my physical body.

My program in North Carolina will meet two more times, this coming June, and again in June 2019.

I have been making annual trips to New York state to teach at Omega Institute and with Fellowships of the Spirit in Lily Dale up near Buffalo; my plan at this point is to play those two programs by ear, seeing how I feel about them as I settle into my reduced travel schedule in 2019.

When I am not off somewhere teaching, I am doing astrological readings. For a long time, that has been a Monday through Friday "job." But my client work goes to a four-day week starting in January. My waiting lists for personal readings are already terribly long, so cutting back my hours will be something of a train wreck. But it feels right anyway – again, Saturn is telling me that it is time for me to *move to the next developmental stage.*

From all that I have written, you would be forgiven for thinking that my fancy talk about my "next developmental stage" could easily be defined in less exotic terms: *semi-retirement.* But, hey, I am a Capricorn with Saturn in Virgo on my midheaven – retirement, even of the "semi" variety, is really not in my DNA. This work means so much to me. It feels inseparable from my identity. I will do some version of it as long as I am capable of doing it.

And I fervently hope that is a long time.

But, keeping perspective, I have been on the road since the 1970s. That is long enough. I am so aware of the passing of the sands of time, and mindful of the remaining grains. That utterly Saturnian sense of the *preciousness of the time remaining to me* makes for a poignant meditation while standing for 45 minutes in a TSA line. The work will continue, but it needs to take a different form.

So what is next?

As I mentioned earlier, I suspect that Tony Howard and I will do more webinars. I have learned to enjoy them and to appreciate the democratic availability of the material compared to my live classes. To better support that intention, Michelle and I are in the process of building a studio; it will facilitate video work much more elegantly than my cramped office ever could.

I am not quite sure what direction those future webinars and videos will take. Email me with suggestions for topics or programs, if you like.

I have written many books and articles, and recorded countless hours of teaching. Taken together, that body of work constitutes an astrological education – but the material is a chaotic mish-mash. Organizing it into a structured, coherent course of study has long been a dream of mine. All that has prevented me from doing that has been my "pressing need to get to the airport" or the fact that a client is knocking on my door. As I move into 2019 and beyond, I hope to create a smoother, more logical road through that material for a beginner to follow to astrological mastery.

When I think of my "next developmental stage" and the breathing space I am creating in my life for it to inhabit, right at the top of the list is the idea of more writing. Books, to me, are the ultimate learning tool. I have written a dozen of them, but right off the top of my head I could easily think of the dozen more that I would like to write. Where is *The Book of Uranus?* Where is *The Book of Houses?*

In my southern California apprenticeship program, in sixteen days of teaching spread over two years, I explored astrology's four Elements: Fire, Earth, Air, and Water. I have launched an ambitious project: turning that material into four books. I am currently about halfway into the first draft of the first volume – *The Book of Fire.* I find I am actually *writing* this book; it is not an edited transcript of the classes I offered. I want it tighter and more succinct than my usual rambling spoken-word style. *The Book of Fire* is not simply about the element Fire. It is an in-depth study of the life-giving role of the three fire signs: Aries, Leo, and Sagittarius, along with their corresponding houses, the first, the fifth, and the ninth. Completing the picture, I am exploring the roles of Mars, the Sun, and Jupiter – the ruling planets of those Fire signs. *The Book of Fire* will contain a lot of "cookbook" material – that is, specific discussions of those three planets as they function in each of the twelve signs and each of the twelve houses.

Doing the same with Earth, Air and Water is a huge project, so completing this series will take me a long time. My hope is to create something of a reference "Bible" for the style of astrology I have been teaching all these years: a set of books to which students and practitioners can turn when they need some help kick-starting an interpretation.

So that is my master plan, compliments of our friend Saturn – assuming old Cosmo chooses to keep my heart beating for a few more years. I feel like I am doing my own part by listening to Saturn, walking my own talk, being mindful of the aging process, and trying to embrace my next developmental stage.

One more point: *The excitement and sense of engagement that I feel as I contemplate this path is my confirmation that it is the correct one.* Even with Saturn, feeling life renewing itself within you is always the sign that we are on the right track.

37

I continue here with the theme of trying to understand the lessons of my own life by contemplating my experiences through the lens of astrological symbolism. In this essay I talk about the very Uranian "evolutionary necessities" created for me by the seemingly simple "good luck" of winning a major professional award. What I write here illustrates the notion of an "astrologically-assisted" life pretty clearly – I honestly do not think I could have learned what I needed to learn here without the supernatural boost in self-awareness that evolutionary astrology provides.

WINNING THE REGULUS AWARD

(Newsletter – June 2018)

Uranus is famous for providing surprises and it sure worked for me a couple of days ago! I was speaking at the United Astrology Conference in Chicago. At the time of the big banquet on Monday night, transiting Uranus was just 0° 28' from conjuncting my natal north node of the Moon. "Expect the unexpected" is the classic advice. And it sure worked! I won the Regulus Award for Astrological Education.

I don't mean to sound disingenuously modest here. I know my work is popular and that I have a high profile in the world of astrology. It seems that winning an award should not come as a total shock. But it really did.

Some of my surprise derived simply from past experience – I had often been nominated for a Regulus, but never won one. I had no reason to think this time would be any different.

This was the ninth UAC. I did not attend the first one, which happened in San Diego in 1986 – relatively few people in AstroWorld knew about my work back then, so I wasn't invited and I was too much of a Capricorn to simply go as an attendee. I've spoken at every one of them since then.

Of those eight conferences, if memory serves me correctly, I was nominated for a Regulus seven times. "Seven" was obviously my lucky charm here – but after six nominations and no prize, a certain *deja vu* inevitably sets in. My friend Michael Lutin started calling me the "Susan Lucci of the Regulus Awards," referencing the actor who was nominated for an Emmy fully *eighteen* times before actually winning one – and, by the way, what it took for Lucci to win was transiting Uranus hitting *her* north node, via a trine aspect in her case.

I bet she was even more shocked than I was.

There are simple things to be said here, and they are no less true or less sincere for being obvious and a bit *pro forma*. I am happy and grateful to receive this honor. I want to thank everyone in the sponsoring organizations who voted for me. Blessings to those who did not vote for me too – I know there were other worthy nominees. I also extend my gratitude to the people who volunteer their time to keep the organizations going, and reserve a special bow for the long-suffering, head-banging souls who made UAC happen. It is an epochal undertaking.

All that is absolutely sincere.

But there are deeper waters here. To understand my honest surprise at winning the Regulus, I need to explore them in a somewhat autobiographical way, complete with a few squirmy issues.

I mentioned that I did not attend the first UAC back in 1986. I didn't really know anything about the larger astrological community back then. At that time, I had actually *never even met* another professional astrologer.

My first book, *The Inner Sky*, came out with Bantam Books in 1984, but it took a while to catch on in the astrological community. It was – and still is in some ways – a maverick piece of work. Evolutionary astrology has always been . . . well, about *people evolving* – while much astrology, especially back in those years, was essentially *descriptive*: this configuration in your chart correlates with the following issues, strengths or debilities, now and forever.

Static description and ever-changing evolution are not easy to reconcile.

Challenging the *status quo* does not always make you friends in high places.

I have been involved in the two biggest astrological organizations – ISAR and NCGR – all through my professional life, and, with one exception, I have no complaints about how I have been treated.

But I have always felt like I was marching to the beat of a different drummer.

That feeling only increased as my work became increasingly centered on nodal analysis" – that is, on understanding the way unresolved issues from prior lifetimes show up in the present birthchart. Some trauma soon entered the equations – as my past-life work became more publicized, there was also some villainous misunderstanding introduced into the astrological community on one crucial point: a false idea was promoted that I was claiming to be able to discern specific "name and date" details of prior lifetimes in the chart.

That was obviously an indefensible claim, and one I never actually made. The situation took some ugly turns, which pushed me further away from the organizations.

All the while that mess was playing out, my Astrological Apprenticeship Program was taking off – and also absorbing most of my teaching time. It has in fact grown to be almost the same size as ISAR itself.

The upshot of all of this was that my active involvement with the organizations diminished. Along with that diminishing involvement, my self-identification as "an astrological outsider" grew.

I emphasize that this was any kind of "bitter feeling that consumed me." I still supported the organizations and would occasionally speak at their events. The whole thing felt more like a harmonious, mutual agreement to de-escalate a relationship, with blessings and good wishes all around, plus an occasional lunch together to catch up on the news.

Cut to twenty years later. There I am in my necktie, sitting in the banquet hall at the *chi-chi* Chicago Downtown Marriott hotel, waiting for someone else to win the Regulus Award yet again. The envelope opens and I hear, "*And the winner is . . . Steven Forrest.*"

Thank you, thank you, thank you.

Transiting Uranus is just one half a degree from a conjunction with my lunar north node – expect the unexpected, Steve. Prophecy and reality sometimes fit like a bolt in a nut. I was sincerely surprised. In my own mind, I had calculated that even though my work was popular, my diminished relationship with the astrological organizations had also decreased my visibility among the relatively small group of people actually qualified to vote in the Regulus awards.

Sometimes being wrong is a great joy.

Let me take it further. At a deeper level, transiting Uranus is about *breakthroughs in individuation* – the endless process of becoming ourselves. On the north node, these potential breakthroughs depend upon *loosening the blinding stranglehold of the unresolved karmic past.* With my lunar south node in Scorpio conjunct the cusp of my twelfth house, that loosening must address my inborn *attachment* to my "outsider" status – so much of my own prior-life conditioning is related to immersion in some deep *woo-woo* stuff and clandestine initiations, along with hidden shames and taboo esoteric knowledge. My relationship with the astrological community was just another echo of that ancient, ingrained pattern – that's how karma works.

With my north node in Taurus, in this lifetime I need to try to be simpler and more straightforward. With the node on the sixth house cusp, I have needed to be open about these former "secrets," sharing them as widely as I can. Sixth house fashion, I have needed to pass them on to my students. With Venus ruling that north node, *loving – and letting myself be loved* – are critical evolutionary steps too.

As ever with this craft we practice, synchronicity triggered a set of events that allowed me to become more conscious of the extent to which the past was living on inside my head and that it was time to release it. *It was time to let go of being an outsider.*

I won the Regulus. I will admit it: as hard as it is to admit it, *that means that a lot of you love me.* I am blushing, and I am dealing with it.

And, just maybe, evolving.

Thank you!

38

This essay comes a little further down the time-line, a little closer to the present. The four years or so starting in 2018 were a major turning point for me – my beloved apprenticeship programs came to a natural end, only to be replaced with what became the online Forrest Center for Evolutionary Astrology. I wrote my voluminous "Elements" series – four volumes which ultimately ran nearly two thousand pages in length. I put a huge amount of work into "Lila" – my astrological cell phone app project. Meanwhile, Covid-19 struck, which removed me even further from the constraints of the itinerant life I had been living ever since The Inner Sky came out. Naturally, my chart was lit up while all of this was transpiring – astrology works, in other words. I've already written quite a lot about that. If you will forgive a little more "me, me, me," yet another dimension of what was happening astrologically was the passage of my progressed Moon through the twelfth house, which is my topic here. Once again, even though I am yammering about my own life, my hope is that others of you, as you go through your own twelfth house lunar progressions, can get something helpful out of the personal experiences which I relate here.

MY 12TH HOUSE
PROGRESSED MOON

(Newsletter – June 2019)

As I described in a previous essay, Saturn is transiting over my natal Sun, so I am trying to walk my talk – working like a maniac, in other words, trying to keep my eye on the prize.

At the same time, my progressed Moon is passing through the twelfth house. True to form, *I don't know exactly what I am doing.*

That is a strange astrological combination platter, as you can plainly see.

At times such as these, my appreciation of astrology really goes through the roof. I look into that bright mirror in the sky and, among other benefits, I feel a whole lot less crazy than I might feel. I bet that you feel that way too, or you wouldn't be tuning into my monthly astrological ramble. I wish that everyone else on the planet knew about the *simple soul-comfort* our sacred craft provides, along with all the practical guidance about what we are learning, how to do it in the most harmonious way, how to time things in our lives, and so on. I think we are already making good progress in that public relations direction as astrology becomes more widely accepted.

A while back, when I saw that my Moon was about to start progressing through the twelfth house, I knew that many "contracts" in my life were about to expire. That progression always marks a time to *let things go* – or to expect them to fall away naturally. Much twelfth house wisdom lies in accepting that fact rather than fighting it.

Meanwhile, during a twelfth house Moon time, if you *keep the faith* and *clear some space* in your life, a *new vision* begins to take form – and that new vision is something you will really run with, once the Moon starts its new cycle when it hits Ascendant. For me, that epiphany will not happen until the middle of the coming year – so for now it is *a time of overt endings, along with subtle new beginnings.* Those beginnings are unfolding more at the energetic level than in the realm of the obvious.

In writing these words, I am talking about myself – but, hey, simple statistics suggest that I am also talking about approximately one out of every twelve of you. Those are the odds that you might have your own Moon progressing through the twelfth house at this very moment, just as I do. And even if you don't, you will – in fact, you will very likely have this experience more than once in your life. That is because for all of us, the Moon gets around the chart by progression every twenty-seven years and four months.

In other words, my hope as always is that this newsletter proves to be of general benefit to our community – that it does more than provide me with a chance to yack about myself.

This one will be a little more personal than usual though.

Seeing my Moon making a bee-line for the twelfth cusp, I gave notice on my annual teaching trips to Europe and Australia. This past April, I missed seeing Italy and all my friends there – and I know I will miss being "Down Under" in August. That marks the first time in twelve years that I won't see a kangaroo that month.

This month also marks my last annual visit to North Carolina, my old home state.

That's three Apprenticeship Programs wrapped up after all these years.

Every summer, I've been making two cross-country runs to New York state, one to Omega Institute and one to the Fellowships of the Spirit in Lily Dale. I love both places, but getting to them is rough – usually the trip has required three airline flights, with two connections . . . what could possibly go wrong, right?

I'll only be teaching at Omega this summer. I plan to alternate years with Lily Dale. Less stress, more time . . . and yet another example of the twelfth house Moon making space in my life for . . . *what?*

I do have some answers to that question, and I will get to them in a moment. But my best answer is a mantra: *om – I don't know . . .*

I am planning to continue my yearly teaching trip to China, along with my two bi-annual Apprenticeship Programs here in California, but bottom line: my travel commitments are now much reduced. That extra time has opened up possibilities for me that did not exist a year ago. Some of those possibilities are things I can describe – but some are still mysteries to me. Back to my mantra: *om – I don't know . . .*

For all of us, the beginning of wisdom with the Moon progressing through the twelfth house is to create exactly that kind of space for serendipity to happen. Unless that space exists, there is no place for the new vision to take hold. If you think you know what you are doing, a) you are probably wrong about it, and b) you are gumming up your own visionary imagination at a time when you really need it.

By "new vision," I really don't mean anything like a specific "business plan" – it's a lot more subtle than that. I always think of my old friend, Robert A. Johnson, the Jungian who wrote the *He*, *She* and *We* trilogy, as well as many other fine works. He spoke often of how he had followed *the slender threads* all his life. By that expression, he meant signs, synchronicities, clues in his dreams, and strange coincidences – and how by paying attention to those kinds of *guiding omens*, surrendering to them, the new vision forms and is nurtured.

For me, the astrological situation is somewhat confused by the fact that Saturn is transiting over my natal Sun at the same time that the Moon is in my twelfth house. That combination of energies is a bit like trying to accelerate with the brakes on. Normally, Saturn times have the stamp of "Just Do It" on them. And that is the polar opposite of the more patient, reflective energies indicated by any big twelfth house (or Neptunian) influence.

All astrologers are accustomed to wrestling with these kinds of dilemmas – life is complicated and full of paradoxes, and astrology simply holds a mirror before life. All of us are constantly balancing differing, contradictory testimonies in our own charts and in everyone else's.

Tying these two contrasting streams – Saturn and the twelfth house Moon – together does not require any real voodoo. I am staying Saturn-busy, *building some foundational pieces* (Saturn) that I *sense instinctively* (twelfth house Moon) will be important for the future, even though the future is not totally clear – and I am trying to *trust and celebrate that lack of clarity* because of the space it leaves in the equations for the unexpected to appear, as it certainly will.

It is actually as easy as walking and chewing gum at the same time. All it takes is some faith.

Specifically, I have now joined forces with two of my students in order to create an online School of Astrology. As you've read in some previous chapters. I had been anticipating doing something very much like that with Tony Howard, but he's already too busy running his very successful Astrology University, which is a different beast than what I want to create. My two students and I will make a formal announcement about our own school when we are ready – and when we know exactly what we are doing, which we do not at the moment . . . at least, not exactly.

Here's what I do know so far: with all my books, videos, and recorded lectures available at forrestastrology.com, we have a gigantic mish-mash of material that, taken all together, potentially constitutes the building blocks of a fine education in evolutionary astrology. Unfortunately, it is like a library that was hit by a tornado – it is in total chaos, in other words. In establishing our School, we are working toward putting all of that information into some kind of order – and figuring out a way to present it in an online form so that it is widely accessible.

At the same time, we do not want to ignore the "human" component that has been so central to my Apprenticeship Programs, so this whole program will be integrated with mentors and live classes.

Not to be overly mysterious about my two partners in this enterprise – one of my co-conspirators in the project is Dr. Catie Cadge, who is a tenured professor at DeAnza College in Cupertino, California. She is also a fine astrologer. She brings a lot of skill and experience in online education to the table – something about which I know almost nothing.

My other co-conspirator is Jeff Parrett. Along with generous philanthropic support, he is providing us with his enormous knowledge of business, computational, and financial structures, plus some basic visionary perspectives that lie outside the realms of experience that Catie and I inhabit.

The three of us are a good team, and together we are feeling our way through the fog, twelfth-house fashion.

If it weren't for astrology, all my Capricornian mental circuitry would be worried about the many unanswered questions regarding this school project. Now I know that those questions and uncertainties just leave "some cracks for the light to get in." Faith! That is so important in a twelfth house Moon time – give the vision time to form, and above all *don't nail it down to make it fit the limits of your present knowledge and understanding.*

I will of course keep you posted as the school takes shape and eventually opens its digital doors.

The other deal I have made with Lord Saturn lies in the "Elements" series of books that I am writing. As most of you probably know, *The Book of Fire* came out earlier this year. As you read these words, I have just finished work on the manuscript of *The Book of Earth*. With *The Book of Air* up next, then *The Book of Water*, I've still got a long road ahead. But, God willing, I will finish this project in the next couple of years – and then these four volumes will provide basic texts for the School, as well as being available to support anyone who practices the kind of astrology I do. In them – and they will probably total at least twelve hundred pages – you will be able to simply look up the meaning of any planet in any house or sign, or in aspect to any other planet. For each combination, you will find a few seed paragraphs of basic interpretation.

These Elements books are essentially a compendium of the first thoughts in my head when I look at any configuration in any chart – the same seed ideas that have served me well in countless thousands of astrological consultations.

It feels like it is time to share them. Ultimately, one must go beyond such "cookbook" astrology – but most of us find such seed-ideas helpful, especially in the earlier stages of astrological study.

Meanwhile, with the time I have provided for myself by letting those travel commitments go, I am working on a third project. This one is a synastry-based cell phone app called *Lila*. My students and dear friends, Ricky Williams and Linnea Miron are my partners in this one. Ricky, as many of you probably know, is a former National Football League great who is now a fine astrologer as well as an herbalist and practitioner of Chinese medicine. Linnea is – or was – an attorney, so she now brings that legal skill-set to the table. Together, Ricky and I have already written some of the text for the app, which is currently in technical development and getting established on a financial basis, as we assemble our team.

Again, I'll keep you posted about all that as the wheels turn. *Lila* will be simple astrology, at least at first – but it will be many miles from "stupid" astrology. There's a difference! We'll be proud of it or we would not do it. The details are under wraps at this point, but, fear not – it will not just be "Sun signs."

At a practical level, I am hoping that *Lila* will finance my ability to write some more books and to devote more time to the School we are developing. But who knows? We'll see – with my Moon progressing through the twelfth house, I know better than to make any assumptions or even any promises. I'm in the hands of the Universe now, trusting it to remove what I do not need – even if I think I need it. At the same time, I have faith that the universe will slowly feed me the "slender threads" that nourish the new vision – the one that will guide me when my Moon finally enters the first house a year or so from now.

Once again, I am so grateful to hold the mirror of astrology before my own life. I spend so much time teaching it, writing about it, and helping other people with it one at a time in my counseling practice – I wonder sometimes if anyone realizes how much I use it myself and what a difference it has made in my own life.

So: even with Saturn dancing on my Sun, I may be tired, but I am grateful to be alive – and doubly grateful that I will be able to leave something meaningful behind me in the world.

39

*If astrologers had a list of banned books, I fear that Rafael Nasser's
Under One Sky would be up there with the Malleus Maleficarum.
Tired of listening to the sniping among the various astrological schools
of thought, he paid twelve astrologers representing twelve different
traditions a fat fee to interpret a chart – blind. They had nothing but
the person's gender, a false name, plus the date, time, and place of a
birth – nothing else at all. The results ranged from impressive down to
flat-out embarrassing, with the weight at the bottom end of that scale.
Hence, the "banned book" angle – there are some astrologers who wish
this project had never happened. Not me – I think it was a healthy dose
of reality for the astrological community, which perhaps explains my
own commitment to seeing the work come out in a second edition. Truths
collectively denied can become rabid beasts.*

UNDER ONE SKY

(Newsletter – June 2020)

We say "astrology" as if it were one unified entity, but of course it is
not. How many house systems are there? Do we use asteroids or
not? What about Uranus, Neptune, and Pluto? (Many traditionalists prefer
to ignore them.) Meanwhile, Uranian astrologers use hypothetical planets
that no one has ever seen – Poseidon, Zeus and so on – and swear by them. I
hear they get good results too. As an evolutionary astrologer, much of what

I say revolves around the lunar south node – but most commercial astrology programs do not even show its position unless you ask them to.

Even more fundamentally, *is astrology about the stars or the seasons?* To a Vedic astrologer, the sign Aries and the constellation Aries are the same thing – but not to a western "Tropical" astrologer, where Aries starts with the northern Vernal Equinox, which has actually drifted back into Pisces over the centuries.

To put it charitably, astrology is a "big tent."

To put it more pointedly, the many different branches of astrology contradict each other in fundamental ways. Inevitably, these differences lead to the question of which form of astrology is "the right one" – and there begins a slippery slope.

"Nice" astrologers tend to take a tolerant, supportive attitude toward each other, while the "nasty, ill-bred" ones spend a lot of time either attacking other systems directly, or doing so indirectly by saying "my astrology is best."

I mentioned Uranian astrology a moment ago. I know very little about it, so I had to Google it in order to get my references to "Poseidon" and "Zeus" right. The first website to which my Google Search brought me opened with the words, *"The Uranian system of astrology is really our most advanced and evolved system of astrology to date."*

I really aspire to be one of those "nice" astrologers, but obviously the person who wrote those words has it all wrong – anyone can see that MY style of astrology is actually "the most advanced and evolved system of astrology to date."

I am laughing of course – and please laugh too. But, in truth, I have never met an astrologer who knowingly practiced the "second best" kind of astrology he or she had ever found.

Bottom line, the contemporary world of astrology is a chaos of diversity. We are like the biblical "Tower of Babel," with many, mutually-incomprehensible languages spoken all at once. It is like riding the subway in London with your ears open.

The situation has grown much more complex over the last few decades as more astrological systems and styles have emerged and grown popular. When I was a young astrologer, we all at least had enough language in common that we could argue with each other. Nowadays, as I listen to a Hellenist or a Vedic astrologer, I often honestly feel as if I am trying to follow a conversation in *Bantu*. I just don't understand their jargon – and they would be just as confused as I am were I to ask them for their views on the karmic implications of Pluto transiting through a quincunx to a Leo south node in the (Placidus!) eighth house.

All of this brings me to the point of this newsletter. About twenty years ago, a young man of means in New York City decided to put some serious weight on the branches of astrology's tree, and see which ones broke and which ones were strong enough to stand. The young man's name is Rafael Nasser, and he is not quite so young anymore. His friends call him Rafi. He is alive and well and living in Connecticut with his wife and son.

As Rafael dived into the maelstrom of our field back, he found that "I was encountering too many overly self-assured experts making extravagant claims." He added, "Increasingly, I heard astrologers vaunt their particular system as *The System*." (Steven's note: those were the "mean" astrologers.) Tellingly, Rafi also observed the well-intended – but unwittingly deleterious – effects of the "nice" astrologers. He wrote, "At the other end of the spectrum, I was encountering astrologers who indiscriminately accepted far-flung astrological claims notwithstanding their irreconcilable underpinnings."

In his own words, Rafael Nasser had "stumbled upon the collective shadow of astrology." *What was it that astrologers were afraid to look at?* He wondered, "how far do the symbols stretch before they snap?" Being a practical, discriminating Virgo, he decided to actively do something about the situation. His inner voice gave him a command: *"Gather ye twelve astrologers from twelve different traditions and they will interpret the same anonymous birthchart."*

That is how the book *Under One Sky* was born. We are proud to re-release it this month under the Seven Paws Press banner, both in print and in a Kindle version. If you want a copy, just go to forrestastrology.com and enter the title in the search engine.

What Rafi did was simple and elegant, not to mention generous. Twelve very different astrologers were given only the date, time, and place of a woman's birth, along with a false first name. We had no further information about her at all. From that moment on, it was all pure astrology and nothing else. Rafi gave us each $1000 for our troubles and the light turned green – we were off and running, writing out an interpretation of her chart based on nothing but her birthchart in whatever fashion we wanted to set it up and using our own disparate astrological techniques.

Rafael Nasser, in other words, presented us all with a classic *OK, show us what you've got* situation. No more boasting or posturing – just all of us turning our playing cards face-up on the table

Meanwhile, Rafi asked the woman – who was given the pseudonym "Joyce" – to write an account of her life. That portrait, annotated with the dates of turning points in her life to compare with any timed predictions the astrologers might want to make, stretched out to forty pages.

Each astrologer also responded to a series of technical and philosophical questions which Rafi posed. In the end, everything was bound under one cover and the result was a big, fat tome called *Under One Sky*.

For anyone serious about *beginning to learn* astrology, I cannot think of a better investment of time than reading this book. I am a "nice" astrologer – I don't want to make anyone else wrong unless they are actually hurting people. But I am also practical and I do not think it is possible to practice all of these forms of astrology at once. That would be too complicated and too fraught with contradictions, both technical and philosophical. At some point, you have to choose your path. *Under One Sky* is a long read – the book is about 500 pages long – *but it has the potential to put a serious beginner in an informed position about which style of astrology best speaks to his or her heart.*

That may be Rafael's greatest gift.

Under One Sky was published originally in 2004. Some of the astrologers included in it have evolved in their orientations. At least one has passed on, but most are still practicing as I write. Here they are, listed in alphabetical order by first name, with their speciality indicated:
- Demetra George – *Asteroid-centered*
- Evelyn Roberts – *Archetypal*
- Gary Christen - *Uranian*
- Hadley Fitzgerald - *Psychological*
- John Marchesella – *Modern Western*
- Ken Bowser – *Western Sidereal*
- Kim Rogers-Gallagher – *Light-hearted*
- Robert Hand – *Medieval*
- Robert Schmidt – *Hellenistic*

- Ronnie Gale Dreyer – *Vedic*
- Steven Forrest – *Evolutionary*
- Wendy Z. Ashley – *Mythological*

For the record, I know that there is potentially an "appearance of impropriety" in that my own Seven Paws Press wound up publishing *Under One Sky*. Was I in cahoots with Rafi Nasser, with him slipping me the inside scoop about "Joyce?" That unfortunate appearance was perhaps exaggerated when DELL HOROSCOPE reviewed the book, and included this passage: "Readers will come to their own conclusions about which astrologer was most on target, but for me, the clearest, most consistently accurate statements were given by Steven Forrest. He places great weight on the position and standing of the south node in the natal horoscope, and from this was able to see her professional direction, her periodic disasters, and her self-proclaimed path toward personal growth."

About that "appearance of impropriety," here is what actually happened.

Rafael Nasser has a Venezuelan cousin for whom I did some business-oriented astrological consulting many years ago. Through him, I met Rafi. I am guessing that our first encounter probably happened around 1992 in Manhattan. When Rafi started talking about his *Under One Sky* project, he asked me for suggestions regarding any respected astrologers of various persuasions whom he might contact. I helped him out that way, pointing out two or three of the people who ultimately wound up in the book. Rafi's intention – and my assumption – was that he would find an existing astrological publisher. When he sadly hit a brick wall in that search, he turned to me and my then-wife, Jodie Forrest, as a last resort. She and I both thought the project was hugely important and needed to be out there in the world, so we published the book ourselves, with Jodie as the editor.

I did not see Joyce's biography until a year or two after I had written my interpretation of her chart, nor did anyone else involved in the project, except for Rafael Nasser himself.

While I am at it, there is another concern that I would like to address. Many astrologers would refuse to do a "blind" reading at all, instead feeling that for astrology to work, there must be a trusting conversation between client and astrologer. That is naturally a legitimate position for any counseling astrologer to take. I think it is certainly fair to say that the vast majority of us would prefer it that way – obviously, there is much that we cannot see in a chart that is quite relevant to any practical reading of it: the client's relationship status, professional situation, gender orientation, and so on.

My attitude trends along those same lines – that there is an obvious place for conversation and an exchange of information in the astrological counseling room – but with one important ethical divergence. *I never assume that my clients should trust me with any private information of that nature; instead I assume that it is my job to earn their trust.*

- If someone wants to come sit with me, fold his or her arms akimbo, hide behind dark glasses, and just say "show me what you've got," I trust the symbols enough to accept that challenge.

The question of whether or not "astrology can work blind" is what Rafael Nasser was testing in *Under One Sky*. No astrologer was forced to participate, of course. For the sake of proving that astrology can actually stand on its own two feet, they all volunteered for that challenge. In Rafi's own words, "One memorable reaction was expressed by an older astrologer who was horrified by the premise of a blind reading as a means of validating astrology. He said, "You're going to make astrology look bad."

Rafi added that this older astrologer's "fear inspired the project." Again, here are Rafael Nasser's words: *My intention was not to make astrology look bad, but to raise a mirror to the face of astrology and take a serious look at the image staring back. The project was prompted by the Plutonian impulse to invite the reader into the shadow of astrology – blind readings apparently invoke the greatest fear – and to turn on the light."*

The healing power of astrology is certainly enhanced if we have personal knowledge of our clients. But I believe that astrology is powerful enough to speak meaningfully to anyone, and to do so based purely on knowledge of that person's date, place, and time of birth. By the way, I walk that talk several times each month by recording readings for strangers who choose to only offer me their birth data, and nothing more. It works fine, just as it did with "Joyce.".

After the project was complete, Rafael Nasser elected not to write a conclusion which awarded any "Best in Show" prizes. That was probably wise. Suffice to say, some astrologers did better than others. There is always something subjective about such judgements anyway. When I watch the Olympics, I can see why someone wins the Gold Medal in the 100-meter dash – they got to the ribbon first, end of story. But I have never been comfortable with awarding medals for figure skating, for one example – many of those skaters look lovely to me, and I can see that beyond their impressive physical skill, each one has also made many purely aesthetic decisions. What is beautiful to one person might be less so to another – and giving anyone the Gold Medal in such categories always strikes me as being just as false and ultimately just as silly as any other subjective "Top Ten" list.

If you read *Under One Sky*, you will come to your own conclusions. More importantly, if you are new to our field, you will be in a much clearer position when it comes to cutting through all the "my astrology is better than your astrology" posturing and chest-thumping. You will see the direction which you actually want to pursue illuminated – and that is Rafi's rich gift to you.

Taste and see, in other words.

Contemporary astrology is a huge buffet. *Under One Sky* is like a chalkboard menu up on the wall. Everything on it might look delicious, but your tummy is only so big.

What are you having?

40

This final personal essay comes a little further forward on the timeline, with Pluto and Saturn having moved well past my Sun and the progressed Moon having arrived in my first house. The signature of those changes was pretty obvious in my life too – as you read, you'll see me moving in far clearer and more defined terrain, with my wheels turning, my eyes on the future, and bridges burning behind me. The sense of having moved to a new level of possibility is vivid here – a successful passage through an astrologically-challenging time always leads to more than "rearranged biographical furniture." The prize is a breakthrough into territories of sanity and self-actualization that were not only previously unavailable – they were previously unimaginable.

A GOOD PROBLEM
TO HAVE

(Newsletter – August 2020)

Despite my books and my teaching, the bulk of my income and the lion's share of the hours of my working life have always been about private astrological consultations. Along with face-to-face work in my office, people often contact me for recorded readings, which I send them via MP3 files. Lately when I get such a request, I put them on the waiting list and I tell them that I *"hope to be able to do one for them one day."*

The problem is that those recordings are booked at least five or six years ahead.

In a few months, I will turn 72 years old. At my age, making promises about anything that far in the future feels like tempting the Lord to offer me a little lesson about hubris, perhaps punctuated with a lightning bolt.

I also do live counseling sessions here in my office, in person. Those are my favorites. I usually enjoy the human interaction. I also like learning more astrology directly from other people's lives. Years ago, when the recorded readings (an international market) threatened to eclipse my face-to-face work, I started booking the two forms on separate tracks. The local work is more available. The wait for an in-person session currently runs something like three years, although right now, because of Covid-19, it is entirely stalled. I'm not seeing anyone in my office. Lately, potential clients always ask me if I do Zoom sessions or phone work. I never do. The main reason is purely practical – with the other two methods booked so far ahead, how crazy would I have to be to open up a third channel, one that was accessible to the global population?

Being in demand that way is naturally a good feeling. I am prosperous and my life feels meaningful. Those are two great blessings for which I am always grateful. Given my age, people often ask me if I plan to retire. I could, but I don't want to. My intention is to continue doing this work in some form until my heart stops or my brain goes blooey. It feeds my soul and gives purpose to my life. I used to say, "would the Pope retire?" Then Pope Benedict XVI did. But that is the right category: for me, being an evolutionary astrologer is a *spiritual calling*, not simply a job. Retiring would feel almost like a spiritual failure of some sort.

Still, committing to appointments six years down the road is a bit crazy-making, not to mention simply unrealistic. From a selfish perspective, being booked so far ahead is "a good problem to have." What's not to like about job security? On the other hand, who wants to say exactly who they are going to be years from now, then sign it in blood?

Long ago when I decided to become a professional astrologer, people would sometimes praise me for "being brave" – but of course what they really meant was "stupid." In those days, if you had a job with a corporation, they'd take care of you. You'd have the job for the rest of your working life if you wanted it. You could retire. You'd have a pension.

Why would anyone be crazy enough to step out on the thin ice of being an astrologer?

The joke was on them, of course. Corporations seemingly ceased to care about anyone. Many of my "more practical" friends found themselves "downsized" or "redundant" in their fifties – and clueless about how to navigate their own lives without a corporate shepherd.

I've been lucky. Call it my Sun-Jupiter conjunction, I guess. My long waiting lists do have a gratifying component – but, given my age, they are also starting to present me with a big ethical problem.

Am I knowingly making promises that I will never be able to fulfill?

Currently, especially with Covid-19 in the mix and me not seeing "live" clients, I am actually booking more readings per week than I am able to do. The problem – even if it is a good one to have – is steadily getting worse.

Whenever people contact me for a consultation, I explain the uncertainty of the situation, and I routinely refer them to other astrologers. Referrals are the obvious solution to my dilemma. As a result of my Apprenticeship Programs, I'm in a good position to make them too. Something like two thousand people have passed through the "AP" in various countries and states. Many of them are listed in a Directory of Forrest-Trained Astrologers on my website. Many potential clients of mine, daunted by the long wait, have turned to my students and had good experiences.

That's win/win all around, and a source of real joy for me.

But still my bookings grow, and all the while "the Closure Fairy" looms on the edges of my radar screen.

Around three or four years ago, I saw that the progressed Moon was going to enter my 12th house. I knew that much of my life would fall away to make room for a new start. I also understood that it would be better for me to go with the flow rather than trigger any of the baleful "house of troubles" predictions of the astrological doomsayers.

While my Moon was still passing through that reclusive 12th house, Covid-19 struck. One effect of it, as I mentioned a while ago, was that I stopped seeing clients in person. That was out of respect for their health and my own – but it sure freed up a lot of time for me to work on writing. *The Book of Water,* the final volume in my series, is now done and in its final edits, many,

many months ahead of schedule. *I actually wrote "amen" on the first draft of it on the very day that my progressed Moon hit my Ascendant* – that just happened naturally, nicely illustrating our principle that "you can't make this stuff up."

I want to insert a big thank you to those invisible gods and goddesses in the sky. I saw that twelfth house lunar progression coming, and I adjusted my life accordingly. But as usual that intelligence in the sky knew more than I ever could. One thing I did not see coming was the pandemic. How much easier it has been for me to surf that "shelter-in-place" imperative with most of my apprenticeship programs cancelled anyway, and what a blessing to have been given all this time to write.

Another big development that I didn't see coming – even though the planets guided me to make room for it – was the birth of the Forrest Center for Evolutionary Astrology. On March 6, 2019, with my Moon just over the line into the 12th house, I met for the first time with Jeff Parrett and Catie Cadge to discuss the possibility of creating a mostly-online school. It would support people who wanted to learn how to do the kind of astrology I do. Jeff brought years of business skill and visionary leadership to the mix, along with enough financial support to make it happen. Catie brought thirty years of teaching experience, much of it online, as an art professor. Our individual skills definitely formed a perfect "trine," and with their help, I sensed that I could be part of something that would take my work to the next level – something fresh, and something which I could never do alone.

I don't want to write too much about the FCEA in this newsletter. Suffice to say that, while we are hoping to launch it around the Jupiter-Saturn conjunction at the end of this year, our first commitment is to quality and integrity, with deadlines and schedules taking second place. As I write these words, our website is basically a placeholder, but if you are interested in the school, you can sign up for further announcements at www. forrestastrology.center. Very soon, we will post a long interview about the project there. We shot it a week ago, and it is being edited now.

Let's go back to the dilemma that is the heart of what I am talking about in this newsletter: *that I am in my seventies, and I am afraid that I am "booking consultations into my next incarnation."* It's an intractable problem, and I am not sure how to solve it.

My business-oriented friends have always suggested the basic capitalist solution: *that I should simply raise my prices.* Doing that would surely work, but I cannot seem to sprout the requisite dorsal fin. I have enough money. I grew up very working class and those are my roots. I appreciate *la lucha*. Still, I cringe when I read someone post on Facebook about "all those selfish rich people." My work has brought me into intimacy with a lot of very wealthy folks. In general, I find them to be as human as anyone else, with the good, the bad, and the ugly all fully represented.

Bottom line, *I simply do not want my work to become exclusive.* I do not want to serve only the very affluent, even though they are as welcome as anyone else. My prices are already high enough. I cannot bring myself to solve my booking problem that way.

Really, the only truly long-term solution I can see is to have more astrologers working in my style. I came to that realization a quarter-century ago and so I began to put more focus on teaching the methods I had evolved – methods which had obviously struck a chord in the collective. We have two things in abundance in our field: one is *myriad forms of astrology* and the other is *starving astrologers.* I do not want to put any energy into criticizing other forms of our craft unless they damage people – many of these forms undoubtedly work in helpful ways.

Still, it is my own style of evolutionary astrology that I want to pass onward. That is the flame I want to still see burning after I am gone. To that end, my apprenticeship programs are currently evolving into the FCEA. I am busily recording hours of instructional videos for that project, and I am very excited about it.

Someone asked me about the difference between the FCEA and my older teaching programs. Along with all the material that is already available on my website. The answer in one word is *structure.* With the FCEA, students will be guided to astrological proficiency in an orderly, efficient way. They can start at zero, or they can start where they are – but we will hold their hands for the rest of the way, and they will emerge as Master evolutionary astrologers.

With my progressed Moon in the first house now, I know that I am laying the foundation of the next twenty-seven years of my life – which is very probably the rest of it. I also know that I need "to let the Moon make my decisions," which is to say that I simply need to *follow my heart.*

In honest Goat-fashion, my heart has me working harder than ever, but my focus is more on writing and preparing material for the FCEA than upon individual client work. That decision feels right, but I can do the math – with my focus shifting ever more toward teaching, even my being "booked six years ahead" might be too optimistic a projection. Yet *I continue to add people to the list*. Ethically, all I know to do is to be honest with them and to continue to offer referrals. I intend to always do some private astrological work – I would be suspicious of any astrological teacher who didn't face that particular test on a regular basis. But the way the wind is blowing, I seem to be doing less individual client work and more "legacy" work.

My mom lived to almost the age of ninety-six and she "still had all her marbles." Sometimes I have a happy fantasy of my doing a reading for a young man or woman – perhaps someone not even yet born – when I am ninety-five. I imagine that the experience will be as meaningful for me then as it is today.

Anyway, if you are on my waiting list, please understand and be patient – and please pray for my longevity.

Note: as of August 2021, I have decided to stop adding people to the waiting lists at all. They are about ten years long and I need to be as realistic and as wise as I can be about how to best use the time I have left in this world.

SECTION SIX

MUNDANE ASTROLOGY –
PLANETS AND THE BIG
WORLD

Whenever a planet enters a new sign, the change in the collective atmosphere is palpable. Naturally everyone is interested in what the event might portend for themselves personally – and that's where writing about these sign changes can become a bit delicate. When, for example, Jupiter crosses into Scorpio, there are many helpful, universal points we can make, but its individual meaning *depends greatly on the specific house Jupiter is passing through in your own chart, what aspects it will make, and how it fits into the general tenor of your natal map as a whole. Understanding those intimate dimensions of the transit requires an individual consultation, but in all of the essays that follow, I am addressing a broader audience, trying to understand how various sign ingresses and slow-moving aspects among outer planets impact everyone. You may feel them in the bedroom, in other words – but where you will see them most clearly is in the headlines. By the way, this section is more or less chronological. I was tempted to group all of the pieces about Jupiter entering a new sign together, but elected instead to flow with the river of time.*

41

This first newsletter is short and sweet – just a quick introduction to the epochal entry of Neptune into Pisces. We will have a deeper look at the meaning of that portentous event in chapter sixty-six, "Spiritual But Not Religious." Here, to avoid redundancy, I only offer an initial taste of it.

NEPTUNE ENTERS PISCES

(Newsletter – July 2011)

In early April, as tentatively as a cat sniffing the night air through an open door, Neptune entered Pisces. Immediately, the cover of TIME magazine blazed with the question, *What If There Is No Hell?* Neptune's passage into its own sign is a complex subject, but the bottom line is the turning of the collective consciousness of humanity in the direction of life's ultimate questions. TIME's cover story reflected that Neptunian principle perfectly – where normally we would see news, suddenly we saw theology.

On June 2, not even having reached one degree of Pisces, Neptune got cold feet and started heading back toward its hideout in Aquarius, where it has been since 1998. It re-enters Aquarius on August 4, turns around again on November 9, and re-enters Pisces definitively early in the coming year, on February 3.

Once back, Neptune will remain in Pisces for about thirteen more years. It will change the world too. It always does.

To understand where Neptune is going, let's start by understanding where it has been. Aquarius is an Air sign, so it is about *ideas and concepts*. It is also a Fixed sign, which indicates *sustainment and stability*. As with all the pieces of the astrological puzzle, there are potentially good things and bad things about this combination.

On the dark side of the equation, when Fixity and Air combine, we can find ourselves in an arid wasteland of bodiless, lifeless intellect – *rigid* (Fixed) *ideas* (Air) can freeze all vitality out of the intellectual equations. That's dark Aquarius. Think of the most boring class you ever took in college. Think of the dried out academic prune of a professor who was teaching it.

Now try mixing that unpleasant elixir with mystical Neptune.

Not easy, right? In Neptune's 165 year cycle through the signs of the zodiac, its passage through Aquarius is the salad course for its arrival back on its home ground in Pisces – and a much-needed fresh start.

In Pisces, we see an explosion of enthusiasm around mystical and spiritual subjects – a vast *visitation of energy*. TIME magazine's cover as Neptune first touched Pisces is only the beginning.

Think of St. Paul coming to the "seven churches of Asia."

Think of the meteoric rise of Islam.

Think of the Protestant Reformation, the coming of Buddhism to Japan, the rise of Spiritualism in the 19th century.

All of these epochal events in the history of world religion occurred with Neptune in Pisces.

What sets the stage for such a renaissance? In a word, *boredom*. When *religion takes over from spirituality,* when things that separate us from each other are mistaken for a spiritual path, when being "right" becomes more important than dissolving in an ecstatic relationship with the Divine, when we have all *mistaken ourselves for ideas* and theological position papers, the stage is set.

Thus the dark side of Neptune in Aquarius triggers the readiness and openness that allow Neptune to work its Piscean magic.

Between August 4 and February 3, 2012, with Neptune back in Aquarius for one last time, all of us can participate actively in helping humanity achieve this spiritual renewal. We can do that by reflecting on our own attachment to increasingly useless and dysfunctional theologies and beliefs. We are all invited to root out the inner Fundamentalist, the inner

Inquisitor, even the inner "Expert Philosopher Who Is Right About Everything." We are invited to clear away all the mental debris that insulates us from each other. *We are invited to become spiritual beginners again.*

That is what getting it right looks like. Getting it wrong? The Fundamentalists – of every possible persuasion – begin their violent defense of their dying theologies. The Holy Inquisition rides again.

42

*What follows is a bit of "hellfire and brimstone" – an intense
newsletter about an intense topic: Saturn entering Scorpio. Humans
have projected a lot of fear onto both of those symbols, and that
projection is not entirely unwarranted – we just have to be careful not
to throw out the baby with the bathwater. As ever in astrology, there
is a higher purpose in this passing configuration. If we get it right,
the soul-victory comes with a rich prize. Perhaps the real source of
astrologers' fear of Saturn's passage through "the sign of the scorpion" is
that, if we get it wrong, the price is bitterness, loneliness, and a sense
of defeat so deep that it leaches into the marrow of your bones.*

SATURN ENTERS SCORPIO

(Newsletter – October 2012)

Beware, beware, on October 5 the Greater Malefic enters the Sign of
the Scorpion! Hell will rain down upon the innocent and the guilty
alike! Rising prices! Falling stocks! Earthquakes! Bad relationships, bad
luck, and bad hair days!!

You can just about predict what the fear mongers are going to say. But
of course, with Saturn's orbit of a bit under three decades, humanity has
survived this transit countless times. As with everything else in astrology,
it is not something to fear, it is something to use.

What are the tools here? And to what purpose might we put them? And before we attempt to answer those questions, let's recognize that if we do not use the tools, they will surely use us. While I do enjoy lampooning the more fearful readings of Saturn's passage through Scorpio, I take them seriously as a warning about any weak response that we might make to the challenges. I always think of Saturn as the Biblical Jehovah – a god that is far more inclined to dish out Justice than he is at offering Mercy. In other words, don't try to get away with anything with Saturn. As Grant Lewi put it, Saturn is "the cosmic paycheck" – *you'll get what you deserve.*

Meanwhile, of course when anything is in Scorpio, we are playing an intense game for high stakes. Freud was once asked for a succinct definition of psychoanalysis. He said it was *the process of making the unconscious mind conscious.* I've always felt those words to be about the best description of Scorpio that I have ever seen, at least from the evolutionary perspective. *Scorpio is about facing what we do not want to face.*

And back to Saturn? One way I love to describe Saturn to my clients is that this is the planet that *gives us the ability to do what we do not feel like doing.*

- Put Saturn and Scorpio together and you have it – the very last thing most of us "feel like doing" is looking at our own denial, rationalization, and culpability. Yet it is now time to do that, individually and collectively.

The alternative? Basically it is a big dose of reality, right up our noses. Denial, rationalization, and culpability are expensive luxuries, but the "good news" is that we can put the bill for them on our existential Visa cards – that works . . . *for a while.* The bad news is that sooner or later the bill comes due, and usually with 18% interest.

Saturn's entry into Scorpio means the mailman is on the way.

Discipline is a fundamental Saturn word – again, that typically means doing what we do not feel like doing. Here are some more Saturn words: *Persistence. Focus. Relentlessness. Patience.* Perhaps the uber-myth of Saturn is the parable of the tortoise and the hare. "Slow and steady wins the race." We can all actually take some comfort in that notion – Saturn is in Scorpio for quite a while, moving in and out of Sagittarius between December 2014 and September 2015. That gives us almost three years to accomplish this task – a lot of time. Given the magnificent order of the universe, we can confidently know that those three years are *exactly enough time to get it right* – there's not a minute to waste, but there are precisely enough minutes to nail it.

Saturn can be associated with feelings of *depression* and *defeat*, while Scorpio is not the most lighthearted sign of the zodiac. The combination, in other words, can trigger a bleak mood. But keep perspective – you know how you feel early in the morning on the day you have resolved to give your house a major clean-up. It feels overwhelming just to contemplate it. You feel heavy-hearted. You are sorely tempted to blow it off and go play. But then you get out the vacuum cleaner and you get started. *And you quickly feel better.*

As Confucius said, "the journey of a thousand miles starts with a single step." What Confucius left out was that by about the third step of that journey, you are *engaged*. By the sixth step, you are probably whistling while you work.

Saturn tasks are like that. *There's an aliveness in actually doing them.* Simply getting started dispels the sorrow and the gloom. But simply getting started is always the hardest part.

What will Saturn's passage through Scorpio mean for you personally? To be precise, we would naturally need to place the transit in the context of your actual chart. What house is it in? What aspects is it making? That information will focus all this theory to a pinpoint.

- Maybe Saturn's transit is connected with the tenth house, and so it's about your work. Here's a Scorpionic question: have you rationalized the fact that you are pouring your life down a rat hole for the sake of money? Do you really want to live that life? Again, your career may not actually be that bad – the point is, *that's the right question to ask.*
- Maybe Saturn is in your ninth house and the questions are about your religious or spiritual beliefs. Do you really believe them anymore – and if not, is there anything at all beyond them, anything at all in which you can truly believe? Perhaps facing that is better than resolving to be a hypocrite for the rest of your life.
- Maybe Saturn is on your Venus and it's about a primary relationship. Did it die a year ago and has it just not fallen over yet? Do you want to live that lie for the rest of your days on earth?

You may have noticed that my language here is harsh. That is intentional. This is the natural language of Saturn in Scorpio. It is not a gentle energy, nor a diplomatic one. With Saturn passing through Scorpio, you might face some dark hours. We cannot rationalize that reality away or hide it behind happy-faced philosophy. This is a time for real, pedal-to-the-metal, inner work – medicines that are merely comforting are too weak for the job.

Here on the other hand is some medicine you can count on: *the time has come for this work, you are strong enough to do it, and you have exactly enough time.* Be patient, be relentless, and do not swerve.

Do that, and Lord Saturn will bless you with wisdom and a new level of maturity that you have never before had – and the freedom that comes with them.

43

At one level, the following essay is about an unusually thick concentration of planets in Water signs that happened way back in 2013. It was interesting and relevant at the time, but today it is as meaningless as a weather report for a rainy Tuesday in Lithuania in 1832. I include it here because that years-ago configuration gave me a bully pulpit for writing about the Water element in general. I describe the mechanisms that link our ability to be of solace to other people to our willingness to heal ourselves – and that's still as true today as it was on that rainy day in Lithuania.

WATERY WEATHER

(Newsletter – June 2013)

Contemplating the astrological weather for the month of June, three "warm fronts" capture my attention. They all promise rain, at least in the symbolic sense.

- First, Neptune makes its station in Water-sign Pisces on June 6th. Planets making stations are always at their strongest.
- Second, Jupiter enters the Water sign Cancer toward the end of the month – on the 26th.
- Third, Mercury and Venus pave the way for Jupiter's Cancer ingress, with Mercury arriving in that sign on May 31 and Venus following on June 3rd.

Bottom line: we will have a lot of Cancer steam in the air for the entire month, and it will be getting an assist from Neptune in Pisces. Throw in Saturn's continuing passage through Scorpio, and that's a lot of Water energy!

The four Elements – Fire, Earth, Air and Water – lie at the foundation of all astrological thought. And they each mean pretty much what anyone would think they mean, provided that person didn't fail poetry back in high school. In plain English, Fire is "fiery, Earth is "earthy," Air is "airy," and Water – well, let's think about it . . . in fact, we will all automatically be doing a lot of thinking about Water over the next few weeks, although "thinking" is probably not the most precise word to use. Water is more emotional and intuitive.

Show a random group of people a photo of a woman with watery tears running down her cheeks. Ask them what they think is going on with her. 95% will interpret those tears as a sign of *sadness*. They think that the woman is weeping because she is feeling sorrow. That might be true – *but why do the bride and groom cry on their wedding day?* Why does Miss Universe cry when they put the crown on her head? Why do you cry in the movies when the brave hero dies or the lovers finally connect after surmounting terrible adversity? Why do I cry listening to Van Morrison's *Astral Weeks?*

Tears come when any emotion reaches a certain threshold inside us. It does not matter what the actual nature of the emotion is. When we feel that deeply, water – literal water – comes out of our eyes.

- Water does indeed represent emotion. *But more broadly, it represents all the forces that animate and pervade the inner, subjective world.*

Water is the place you go when you close your eyes. Water is the perceptual faculty through which you just "know things" . . .things that come to you from outside the realm of reason. These are typically the most important things in life, by the way. For example, *whom should you love?* Who could ever answer that question via logical analysis alone? Here's another: *in what should you believe?* Even this one – what color should you paint your living room? Somewhere on the earth is a person whose angels are whispering, *"Chartreuse . . . paint the living room chartreuse . . . trust us, we're angels."*

That might sound silly, but in fact the color of your living room is a significant daily subliminal message.

The big point here is that an awful lot of the truly pivotal decisions in life have to be made *trans-rationally*. I could say "irrationally," but that word carries the ghost of negativity. Water isn't negative. It is the soul of life. And it *transcends reason.*

- Water is the part of you that knows that life is inherently meaningful, even though you can't prove it. Water is the part of you that doesn't *need* to prove it.
- Water is the part of you that just knows that your cat loves you, even if some science-side people might dismiss that as "an anthropomorphic projection onto your cat, who would actually eat you if it were larger."
- Water is the part of you that feels knocked out by the vibes when you walk into a cathedral where people have been praying for a thousand years.

All humanity is moving into a Watery period. Jupiter's entry into Cancer opens the big sluice gate, although Mercury and Venus will have already set the stage. Once Jupiter arrives, it will be there about a year – until July 2014. Neptune will not be done with Watery Pisces until 2026, while Saturn remains in Watery Scorpio until September 2015. So the Sun, Venus and Mercury are really just the frosting on the cake. They are much more transitory – but while they are there in Cancer, they really underscore this Watery flood.

Venus exits first, on June 27. But Mercury is retrograde in Cancer from June 26 through July 20, and only enters Leo on August 8th. And of course the Sun will remain in Cancer, as usual, until July 22nd.

Cancer is the energy of the Great Mother. Its highest expressions are kindness and caring. Cancer represents healing energy. These sweet words all refer to the outward behavior of Cancer, at least at its best. It is disposed to behave gently toward others, as a good mother would behave toward her baby. But all positive expressions of Cancer begin with the expression of *caring toward ourselves* – and that caring begins with simply knowing where we hurt.

Illustration: maybe you wake up one morning feeling a little sick. You take your temperature and you realize that you have a slight fever. You call into work saying that you're ill and that you are going to stay in bed and take care of yourself.

That's high Cancer energy.

You add, *"I don't want to give this bug to anyone."*

That's exactly how caring for others derives from the foundation of self-care. That is why, during this time, we are all invited to pay a little more attention to our own woundedness, tiredness, and sadness. *The aim is not self-pity, but rather the generation of self-awareness relative to areas where we are bleeding, and to correct them.*

Jupiter's big question is always, how have I been settling for too little? All of us are invited to attend more effectively to our own self-care – and to not "settle for less than that." The planet needs it and you need it too.

Meanwhile, Neptune is in Pisces. At their best, these two mystical influences – the planet and the sign it rules – reinforce each other. One quality that emerges is *compassion.*

What about Saturn itself being in Scorpio? How does that fit into the picture? Saturn is serious and real, and inclined toward melancholy. Scorpio deals with everything in an emotionally authentic, unvarnished way. *Thus, Saturn in Scorpio represents a realistic, grounded appraisal of our limits and of life's more exhausting and dispiriting dimensions.* Mixed with Neptune's energy, this combination spells *sweet sorrow.*

Sometimes people need a good cry. Maybe you are one of them.

Put it all together and we have a formula for *compassionate, healing engagement with our own hurt* – and to the extent that we can succeed at that first step, there arises in us *an urge toward compassionate, healing engagement with the hurts of others.*

Tune in to your own intuitive Water-world. *Doesn't all of this feel timely?* Isn't this what the world needs now? Isn't this what *you* need now?

As ever, astrology illuminates the path – and, as ever, it is our task as conscious humans to follow it.

44

I still believe that most of what I wrote in this 2015 piece is solid and worth reading, but let me be the first to trumpet one of the biggest astrological blunders I have ever committed to print. As you read these words, you will encounter this sentence: "But seeing the Pluto–Uranus square slowly breaking up does lead me to expect that humanity is heading for some relatively calmer waters." Mea culpa, obviously. In my feeble defence, I had not yet fully grasped the significance of the Eris–Pluto square, and what tests still lay ahead for all of humanity.

THE URANUS-PLUTO ENDGAME

(Newsletter – March 2015)

On March 16, Uranus and Pluto form a square aspect at a little over 15° of the signs Aries and Capricorn respectively. This represents the final exact square in the long series of seven of them which began on June 24, 2012 at a bit over 8° of those same signs.

This is the first time both planets have been in direct motion at the moment of the exact square.

- Over a period of about three years, the furious, violent "Lord of Earthquakes and Lightning Bolts" has been "squared off against" the uber-controlling "Lord of the Underworld – also known as the "God of Hell."

Don't you love this language? The words ring of *Alien Vs Predator*. They sound like a hormone-addled fourteen year old boy's wet dream.

And of course, astrology is working just fine – it always mirrors reality. All that archetypal mayhem has been reflected almost daily in the horrific news of the world. Just when we thought things could not possibly get any worse in terms of the way humans behave toward each other, we get government-approved torture, mass graves, beheadings, murdered journalists, and so forth. The dark, log-jammed logic of this potent square has been evident everywhere.

Thank God it is ending, right?

Well, not so fast. These planets move slowly and, while March 16 represents their last *exact* square, they're not exactly finished with each other. Pluto turns retrograde in April as does Uranus in July. On Christmas Day, 2015, Uranus will be standing Stationary at 16° 33' of Aries, with Pluto at 14° 51' of Capricorn.

That 1.5° spread is "close enough to count," for sure. After that, the epochal power of this square will then fade out through 2016 and 2017 as Uranus slowly pulls ahead of Pluto.

Their dance, in other words, will end with a whimper, not a bang – although 2015 may very well hold another bang or two.

Looking at the mass of humanity and how we respond collectively to celestial events can be dispiriting. There's a clear tendency for the lowest common denominator to make itself felt in the litany of daily horrors. We have surely seen that principle evident recently. *Angry* (Aries) revolutionaries (Uranus), often *armed with technology* (Uranus again) have been pitted in life-and-death battles (the square aspect) with *controlling* (Capricorn) *governments* (Capricorn again) willing to use d*ark means* and every *treachery* (Pluto) to destroy them.

Meanwhile, *conservatives* (Capricorn) have been in the teeth of *progressives* (Uranus), each projecting inhumanity upon the other. *Irreconcilable differences* (the square aspect) have actually created a tense, unchanging, profoundly uncomfortable *stability* in human affairs – the domestic and geopolitical logjam, with all its venomous frustrations leaking out in the nightmarish grotesqueries of the nightly news.

Oi!

And that's just the human world. Think of the increase in terrible earthquakes, volcanoes, and super-storms we have been experiencing since 2010 or so, when these giant planets began smelling the square. For one example, the exact day that Uranus returned to Aries (after briefly retreating into Pisces for several weeks) was the day the tsunami struck the Fukushima reactor in Japan – *a Uranian earthquake released Plutonium from a Capricorn containment structure.*

As they say, you can't make this stuff up.

Speaking of which, I've never met anyone with the following two traits: *they disbelieved in astrology and they knew a damned thing about it.*

Prediction isn't my thing. I believe too strongly in the power of the human will to have much faith in any mechanistic model of astrology. But seeing the Pluto-Uranus square slowly breaking up does lead me to expect that humanity is heading for some relatively calmer waters. Even though we often do behave mechanically, we are not marionettes hanging from the planetary strings – at least not necessarily. But the crowning irony of freedom is that *we are free to not be free*, if we so chose. So often our responses are indeed reflexive and unconscious. Collectively, the human response to the Pluto-Uranus square has been quite instinctual: *rampant projection, rampant demonizing of "the other," spiced with a war of slogans and an appalling body count.*

Even if humanity simply continues in the same unconscious, reflexive vein, we will probably find ourselves losing some interest in the endless war, "getting over it," listening to each other a little more clearly, and generally being more willing to tend our own gardens. That in itself would be a mechanical response to diminishing tensions in the sky – mechanical, but welcome. Comparatively speaking, I'd celebrate that – I mean, compared to grandpa crawling up our legs with a knife in his teeth, which is what we have been experiencing.

Individuals, however . . . human individuals are an entirely different beast than human societies. Sting said it so well in his tune, *All This Time:* "Men go crazy in congregations, but they only get better one by one." The "least common denominator syndrome" that is so obvious in the news is far less relevant to the individual.

- We individuals are the *quanta* in a kind of collective social quantum theory. Some equivalent to Heisenberg's Uncertainty Principle rests inside of each one of us.

One expression of that principle is that some of us will always respond to any astrological stimulus in the worst possible way. Examples would be those who have actually *beheaded* other people for what they symbolized – or police officers who've pulled the trigger on unarmed kids with their hands up, or kids who've attacked police officers because of their uniforms or their skin color.

If you've come this far in reading this piece, thank you. I know the emphasis so far has been negative. I am about to turn all that around and celebrate the soul-victories that this Pluto-Uranus square has represented in so many lives. I never want to turn away from the darkness – pretending that it is not there only makes it more powerful. But it is the Light that gives us the strength to endure the truth.

We need it and it is always there.

Reflecting the higher possibilities of this Uranus-Pluto square in the lives I see from the front-row seat of my astrological counseling practice, I have observed individuals integrating tense opposites within themselves – reconciling the inner conservative and the inner liberal, so to speak. Through conscious work, I've seen potentially devastating existential earthquakes eased before they broke. I've witnessed new-born wisdom, sobriety, empowerment, and grace.

These processes have been available to one and all, but they've been particularly pressing for people with planets in the four Cardinal signs between about 6 and 17 degrees, where Pluto and Uranus have been sweeping along, conjuncting, squaring, or opposing them.

These are the folks who have been on the front lines. Some have fallen and some have soared.

This subject is too vast for a short essay such as this one. But I've learned that there are a few principles which underlie all the successful, integrative, life-healing responses I have seen people make to these intense, paradoxical stimuli. Here they are, presented as the little formulas I used in my Apprenticeship Programs as I prepared my students to help themselves and others through these stormy times:

- Breaking points can be breakthrough points
- Crisis relieves chronic stress
- Facing one's woundedness leads to personal liberation
- Via synchronicity, successful inner work triggers magic – walls can turn into doors

- Sudden changes often reveal underlying issues
- Bold moves can lead to empowerment and insight.

Nobody can be equated with a little formula, of course. But think back on your life over the last few years, especially if you have that Cardinal sensitivity in your chart. Take the houses through which Uranus and Pluto were transiting into account. Think about the specific aspects they were making. And see if any of these little formulas have biographical, evolutionary relevance to you.

I know they do for me, profoundly.

As you reflect, you integrate. You gain the full benefit of your own hard evolutionary work. You nail down the victories you've won.

Soon the long-running Uranus-Pluto square will be over. It's nightmarish exaggerations of everything grotesque and impossible in human nature will likely diminish. But there are two things I have learned about these kinds of global astrological events:

- First, the kids born under them will carry these questions forward and wrestle with them throughout their lifetimes. Often that piece of the astrological puzzle – *the lives of the children themselves* – is really the biggest one, once the immediate fireworks are over. You see its effects for a century, not just a few years. Think of the fabled 1960s – and now think of the impact on human history of the children born in the 1960s with that Uranus-Pluto conjunction hard-wired into their consciousness. Many of them are just now coming into their full power as voices, artists, and leaders.
- The second thing I have learned about these global astrological events is that the inner work we do under them lives on, not only in our own lives, but in the form of the contributions we are empowered to make to our communities, both visibly and on the subtle plane of the vibrations we all emanate – vibrations of madness or of wonder ... vibrations of despair and defeat, or of love and the miracles of kindness and forgiveness.

45

Here we begin a long romp through some basic Jupiter theory, along with a refresher survey of the meaning of the sign Virgo. More importantly, we get a quick lesson in how to integrate the messages of any two very different symbols. Remember, Jupiter is often described as being "in detriment" in Virgo. Let's prove those pessimistic astrologers wrong. Let's watch what happens when Jupiter and Virgo bring out the best in each other.
As this section of The Endless Sky unfolds, you'll come to several other essays about Jupiter changing signs. In each one, the planet becomes a very different beast – the same way that you do when you hang out with your friends after a weekend spent with your relatives.

JUPITER ENTERS VIRGO

(Newsletter – August 2015)

In pop astrology, Jupiter is celebrated as the lucky planet. So if you are a Virgo, lucky you! Jupiter enters that sign on August 11. Meanwhile, all of you Leos better drink up because your year of glory is drawing to a close. Jupiter's sweep through Virgo will run for about thirteen months, finally – allegedly – bringing sunshine to all the world's Librans starting on September 9, 2016.

We will have deeper things to say, fear not! But for a moment, let's contemplate the phenomenon of good old plain dumb luck. Who knows what that wild card signifies in the larger scheme of the universe? Is it random – as simple as saying "every dog has his day?" Is it good karma coming home to roost? That's my own guess – I've never had much faith in the "random universe" model.

Whatever "dumb luck's" origins and possible deeper meaning may be, it's a real phenomenon. We all recognize it when we see it. And when it raises its welcome head in your life, there's a good chance that Jupiter has simultaneously stepped into the spotlight of your chart.

So for all of you Virgos, good news: there is an excellent chance your stock is going to go up between now and September of next year. And think about it: *couldn't you use a victory about now?* That line is our doorway into some deeper territory. Jupiter isn't only about dumb luck in some random way that's pleasant but pointless. In common with all the transits of all the planets, Jupiter's arrival at a sensitive point in your chart represents an *evolutionary opportunity* – or to put it more accurately, an evolutionary *necessity* whose moment has ripened. In this case, that necessity has to do with you *needing a victory* – needing something to go your way, in other words.

"Change" is a word that functions as astrology's basic "Swiss Army knife." All transits are about "change." With Jupiter, the pressing necessity is a *change for the better*. The evolutionary questions which trigger making that breakthrough healthy are:

- How have you been underestimating yourself?
- How have you been settling for too little?
- How have you sold yourself short?

As you reflect deeply on those questions, you are doing the necessary evolutionary work implicit in a Jupiter transit. You are using it consciously in service of the growth of your soul rather than being knocked around like a billiard ball on life's little pool-table – even if you happen to be knocked triumphantly into the corner pocket.

Synchronicity provides the next link in the chain. Once you have opened your heart to those three uplifting questions we just mentioned, simultaneously *doorways to opportunity* open in the world. The irony is that those doors might actually be open anyway – *but unless you had been brave enough to see your own discontent, unless you had acknowledged that you really needed a victory, you would not even notice that they were open.* The opportunity would be sitting right there before you and you would sleep right through it.

So, in order to make Jupiter work for you, you need to start by cultivating two qualities: the first is a sense of *self-worth*, and the second one is *hunger*.

You've got to really want it.

We will get back to all those general Jupiter principles in a minute, but first let's tie all that we have said more specifically to Virgo. So far everything that I have written is about Jupiter transits in general.

If you are a Virgo, then this season of opportunity really has your name on it. But a deeper reality is that all of us are Virgos in some way. That just means that Virgo figures in everyone's chart. Even if you have no planets there, Virgo is still probably on the cusp of one of your houses, for example. Astrology is not "one size fits all" – Virgo's mark on you might be subtle or very narrowly defined. Or it might be as central to you as your spine. Your exact and specific astrological sensitivity to Virgo says a lot about *exactly where* you might look for this "luck" we are predicting.

- Maybe Virgo is on the cusp of your 7th house, maybe it's time to ask more of your partner – or to look for a partner who is worthy of you.
- Maybe Virgo is on the cusp of your 2nd house. That's often about money; ask for a raise at work, and you'll probably get it.

Those are two quick examples of how your chart points your nose at the likely source of the good fortune that is available to you – just remember, you've got to *feel worthy of it* and you've got to feel *hungry for it*. Those attitudes are what triggers the synchronistic magic. Without them, nothing happens. There really is a "magical" feeling about how synchronicity works, but there is also a lot of plain obvious common sense to it.

If you don't ask for that raise at work, you probably won't get it.

Jupiter-in-Virgo is a different beast than Jupiter-in-Leo. One key word for Virgo is *competence*. Another is *skill*. A common one is *service*. The underlying idea is that there is a basic, nearly universal – and very Virgoan – human desire *to be good at something* which other people value. Add Jupiter to the mixture, and it's time to claim a bracing dose of self-improvement in those arenas.

Obviously that can often connect directly to *vocation* or *career*. Maybe, for example, you've been studying astrology for a couple of years. *Maybe it's time actually to start doing readings for people you don't know and getting paid for them.*

You don't feel ready for that? Well, maybe you are right – but remember our key question: *are you underestimating yourself?* Maybe you truly *were* not ready to practice astrology last year. That was then, this is now. Update your files on yourself. You are better than you think you are.

For all of us, universally, while Jupiter is in Virgo, there is a need to improve our skills. To get better at what we do. *To do work that matters to you.* And if you let yourself feel that desire inwardly, doors open in the outward world of circumstance.

That's synchronicity again. .

Virgo is not only about working – it is also about the *routines* of life. They too can be lifted up to higher levels of expression and efficacy under this planetary ray. To illustrate this, I will sound a little silly for starters – *maybe your toothbrush needs an upgrade.* (You know how they get after a few months . . .) You probably use your toothbrush at least twice a day. You probably hardly notice it. But one night, you recognize that your old toothbrush needs an upgrade, so you junk it and buy a new one. *And your life is just a little bit better in the Virgo department.*

Now take a look at your chart – transiting Jupiter is trine your Moon, which is always connected with *self-care.* You might not even connect that transit with the new toothbrush – you may even scratch your head, wondering "why your Jupiter-trine-the-Moon isn't working."

Meanwhile, your angels are laughing at you. Your new toothbrush was actually part of it.

The toothbrush illustration is trivial – I promised a silly example, didn't I? But let's multiply it a thousand times. Virgo is about *details*, no single one of which is so mission-critical individually, but taken together, they define the quality of your daily experience.

A toothbrush may just be one of the basic tools of life, but Virgo is about the *whole toolshed.* Your tools need an upgrade; they need to work better.

Maybe you replace your ancient vacuum cleaner. Maybe you spring for an uber-modern, uber-cool, new blender for your smoothies. Maybe you free up your windows so they actually go up and down.

Again, none of this is crucial if we take it piece-by-piece – but put the whole package together and your life hits a lot less static. Things work better.

Go further – maybe you go through your closet and get rid of the clothes you don't wear anymore. Maybe you organize the work bench in the garage. Maybe you detail your car. Again, *things work better.*

They say "the devil is in the details." True. It is time to turn those devils into angels.

46

At the risk of sounding pretentious, if anyone were to ask me which of my monthly newsletters I felt was the most important one that I had ever written, the following essay would come instantly to mind. Nominally, it is an exploration of the then-current Uranus-Eris conjunction, but in a deeper sense, these are my initial observations about Eris, a "new" member of our solar system – and thus a new word in our astrological vocabulary. History teaches us that the discovery of a new planet stretches people to their edges. It is never an easy thing to integrate. When this piece was first published, I got more than a few critical emails from people who felt that Eris represented world peace, gender equality, LGBTQ rights, and a renaissance in environmental sensitivity. I'm in favor of those things! But the sky always mirrors the world, and anyone who thinks we've only been looking at nothing but the flowering of those virtuous realities since 2005 has been smoking something. There is no way, in my view, to understand the contemporary mortal struggles of the world astrologically without looking at them through the lens of knowing that we are now – like it or not – launched upon the stormy seas of The Age of Eris.

THE CURRENT URANUS-ERIS CONJUNCTION

(Newsletter – September 2016)

If Pluto is a planet – and most astrologers, myself included, still say it is – then, like it or not, distant Eris must be a planet too. The two bodies are about the same size. Both orbit in the dark deep-freeze out beyond Neptune. In many physical ways, they are equivalent. We astrologers know all about Pluto's direct impact on our lives. Most of us have scars to prove it. Should we expect anything less of Eris?

The astrological jury may still be out on the power of Makemake, Haumea, Sedna, and the rest of the "trans-Neptunians." But Eris is way bigger. I believe it is time to say that everyone who claims that the jury is still out on Eris is simply not paying attention.

I have also come to believe that Eris's current explosive conjunction with Uranus underlies much of the chaos in the world's current headlines. Notice how you can hardly post "have a nice day" on Facebook without someone drawing parallels between you and Adolph Hitler? Notice how whatever you say about race or gender, someone accuses you of insensitivity? Notice how the comedians are all walking on eggshells? All of that bears the fingerprint of Eris, or at least one dimension of it.

To the Romans, the goddess the Greeks called Eris was named *Discordia*. I prefer that name; it is so telegraphic. Meanwhile, Uranus, famously, is the Lord of Earthquakes and Lightning Bolts. *So what might we expect when "discord, earthquakes, and lightning bolts" form a conjunction in Aries, the sign of the war-god?* As I mentioned, we are all staring the answer in the face – it's happening in all our lives right now. Uranus caught up with Eris on June 9. They conjoin again, both retrograde, on September 25, and one final time on March 16, 2017.

Of course, these are very slow-moving bodies and so their interaction is only *peaking* on those dates. We can run it a couple years before and afterwards – we've been in it a while and there is more to come, in other words.

Pluto is slowly moving into place as well, via a square aspect to Eris that will run pretty much until Pluto crosses into Aquarius in a few years.

Eris was discovered in 2005, so we know that its meaning has been synchronistically tied to the mood of the world for several years now – just as the discovery of Uranus was tied synchronistically to the revolutions in France and America in the late eighteen century. My main point here in this month's newsletter is that *the current conjunction of Uranus and Eris is essentially the moment in which the reality of the Era of Eris is breaking through into collective consciousness.*

- If 2005 was Eris's opening, then 2016 is the Grand Opening.

As in all things astrological, we might say that is both good news and bad news – or, more precisely, that Eris, just like the rest of the symbols in astrology, represents a *spectrum of possibilities*, both high and low. It is not the planet itself but rather how human consciousness interacts with its wide archetypal field that determines what will actually happen. That is a principle I have never once seen fail in astrology.

- *Let's echo that the discovery of a new world out there in space means the discovery of a new one inside us all as well – and, if history serves as a mirror, this integrative process always stretches humanity pretty close to its edges.*

Such a discovery represents something humanity can *barely* do, although we've generally squeaked by. Witness the discovery of Pluto in 1930 and the corresponding release of shadow-energy into the world, along with the psychological tools for wrestling with it. Could, for example, the nuclear age have killed us? Yes. Did it? No. The Cold War was scary, but humanity passed the test. We need to be sober about Eris, but we don't need to be pessimistic.

Eris, sister of Mars in many of her myths, *"delights in the groans of men dying in battle."* She walks merrily among the dying *"increasing their pain."* Virgil describes *"her snaky locks entwined with bloody ribbons."*

In mythology, she is, in other words, a hell-ish creature, almost more Plutonian than Pluto.

As we will see, there is another side to her – one not so negative. In a nutshell, *competition is not always a bad thing.* But Eris is sometimes competitive in the darkest sense. It can be violent, and delight sadistically in the pain of others. In her negative aspect, the goddess Eris *likes to win, but not so much as she enjoys seeing you lose.*

Nothing satisfies her like your suffering.

If you think about for a moment, doesn't this sound like the twisted logic of terrorism? Doesn't this sound like weddings bombed by robots in the sky? Doesn't this sound like psychotic morons armed with automatic weapons blowing away fifty strangers in a nightclub? Or running down innocent people at a festival with a truck? Or people shot for their skin color or for their uniform? *Doesn't this, to stand back a bit, sound like the headlines of the world we have been living in since Eris was discovered?*

Let's remember the dramatic synchronicities around the discoveries of Uranus, Neptune and Pluto – and recall the detail that some of those correlations unfolded *before* the actual physical discoveries of the planets. That's important! The most obvious example here would be the American revolution of 1776 beating the discovery of Uranus by five years, and yet perfectly embodying the Uranian spirit.

- The astronomical discovery can often be pinned down to a specific date, but the *collective psychic discovery* of the planet might be understood to take a generation.

For modern Americans – and I think for much of the western world – we might say that "everything changed" on the morning of September 11, 2001. That violent moment when the Twin Towers came down beat the discovery of Eris by four years, but it totally embodies the violent, sadistic dimension of this new addition to our daily astrological vocabulary.

Here's the core insight: a planet is discovered at a moment of time – but deep psychological and mythic change in the *zeitgeist* cannot be pinned down to a single day on the calendar. *The discovery of a planet leaves its stamp on generation, not on a moment.*

Please bear with me. So far, I have made the discovery of Eris sound like a dumb action movie designed to pander to the bloodlust of fourteen-year-old boys. That is surely part of it – but with this new planet, the Greek myths offer some deeper, more complex insights, and maybe some more comforting ones. The most commonly told Eris story in Greek mythology is also about war and violence, but it is also kind of funny. And beneath the comedy lie some real insights. The tale recounts how the goddesses Hera, Athena and Aphrodite had been invited, along with the rest of the Olympians, to a wedding. Eris had been snubbed because of her ugliness as well as her trouble-making inclinations. In revenge, she tossed a golden apple inscribed "For the Fairest One" through a window into the party.

This little gift provoked the three glorious goddesses to begin an unseemly cat-fight about the appropriate recipient.

Which of them was the prettiest?

To settle it, the hapless Paris, Prince of Troy, was appointed by Zeus to decide the winner. The goddesses *stripped naked* to try to win Paris' decision, so hungry were they for that apple. They also attempted to bribe him. Hera offered political power; Athena promised infinite wisdom; but sly Aphrodite tempted him with his choice of the most beautiful woman in the world: that was Helen, who unfortunately happened to be the wife of Menelaus of Sparta.

Paris chose the girl, of course – and thus Aphrodite won the beauty contest. And the upshot of it all was the Trojan War, in which Paris's city was destroyed.

Eris presumably ran away laughing.

There is much in this myth for us to contemplate. Note for starters that the root cause of the violence was *competitiveness* among the three goddesses. Let's dwell there for a moment. In war and almost all violence, people are always fighting over something they want – money, land, power, status, sexual partners. Without desire, greed, and competition, there would be no war at any level. The dark face of Eris would not exist.

There is another side to it, though: *without such competition, there might also be no progress.* That insight is what brings us to the higher ground. The ancient Greek bard, Hesiod, points out that Eris *"stirs up even the shiftless to toil; for a man grows eager to work when he considers his neighbor, a rich man who hastens to plough and plant and put his house in good order; and neighbor vies with his neighbor as he hurries after wealth."* Tellingly, he adds, *"This strife is wholesome for men."*

Hesiod points out that much effort and creativity is triggered when *"potter is angry with potter, and craftsman with craftsman and beggar is jealous of beggar, and minstrel of minstrel."* As a result, they might all make an effort to improve.

It may not be pretty, but we all get better pots and better music.

Hesiod was writing two and a half millennia ago. For a contemporary illustration, think of the enormous success of the Toyota *Prius*. You can't drive far today without seeing one. Dwindling oil supplies triggered competition among car companies. The creation of these kinds of more environmentally-friendly vehicles followed. Simultaneously, and for similar reasons, the price of solar panels has been coming down while their efficiency increases.

Whoever comes up with the best idea wins the money. Like it or not, it remains a fact. In these two cases, I think it is fair to say that we all benefitted. But then along comes *fracking* – another new idea based on competition over petroleum resources. You can judge for yourself whether cheaper fuel for a few years is worth poisoning our water supplies for centuries.

- The point is only that Eris – also known as *human competition* – has two sides: it can better us all, or it can worsen everything. To keep balance in our understanding of Eris, we need to keep an eye on both perspectives.

Competition has naturally always been with us – it did not come into existence suddenly in 2005. As astrologers we might simply say that we always have Mars and Aries in our charts – nothing new there. But very clearly the *scale and intensity* of worldwide "competition" has gone through the roof in the past generation or so. One force driving it is resources dwindling while populations increase.

I think it is also fair to observe that competition has taken on a new Eris-flavored edge of sheer *sadism* – the evil joy in the suffering of others. What would you see if you looked into the eyes of "shooters?" Or suicide bombers about to pull the trigger in a crowded marketplace? Imagine people cheering as they saw human beings leaping from the windows of the Twin Towers in September 2001.

It would chill you to the marrow. That is dark Eris. It's not exactly new – the point is that it is now *epidemic*.

Go back to the myth. What are Hera, Athena, and Aphrodite fighting over? An apple? In a way, yes. But they are really fighting over the most quintessentially trivial question imaginable: *who among them is prettiest?*

Doors open for physically attractive people – and often close in the faces of those who are less attractive. I believe that one thing the discovery of Eris signals is that the time has come for humanity to deal with the "beauty myth" and all the distortions, pain, and unfairness it creates among both women and men. To me, that is a significant part of what the collective discovery of Eris actually means.

- Maybe we can finally begin to question the endless "beauty contest" of modern life.

The beauty myth, while fascinating, is a specific Eris subject. Here I want to spotlight a broader point: Hera, Athena, and Aphrodite made perfect asses of themselves over a high school issue. Which one of them is prettiest? They were so desperate for that particular golden apple that they stripped naked and paraded in front of Paris. For the sake of winning the trivial "apple of ego," the goddesses made themselves into pole dancers at a "Gentlemen's Club." Add twelves square inches of Spandex and they could have been on MTV today.

Humans are naturally somewhat competitive and sometimes fierce about it – we all have Mars in our charts, in other words. Most of us would attack a bear with our fists if it were threatening our children. *But what happens when we bring that same fierceness into competition over trifles whose value we have inflated* – trifles such as status and money? As Bono of U2 sang, *"You can never get enough of what you don't really need."*

But if you have decided, delusionally, that you truly *do* need it, you might very well make someone else bleed in order to get it.

Broadly, the discovery of Eris coincides with a time of mounting competitiveness all over the earth. The questions it raises are not simple – no simpler than were the questions raised by the discovery of Uranus, Neptune, and Pluto. Humanity answered those questions; I have faith that humanity can answer Eris's questions too. But they are pressing at us, and vexing us, and the stakes are extraordinarily high.

In a nutshell, with resources dwindling and population exploding, what will happen? On what kind of future will humanity decide?

Here's one more example of a question arising in synchronistic lockstep with the discovery of Eris – think for a moment about the issue of *international migrants*, some of whom are escaping from war, others from poverty.

- One perspective: Who likes the idea of their country being taken over by hordes of desperate, penniless outsiders from violent, alien cultures?
- Another perspective: Who among us, if we ourselves survived a poison gas attack in Syria, would not do anything to get into Europe or America?

Passions run high. "Kill them all" is heard on both sides. People run for political office with little more to say than that. Meanwhile, dark Eris stalks among the dead and the dying, "increasing their pain."

I am not happy writing any of this, but hiding behind a smiley face doesn't make it go away. Who can doubt that humanity is approaching some hard limits? As of this past March, the world's population was about 7.4 billion – already enough to be a calamity in many places. The United Nations estimates it will be 11.2 billion by the end of the century, barring disasters – or an outbreak of wisdom. Meanwhile, we are poisoning the water that remains, destroying arable land, and heating up the planet in ways whose full effects are utterly scary, but hard to foresee accurately. That is all physical stuff, and familiar territory to most of us. I won't belabor it here.

To me, this sense of "shrinking, crowded space" *and the competitiveness it engenders* has been exaggerated further by something not so well understood: *the digital revolution.*

A year ago, for example, Facebook reached 1.39 billion subscribers worldwide. In that moment, it became, in a sense, "bigger than China." One way of saying it is that Facebook is now "the biggest country in the world." The potential benefits for community and communication are huge – but try this: *imagine an Afghan farmer in 1843 feeling that his culture was threatened by the encroaching immorality of French can-can dancers.*

No problem, right? He obviously would have lived his life in blissful ignorance of them. Not today. *Today everyone's psychological and cultural space is shrinking, converging, and tightening, right along with the physical environment.*

Those who are committed to defending a dying world order are cornered and frightened, and Eris is calling them. It is a slow-motion train wreck and anyone who believes it will only bring out the best in people is being unrealistic.

But anyone who believes it will inevitably only bring out bestiality, violence, and destruction has also not paid any attention to history.

Fear-mongers, many of them astrologers, have predicted the end of the world almost annually since the beginning of recorded history. But humanity often rises to these kinds of challenges. Solar panels and the Toyota *Prius* are not going to save us – but they do symbolize a positive, creative response to the Eris's stimulus of free-for-all competition.

Did engineers at Toyota want to "kick the butts" of Ford's engineers or Honda's?

Probably! Can you doubt they talked that way?

And maybe that was not such a terrible thing.

I have a lot of faith in the human capacity to innovate, especially as Eris aligns with the planet of pure genius, Uranus. Good science, truly in the human interest, is almost inevitably going to be part of any attractive picture of the human future.

Underlying all of this is the root issue, the very essence of Eris: *the two faces of competition.* The bleak side of it brings us back to the ugly spectacle of Hera, Athena, and Aphrodite dancing naked in their fight over an apple.

- Simply said, there are things worth competing for and there are things that are not. Similarly, we can compete in creative ways or brutal ones.

Once we get the scent of blood in our noses, humans – and Greek goddesses – are not very good at discerning between the two paths. Would I fight to protect myself or those whom I love? Of course – and you probably would too. But would I poison the water in order to keep the price of gasoline down? Would I live in a big house if it meant that someone else had to live in a packing crate?

While we are at it, let's add some urgency to that last point – say that person living in the packing crate held two more playing cards: *hopelessness and a gun.*

There's the world that is dawning before us with the discovery of Eris. The alignment of Eris with Uranus has brought forth these choices in vivid, blood-red terms, spiced with an added dollop of pure Aries energy. We read about it in the news. We see it all, real or projected, in the politicians. Humanity can compete for the grand prize, which is human survival. Or we can slip into the dark, no-win Hollywood terrain of imagining victory as a sea of corpses around us – each corpse with a different skin color, religion, uniform or ethnicity.

The higher ground?

Innovation and *new thinking* are central. Let's honor and reward those who truly create. We need scientists and engineers – but let's not forget that we also need artists who can inspire us with a new vision for a new world. We need geniuses of all stripes now, and we need to recognize, honor and support them. We might call this idea of *rewarding the creators* a "conservative" Eris idea – that innovators should be rewarded with prosperity, while those who contribute less naturally receive less.

Before anyone hits the roof, let's balance that perspective with a "liberal" idea: let's dump the destructive notion that "you can have it all," at least speaking in material terms. If we are honest with ourselves, we realize that much of that "all" was only a golden apple anyway – one which never actually brought anyone much joy. Let's replace it with a little more emphasis on, "Live simply so that others may simply live." In the long run, there's more joy in community than there is in a private jet.

It will take decades for all this to be clear. The brighter Eris-vision is struggling to rise up out of the collective unconscious. Right now, the various pieces of the puzzle often appear to be opposites arguing with each other, often in bloody-minded fashion.

There is another huge part of all this that we must not forget: *there are children being born right now who carry this Eris-Uranus signature in their birthcharts.* They are part of the answer, for good or for ill. They are humanity's ace-in-the-hole.

And right now, they are just kids. It will be a while before we hear from them.

Meanwhile, for each of us individually, it is time to sort out how much we are willing to pay for the various "golden apples" in our lives. What we see "out there" in the world is simply the *out-picturing of the sum of our individual consciousnesses.* Maybe you can't personally stop a crazy person with a gun or a bomb – but I believe that as you temper the rage of your "inner bomber," the world as a whole moves an inch closer to serenity.

Even if I am wrong about that, I am surely right about this: *if you succeed in that inner purification, you yourself will have moved many miles in a better, happier direction.*

Do that, and you are not parading naked for golden apples anymore.

At the personal level, the current conjunction of Eris and Uranus comes down to these questions:

- Where have selfishness and rage taken a bite out of my heart?
- What price has my soul paid for material comfort, perceived beauty, or social advantage?
- Where have I squandered my genius on the pursuit of trifles?

Eris and Uranus are conjunct early in the third decanate of Aries. Where does that fall in your chart? In what house? What aspects does it make? There are some of your answers.

As we contemplate those lofty questions, let's not forget the other, edgier, side of the equation.

- Where do I actually need to claim victory, status, or territory?
- Where is that competitive behavior not only fair and legitimate, but also something that contributes to the greater good of us all?
- Where have I bowed down when I have a right to stand tall and insist on being heard?
- Where do I need, above all, simply to win a personal victory which also benefits my community as a whole?

Those latter questions are a philosophical and spiritual quagmire, but they will not go away. How do we avoid rationalizing? How do we sort out simple ego hunger from the higher ground? To do that, just remember the big hint: *the higher ground with Eris ultimately helps everyone.* For the answer, we go back to Hesiod, who saw the bright side of Eris so clearly when he wrote, "This strife is wholesome for men." He saw that it made for better potters and musicians. Healthy competition benefits the human community.

So here is how you sort it out: in putting yourself ahead, are you making the world a better place – or just parading naked in front of strangers for the sake of a golden apple? Do you want to win for the *right reasons* – or do you really just want to see someone else lose and suffer the pain of loss?

Honest answers to those questions can literally save the world. Dishonest ones can destroy it.

As it was written in the Upanishads many centuries ago, "Such verily is truth. Now do as you will."

47

Much media hoopla was generated by the spectacular solar eclipse of 2017 which swept across the United States. I was commissioned to write an article about it in advance for a glossy one-off newsstand publication in the New York City area. With their kind permission, I also published a somewhat more technical version of the same piece as one of my newsletters. That's what you will see here. In all honesty, I have a strange relationship with eclipses. Often they do not seem to affect me very much, while other times they have knocked me for a loop. I am not sure how to explain that discrepancy. Some of what I write here is connected to my own experience, but I've also distilled the perspectives of a few other astrologers whose work I respect and who seem to be more deeply and reliably affected by eclipses than I am.

THE BIG AUGUST ECLIPSE: WHAT DOES IT MEAN?

(Newsletter – August 2017)

A longer version of this article appears in Athlon Publication's "The Great American Eclipse," which is available at many newsstands, including Barnes & Nobel, Hudson News, etc. I am grateful to them and to my intrepid editor there, Brad Tolinski, for permission to publish this abridged and somewhat more technical version in our newsletter this month.

A miracle of nature looms on America's horizon. On August 21, starting in Oregon, racing in a grand arc across the United States, finally going offshore in South Carolina, a shadow of night will fall in the midst of the bright day. Along the centerline of the solar eclipse's path, stars will shine at lunchtime. Birds will go crazy. Some people probably will go crazy too. Eleven states will experience the eerie surreality of Totality, but no state in the contiguous 48 will escape the shadow of our first American total solar eclipse since February 26, 1979 – and that one just touched the Pacific Northwest and was mostly hidden behind their famously gray skies.

Meanwhile, long ago in a galaxy far, far away, Little Green People are drooling over UFO travel brochures, dreaming of visiting Earth on August 21. From their point of view, our giraffes and hummingbirds may be cool, but you can't beat Earth's most famous attraction: *a total solar eclipse*. It is just possible we are actually the only planet in the galaxy where this particular spectacle is available. Think about it – the Sun and the Moon, even though they look very different, are *almost exactly the same visual size*. That means that the Moon fits over the Sun almost perfectly. It's not so small that it's nothing at all – but also not so big that it blocks out the magnificent solar corona.

The odds against striking that happy balance are "astronomical." Hence those UFO travel brochures.

A dark shadow sweeps across America . . . who could read that line without feeling a little Neanderthal twinge of fear? What are the gods and goddesses telling us? On the face of it, "a dark shadow" doesn't sound like good news.

Enter the astronomers. Patiently they explain that the Moon is just a rock and the Sun is only a ball of gas. They both lie at safe distances, and anyway all this is predictable, so never listen to superstitious charlatans, a little shadow never hurt anyone . . .

I am sure you've heard it all before – and you will hear it repeated *ad nauseum* as the date of the eclipse approaches.

Being an astrologer, I am of course on the other side of the fence. It is not about fear, but while I love scientific astronomy, I also believe that events in the sky always *signify something*. My only personal fear as August 21 approaches is about the avalanche of nervous emails I am surely going to receive from my clients and readers.

People are often spooked by eclipses, and some astrologers are guilty of fanning those flames. It's instinctual: there's just something wrong about the Moon eating the Sun. The willies such an event generates are truly primal. "A shadow falls across the earth" is an edgy line whether we are sophisticated denizens of the Metropolis – or perhaps the indigenous 16th century Jamaicans hoodwinked by the late, great Christopher Columbus. When, in response to the rapacious misdeeds of his crew, the Natives stopped supplying them with food, Columbus took a look in his almanac and saw that an eclipse was due – in this case, it was a lunar eclipse. He summoned the Native leaders and threatened to "destroy the Moon" unless catering services were promptly renewed.

The Natives laughed – until the moon began to disappear. In the words of Columbus's son, Ferdinand, "with great howling and lamentation they came running from every direction to the ships, laden with provisions, praying the Admiral to intercede by all means with God on their behalf; that he might not visit his wrath upon them . . ."

Kindly, Christopher Columbus agreed to discuss their case with the Lord. Thus was the Moon – and prompt Jamaican food service – restored.

Like an erupting volcano or a tornado, like hurricane winds or a waterfall after torrential rains, there is something simply awesome about an eclipse. Even kings and emperors have feared them and have felt dwarfed and threatened by them. Way, way back on October 22, 2137 B.C., the two royal Chinese astrologer-astronomers, Hsi and Ho, were allegedly drinking booze when they should have been observing. They failed to predict a coming eclipse. When it occurred without them warning him, the Emperor, Chun King, was not happy. His decree: off with their heads.

Since then, I have never accepted a single Chinese Emperor as a client.

To astronomers, the sky is merely an objective fact. To astrologers, it is *poetry*. Any argument between them is as silly as debating the relative merits of physics and English.

So what is the *poetry* of a total solar eclipse? And what specific meaning might we find in the sky-show of August 21?

Start by realizing that we come very close to a solar eclipse every month. That event is simply the New Moon – which of course means no Moon at all. At that time of the month, the Moon is aligned between the

Earth and the Sun so the brightly lit side of the Moon is aimed away from us. *We can't see it,* in other words. The only astronomical difference between a New Moon and a total solar eclipse is that in the former, the Moon is a little above or below the Sun, so it doesn't cover the Sun's face. Close, but no banana, so to speak.

For those of you with a more technical interest in astrology, let me express this a little more deeply. Eclipses, both solar and lunar ones, only occur when the Sun, Moon, *and the axis of the lunar nodes* are aligned. The nodes represent where the plane of the Moon's orbit crosses the ecliptic. The Sun is always on the ecliptic, by definition. Thus, when the Sun, the Moon and the lunar nodes are all conjunct, the Sun and the Moon are aligned *center-to-center* and so we get an eclipse instead of just the normal monthly New Moon.

If you want to dive more deeply into the astronomy behind all this, have a look at chapter three of *The Book of the Moon.*

Out of the New Moon emerges the Crescent, the Quarter, the Full Moon, and eventually it all wanes back down to another New Moon. *So a New Moon is both an ending and a new beginning.* A total solar eclipse is simply an intensified, special-case version of exactly the same thing. In essence, it is a New Moon on steroids: an *epochal* new start – and of course any such start must be preceded by some dramatic ending. Space must be made for the new beginning.

Now, to be true to the sky-poetry of an eclipse, add that little tingle of fear everyone feels in his or her bones as the Sun disappears – or at the very least a dose of humbling, knee-knocking awe. Death is scary, *and something must die for something to be born.* A good thing or a bad thing? That depends on whether you are the baby bunny rabbit or the pregnant coyote.

An example: Julius Caesar crossed the Rubicon on March 7, 51 B.C.– the day of a solar eclipse. Thus died the Roman Republic to make way for the Roman Empire. Momentous events – such as Caesar crossing the Rubicon – often occur right around eclipses, although their effects can sometimes be triggered even months later as planets contact the place where the eclipse occurred – a fact that quickly gets into deeper technical astrological territory. Bottom line, the degree of the solar eclipse seems to remain "charged" for a while, waiting for transiting planets to form aspects to it.

We will point to some post-eclipse dates connected with the August 21st event in a little while.

Here's the easy part – there is a big difference between the "poetry" of the days leading up to an eclipse and the days immediately afterwards. Right before an eclipse, something is dying – the visibility of the Moon itself. *Events rooted in those two weeks or so often go awry.* Intentions are thwarted. Things "beyond our control" change the landscape.

Keep that in mind as you make any personal plans – or as you watch any news that might be unfolding – during the "fortnight" before August 21st.

Prince Charles and Camilla Parker Bowles, for one example, had long planned to marry on Friday, April 8, 2005, which happened to be the day of an eclipse. Pope John Paul II died on April 2 that year. The result was that their wedding had to be postponed for 24 hours so Charles could attend the funeral. Not such a big deal – but try this one: I know a man who moved with his wife to their dream house in a different state at the end of July 2008. There was a solar eclipse on August 1, so their move had happened squarely in that "dying" period that clears the way for new starts. Within a couple of years, they had divorced and the wife was married to the gentleman who had actually built the house.

It will be intriguing to watch the daily headlines through this crystal ball – both the newspaper headlines and your personal ones – from about August 7 onward to the date of the eclipse. Wheels that start turning during that time are dying wheels. From the actual eclipse-day – August 21 – onward to about the end of the month, the energy is different. It has more momentum and staying power, for good or for ill.

Sabre-tooth tigers must have been magnificent beasts, but when I go hiking I take some comfort in their extinction. Without endings, there could be no beginnings. When you are touched personally by an eclipse, that is essentially your situation. In your life, something must die so that something new can be born. One really helpful psychological trick is to *take it on faith that something is being born even though you can't yet see it.* Recognize that whatever is dying needs to get out of the way. You can take comfort in that perspective now – or you can take comfort in it later.

I said "when you are touched personally by an eclipse." Eclipses do not affect everyone equally. You might possibly be immune to this one. Your astrological radio has to be tuned to the station where the broadcast is happening – which in this case is near the end of the sign Leo. What if you are not a Leo? Are you then unaffected by this eclipse? Again this quickly gets into technical territory. Does the eclipse occur, for example, on the place the planet Venus occupied when you were born? Then something must die in an important relationship – that is Venus territory. Does it happen near the sign and degree that was on the Midheaven when you were born? That suggests a career focus. Maybe you lose your job – and maybe you find a better one.

Any competent astrologer can help you sort all that out. Here, in the one-size-fits-all context of an article, all I can offer is that if your birthday falls within a week or so of any of these four dates, the August 21 eclipse has your name on it: February 17, May 19, August 21 itself, and November 20. That means it is connected with your Sun via a hard aspect – and the Sun is the center of everything, both astrologically and astronomically.

The central shadow-path of this eclipse slices across America. It first touches U.S. soil at Government Point, Oregon, at 10:16 a.m., local time, then it crosses Idaho, Wyoming, Nebraska, Kansas, Missouri, Illinois, Kentucky and Tennessee. It clips the northeastern corner of Georgia, then sweeps across South Carolina before heading out to sea. Those are the states where actual Totality is visible. Weather permitting, the rest of the continental USA will at least see a partial eclipse. The event has America's name on it, in other words. Furthermore it occurs opposite the "revolutionary" Aquarian moon in the most commonly-accepted birthchart for the United States – the "Sibly chart," which is the one that most accurately reflected the timing of the attacks of September 11. (If you are interested in learning more about that chart, go to my website and search for "The USA Chart.")

So what does this summer's eclipse portend for America? Astrologers are expected to make predictions. It is the bane of our profession, in my opinion. I feel we can predict questions and perhaps make some educated guesses about what answers might arise. But we must never under-estimate life's wild cards, nor life-shaping power of consciousness and wisdom – wise choices, in other words. They can shape the human future. We can all prove gloomy astrologers wrong. And if the people lead, maybe those gloomy astrologers will follow!

With that in mind, let me dive into the soup. Leo is the Lion, the "King of the Beasts." This eclipse involves the archetype of kingship – leadership, in other words. It is triggering that Aquarian Moon in the USA chart, the sign of revolution, genius, and either breakthrough or breakdown. Since we are talking about an eclipse, we know that something must die to make way for a different future. During the second half of August, we are likely to see dramatic events connected with the fusion of these symbols. Might this involve the deaths or "falls" of "stars" in the fields of film, sports, or music? Those are all Leo figures, for sure. And of course, very directly, Leo represents those "kings" that rule us – political leaders and captains of industry and finance. (Remember that not everything would happen right on August 21. The rest of the month is active too.)

Some events rooted in the eclipse will be further triggered by the arrival of Mars on the eclipse-point around September 2, the arrival of Venus there on September 18, and the square aspect of Mars to that point on January 23, 2018.)

Obviously America is currently torn by passions and division at the "Leo" leadership level. I suspect those tensions will reach some kind of major breaking point around this eclipse. Underscoring it all, Donald Trump's Ascendant is right at the end of Leo, almost exactly where this eclipse takes place. His "radio" is definitely tuned to this station. Does Trump get impeached, as many predict? Or simply consolidate his power? Does he stage a coup, as many fear? Does the military step in? Martial law? Massive civil unrest? Assassinations? Do we see the end of the American Republic and the beginning of the American Empire, just as happened when Caesar crossed the Rubicon? Or does Democracy, which has grown so lazy and divided, find renewed life?

And maybe none of that will happen. The August 21 eclipse is just a dance between a big ball of gas and a big rock up in the sky. And that sky is a mirror. It reflects us all down here below.

But what exactly does it reflect? Not our answers, but our questions.

Something has reached a breaking point in our country. Something needs to die so that something new can be born. And the impatient sky is pressing us to choose what to do about it. We are about to reach a crossroads. The choices – but not the timing of those choices – are in our hands.

48

*Some planetary combinations seem totally straightforward –
communicative Mercury entering chatty Gemini, for example. But
then there are ones that feel less natural, such a happy-go-lucky Jupiter
entering serious-as-a-heart-attack Scorpio. To interpret those latter
kinds of configurations, we need to hone our sensitivity to paradox,
irony, and ambiguity, both as astrologers and perhaps even more
so just as human beings swimming in the symbolic stew, trying to
remember which direction we are going.*

JUPITER ENTERS SCORPIO

(Newsletter – October 2017)

When Jupiter, the reigning heavyweight champion of the solar system, enters a new sign, we all need to stand back – the "gravity" of the symbolism is going to pull a lot of events into its synchronistic orbit. Jupiter crossing such a line is the main event this month, as it enters Scorpio. Since Jupiter takes about twelve years to orbit the Sun, it changes signs every year or so. It entered Libra on September 9, 2016. The passage into Scorpio occurs on October 10. After that, it remains in Scorpio until it crosses the Sagittarian frontier on November 8, 2018.

Jupiter's principle effect is to *expand anything it touches*. It symbolizes *abundance* – hence, its historical reputation as the "Greater Benefic." But before we leap into paroxysms of ecstasy here, let's reflect on exactly what Lord

Jupiter is going to be expanding. The answer lies in the symbolism of Scorpio, and as in all things astrological, there's both good news and bad news there. Better said, there are ways to get it right and ways to get it wrong.

Scorpio embraces all of the "strong energies" in the human psyche – *instincts, mammal reflexes, appetites, rage, fear*, along with the *wounded places* in us all. It represents, among other strong psychic forces, our *sexuality*. And sex is as good a place as any to start our thinking about this transit.

Imagine a year in which human sexual drive is boosted, say "by 5%," across the board in everyone ... and then think deeply about that idea for a moment. For people in loving relationships, that "5% increase in sex drive" is nothing but merry news. But what if you are in no relationship at all? Then how do you feel about it? And going darker, what about the world's rapists, molesters, and exploitative pornographers? Or people sitting on that borderline?

Their sexual drives will be boosted too.

You begin to get the picture: Jupiter entering Scorpio is a complex event, with potentially high, positive meanings, along with darker ones. And it's not just about sex either – that's just a good place to start because sex is emblematic of the rest of these strong, instinctual Scorpionic forces. Everything in the human unconscious is lit up, in other words. As individuals, we will respond to this stimulus well or poorly. Meanwhile, collectively on the stage of history, we will probably see the expression of the full spectrum of possibilities from dark to light.

- In all cases, the *presence of unconscious material* (Scorpio) will be *vividly, even spectacularly, demonstrated* (Jupiter).

Always, in any kind of Scorpionic time, the bottom line is that *elements of the unconscious mind are becoming conscious*. Spontaneously, humanity generates powerful *collective symbolism* that potentially guides us like a lighthouse into deeper understanding of ourselves. Everything that is taboo is brought to the surface. Individuals do the same thing on a smaller scale. Metaphors of mystery – and of *mysteries unveiled* – abound.

Here's one of my favorite concrete examples – the space probe that let humanity *first see the dark side of the Moon* was launched with Jupiter in Scorpio. What magnificent symbolism that is!

Here's another: *Moby-Dick* was first published – and just take a moment to reflect psychologically on Captain Ahab's obsessive hunt for the "white whale" deep down in the waters of the unconscious mind.

The first Sherlock Holmes tale, *A Study in Scarlet,* appeared in print with Jupiter in Scorpio – and if Sherlock is not a Scorpionic figure, my nephew must be a monkey.

The list goes on ... the U.S. Central Intelligence Agency. was founded. Spies!

At the individual level, we need to *ask ourselves hard questions* – that's the Scorpio process – about *what we really want and what is truly good for us.* There's Jupiter. And then, armed with that hard-won self-knowledge, we need to boldly and audaciously make our moves – that's Jupiter again. Jupiter-fashion, you *need a victory* – but you had first better make sure you "know what's good for you." *Thus, Scorpionic inner work sets the intentions, while King Jupiter leads the charge.*

That's the road to the higher ground.

The lower ground? When Jupiter-in-Scorpio operates unconsciously, the dark and tangled complexes that animate human madness find extravagant outward expression, both individually and collectively. We see our fears crystalized and expressed on the stage of history or the stages of our individual lives. Nightmarish massacres such as the Rwandan genocide of 1994 occur with Jupiter in Scorpio, as did the first execution by lethal injection.

Here's another historical piece of the Jupiter-in-Scorpio puzzle that doesn't fit as neatly into "getting it right or getting it wrong." *Deaths occur that take on broad, eerie symbolism in the collective pages of social history –* think about the passing of Jimi Hendrix, Janis Joplin, and Jim Morrison in 1970 and 1971, or of Kurt Cobain in 1994. Or remember the Kent State massacre. Or the beginning of the murder spree of that iconic dark-Scorpio figure, Jack the Ripper.

All of those *mythic deaths* occurred with Jupiter in the sign of the Scorpion.

In every one of these instances, the collective unconscious spilled out extravagantly into the world of physical manifestation.

What will Jupiter in Scorpio mean for you personally? Well, we know you are soon scheduled to "have a long talk with yourself" about what you really need and what you really, truly feel – that's Scorpio. If you are brave and real enough to get that talk right, the Laws of Synchronicity guarantee that you will have the opportunity to *act on those desires*, plus an excellent shot at realizing many of them.

Technically, the key question is, where does Jupiter-in-Scorpio fall in your own birthchart? What aspects does it make during the year-long transit? Critically, is Jupiter in the 3rd House or the 8th or which of them among the other ten? Most likely the transit will impact *two* of your natal houses and so there will be two phases to this powerful transit for you. Because of retrograde motion, Jupiter might toggle back and forth over a house cusp, spending, for example, several weeks in your 7th house, then entering the 8th for a while, only to return to the 7th, before re-crossing back into the 8th.

I'm fastening my own seatbelts here. As soon as Jupiter crosses the Scorpio frontier, it enters my 12th house and crosses my south lunar node. As synchronicity would have it, that coincides with my heading for Yunnan Province in China to teach – appropriately enough, that is a place where I've always intuitively felt that I had some *Buddhist* (12th house) *karma* (south node). Jupiter hitting that part of my chart suggests whatever karma I have there has ripened – it's time for me to have a look at it.

Then, through much of 2018, Jupiter will be crisscrossing over my Ascendant – so my prayer is that some wisdom arises for me in the 12th house chapters of the transit – wisdom that allows me to take truly helpful and discriminating advantage of whatever outward opportunities arise as Jupiter interacts with my Ascendant.

That's just me – but it illustrates the kind of two-house thinking I mentioned a moment ago.

Bottom line: first be real with yourself, then ask for what you *really* want.

49

Lucky Jupiter! Sometimes I've had to struggle to come up with a fresh newsletter topic that would be meaningful to my readers. Jupiter to the rescue! Every year it enters a new sign and provides me with something fun and meaningful about which to write. Even better, it comes around again every twelve years, and so no one has to wait for Tectonic Plates to move before the essay is again relevant.

JUPITER ENTERING SAGITTARIUS

(Newsletter – December 2018)

Jupiter is in Sagittarius now and it will stay there until December 2, 2019. Since Jupiter "rules" that sign – *and also famously has dominion over Lady Luck* – there's a pervasive tendency among astrologers to view this transit as an innately wondrous thing, as if all of us can expect an avalanche of winning lottery numbers, true love, and attractive weight loss.

Fear not: we are not going to say the opposite! But this big Jupiter event does offer us a chance to think some deeper thoughts about what it means for any planet, and Jupiter in particular, to be "in its own sign."

- Here's the simplest way to say it: when a planet passes through a sign that it rules, it does not become "better;" it just becomes *stronger.* The good or bad of it depends, as ever, on how you *use* that energy rather than on the configuration itself.

In any rulership situation, it is as if you are cutting a piece of wood with a hand saw. When you are cutting across the grain, it's hard work. When you are cutting along the natural lines of the grain, it's much easier. The lay of the grain and the direction of your efforts are in alignment. When a planet is in its own sign, it's very much like "cutting with the grain." You get more bang for the buck, in other words. Your efforts go further.

With Jupiter in Sagittarius, for example, *Jupiter's expansiveness agrees with the damn-the-torpedoes enthusiasm that characterizes Sagittarius.* Jupiter says, "I feel lucky." Sagittarius replies, "Me too."

So what happens? Maybe you make a bold move that pays off in a big way.

Or maybe you do something really, really dumb.

With Jupiter smack in the middle of Sagittarius, the "unsinkable" HMS *Titanic* hit an iceberg and sunk. A lucky day? Not for people who drowned, obviously – although no doubt someone else somewhere on the earth won a lottery around the same time.

Still, sailing "full speed ahead" in darkness in an untested ship into an area where icebergs had already been reported might fairly be construed as an excessive dose of "feeling lucky."

That's the dark side of Jupiter in Sagittarius.

On the other hand, the uber-successful, iconic TV series, *M*A*S*H*, began its long run on CBS with Jupiter in Sagittarius. That happened on September 17, 1972, just a few days before the planet crossed over into Capricorn. That project worked out splendidly for all concerned. The cast and the production team *believed in themselves* and bet accordingly.

Lord Jupiter loves that kind of pluck. As they say in basketball, "You miss 100% of the shots you don't take." The *M*A*S*H* people took the shot, and it paid off. But the captain of the *Titanic* took a shot too – he thought he could really impress everyone with a record-breaking fast passage to New York City.

During this coming year, you should take your best shot too. But what shot? More about that in a minute . . .

Every planet, every sign, every house – every syllable in the vocabulary of astrology – is simply a form of energy. Each one has a higher purpose and darker side. When a planet is in its own sign, both possible sides of the coin are simply *magnified*.

- Confidence, faith in one's self, and faith in life – these are beautiful "Jovian" qualities. Without them life is petty and drab. Think about it: *how much faith does it take to look for a new job, to move to a new city, to get married?* That's Jupiter!

- It would also require enormous faith to believe that you could be the first person to swim naked across the Pacific Ocean. But that might not actually be such a good idea. That's Jupiter too.

As is so often the case in life, the critical ingredient with Jupiter in Sagittarius is simply having some brains in your head – although a better word would be wisdom. *Knowing what is truly good for you* – that phrase really captures it all, at least once we open it up and really reflect on it. The problem is that people always seem to automatically believe that they "know what's good for them." Who, for example, would object to hitting the winning combination of Powerball numbers? Anyone eager to turn down an unexpected $350 million?

And yet, with your wisdom running at full power, *are you absolutely certain that that kind of money would actually make you happier?*

OK, I'll admit it – I'm practically certain that I *personally* could handle $350 million just fine.

And I bet you are too.

And that is exactly the part of yourself of which you must be wary as you navigate these exaggerated Jupiter energies over the coming year. Seductive "all that glitters is not gold" risks – along with genuine golden opportunities – characterize our collective karma until next December.

Not to be too black and white about it, but there is a good chance that in some areas of life – areas specifically spotlighted by transiting Jupiter's position in your chart – *you will get what you want.* So make sure that your wanting is wise.

For everyone, Jupiter-in-Sagittarius is a double-edged sword: don't be afraid to make your move, being careful that you do not settle for too little – while simultaneously being wary of hubris, gross over-extension, and your inflated ego grabbing the steering wheel. It's a question of balance. It's a question of listening humbly to the voice of your own soul – a question of *inviting your soul to be the counselor to your ego's appetites.*

If you can do that, then get ready for the kind of "luck" that will still feel like luck twenty years down the road.

Much of the art of getting this right comes down to knowing exactly where this Jupiter transit falls in your birthchart. It is in that spotlighted area reflected in terms of its house position and aspects, that the true nature of "wise wanting" for you is illuminated. It is in that part of your life that you need to be audacious, to make your move, to ask for what you want. It is there that you have probably been settling for too little, underestimating yourself. It is there that you are ready to move to a new level of self-actualization and empowerment.

It is there, in other words, that you truly need – and deserve – a victory.

Just to get you started, let's take a quick stroll through the twelve astrological houses and try to define the area of life in which it is high time for you to "feel lucky," and to just roll the dice.

(Note that unless the sign Sagittarius is entirely intercepted – that is, completely contained within a single house – you will very likely experience this Jupiter transit in two phases as it transitions from one house to the next. Further complicating everything, it may enter the subsequent house, then retrograde back into the previous one for a while before moving on.)

- With Jupiter in Sagittarius transiting through your *first* house, put some shine on your appearance, try to look like you believe in yourself – and act like it too by initiating some bold, ambitious campaign to improve your position in life. The Force is with you!

- With Jupiter in Sagittarius transiting through your *second* house, we smell money. Ask for it. Look for it. But this transit goes further than your bank account. Beyond money, it is time to look at the entire *resource base* that supports your dreams. To go further in life, what talents or skills do you need to acquire? What new tools? What alliances? If you look for them, you will find them.

- With Jupiter in Sagittarius transiting through your *third* house, speak up. You have something important to say. Don't be shy. Don't let yourself be intimidated by anyone's PhD or air of superiority. Express yourself with panache and verve, and your voice will be heard.

- With Jupiter in Sagittarius transiting through your *fourth* house, look to your roots and to your nest. Maybe your home needs an upgrade. Maybe your family – and that might mean your actual family or your soul-family – are an untapped source of joy, faith, and happiness for you. You need some quiet time, alone or with them, or both. Claim it.
- With Jupiter in Sagittarius transiting through your *fifth* house, you need a dose of playfulness, joy and celebration. Buy yourself some toys. Take a vacation. You need a more visceral reason to be genuinely happy that you are alive. Look for it – the gift is right there before your eyes. Don't let those old devils – duties and "maturity" – trick you into missing it.
- With Jupiter in Sagittarius transiting through your *sixth* house, cast a suspicious eye in the direction of your immediate "work-and-responsibilities" environment. How can you make it more pleasant? What new devices or creature comforts might materially lighten your burdens? Do you need assistance? Ask yourself why things are more difficult there than they need to be, then boldly seize the solutions no matter the cost.
- With Jupiter in Sagittarius transiting through your *seventh* house, reach out to the people you love and ask them for what you need. In all your relationships, the situation can be improved – and that does not mean that the current situation is "bad," only that it is ripe for a breakthrough and a step forward. All you have to do is to be bold enough to light the fuse on the negotiations.
- With Jupiter in Sagittarius transiting through your *eighth* house, don't be prim about expressing your sexual needs, desires, or appetites. Regardless of your age, this is also an auspicious time for you to do some spiritual and practical preparation for the end of your life. Don't get us wrong – there is nothing morbid about this transit. It does not mean that "you will die;" only that the angels of luck and opportunity are here now to support you in your conscious embracing of one of life's primary realities: *that it ends*. Much wisdom flows from that single, inescapable reflection. Write or review your will.
- With Jupiter in Sagittarius transiting through your *ninth* house, dust off your passport or your backpack. It's time to hit the road, time to see someplace you have never seen before. The opportunity – and

the need – to blow out some cobwebs is upon you. You may be busy, but behind the screaming buzz of life, the fact is that you are bored with your predictable routines. And you don't need to be! There's a treasure waiting for you beyond the far horizon. Go seek it.

- With Jupiter in Sagittarius transiting through your *tenth* house, you are ready to graduate to a new level in terms of your place in the community. Step up to the stage and occupy it. You are ready, and they need you. It is always helpful with the tenth house not to limit our attention to "career" in the narrow sense – although, by all means, this is a splendid time to ask for a raise or a promotion at work. It's bigger than that, though. There is great satisfaction in *offering a gift to your community*, even if no paycheck is involved. The critical element here is that the community, whether it knows it or not, is eagerly awaiting you.

- With Jupiter in Sagittarius transiting through your *eleventh* house, raise the level of your long-term plans and your strategies for fulfilling them to reflect the fact that you are better, stronger, and wiser now than you were a year or two ago. *You have outgrown your old priorities.* You are capable of more, and your old dreams no longer mirror the true reality of your capabilities. Once you've got your new aims defined, seek alliances that improve your strategic position. Good people are going the same direction as you are. Look for them; they are there. You can help each other.

- With Jupiter in Sagittarius transiting through your *twelfth* house, the "wisest wanting" you can possibly have now is for some quiet, reflective time. You have come to the end of a major cycle of experience. What's next? The beginning of wisdom lies in realizing that you have no idea! Angels are trying to whisper in your ears. They have some precious advice for you. The thing is, to hear angels whisper, you have to become very, very quiet.

50

The Covid-19 pandemic struck the world and suddenly everything was different. As is so often the case, the whole mess makes perfect sense astrologically — retrospectively. Inevitably, the question arises, "If you astrologers are so good, why couldn't you have seen Covid coming?" Sadly, some astrologers actually buy into that disheartening perspective, putting themselves in an impossible situation. I've said it before and I say it again here: astrology is not a reliable tool for prediction — it is a tool for understanding. Its greatest strengths lie in the present tense. Astrology helps us to grasp the meaning of today, not the nature of tomorrow's events.

PLUTO, ERIS, AND THE EVOLUTIONARY MEANING OF COVID-19

(Newsletter – April 2020)

As I write these words, I am in voluntary self-quarantine. I suspect that many of you are too. It's the right thing to do. A few of you have contacted me, wondering about the astrology behind the pandemic, how long it will last, and how bad it might get. I don't know the answers to the two latter questions, but let's peer into the crystalline mirror of the heavens and see what we can learn about the first question: why is Covid-19 is upon us right now? I do think that we can at least get some sense of its purpose.

Many astrologers have been pointing an accusing finger at the current planetary traffic jam in Capricorn, with the Saturn-Pluto conjunction as the main culprit, and Mars currently helping it along. Neptune in Pisces has a correlation with contagion too, as my colleague Maurice Fernandez has often accurately emphasized.

All that is solid astrology, but it leaves out an important piece of the puzzle – one whose significance has been banging us over the head since 2005, but which astrologers still tend to ignore. That is the planet *Eris*, which is currently squaring the Pluto-Saturn conjunction, and doing so from the edgy sign Aries. That is what I want to explore with you in this newsletter. I believe that with Covid-19, the Eris-Pluto square is actually the heart of the matter.

Many of you are probably only dimly aware of the planet Eris. It still has not gotten the press it deserves in the astrological community. Let me be the first to admit that I have not integrated it properly into my own teaching and counseling myself yet. For one thing, I am still learning about it, and I never want to turn my clients into guinea pigs for my speculative theories – that would be an ethical blunder, obviously. But the more I learn about Eris, the more I am convinced that we need to take it as seriously as we take Pluto, which resembles it in many ways.

Let me prove that to you. I believe we can clearly see Eris's unmistakable fingerprints in the current Covid-19 situation.

In a moment, I'll offer a quick introduction to this new planet just to bring us all up to speed, but first, let me throw some dates at you: Eris and Pluto form five squares before Pluto moves on toward the waning degrees of Capricorn and into Aquarius. This year, the dates of the Pluto-Eris squares are January 26, June 14, and December 10. The dates in 2021 are August 27 and October 9.

Since both of these planets move very slowly, all five of these conjunctions occur within a space of about one degree, between 23° 14' and 24° 18' of Aries and Capricorn. If you've got planets there, hold onto your hat.

Eris moves very slowly. It has been in Aries since 1925. It will not touch the Taurus cusp until June 2044. Eris is not only really slow, it is also at the slowest part of its orbit, close to aphelion. (We have a rare opportunity here to think of Pluto as fast-moving.) Eris is slightly smaller, but slightly more massive, than Pluto. It is also much further out in space. It takes 559 years to orbit the Sun a single time, compared to Pluto's 248 years.

Astronomers currently classify Eris as a "dwarf planet," just as they do Pluto – and since few working astrologers would dare to "dwarf" the significance of Pluto, it makes sense that we should show similar respect for Eris.

In September 2016, I wrote a lengthy newsletter about Eris. (It appears earlier in this volume as well as Chapter Forty-Six.) Because I want to move quickly toward a look at the current Covid-19 situation, I will just say a few brief introductory words about this newly-discovered planet in order to get us going, then cut to the current Covid-19 chase.

In Greek mythology, Eris is a hard goddess indeed. Let's start with the fact that she is the sister of Mars. She delights in "the groans of men dying in battle." She "goes among them, increasing their pain." The Romans called her *Discordia* – a name that works even better than Eris. She sows discord wherever she goes. For one example, she singlehandedly fomented the Trojan War and sat back laughing. Again, if you are interested, you can read all about it in Chapter Forty-Six.

The single most reliable principle I have ever found in astrology is that *every front has a back* – in other words, every symbol has a higher purpose as well as a dark side. *Vicious competitiveness* is the dark side of Eris. She likes to win, but not as much as she likes to see you lose.

Her bright side lies in the way competition can bring out a person's *excellence*. Writing of Eris, the Greek poet, Hesiod, points out that much effort and creativity is triggered when "potter is angry with potter, and craftsman with craftsman and beggar is jealous of beggar, and minstrel of minstrel." As a result of their competitiveness, they might all simply make an effort to improve.

That rivalry may not be pretty, *but we all get better pots and better music.*

Pluto is undoubtedly more familiar to you than Eris. Working at its best, the "Lord of the Underworld" helps to bring unconscious material to the surface. Pluto is the part of us that can squarely face difficult truths. But when we instead make a weak response to Pluto, those difficult truths *manifest in our lives* instead of showing up in our heads and hearts in the form of *liberating insights.* At such times, the Shadow grabs the steering wheel. We get hurt and we often hurt other people too.

The square joining Pluto and Eris is an aspect of *friction.* That is not always a bad thing – friction can be creative, and it is often highly motivating. But with any square, we can also potentially see two planets bringing out the worst in each other. And, given the edgy natures of both Pluto and Eris, that worst case scenario is a scary prospect. I want to look the devil straight in the eye here – but I promise that before we are done, we will consult a few angels as well. Nothing in astrology happens without a higher purpose. That is true of this Pluto-Eris square. It is also true of the Covid-19 crisis which I believe this square has brought us.

To understand all of this, we have to go further. We have to reflect on the *signs* that Eris and Pluto currently occupy. Without signs, planets tend to be too abstract to make much sense in human terms.

- Aries – where Eris lies – is a *self-oriented* sign. It is about our right to behave independently, to set boundaries and to defend them. It is characterized by an attachment to a *high degree of autonomy.* (One can also see that quality very clearly in the natural resonance between Aries, the first sign of the zodiac, and the first house.)

Let all those statements about Aries enjoy some ambiguity. Let them be both potentially good and potentially bad. *In a nutshell, we would all be in trouble if we were never capable of being selfish – but a little of it goes a long way.*

- Capricorn – where Pluto lies – has a natural resonance with the tenth house, and thus it correlates with our *responsibilities* to the big world: society, government, the spirit of the times, styles and fashions, public institutions, along with the weight of customs and tradition.

With Pluto there, that big Capricorn world has been looking quite Plutonian, at least in the darker sense, since 2008 when Pluto entered that sign. We have seen so much pain, division, anger, and trouble everywhere. Capricorn respects tradition; it is thus naturally related to *conservatism* in the broad sense of the word. Pluto brings out the shadow-side of whatever sign it is in. *Who can doubt that we have been witnessing the shadow dimensions of conservatism all around the world for the past dozen years?* It's been a great time to be a tyrant – and not such a great time to be vulnerable or otherwise disadvantaged.

All of that is intensified now. Who can doubt – with not only Pluto, but also Saturn, Mars, and Jupiter in Capricorn – that the "big world" is looking *particularly* scary at the moment? That is not just because of the Covid-19 virus, but the virus nicely encapsulates the point.

In the light of what we all know of Capricorn as a *wintry, solitary, disciplined* archetype, to grasp this encapsulation, we only need to tick off the checklist of the obvious current *specifically Capricornian synchronicities* which have been generated by the pandemic:

- We are exhorted to *isolate ourselves* and to *avoid touch.*
- We must *give up social pleasures,* such as eating in restaurants or getting together with friends. No concerts, no sporting events.
- *Austerity* reigns. Blessed are those with toilet paper – a situation that was literally unimaginable just a few weeks ago.
- If we have any money, it is rapidly disappearing. Many people are facing the prospect of actually starving or of being cast out from their homes. And may God have mercy on those who are "vulnerable or otherwise disadvantaged."

Meanwhile, all of that Pluto-in-Capricorn pressure is grinding away on Eris through that hard square aspect – and let's not forget that Eris lies in Aries, which in its darker potentials is the *angriest,* most *violent,* and most *selfish* sign of the zodiac.

Here are some good rules of thumb: *don't annoy Eris. Don't try to tell her what she can do and cannot do. Don't force rules upon her.*

And of course that is obviously exactly what Pluto is doing – and doing it in ways that reflect a slippery mixture of justice and corruption.

How does Eris feel about that? And how is Eris going to react?

As we have seen, Pluto always brings out truth one way or another – either in the form of liberating realizations or in the form of people "acting out" their wounds. As one illustration of what I mean by "acting out our wounds," in a Plutonian time, *the kid who was once physically abused finds himself hitting his own child.* It does not have to be that way, but it often is –.statistically, being hit while you were growing up often correlates with hitting your own kids later on. Plutonian insights abound in that single human observation.

What about the higher Plutonian ground? That same grown-up child, for one example, enters therapy under a Plutonian stimulus and deals effectively with his hurt and his anger.

Let me add an even edgier perspective – one that we must grasp if we are to understand how Pluto works as a healing force in the mucky realities of life as we actually experience it: perhaps that grown-up child does actually hit his kid – *and is so shocked and humiliated by his own behavior that he then seeks psychotherapy.*

Sometimes, in other words, "acting out" is the trigger for the eventual healing. It ain't pretty, but it sometimes works. Sometimes we need to learn things the hard way. I get the feeling that there is a lot of that going on right now.

Let's get to the point in terms of how this Pluto-Eris square relates directly to the pandemic. To do that, we will contemplate one sadly familiar – and profoundly emblematic – scene from the current state of the world: *someone has selfishly snapped up every bottle of hand sanitizer in the drugstore.* Why would she behave so insensitively? She is obviously reacting to her fear of being infected with the virus. In broader terms, she fears everything symbolized by Pluto in Capricorn – *she feels like the big world is attacking her personally and that her only defense is to let Dark Eris overshadow her.* She behaves selfishly, hoarding the hand sanitizer, not caring that if as a direct result of her actions, others have no hand sanitizer at all.

She does that because she is *frightened,* not because she is inherently mean.

The effect of her selfishness is that her behavior has actually spread the virus by preventing other people from caring for themselves.

In her fear of the dangers of the world – in her fearful selfishness – she has actually made her world a more dangerous place, not a safer one. She is now more likely, not less likely, to become infected with Covid-19. This is a clear example of Pluto and Eris interacting in a way that brings out the worst qualities in each of them.

One bottom line is that, as all the wiser pundits and medical people are saying, we are all in this together. *Our only defense against Covid-19 is to come together as a community.* Only in caring for each other can we effectively care for ourselves. That is not philosophy; that is medical science, not to mention a pretty deep well of spirituality.

- The meaning of the Pluto-Eris square of 2020 and 2021? *Our collective addiction to our separation from each other has reached critical mass.* It is catching up with us.

Humanity has manifested this disease as a mirror of that spiritual crisis. It is pure synchronicity, brilliantly mirrored in the Pluto-Eris square.

Nothing happens in astrology unless it needs to happen. Another way of saying the same thing is that everything that happens in the sky reflects an *evolutionary necessity.* Nothing astrological should ever be considered as simply bad luck – or good luck, for that matter. They always have a purpose. Collectively, we need this virus. Paradoxically, it might turn out to be very good for us.

As Hesiod told us millennia ago, competition makes better potters and musicians. Whoever creates an effective vaccine or medicine for Covid-19 will undoubtedly become fabulously wealthy. Perhaps we shouldn't begrudge that prosperity to anyone. Again, in the words of Hesiod, "This strife is wholesome for men." So let the race for that fortune begin. I am sure it already has. Selfishness and competition can be harnessed for the collective good. We should never forget that face of Eris, along with the scary one. That is partly because it is simply true – but more deeply, if we make Eris "bad," we've slipped into a catastrophic astrological error: we've stripped a symbol of its higher purpose, leaving it with only a negative interpretation.

That "conservative" point about someone getting rich by coming up with an effective medication is worth making, but there are deeper waters here.

Communities that pull together, communities in which people *effectively care for each other* by staying away from each other, washing their hands, voluntarily self-isolating if they have symptoms or think that might have, getting vaccinated if a vaccine is actually invented – those communities are going to survive and thrive.

Meanwhile, communities dominated by Plutonian denial, along with the Eris "combo platter" of selfishness, fear, and anger, will suffer disproportionately.

Nations that help to support people in those good behaviors, making those behaviors as easy as they can possibly be made, will get through this mess with a far lower body count than nations dominated by more selfish laws, customs, and institutions – or nations so stuck in their habitual "conservative" social customs that they cannot adapt to change.

Collectively, as I've indicated, I believe that Covid-19 is fundamentally a manifestation of the Pluto-Eris square. *The essential underlying evolutionary purpose of the configuration is the realization that selfishness – both in individuals and in nations – has just collided with its own end game.* The myth of the rugged, independent individual *separate from everyone else* has finally hit the wall. As we have seen, *we are all in this together.* Denying the reality of that fact simply no longer works in a practical way for anyone. Anyone who does deny it is simply more likely to get sick. Even money can't keep anyone safe. Our anger with each other, our divisions, our brutal competitiveness, and *our sense that political boundaries on a map reflect some immutable law of nature* – all of that is collapsing right now before our eyes.

Even politicians must come together to craft a survival strategy. They must get past this "fan-based" model of rooting for their own political party as if the government were the National Football League.

Do we learn the lesson – or do we "hit the kid?" The universe has set up the question. It is pressing on us all. It will not go away.

The answer we choose to give is our own.

51

I went back and forth about including this newsletter in the book – after a brief introduction, it's just a section of a chapter in my book, The Night Speaks. I've elected to include it, mostly because it fits the "mundane astrology" theme of this section so perfectly. The conjunction of Uranus and Neptune in the early 1990s should never be forgotten. It has set the tone for the present age – something that was true back then when it was happening, but whose truth is becoming increasingly crystallized in the nature of questions that are currently pressing upon the human species. As ever, I am in awe of the power of astrology. When I wrote the words you will soon be reading, I didn't understand their full import. Astrology is forever wiser than the astrologer.

A VIEW OF TODAY FROM FOUR YEARS AGO

(Newsletter – November 2020)

A few weeks ago, a French gentleman named Olivier Clerc contacted me about the possibility of getting more of my work published in his country. Naturally, from my point of view, that is an attractive thought. He has connections to the French publishing industry and there are some encouraging early signs that it might actually happen.

I hope so. Getting this kind of astrology out to the global community is a pretty good summary of my life's purpose.

In an email exchange I had with Olivier this morning, he wrote glowingly about a section of my book, *The Night Speaks*. He suggested that I publish it as an article on my website. I'd come to the time of the month when I needed to be thinking of a newsletter topic, and, well – *voilà*, as they say in France. I put two and two together and followed Olivier's suggestion.

I originally published *The Night Speaks* in 1993, at the time of Uranus-Neptune conjunction in Capricorn. I wrote quite a lot about that epochal event in those early pages, but of course back then it was "pure astrology." No one, myself included, really knew yet what the alignment would bring. I was writing about it in real time, as clueless as a newscaster "on the scene." In fact, I did most of the writing *before* the conjunction actually happened – it was all unadulterated astrology, with no reality checks.

In 2016, we brought out a new edition of the book. I added a "twenty-three years later" perspective on what I'd originally written about the conjunction. That later work is the section of the book that Olivier Clerc was praising and asking me to share with a wider, current audience. He pointed out that many of my long-time readers who bought the earlier 1993 edition would not even know of this more recent 2016 addition.

There was a second reason for me to offer these words again. As a citizen of the United States here in late October 2020, I am of course nervously awaiting November 3rd and the results of our national elections. I do not know how they will turn out, so I can't yet write a meaningful commentary on them. The deadline for my newsletter comes earlier, yet I felt the need to say something relevant to this turning point in my own country's history. As I re-read this section of *The Night Speaks*, it struck me as deeply "current" in a kind of mythic, meta-political way.

So, thank you Olivier – and here is the "Update, 2016" section of *The Night Speaks*. There are a few references to the longer, original historical analysis which appears in both editions, but I think you'll be able to follow along without difficulty.

THE NIGHT SPEAKS, excerpted from chapter 10: "In Practice"

As I mentioned in my introduction to this new release of *The Night Speaks*, my intention is to offer the book essentially as I originally wrote it. One major departure from that principle presses at me now. When I wrote the previous section about the epochal conjunction of Uranus and

Neptune, it hadn't even happened yet. The book was published in 1993, right at the center of the event's time-line. Naturally the actual writing had occurred in the years before that, starting in 1988. In other words, all that I wrote – and all that you just read – was "prophecy" relative to the as-yet unrevealed meaning of the alignment.

Now nearly three decades down the road, we can evaluate the event from a clearer vantage point. Keep in mind that we are only barely into the full 171-year cycle. Perspective: during the last conjunction, in 1821, humanity discovered how to generate electricity. How clearly were the implications of that development understood by, say, 1844 – a similar 23 years later? Nights were still dark and no telephones were ringing.

We are in the same position now. But the handwriting on the wall is clearer now.

Subjectively, it doesn't feel like so long ago since *The Night Speaks* came out, yet I wrote the first sections of it on a very early, very clunky, Windows-based computer using a primitive word processor. Not long before, with my little DOS-based "Commodore 64" machine, I had developed an active business of printing out ugly little "dot matrix" birthcharts for people and snail-mailing them the sheet of paper. We were busy enough with that enterprise that we had to hire someone to do the work for us.

I said "snail-mailing," but back then we didn't use that term at all. To me, there was only one way of mailing anything – that was via the post office. My little computer was not connected to the Internet. In fact, I didn't know what the Internet was. I vividly remember reading letters-to-the-editor in TIME magazine. Some were signed johnsmith@aol.com.

I wondered what "@aol.com" meant.

That's the way the world was back then at the onset of the Uranus-Neptune conjunction.

Launching into a long, obvious discourse about "how the digital revolution has changed our lives" would be tedious for thee and me. We've heard it all before. But that doesn't make the digital revolution any less epochal.

Here's another potentially tedious point: how do those of us with gray hair explain what that earlier world was like to younger people today?

That is what it feels like to live through a Uranus-Neptune conjunction. If you were born before, say, 1980, you know exactly what I mean. If you were born before, say, 1960, it's as if you remember dinosaurs. There has been a paradigm shift. We've lived through it. A new myth of the world has arisen. It has happened fast enough to be shocking – and slowly enough that it kind of slips under the radar screen.

Not to belabor the digital point, but what about Facebook and "social media" in general? What about cell phones? What about Google and Wikipedia? If people had told me in 1989 that I would soon carry a little wireless computer in my pocket with which I could access virtually all of humanity's accumulated encyclopedia of information while standing in line in the grocery store, I would not have believed them.

Then there are some purely human implications. Here's a giggle I saw on Facebook. *"Be kind to your parents. One day you will look up from your cell phone and they will be gone."*

Obviously the digital revolution has impacted family life and social relationships, and not always in a way that feels healthy to an older person such as myself. But who is to say? As we saw last time around with this conjunction, we created the roots of *media* and *rapid geographical mobility.* I'm sure there were older folks back then talking about how the world was going to hell in a handbasket too.

Let me go deeper. Not that it matters, but I tend to be politically progressive – liberal," to use the old word. How you vote is your own business. If we can't honor human diversity, we have no business in the world of astrology, amen. But my Facebook feed is mostly progressive commentary. I don't get much of the conservative perspective, except as it is caricatured by other liberals or progressives.

Of course the same is usually true for politically-conservative Facebook users. They see "liberal jokes" a lot more than they see serious progressive arguments.

On another note, I might add that I sure see a lot of astrological commentary on Facebook too. For obvious reasons, an interest in astrology reflects the people I have "friended" there. I also have a great affinity for Buddhist philosophy – once more, my Facebook feed reflects that interest too.

- So, if I were to judge society by my "social media" experience, *the world is populated by environmentally-savvy, gay-friendly, anti-gun, Buddhist-sympathizing liberals, all of whom believe in astrology.*

In the same vein, I listen to my own music on my iPod or I stream specialty channels on Sirius XM. When I was growing up, Top Forty radio was very diverse. Now my ears tell me that everyone on the planet loves the rock 'n' roll of the period 1955-1985, hard jazz, and a bit of classical music – minus the operas.

See the pattern? *The digital revolution has fragmented culture.* The unifying impact of shared experience and a consensual interpretation of reality has been vastly reduced in the past three decades. Again, it happened so fast that we are all in a state of shock – but slowly enough that the change didn't fully register.

Going further with the same idea, I grew up thinking I was "an American." We still use that language, but how much sense of shared community does a right-wing radio host in Texas feel with an LGBTQ blogger from San Francisco? And, given the digital fragmentation of society, what basis do they have for possibly understanding each other?

Like looking at yourself in a maze of mirrors, the implications of all this just keep on ramifying. Connect the dots. Under the Uranus-Neptune paradigm shift I believe we are witnessing *the collapse of the idea of geographical nations and communities.* Where I once thought I was "an American," I now basically think of myself as a "kind" of American." What kind? I painted it as a cartoon a few lines ago, but here is the underlying principle stated more seriously and broadly: *I now identify with a set of ideals and values rather than with a geographical location.*

I brought up my "being American" a moment ago, but I actually have more of an active sense of shared values, shared interests, and shared experience with friends in Australia than I do with most of the people living in my own little town out in the desert. I even do half of my shopping on the Internet – no need to leave my house. And I am in daily contact with people in China, Turkey, and France with whom I have more in common than with my own neighbors

- In the post-Uranus/Neptune digital age, *identity is becoming non-local.*

Has this broadened my life? Or narrowed it? There's an essay question – one humanity is still answering.

I wonder how much the rise of extreme nationalism is a reaction against this sense of the old world eroding out from under the feet of people who are still attached to it?

Now, I am going to seem to change gears without actually changing them at all. For citizens of the United States of America, the world changed utterly on September 11, 2001 with the attack on the World Trade Center. Before then and since then, other countries have experienced similar fates. Clearly, the rise of international terrorism has been one of the most obvious features of post-1993, post Uranus-Neptune conjunction, global society. What does the rise of terrorism mean? What is really going on? In response to 9/11, the Bush administration elected to invade Iraq. In the words of Richard Clarke, who was an intelligence and counter-terrorism advisor to four administrations, "Invading Iraq after 9/11 was like invading Mexico after Pearl Harbor."

It's a funny line until you start the body count.

I am verging dangerously close to divisive political territory here, but I want to skirt that abyss in order to make a far broader point – and to distill the wisdom that underlies Clarke's quip. On September 11, 2001, America was not attacked by a nation. *We were attacked by a group of people united by a common idea.* That had never happened before. In the language I used when I wrote the earlier sections of this analysis, we were attacked by "barbarians" or by "people who do not matter." *But they were not a nation.* They had no homeland for us to attack in retaliation. In a classical example of "always preparing for the last war," my impression is that the Bush administration did not understand this absolute Uranian-Neptunian change in the underlying form of the human world. They felt they had to attack a nation because a nation was the only "enemy" they could imagine. So they "invaded Mexico." So far history does not seem to support the argument that this was a good idea.

In writing these words, I am aware of perhaps sounding "too American" to my international readers. Guilty as charged. Other countries have suffered far worse than America as a result of this spate of terrorism – this global war of ideologies fought by armies united, not by geography, but by common ideas. France is in shock and disarray. The Middle East has become a hell-world for an awful lot of innocent people. The "Islamic State" – ISIS – is presently looming very powerfully . . . and, in my opinion, it is doomed because they too are operating in the old nation-state, geographical model.

Their *recruiting*, however, is utterly post-Neptune/Uranus. It couldn't happen without the tools of the digital age, both for spreading their ideas, but perhaps even more pivotally by presenting them in a socially-fragmented "bubble" with no reference to other points of view.

And that brings us right back to the Internet and the digital revolution. *The civilized world is fighting a battle against an idea – and the neurons and synapses in the brain of that idea are digital.*

All of this of course makes the digital revolution sound like a bad thing. That is not my point at all. Going back to the last Uranus-Neptune conjunction of the early 1820s, was fossil-fuel driven mass transportation a bad thing? Was the industrial revolution a bad thing? What about electricity?

We may be rightly nostalgic for the good things we have lost, but I doubt that very many of us would turn our backs on the freedom, empowerment, and convenience those developments have brought to us. And remember: the roots of all those inventions lie in the previous conjunction of Uranus and Neptune early in the nineteenth century – see either edition of *The Night Speaks* for the details.

But under this new Uranus-Neptune cycle, we are now confronted by global climate disruption which is, in part, driven by those inventions.

As we explored earlier, in many ways, the previous Uranus-Neptune conjunction of the early nineteenth century marked the beginning of *mass democracy.* How well is that experiment unfolding?

What about the birth of *media culture?* (As we saw, the advent of photography and primitive sound recording, along with electrical communication over long distances in the form of the telegraph marked the germination of media culture during the previous conjunction.) It would be easy to sermonize here about kids "helped" in their passage through puberty by Internet pornography. It would be easy to compare a live performance of Shakespeare to *Blast the Aliens, Part VIII.* Thinking about the current realities of media culture, it would be easy to mount the pulpit and sound the bugle for "a return to the good old days."

But I don't want to do that – and not only because that is a bugle famed for its futility. Truth said, when we hear that bugle it is usually playing *Taps* for the dead and the dying.

The old world will not return.

One further illustration of that principle lies in the changing definitions of gender. Here's a line I quote from back in Chapter Four. "But certainly women, either by nature or by programming, have traditionally been identified with our intuitive right brain/left hand, leaving the "more valuable stuff" to men."

I probably wrote those words in about 1990. When I saw them again in preparing this new version of *The Night Speaks*, they already had begun to seem awkward and anachronistic to me. Much that was controversial and "politically correct" back then is simply assumed to be true today. Who today imagines women to be incapable of logic? And when was the last time you heard anyone use the term, "women's intuition?"

I grew up in an age of activist feminism. The rights of women were a hot issue. Nowadays, many of the feminists of my generation are dismayed by the lack of support and appreciation they feel from younger females. The younger women, in return, seem to feel that the battle is over – they won, so why keep on fighting it? They are free to enter the workplace more or less as the equals of males. They are free to express themselves sexually as they please. They can live on their own and make their own decisions.

They are already, to use the common term, living in a "post-feminist" age.

I will happily leave it to history to sort all that out. Suffice to say that the roles of women before and after the Uranus-Neptune conjunction of the early 1990s bear little resemblance to each other. At least that is true across much of the Western world. Again, this change has happened quickly enough to spin older heads, but slowly enough so that it is easy to miss the enormity of it. We older people see it more clearly than the younger ones since we have lived in both worlds.

But the younger ones "wear it" more naturally.

A similar, if even more dramatic evolution has taken place relative to the acceptance of gayness as a natural condition. As with feminism, that battle is not necessarily over. But it would be folly to fail to see how far we have come. Remembering that the Uranus-Neptune conjunction was at a peak in 1993, consider the following synchronicity: On December 21, 1993, the United States Department of Defense prohibited the armed forces from barring people from service based on their sexual orientation. This policy was famously known as, "Don't Ask, Don't Tell." I believe it is fair to take it as the point where the cultural tide turned, leading to the widespread appearance of sympathetic, multi-dimensional gay characters in the media, people being "out" without shame or hesitancy, and of course to the seismic shift in the collective attitude that has led to the acceptance of gay marriage.

Just to sharpen the point, let's go back to 1977 in San Francisco – a city famous for its openness to diversity. A gay man, Harvey Milk, had won a seat on the Board of Supervisors. He introduced an ordinance to protect gay people from being fired from their jobs because of their orientation and another one pitted against "Proposition 6," which attempted to forbid gay people from being school teachers. That's the way the world was back then. Appallingly, bizarrely from today's perspective, people could be fired from their jobs for being gay.

And on November 27, 1978, Harvey Milk was assassinated.

A couple of years ago, there was some kind of bloody headline in the news. Just to strike a balancing note, I posted a simple statement on my Facebook page about how humans are capable of progress and how we do get things right sometimes. I made a point of how far we had come in my lifetime in three areas: racism, sexism, and homophobia. To my shock, I got some condescending feedback explaining to me about how racism, sexism and homophobia are "alive and well."

And, hey, I know that.

But I was born in 1949 and in the world I entered, racism, sexism and homophobia were actually *the law of the land*. If you weren't white, male, and straight, you were a target of derision, or far worse.

Anyone who says we are not making progress just isn't paying attention. Things were different before Uranus caught up with Neptune and changed the world forever.

I once taught a four-day seminar about the world's current changes in one of my Apprenticeship Programs. One line to which I kept returning was simply "trust the children." I repeat it here. So many of the world's current problems had their origins back at the last conjunction of these two invisible giants, back when that unsung visionary, Mary Shelley, was writing *Frankenstein* – what a prophetic book, as *science creates a monster whose effects it cannot foresee or control.*

Children and young people today have inherited a dreadful world full of seemingly intractable challenges. But they are different from us. They hold the seeds of a new paradigm. Some years ago, they were often called "the indigo children." I don't hear that term much anymore, but the principle behind it was solid.

As I write these words, many of these human beings – born from, say, 1988 through 1995 – have just touched the shores of full adulthood. Most are not yet at full power. I have enormous faith in them.

I also have faith that they will shock and confuse me, and that's because I am a creature of the past and they are creatures of the future.

I have faith that they hold the seeds of answers I could never imagine. And of course, fair is fair – they are not all little saints, geniuses, and moral paragons. Many will just be members of a generation of lost souls, cut off from all that has given meaning to life for the past two centuries, or longer. They all carry an enormous burden. Some will break under the load. Even the best and wisest of them, in fashioning the new world, will surely, unwittingly, sow the seeds of many new problems – but let's not worry about that until 2165, the next time Uranus and Neptune align.

I suspect the scientists among them will begin flowering over the next decade or two – famously, scientists often do their best work before they are forty. Meanwhile, the painters, poets, novelists, and screen-writers among them, like fine Cabernet Sauvignon, may "need another thirty years to age in the bottle."

And these human beings will have children. They will have students and disciples, and the story will go on unfolding just as it has in all the previous apparitions of the Uranus-Neptune conjunction: old problems solved in previously-unimaginable ways, a world created that bears little resemblance to the previous one it displaces. New art, new music, new tools, new styles of relationship – and the faint breath of some unsuspected Frankenstein just below the threshold of detection.

What have I missed in writing this new section of *The Night Speaks?* Probably half of what is important – and half of what will be utterly obvious to future historians. Famously, what can the fish tell us about the sea?

But there are two points which I did not miss and which I feel are the practical center of everything: do not lose faith in the human future, and, above all, trust the children.

52

Once more, Jupiter changes signs and provides me with a juicy newsletter topic. In this case, it is entering Capricorn – a sign that could hardly be any different from the previous one, Sagittarius. One underlying agenda in this short essay was trying to underscore how each planet really becomes almost an entirely different entity as it changes from sign to sign.

JUPITER ENTERS CAPRICORN

(Newsletter – December 2020)

Jupiter dominates the astrological headlines this month. As most of you probably know, it crosses out of Sagittarius and into Capricorn on December 2nd. The old astrologers called Jupiter the "Greater Benefic." One piece of corroborating evidence lies in how nicely it cooperates with astrologers, taking about twelve years to get around the Zodiac – and thus conveniently spending about one year, give or take a little bit, in each sign.

This current passage is no exception – Jupiter remains in Capricorn until December 19, 2020, when it crosses into Aquarius. On the day that Jupiter does that, Saturn will have already been there for three days. The two heavyweight planets of the solar system form their every-two-decade conjunction in very early Aquarius on December 21, 2020.

That conjunction is a big subject. If you are interested in my take on it, a little bit of patience will soon be rewarded – one rather "meta" dimension of it is the subject of our next chapter. On my website, you can also find links to videos I've made about the Jupiter-Saturn conjunction at a more personal level.

My ambition in this short newsletter is more modest. I only want to reflect on the personal meaning of Jupiter's passage through the sign of the Sea-Goat as it affects each one of us. And let's start by emphasizing a core astrological principle: Jupiter in Capricorn is not the same beast as Jupiter in Sagittarius – or Gemini or Aquarius, for that matter. "What does Jupiter mean" sounds like an innocent question, but answering it can get an astrologer into worlds of trouble. The best response is always, "Show me your chart." In astrology, context is everything. A sign flavors a planet with motivations and values – and Capricorn's values are quite different from those of Sagittarius.

Here are three really dumb statements. As you reflect on the *reasons* that they are dumb, you can learn a lot about how astrology actually works in human terms.

- Everybody should get married.
- Everybody should like anchovies.
- People are crazy to live in the country when they could live in a big city.

The problem with each of these statements is that in each case we have left out a critical ingredient: *exactly who are we talking about?* In each case, it's "different strokes for different folks," in other words. In every one of these examples, some people will benefit from turning left, while others will benefit from turning right. It works exactly the same way with planets. *Signs give them specific tastes, interests, and values, making them as different as people.* For example, Jupiter enjoys having some *risk* – and therefore, some sense of *serendipitous possibility* – in its life. But risks come in a lot of flavors.

Hey, Jupiter – how's about going bungee-jumping over shark-infested waters with me this weekend?

Jupiter-in-Sagittarius: *Let's go!*

Jupiter-in-Capricorn: *Are you nuts? I mean, why would I ever want to do that?*

Capricorn tends to be "practical," although there are deeper words we can use. From Capricorn's perspective, the best possible outcome from bungee-jumping over shark-infested waters is that nothing goes wrong and you survive the experience. There is no "upside" to it at all. And that raises the question of why you put yourself in that position in the first place. What was in it for you?

Capricorn's answer: *nothing at all*. So why do it?

All of this could make the Sea-Goat sound pretty boring – and from the Sagittarian perspective, *it is* – once again, there are good people who like anchovies and there are good people who don't.

The Jupiter-risks that excite and motivate Capricorn are more long term in their orientation. Here's a way to think about it – Capricorn reminds me of that famous child psychology experiment where you ask a bunch of kids if they would like *one* cookie right now or *four* cookies if they wait for half an hour.

You guessed it: that experiment will nicely sort out the Sagittarians from the Capricorns.

Capricorn, in a nutshell, likes a *long-term project*. It likes to keep its eye on the prize – and if the prize takes a while to win, the joy is intensified by the anticipation.

Now let's add Jupiter to the mix – and while we are at it, let's let go of the silly, ungrounded notion that Jupiter is always simply "lucky." That word has some relevance, but it can also get you into a world of trouble with this planet. To me, the key question with Jupiter boils down to this: *How have you been underestimating yourself?* Jupiter wants you to *believe in yourself*. It wants you to act like the king or queen of the gods. That's not about being haughty or bossing anyone around; it's about comporting yourself with confidence, faith in your abilities, and high aspirations.

Put Jupiter in Capricorn, and here's what happens – at least here is what is *supposed* to happen: you set a *worthy goal* for yourself and you *work relentlessly, logically, and systematically to attain it.*

What kind of goal? To answer that, we need to ask a few more questions: where does Capricorn fall in your chart? What is the condition of your natal Jupiter? What planets will that transiting Jupiter be contacting by aspect while it is in that sign?

Answer those questions, and you will see that worthy goal clearly illuminated.

Remember that the prize might not be something obvious or worldly – it doesn't have to be about any of the usual cultural obsessions around money, reputation, and career. It might be a spiritual goal or a psychological, attitudinal one.

Again, the specifics of your chart come into play here.

If you set that goal and thus harness the energies of Jupiter-in-Capricorn in pursuit of it, *magic happens.* That is where that slippery word "luck" steps onto the stage. Get it right, and doors open. The right people show up. Resources become available.

What triggers those fortunate synchronicities? *The answer is your own faith in yourself.* It boils down to believing that you are capable of *meaningful accomplishments* that go beyond any victories you have previously won. You are ready to take a significant step forward in your soul's journey – and the universe is ready to support it. All you have to do is to believe in yourself, stretch beyond your old limits, roll up your sleeves, and actually do the work.

Capricorn is not about dreaming; it's about doing.

53

The Jupiter-Saturn conjunction – which happens like clockwork every twenty years – always dominates the astrological headlines for a year or so. Naturally, people are interested in what it might portend for them personally, and that's always a fair question. In this piece however, I take a far, far longer view of it . . . really too long a view for my words to have much personal meaning at all. This essay starts with some visual astronomy, but it is really about changes that unfold over centuries rather than over a couple of decades. Every couple of hundred years these Jupiter-Saturn conjunctions begin to happen in a new Element and, with each of these "Mutation Conjunctions," it is as if the zeitgeist of the world shifts on its axis. All of us have front row seats for this one – it is all happening now right before our eyes. Prepare to be astonished by a relatively little-known area of mundane astrology so powerful that I'm sure it could make believers out of astrological non-believers, provided they knew a bit about history.

JUPITER, SATURN, AND A CHANGING WORLD

(Newsletter – December 2020)

All eyes are on the sky this month. As most of us probably know by now, Jupiter and Saturn come together and form their every-two-decades conjunction on December 21. And this time they *really* come together – they stand only one-tenth of a degree apart. That's close! They won't "blend into one star" as some people have erroneously said – you will still see two points of light. But it will be a striking sight, something you may have never before seen in the sky.

How close is one-tenth of a degree? Here's a way to visualize it. Hold your arm straight out and stand your pinky-finger straight up. The span across your fingernail is about one degree.

One tenth of that. Close!

Hey, but what if it's cloudy on the night of the 21st? Have you missed the whole thing? Do you have to wait another twenty years? Well . . . it's both worse than that and better than that.

The next Jupiter-Saturn conjunction occurs in October of 2040, but it's a just pale version of this one – the two planets are much further apart (because of very different declinations) and also somewhat lost in the Sun's glare.

Twenty years after that one, they are at it again – but once more, conditions are similar to 2040.

All of that is the "worse than that" side of the equations. What about "better than that?"

Start with the fact that this is a very slow dance we are watching. Jupiter and Saturn are *already* really close together. Right at the beginning of the month, on December 1st, they are only separated by a little more than two degrees. (Hold your middle three fingers up against the sky at arm's length. That is about five degrees. Less than half of that – which is close enough to be strikingly beautiful.)

Like everyone else who pays attention to the heavens, I am awaiting our once-in-a-lifetime moment on December 21st, but who knows about the weather? Clouds could blow the show.

Again, take comfort – there's another date that may actually be even more memorable and more lovely: December 16. On that day, Jupiter is closing in on Saturn, standing only half a degree away – just half the breadth of your pinkie. But what promises to make the view totally magical that evening is the Moon. It will be in its pretty waxing crescent phase and just five degrees below the two planets. If you are lucky enough to find yourself under dark, clear skies, you'll see *earthshine* softly illuminating the dark portions of the Moon, and the whole thing will be glorious enough to put tears in your eyes – maybe an even more memorable sight than the true maximum conjunction itself just five nights later.

Still, here's my prayer: may the whole Earth be blessed with clear skies on the evening of December 21st. That will be a moment for the history books.

By the way, as most of us know, the conjunction will happen right at the beginning of the sign Aquarius. Meanwhile, on December 21st, the Sun is just into Capricorn. That puts the Sun about thirty degrees away from Jupiter and Saturn, just one whole sign before them in the zodiac. Jupiter, Saturn, and the Sun are all fairly close together, in other words. *So the Sun sets, then Jupiter and Saturn set.* What that means in practical terms is that you want your lawn chair set up *facing west just after sunset.*

People who say "let's have a beer and catch the conjunction later tonight" will be disappointed. It will be over by then, at least in terms of our ability actually to see it. Everything will be below the horizon.

Like most astrologers, I have explored the meaning of the Jupiter-Saturn conjunction in a lot of detail elsewhere. Go to my website, and enter "Jupiter Saturn conjunction" in the Search engine. You'll see three different talks I've done on the subject. I don't want to rehash any of that material here. Instead I want to take a longer, more historical view.

These Jupiter-Saturn alignments happen every 19.85 years. Usually there is just one exact conjunction, but sometimes, due to retrograde motion, there are three of them, all happening within a few months.

- One interesting feature of the Jupiter-Saturn conjunctions is that these alignments cluster for a couple of hundred years in Fire signs, then about two hundred more years in Earth signs, then in Air signs, then in Water signs.

The transition from Element to Element is a bit blurry. For example, after two centuries in Earth signs, three Jupiter-Saturn conjunctions happened between December 1980 and July 1981, all in the Air sign, Libra. But May 2000 brought us a conjunction back in the Earth sign, Taurus. Our current one is of course in the Air sign, Aquarius – even though a lot of the action occurred in earthy Capricorn.

- Bottom line: when we take the long view, there is an unmistakable pattern of approximately two-century Element cycles in these Jupiter-Saturn alignments.

The astrological community is indebted to Richard Nolle for posting much technical material on his website. Here is a table of Jupiter-Saturn conjunctions from the year 1425 to the year 2219, all gleaned from www.astropro.com. The table on his website covers an even longer span of history and gives even more information. I've shortened it here to better fit our purposes. Thank you, Richard!

JUPITER-SATURN CONJUNCTIONS 1425-2219
(Kudos to Richard Nolle at www.astropro.com)

DATE	POSITION	CYCLE
FEB 14, 1425	*17SC18*	**Water**
MAR 18, 1425	*16SC33*	
AUG 26, 1425	*12SC40*	
JUL 14, 1444	08CA57	
APR 08, 1464	04PI35	
NOV 18, 1484	23SC11	
MAY 25, 1504	16CA25	
JAN 31, 1524	09PI14	
SEP 18, 1544	28SC05	
AUG 25, 1563	29CA10	
MAY 03, 1583	20PI11	
DEC 18, 1603	08SA19	*Fire*
JUL 16, 1623	06LE36	
FEB 24, 1643	25PI07	*(Out of quality)*
OCT 16, 1663	12SA58	
OCT 24, 1682	*19LE09*	
FEB 09, 1683	*16LE43*	
MAY 18, 1683	*14LE30*	
MAY 21, 1702	06AR36	
JAN 05, 1723	23SA19	
AUG 30, 1742	27LE09	
MAR 18, 1762	12AR21	
NOV 05, 1782	28SA07	
JUL 17, 1802	05VI08	**Earth**
JUN 19, 1821	24AR39	*(Out of quality)*
JAN 26, 1842	8CP54	
OCT 21, 1861	18VI22	
APR 18, 1881	01TA36	
NOV 28, 1901	14CP00	
SEP 10, 1921	26VI36	
AUG 08, 1940	*14TA27*	
OCT 20, 1940	*12TA28*	
FEB 15, 1941	*09TA07*	
FEB 19, 1961	25CP12	
DEC 31, 1980	*09LI30*	**Air**
MAR 04, 1981	*08LI06*	
JUL 24, 1981	*04LI56*	
MAY 28, 2000	22TA43	*(Out of quality)*
DEC 21, 2020	00AQ29	
OCT 31, 2040	17LI56	
APR 07, 2060	00GE46	
MAR 15, 2080	11AQ52	
SEP 18, 2100	25LI32	
JUL 15, 2119	14GE52	
JAN 14, 2140	17AQ05	
DEC 21, 2159	07SC59	*(Out of quality)*
MAY 28, 2179	23GE03	
APR 07, 2199	28AQ19	
OCT 31, 2219	14SC42	**Water**

Let me explain what you are seeing here. Mostly the listing is straightforward, giving the dates of the conjunctions, their exact degree positions, and the Element in which they took (or will take) place.

You may notice that some of the dates are italicized. I do that only with the *triple conjunctions*, where the two planets come together three times over a period of a few months. The very first entry is an example of that as Jupiter and Saturn formed three alignments in Scorpio over a period of about six months back in Ye Olde Year of Our Lord, 1425.

Glancing at the Table, you can easily see the blurry clustering of conjunctions in successive Elements over cycles of around two hundred years. I say "blurry" because after entering a new Element, there is usually a "throwback" conjunction in the previous one – that, or an early harbinger of the next Element before the old one gives out. In the Table here, I have labeled those "throwbacks" as *out of quality* conjunctions.

At our present moment in history, we are staggering out of a long cycle of Earth conjunctions. We had a taste of Air in 1980, then back to Earth in 2000. With this conjunction in Aquarius, we are entering a solid Air cycle that will carry us all the way to Halloween 2219 – with one early taste of Water in 2159.

What we are seeing here is admittedly somewhat messy, but the basic pattern is ultimately clear:

- These conjunctions form long cycles in specific Elements, then they make a halting transition into a new Element cycle.

The term *Mutation Conjunction* is often used as we enter a fresh Element – but once again there are often a couple of candidates in each case for which conjunction gets that title. In thinking about this epochal pattern, it helps to take off your close-up "Virgo glasses" and instead view it through your broad-pattern "Sagittarian" ones.

- Looking at this Table in broad, impressionistic terms, we have a Water cycle that ran approximately from 1425 to 1603. What was happening in that period? The *Renaissance*, for one thing – a great flowering of Watery human imagination, not to mention the European exploration of the world via sailing ships *moving on water.*

- Water gave way to a Fire cycle, running approximately from 1603 to 1802 – and we had two hundred fiery years of war, conquest and colonization.
- Fire gave way to Earth, running approximately from 1802 to either 1980 or to today, depending on how you define the Mutation Conjunction. What did we have? *The Industrial Revolution*, which was driven by *fossil fuels* and *metals* taken from the bones of the earth itself. We have an epoch of *building, building, building*. You can easily feel the Earth signature in all of that.
- Earth gave way to Air – again either in 1980 or 2020, depending on how you think about it. Our current Air cycle, which is *unambiguously* underway starting on this December 21st will last for another two hundred years or so . . .

. . . and what do we have? Well, this is a good time for me to invoke that reliable cliché, what does the fish know of the sea? Certainly the familiar term, *The Information Age,* is profoundly and obviously relevant to our moving under the wings of the Air Element, and it also fits the timing perfectly. But Air is not just about cell phones and microchips. Here are some words I wrote in *The Book of Air:*

Air is what connects our hearts and our minds to the world around us. Astrologically – but also in plain speech – it is the linking element, telegraphing an endless stream of information to us – and letting us send a few telegrams in return. Air makes a mockery of the delusion that we are separate from each other – or, for that matter, from anything else. Air connects. It is what allows us to pay attention, and perhaps to create some good reasons for other people to pay attention to us.

Humanity is becoming literally more crowded and more interconnected in so many ways, digitally, but also in literally *sharing the planet's air* with all of the attendant implications regarding climate change and the possibility of contagion.

The pressing question is, can we *listen to each other?* Can this new Renaissance of the Air Element, beginning this very month, herald a vibrant, creative future for the human race – one with maybe a little dollop of *Star Trek* social culture, not to mention some *Star Trek* technology in the mix?

Can simple Airy *interest* in each other replace some of this Pluto-Eris rage and the current need constantly to make everyone else "wrong" somehow?

I don't know. I have never claimed to have a crystal ball. But one thing is certain: with the conjunction of Jupiter and Saturn in Aquarius on December 21st, we are entering the uncharted territory of a new, and far more Airy, world. One look at the Table and you can see that this principle has never failed to be true. It has worked for centuries. It will not fail this time either. We can already see it happening.

So point your lawn chair to the west on the evening of the 21st and have a look at the human future. And let your faith bring faith to those who doubt that humanity can create a future worth living.

54

What's happening to the world today? Astrologically, that is a huge question. When people ask, I often say that once my students asked me the same question and it took me talking for four days to answer it. (That generally changes the subject pretty quickly. And it's true too – at the end of this piece, you see a link to a recording of my four-day "Generations" program, which proves it.) In the relatively short-term, we can cast light on such macro-questions by considering major outer planet transits – for example, the Pluto-Eris or Uranus-Eris squares we have already explored earlier in this section. For a bigger perspective, embracing 171 years, we can take in the long-range, epochal implications of the Uranus-Neptune conjunction, as we have also seen. But for the really big picture, nothing explains the changing world more effectively than a reflection on the fact that . . .

IT IS THE DAWNING OF THE AGE OF AQUARIUS . . . OR IS IT?

(Newsletter – January 2021)

The fabled Age of Aquarius – does it mean anything at all? Ever since the musical *Hair* was first performed back in 1967, there has been a vague sense that the Aquarian Age had something to do with hippies or free love or world peace or . . . *something*.

Anyway, from that long-haired point of view, the Age of Aquarius probably ended about fifty years ago . . . unless you bring up the subject among a group of astrologers. Then what you will typically see has very little to do with *"harmony and understanding, sympathy and trust abounding . . ."* Then what you will typically see is closer to World War Three.

Opinions on the subject of the astrological ages tend to be trenchant – and the general thrust of them usually runs down the road of claiming that the Age of Aquarius is real enough, but that it is still way off in the far distant future.

I disagree. I think we are in it now. I think we have been in it for over a century already.

In this newsletter I want to make my case that the Age of Aquarius dates back to 1903-1905.

Let's start with Science Class.

Earth's north pole describes a slow circle in the sky, sort of like a child's spinning top winding down. This cycle – called the *Precession of the Equinoxes* – takes 25,771.5 years to go around the circle once. As the north pole leans first this way, then circles around that way, naturally the position of the Celestial Equator shifts along with it too – tilt the child's top and you can't help but tilt the painted stripes on its sides as well. That point will soon become important.

- At the Solstices, the Sun is maximally far north or south of the Celestial Equator, while at the Equinoxes, the Sun is aligned with it.
- Remember: the Sun is *always* on the ecliptic – the path of the Sun is what defines it.
- Two plus two makes four: *at the Equinoxes, the Sun is where the Celestial Equator and the Ecliptic cross.*
- That junction is the point that is slowly moving backwards, taking 25,771.5 years to return to where it started.

What all this astronomy boils down to is the fact that the Sun's position on the first day of Spring (or the first day of Autumn) *relative to the starry background* is slowly *precessing* in retrograde fashion. Gradually it shifts backwards from constellation to constellation, in other words.

Four or five millennia ago, on the first day of northern Spring, the Sun rose into the *constellation* Taurus. After some centuries, it began to rise into the *constellation* Aries, then into the *constellation* Pisces . . .

I emphasize "constellations" because they are different from signs. That, as we will see, is the key to the entire mystery.

We Western astrologers define "the first degree of Aries" as the position of the Sun on the day of the northern Vernal Equinox. Long ago, there was a period of centuries in which the Sun on that day happened to align with the actual constellation of stars we call "Aries." That period also apparently coincided with the birth of the kind of astrology we practice today.

No longer.

Here's the whole thing in one sentence: *Astrology, as most of us practice it in the West, is based on the seasons, not the stars.*

(Vedic astrologers and the Western *siderealists* use the constellations.)

All of that sets the stage for us understanding all the arguments around whether or not we are in the Age of Aquarius. Theoretically, defining these precessional Ages is very simple: the "Age of Pisces" began when the Vernal Equinox left the constellation Aries and entered the constellation Pisces. And the Age of Aquarius began – or will begin – when it enters the constellation Aquarius.

Simple? Not really.

The question is, *where exactly* does the constellation Aquarius begin? That's tricky, because actually, when you think about it, all we have up in the sky is a bunch of stars. There are no natural boundaries around them. Different cultures have "connected the starry dots" in different ways.

Constellations are *folklore*, not any kind of objective, measurable reality.

That fuzziness about constellation boundaries was an inconvenience for astronomers. They solved it, innocently enough, by forming a committee. The boundaries of the 88 official constellations were adopted by the International Astronomical Union in 1928 and published in 1930.

If we take the word of the IAU to be the holy gospel of truth, the Vernal Equinox will enter Aquarius around the year 2600 A.D. By that standard, we are not even close to the dawning of the Age of Aquarius, so put away your guitars and your bell-bottom bluejeans.

As I mentioned earlier, many serious astrologers pooh-pooh the notion that we have already entered the Aquarian Age. Their argument is founded upon their great and unquestioning faith in the map of the sky that the International Astronomical Union published almost a century ago.

There are some problems with that kind of thinking however. Have a look at this diagram:

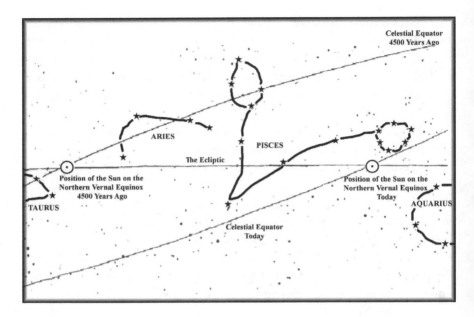

On the left, you can see the position of the Sun on the northern Vernal Equinox around 4500 years ago. Did it fall in Taurus or Aries? How do you read that? This represents what our ancestors were looking at – the actual sky, not a *map of the sky* published by the IAU almost seven thousand years later.

There are no boundaries in the sky, but we might say our answer is that the Vernal Equinox over four millennia ago "leans Taurus."

On the right, you'll see the Sun's Equinox position today – *and it is clearly still very much in the constellation Pisces.*

Case closed? Again, many astrologers are adamant about that claim. Personally, I think that they are taking the International Astronomical Union too seriously. For one thing, if we follow the IAU's lead scrupulously, we'll all need to add a thirteenth astrological sign – Ophiuchus. It is now on the ecliptic too.

Back to our diagram. Note that the constellation Aries is *tiny* compared to Pisces. *Constellations vary enormously in size.* Virgo is the biggest zodiacal constellation by far. Capricorn is the smallest, at least in terms of the number of "square degrees" it occupies.

But absolute astrological bedrock is the idea that all twelve signs are equal in size.

Should we abandon that principle? Twelve *equal* divisions – that is the core of astrological geometry.

Nothing against the International Astronomical Union, but let's try thinking like astrologers. Let's take a leap and postulate that there are twelve equal "constellations" up there in the sky, each one 30° wide. I put "constellations" in quotation marks because we would no longer be thinking according to the IAU's boundaries, nor would we be bound to *Eurocentric folk traditions* about how to arrange these configurations of stars.

These new "constellations" would not be our familiar signs of the zodiac either, although they'll retain the same names.

Fine – but all this brings us back to our central problem: where does our "constellation" Aries begin? We still cannot see a mark in the sky.

- Go back to astrological bedrock: *"as above, so below"* – but of course that also means "as below, so above." Maybe if we can't answer our question by looking at the sky, we can answer it by looking at human history. Astrology works; each one should reflect the other. If we want to learn about the sky, there is no reason that we shouldn't look at history.

Twelve equal "constellations" would mean that each astrological Age would last for one-twelfth of 25,771.5 years. Each one would then be 2147.5 years long – that's another link in our chain.

When did the Piscean Age begin? We can write volumes about Pisces, but let's cut to the chase by simply thinking of it as the most *mystical* sign. Reasoning from history rather than from astronomy, we might make a start by arbitrarily splitting the difference between the births of the two great Piscean Age mystical Teachers, Buddha and Christ, born in approximately 563 and 4 BC respectively. (We might include Muhammad, but he was not born until much later, in 571 A.D.)

Splitting the difference, using Gautama and Jesus, that would give us 283 BC for an *admittedly wildly hypothetical guess* about the start of the Piscean Age.

This is obviously very quick and dirty thinking! But let's see where it leads us.

We do know that sometime around then, we would also have been emerging from the Age of Aries – an epoch of bloody conquest, swords, and cities laid to waste. And that is about right impressionistically – the late Bronze Age was no picnic.

As Aries gave way to Pisces, it seems reasonable to speculate that people might be ready to hear a few words from "the Prince of Peace."

Skipping ahead a couple of millennia, what is Aquarius in a nutshell? Limiting ourselves to one word as we did with "mystical" Pisces, let's say Aquarius represents *genius*.

- One might speculate that the outset of an Aquarian Age would be heralded by some startlingly brilliant, rule-breaking human innovations.

Adding 2147.5 years to 283 B.C. (and remembering that "A.D." started with 1 A.D., not 0 AD), would yield the year 1865 for the hypothetical beginning of the Aquarian Age – presumably an Age of genius. But please do recall that we arrived at "283 B.C." in very crude fashion. There is no compelling reason to be rigid about that date – if we had a good reason to shift it by a few decades, there would be no reason to worry about doing that.

Personally, I like 1903-1905 for the cusp of the Aquarian Age – that's just forty years or so later. It coincides with *the first powered airplane flight* – the Wright Brothers taking off from Kitty Hawk on the Outer Banks of North Carolina on December 14, 1903. *Humans learning how to fly!* Doesn't that sound like an Aquarian rebellion against all limitations? Doesn't that sound like a new level of human freedom? Doesn't that ring of human genius?

I also like the publication of Einstein's Special Theory of Relativity on September 26, 1905, right around the same time. Albert Einstein – just say the word *genius* and it takes most people under ten seconds to free-associate to his name. One could make a case that the Theory of Relativity is the greatest intellectual triumph in human history.

1903-1905 is not quite the same as 1865, but with Ages running over two millennia in length, forty years is only a drop in the bucket.

- My favorite line here is that *we went from Kitty Hawk to the Moon in 66 years.*

Doesn't that sound like the cusp of a new age? Doesn't that sound like leaving the Age of Pisces and entering the Age of Aquarius?

Again, in all of this, we are reasoning from "below" to try to figure out what is going on "above." We don't know in any meaningful, confident way where the constellations start and finish – that's our basic problem. *So we instead turn our usual astrological methods on their heads.* We look to events on earth in order to understand the sky.

Reflecting on how the 20th century changed the elemental texture of human life makes a compelling argument that we are on the right track with this kind of thinking. And it of course goes way beyond airplanes and Einstein. Think of electricity, automobiles, the Internet ... you know the list.

The implications for the global community moving out of the Age of Pisces and into the Age of Aquarius are vast. In this brief essay, I have only wanted to spell out the technical challenges we face in trying to decipher these mysteries – and to begin to make my case that we actually entered the Aquarian Age over a century ago.

In June 2018, I offered a four-day seminar called *Generations* to my Apprenticeship Program in Durham, North Carolina. It ranged widely, looking not only at the astrological ages, but also at the meaning of various outer planet configurations that have helped orchestrate the transition – the Uranus-Pluto conjunction of the 1960s and the Uranus-Neptune conjunction of the early 1990s, for two examples. We also explored the generational impact of the outer planets passing through the various signs. The underlying theme in that seminar was *"trust the children."* I've recently extracted a two-hour presentation from that longer program. It is specifically about the astrological ages, with a deep focus on what it means to be moving out of the Age of Pisces and into the Age of Aquarius. If you feel drawn to going more deeply into any of this material, go to my website and enter "Generations" in the search engine. You will find links to both programs.

SECTION SEVEN

A FEW LOOSE ENDS

There are six "loose ends" in this short section – topics that did not fit easily into any of the other categories, so I gave them their own boneyard. The first es-say deals with the burgeoning diversity of techniques in astrological thought. I wrestle with my own uncertainty about whether to think of that as a problem or not. The second essay started out as a playful "Happy New Year" message, but it quickly dived into deeper waters. In it, a meditation on the wild Roman feast of the Saturnalia was the launching pad for what turned into an investigation of what's missing from our contemporary view of Capricorn. In the third essay, I step out onto the exceedingly thin ice of talking about gender in the modern world and what that might portend for astrologers who persist in calling Venus "she" and Mars "he." (I bet you already sense which way the wind is blowing on that one!) Then there is a piece about 12-step programs and how they seem to share some primordial DNA with the original 12-step program: astrology itself. The fifth essay deals with a modern form of anxiety attack – what if I'm not really a Leo? What if I am an Ophiuchus? Finally, I take a close look at the often-overlooked quincunx aspect.

54

It's been ten years since I wrote this next piece and the circumstances I describe remain about the same: contemporary astrology has split into a number of highly distinct branches, most of which don't understand each other's vocabulary or techniques very well at all. Inevitably this has led to a massive communication breakdown, as well as some partisan mudslinging among certain astrologers whose behavior suggests to me that they did not enjoy the advantages of good potty training as children. Calling this situation "a problem" is fair enough, so long as we are careful not to imagine a "solution" in which one form of astrology conquers and silences the rest. The problematic part is pretty obvious though – it is hard to have a community without a common language, and the contemporary astrological world is rapidly careening in that direction.

THE ASTROLOGICAL
TOWER OF BABEL

(Newsletter – March 2012)

The United Astrology Conference is happening in New Orleans, May 24-29. I am shaking in my boots. There is something good about the big pow-wow aspects of the event. It is a gathering of astrology's far-flung clans, a chance to catch up with old friends and maybe encounter some new ideas. UAC is a good thing! Experienced astrologers can always learn something new there. Beginners can get a taste of the various current styles of astrology, and decide what approach best fits their values and interests. It is a *smorgasbord* of teachers. A lot of good people work very hard to make the event happen. I am grateful to them all.

Why am I shaking in my boots? One reason is that UAC is not exactly a semi-introvert's paradise – I quickly start feeling like the proverbial deer-in-the-headlights when I am there in those crowds. Playing the role of "a famous astrologer" makes it tougher in that department too. Mostly, the "famous astrologer" thing is kind of a joke – it's like being world famous . . . i*n the southwestern corner of Moldavia.*

That's mostly what it feels like to be a famous astrologer . . .

. . . except at UAC, where I feel like Elvis Presley, except that Elvis never had to walk across a lobby filled with a thousand people all looking to get him to sign a book or listen to a theory. The attention is gratifying at first, and I genuinely appreciate the love and support I get. But after a few hours of it, I feel like hiding under my bed in my hotel room. And UAC lasts for days and days . . .

So that is the main reason I am shaking in my boots.

But there is another one, and that's what I want to write about in this newsletter. UAC embodies a situation I am concerned about in the contemporary world of astrology. I am not sure if it is fair or right to call it a "problem." You can decide. *The issue is that there are so many forms of astrology nowadays that even astrologers can barely talk to each other.*

When I was a young astrologer, most of the books and teachers I encountered were speaking essentially the same language. There were arguments and disagreements, of course. But we all had a common vocabulary. We called it "astrology" and we all meant basically the same thing by the word. Then, pretty much coinciding with Neptune's entry into mind-expanding Sagittarius in 1970, astrology went into a period of cross-cultural expansion and fragmentation. In the western world, there was rather suddenly a lot of popular interest in Vedic astrology. Simultaneously, Renaissance astrology had a . . . renaissance. The older Hellenistic and Arabic texts began to be translated, and spun off into the "traditional astrology" schools of contemporary astrological thought. There was also a burst of interest in asteroids. Uranian astrology expanded its circle of advocates, as did Harmonic astrology.

At the same time, personal computers appeared on the astrological scene, making all sorts of abstruse calculations and techniques available. Each one of them developed a passionate following, at least for a while.

We still talk about "astrology," as if it were one field. *But the truth of it is that there are now a great many astrologies, all seemingly drifting further and further away from each other with each passing year.*

The issue that I am focussing on here is that these various astrologies are mutually incomprehensible. The situation parallels the way the Latin language of the Roman empire metastasized into half the languages spoken in Europe today. And speaking good Spanish does not mean that you can understand French.

An even better metaphor might be the Biblical "Tower of Babel." In the Book of Genesis, humans were getting a little haughty and decided to build a tower that would reach up to God's realm in the sky. God came down to see what they were up to and He said: *"They are one people and have one language, and nothing will be withholden from them which they purpose to do."*

And then God got an idea. He said, *"Come, let us go down and confound their speech."* And so God *"scattered them upon the face of the earth,"* confusing their languages.

In the resultant chaos, no further construction on the Tower of Babel building was accomplished. The modern astrological community is in a "Tower of Babel" situation very much like this.

As an evolutionary astrologer, I am confident of my skills and techniques. I have more clients and students than I can handle, and I am grateful for my good life. But at UAC I know I will hear, for one example, Hellenistic astrologers talking – *and I will not have the slightest what they are saying.* I wouldn't even be able to have a creative, respectful argument with them. It would be like me trying to discuss philosophy with a professor in Moscow. I don't speak Russian.

Everything boils down to one word: *diversity.* Is astrological diversity inherently a problem? No, of course not. There is not "One True Astrology" anymore than there is One True Faith. All these paths are welcome. All have skillful practitioners who help people – and all of these separate branches of astrology number egocentric goofballs in their ranks as well.

But does this diversity present something more troubling? Does it pose difficulties around communication? And is communication not the basis of community?

Those are easier questions. Yes, yes, and yes are the answers.

The actual astrology-in-the-sky of the UAC event is telling – and adds fuel to my shaking boots. UAC runs from May 24-29. On May 26, Mercury, along with the Sun, conjuncts the Moon's south node in Gemini. To me, that suggests *a ripening karma of too much intellect and chatter, and not enough soul, human feeling, and "embodiment."*

I think that contemporary astrology's "Tower of Babel" karma is going to be a very dominant theme there in New Orleans this year. I fear the conference will be characterized by a nervous, mentally-overdriven energy – something that just feels like way too much coffee. With Sun in the mix and the auto-referential qualities of Mercury being in its own sign, I fear a crowd of people talking in order to be heard, but no one really listening to anyone else.

Hiding under my bed might be very appealing.

But good astrology never just leaves us hanging. It always aims our attention at *effective answers* too. What I am going to try to hold in my own consciousness at UAC is the healing message of the north node of the Moon in Sagittarius. That makes a reference to a resolution of the hyped-intellect problem via *integrative, wholistic* views, driven by *intuition* and animated by a spirit of *generosity* – Sagittarian virtues, in other words.

Let us "embrace the foreigner."

I am also going to try to be very aware of the Neptune/Chiron conjunction in Pisces, which is squaring that nodal axis. It is telling us that we, as the astrological community, have something sweetly mystical *left unresolved* here in terms of our group-karma. *As a group, our path forward lies in celebrating and healing the softer, more unitive energies of our wounded collective spirituality.*

We are not talking heads. Astrology is not simply scholarship. It is far more soulful than that.

Faced with that Russian professor of philosophy, neither one of us would understand a word the other one was saying. But I could look into his eyes, and connect with his mysterious, luminous humanity. I could let him look into my own eyes and, hopefully, he would see the same thing in me.

I can do the same with the Vedic astrologers, the Renaissance astrologers, the Hellenistic astrologers, and the rest.

Maybe that way, when I am brave enough to crawl out from under my bed at that hotel in New Orleans, I can be part of the solution rather than yet another living, breathing embodiment of the problem.

56

*This started out a fluffy "happy new year" piece, but as I pulled threads which
led me to thinking about the ancient Roman feast of Saturnalia, it quickly got
into far deeper territory. It turns out that there is still a residual wisdom about
Saturn and Capricorn woven into our holiday customs – a wisdom that has
strangely been missing from astrology books for many years. We can still learn
from those books! But we can also learn something astrological – something the
Romans understood very well – from our current customs and traditions around
"the holiday season" where some old traditions about Capricorn have had better
luck surviving than they have in our current crop of astrology books. Let's see
what our drunken Uncle Joe has to teach astrologers on New Year's Eve . . .*

HAPPY NEW YEAR . . . OR IS IT SATURNALIA?

(Newsletter – December 2015)

Light soon returns to the world. *Hallelujah, hallelujah* . . . but you have
heard it all before and so it's not exactly shocking news. I'll refrain
from pommeling you with a cascade of platitudes you've been hearing
since you were a kid. Of course I am talking about the Winter Solstice.
And you might be yawning already. You don't have to be an astrologer to
know that the tide of ever-lengthening nights is now about to turn, at least
up here in the northern hemisphere.

Yet, buried beneath the veil of numbing familiarity, this yearly turning of the tide of light still holds some riddles – and some answers – for us.

For people in the north, the coldest parts of winter still lie ahead, but at least there's a reason for hope. As the eloquent jazz pianist, Bill Evans, titled one of his albums, "You Must Believe in Spring." If you live in the snow-belt, there's a lyric to tape to the door of your refrigerator!

Even here in the southern California desert where I live, I am looking forward to the days getting longer again. Who can reflect even for ten seconds on the notion of "the return of the light" without a little whisper of optimism arising? Who can think of the winter solstice without hope?

But, astrologically, *what is the sign of hope and optimism?* Probably the most obvious response would be Sagittarius, with Jupiter ruling it. Yet the Winter Solstice marks our exit from that domain, not our entry into it. At the Solstice, the Sun enters Capricorn. We fall under the shadow of Saturn. That symbolism has often been saddled with negative connotations – and even a more balanced view of Capricorn and Saturn generally doesn't invoke words such as hope or optimism.

So what is going on here? Do we have the zodiac backwards?

Capricorn and Saturn are usually taken to reflect the values of patience, endurance, and hard work. I think of Saturn as representing our *ability to do what we don't feel like doing.* And if you are living up there in the snow-belt, all you have to do is peer out your frosty living room window and behold your car buried under 18" of fresh snow. Instantly you are an expert when it comes to Saturn: winter is indeed a season of "doing what we don't feel like doing." Get out that shovel and put on your mittens, in other words. You've got to dig out the car so you can get to work.

So where is the hope? Where is the optimism? Where is the joy that should come with the "return of the light?"

Winter is *tough* – that symbolism quickly clicks. But the light is returning . . . how does that piece fit into the puzzle? That's what leads to our pivotal question: *are we missing something about Capricorn and Saturn?*

Long ago, the Romans didn't miss it. Every Winter Solstice, they celebrated their feast of the *Saturnalia.* And it was wild. According to Cato the Elder, *"Rampant overeating and drunkenness became the rule, and a sober person the exception."*

- Citizens wore funny felt hats and bright-colored clothing instead of the usual monochrome togas.
- Gifts were exchanged, including many "gag gifts."
- Kids were given toys.
- Gambling and dice-games, normally viewed with judgement, were played in public.

In one interesting custom, masters would serve sumptuous meals to their slaves, taking on the reversed role. During Saturnalia, slaves enjoyed at least a pretense of disrespect for their masters, and were exempted from punishment for it. Free speech, hell-raising, and wild, uninhibited abandon reigned.

This was how the Romans celebrated Capricorn?

One obvious response is that actually most of us – astrologers possibly excepted at least when we are working – aren't missing anything at all. Clearly, the Roman Saturnalia has reincarnated pretty much intact in our current celebrations of the Winter Solstice: *Christmas, New Year's Eve, Chanukah* – the festivities connected with all of them would be quite recognizable to a Roman citizen two thousand years ago. We still celebrate the "Return of the Light" with gift-giving, dressing up, and general debauchery.

Our word *capricious* – suggesting one who acts impulsively on sudden whimsies, desires, and changes of mood – clearly has its linguistic roots in common with Capricorn. Just think of a frolicking goat. Or think of your alcoholic Uncle Joe late on the evening of December 25th.

So what happened to us astrologers? *How did Capricorn and Saturn get such dure reputations?* And, more importantly, do they actually deserve them?

Well, in a word – yes. Capricorn and Saturn are clearly about *duty* and *integrity.* They are about *impulse-control.* They are about *boundaries, limits,* and the eternal *law of consequences.* I stick by my definition of Saturn as the planet that gives us "the ability to do what we don't feel like doing." All of these observations are easily demonstrated.

But how much of that self-denial can you stand? As Bob Marley sang, *"Every day the bucket a-go a well, one day the bottom a-go drop out."*

Bottom line, we've all got breaking points when it comes to an unrelenting diet of "being good." Living in society of course involves constraint, but at some point, the raw, appetite-driven, animal inside us all has simply had enough of those rules. And that animal can, at that breaking point, become very dangerous.

- Repress anger and it eventually turns to pathological violence.
- Repress sexuality and it turns to perversion.

With what planets do we associate exactly those kinds of explosive outbursts? The obvious answers are Uranus and Mars. Their impulsiveness can be accurately understood to balance the constraints implicit in Saturn. *But what if we are short-changing Saturn (and thus Capricorn) here too?* Saturn is, above all, *realistic.* And how realistic is it really to imagine that humans can eternally toe the lines of mechanical propriety?

We all need an occasional weekend – and think about the clue built into the weekly calendar: *are you perhaps looking forward to this coming Saturn-day, the day before Sunday?*

Every effective high school teacher knows the usefulness of giving the kids a break from endless Algebra from time to time. Corporations have "casual Fridays." Married Celtic people merrily fornicated without shame every Beltane Eve.

Saturn correlates with *structure* – yes, but what we have forgotten is that Saturn's blueprint also includes realistic safety valves that let us endure all that structure. In the words of the proverb, all work and no play makes Jack a dull boy.

The Roman poet Vergil said of the god Saturn that *"he gathered together the unruly race of fauns and nymphs scattered over mountain heights, and gave them laws . . ."*

They were still fauns and nymphs, of course – just better behaved because "laws" gave them a Saturnian sense of the proper time and the place to express the more feral aspects of their own natures.

Tellingly, Vergil added, *"Under his reign were the Golden Ages men tell of. In perfect peace he ruled the nations."*

We are all actually happier with Saturn-structure – provided that the structure includes time for release.

The Sun enters Capricorn this year on December 21 or 22, depending on your Time Zone. Meanwhile, Saturn of course remains in early Sagittarius – an astrological reality that will flavor our collective response to this particular holiday season. Sagittarius – ruled by the fabled King of the Gods, Jupiter – does not enjoy limits. Quoting Oscar Wilde, Jupiter "can resist anything except temptation."

At this holiday season, there is thus in the collective air a pent-up hunger to bust out, to break some rules, and to wreak some merry havoc. While in Sagittarius, Saturn has been holding back the Jovial flood waters. We are all hungry for release. Our inner "fauns and nymphs" are feeling their appetites – for food, for drink, for sexual release, for whatever gets our ya-ya's out.

Interestingly, Saturn makes not a single major aspect to any planet except the Moon during the entire month of December. Thus, there are no constraints on it beyond those limits it supplies itself.

How to handle all this potential for hell-raising? Reflexively we might say keep the whiskey away from your alcoholic Uncle Joe – or yourself too if you tend to overdo it. Zippers up. Think of your waistline. Behave in such a fashion that you will respect yourself in the morning.

But those virtuous admonitions are not . . . well, *Saturnalian* enough. They reflect the modern astrological error of seeing Saturn in strictly "Thou-shalt-not" terms, which is not really, fully, correct. Saturn, as we saw earlier, is utterly realistic – and it is realistic to accept the fact that you need some release. You may be healthier in every sense of the word if you recognize that.

Saturn gave laws to the fauns and nymphs – but in doing so *he didn't turn them all into prim little Puritans drinking non-caffeinated herbal teas with their knees pressed chastely together.* He knew that would only annoy the nymphs and fauns, and turn them mean.

If there were a relevant cliche here, it would probably be, "Moderation in all things" – *including moderation.*

So, from all of us at www.forrestastrology.com to you and yours – Happy Holidays! Have some fun, and take good, conscious, compassionate care of yourself. Indulge yourself – gently – remembering that it's time to be kind to your inner "fauns and nymphs."

That's one way of being in harmony with the Return of the Light – one way of being in harmony with the true spirit of Capricorn. Comfort the parts of yourself that need to have a good time – those *are* your inner "fauns and nymphs." Listen to them. Make a deal with them. Let Virtue and Vice come to an arrangement that allows both of them some breathing room. Be Saturn-realistic: "vice" is part of you too. You can't just "legislate" it out of existence. Throw it a bone – but don't let it grab the steering wheel of your life.

And go ahead and wear that funny hat.

57

Evolving gender politics is one of those areas where wide-open public discussion seems so potentially helpful and healing for all concerned, and yet nowadays one can hardly say anything without eliciting the Holy Inquisition from one direction or another. I step into the fray here, making a modest argument for astrologers getting past the custom of calling Mars "male" and Venus "female." The heart of what I am trying to say in this essay is simply that at a cultural level everything is always changing. To remain relevant, astrologers must be nimble enough to adapt their language to emerging realities, whatever they might be and however they might personally feel about them.

PLANETS AND GENDER

(Newsletter – January 2015)

Stored deep in the antiquarian depths of my memory banks is an old giggle about the dance that heterosexual people do: "she ran away from him until she caught him." What happened to the time when people believed that gender-script? Is it truly extinct? That seems to have become a bit of "an essay question" nowadays as the old assumptions about the meaning of male and female pass through the wringer of cultural change.

In any case, that old saying I mentioned comes to mind as I watch Venus chase Mars around the Zodiac this month.

At the beginning of January, Venus is speeding through the last degrees of Capricorn while Mars lies safely ahead, deep in Aquarius. Venus joins "him" there on the 3rd – but "he" quickly escapes into Pisces on January 12th. Venus tracks Mars down and enters Pisces "herself" at the end of the month, on the 28th. Mars nearly makes "his" getaway yet again – "he" just manages to cross the line into Aries in mid-February, but Venus finally catches up with "him" there on February 22nd. Mars rules Aries though, and Venus is said to be debilitated in that sign, so who wins?

We'll all wait for the *denouement* with bated breath and popping popcorn.

In the previous lines, I am sure that you noticed me putting "he" and "him" in quotation marks. Should I? There are good astrologers who still think of Mars as masculine and Venus as feminine. They have objective reasons for doing that too. For example, they observe that Venus transits often signify contact with women and Mars transits contact with men.

Some astrologers, more Jungian in their language, will affirm that "of course everyone has masculine and feminine sides," with Mars referring to the former and Venus to the latter.

Other astrologers roll their eyes at "political correctness" and claim that *anyone can see* that women are Venusian and men are Martial.

These are some of the most pressing astro-psychological questions of our Age. *Do planetary gender associations still work?* Are they relevant to the actual realities of modern people? Might the whole situation be in flux? As our culture evolves, might this kind of astrological thinking still fit older people – but fail to be meaningful to younger ones?

With Pluto in Capricorn, there has very obviously been a significant swing back in the direction of more traditional values. Will that shift the fabled "revolution in gender roles" back in a more conservative direction? Is that revolution a cultural whimsy, like hairstyles, or does it represent something more fundamental?

Personally, I am only 100% sure of one thing: I wouldn't much enjoy having dinner with anyone who has a quick answer to any of those questions. They are complicated and multi-dimensional. I don't know the answers. My guess is that no one does, at least not yet.

The phenomenon that, when I was young, we used to call "women's liberation" and later came to be called "feminism" is so broad in its implications that it is hard to pin down. It seems to be a fundamental review of the entire collision-zone of history, biology, and myth. I suspect it will be many generations before the dust settles, if it ever settles.

There is another practical point of which I am sure: *astrologers must constantly adapt and re-adapt to the realities that people actually experience.* In my time in the world, with the kinds of people who have been drawn to me as clients, I've personally found that refraining from calling Mars "masculine" and Venus "feminine" has worked best. Both planets are "it" to me, not "he" or "she." That is because clearly, the classic domains of Mars – *independence, competition, assertiveness, and adventure* – are enthusiastically populated nowadays by females, while traditionally Venusian domains – *aesthetics, intimacy, grace, and fresh underpants* – are not off-limits to males.

It seems to me that in the pursuit of wholeness, astrologers today need to be wary of adding to the piles of outdated cultural obstacles we all face. Can I get an "amen?"

But, hey, *get a grip, Steve. Anyone can see that the girls are still out there buying shoes while the guys are drinking beer and watching the game.* That has not gone away.

Do I need some lead in my shoes here, in other words?

I am not convinced that I do – but I am certain that there are many people who would think that I did. Their arguments would be based on what was "obviously true" about the differences between males and females – trouble is, all that was a lot more "obvious" thirty years ago than it is today.

Like most astrologers, the majority of my clients are female. That is no surprise – Venus seeks help, intimate conversation, and relationship, while Mars would rather "solve things himself." Right there in the male/female ratio of my practice is some hard-to-deny evidence for the old gender/planet connections.

When I do sit with male clients, which is probably about 25% of the time, they are often interested in *career*, while the women often bring *relational issues* into the conversation. Again we see the fingerprints of the old mythic script, alive and well, right here in 2015.

But here's another observation: *these patterns I describe hold better with my clients who are in the second half of life. They are less evident with the younger ones.*

Most of us laugh at the silent, stone-faced "John Wayne" view of "cowboy" maleness. Ditto for the chirpy "Doris Day" kind of hapless, kitchen-bound female. They seem too extreme – and of course, to find these stark examples, I have to go back to the heyday of John Wayne and Doris Day, which is even a bit before my time.

There can be no reasonable doubt that there has been change in this Mars-Venus mythology over the past few generations – and little doubt that the changes have taken stronger hold among younger people.

So the big wheels are still turning. Will they continue to turn or will there be a swing back in the old direction? I don't know. As an astrologer, I don't really *need* to know. *I just need to speak the language of the present world.*

What about gay people? Are gay men more "Venusian?" Are gay women more "Martial?" All the old cliches about gayness run in those directions – but in my experience, the majority of gay people don't actually embody the cliches very well.

Acceptance of gayness is increasingly widespread in our society at this point. *My guess is that this social sea-change is just one piece of an even larger re-framing of our relationship with the archetypes of Mars and Venus.* And again, younger people seem to be in the forefront of the changes, not only in terms of being accepting toward gay folks, but also in their blurring the boundaries of gender roles, sexual orientation, and even biology.

I'll turn sixty-six years old about the time you are reading these words. So, as Paul McCartney put it, I am experiencing a state called "Memory Almost Full." As a young boy in the America of the 1950's, I remember getting programmed not to cry. I was taught to be stoic. In essence, I was taught to think of *Superman* – the Man of Steel – as a regular guy to whose standards I had better adhere. I remember a time when I was taught to assume that all women were "girls" – and that all gay people were nice, but inherently comical.

Getting older gives a person the catbird seat watching these kinds of changes. I cringe when I hear or read a fellow astrologer of my own age still making the old uncritical assumptions, still treating Venus and Mars as female and male, as if it were still 1955. They embarrass themselves without knowing it.

And they lose their audience, at least its younger members.

So Venus is chasing Mars around the zodiac all this month and they come together in Aries on February 22nd. Their cycle of conjunctions is erratic; sometimes it's just weeks between them, other times a couple of years. We'll get two such conjunctions this year, with a second one happening in Leo on September 1. After that, we'll wait until early October of 2017 before a Venus-Mars conjunction forms again.

For all of us as individuals, these alignments represent a fresh start in our intimate lives. I also have the feeling that, at a cultural level, such conjunctions reflect a collective attempt to integrate these two ancient energies in fresh ways. Seeing that 2015 holds two such conjunctions, both of them in Fire signs, leads me to believe that this year will be a "hot" one in the ongoing debates and discussions about gender and sexuality around the planet.

And angels will be laughing about how the humans think they are only talking about our biological plumbing when in actuality we are talking about how everyone has a left arm and a right arm and how much better life goes if we use both of them.

58

Let me begin by belaboring the obvious: when you stop and think about it, astrology itself is a twelve step program, maybe the original one. I've often wondered about the connection between the two – and I have always simply assumed the connection to be there. Is the link between astrology and twelve step programs simply archetypal or is there some "secret history" involved? When I wrote the words that you are about to read, I wasn't sure of the answer. After I published this piece, I received several scholarly emails detailing various common origins and linkages. Rather than re-writing this essay to include all of that research, I am happy to leave it as I originally wrote it, and leave any further academic sleuthing up to you.

ASTROLOGY AND THE TWELVE STEP PROGRAMS
(Newsletter – January 2020)

Throughout the centuries, many people have been brought to their knees by addictions of various sorts. Many of them have found healing in twelve step programs based on the model of Alcoholics Anonymous. As most of us know, these programs of recovery are not limited to alcohol issues. They have spun off similar programs for drug dependencies. With only a few modifications, there are also twelve step programs for food addiction, sexual addiction, and codependent behavior.

In a similar vein, there are the ancillary programs called Al-Anon and Alateen for people who experience intimate involvements with friends, lovers, or family members who have suffered from such addictions. Those programs are based on the same twelve steps too.

No surprise: many people engaged in recovery via such programs have also turned to astrological counsel for support. Over the years, many such souls have found their way to my office. As a group, I have found them impressive. I have learned a lot from them. To overcome a disease such as alcoholism requires two virtues in abundance: first, *courage* – and, second, enough *humility* to recognize and admit the existence of the problem.

Inevitably, as an astrologer, I've often wondered about why there are *twelve* steps, not ten, or some other round number. Could there be some interlock between astrology and these life-saving systems?

At one level, I'm confident simply saying "of course there is a connection." No one needs to believe in astrology for it to work. Twelve is an organic, magic number, woven into all archetypal processes, not just astrology.

That's actually enough evidence of an interconnection for me right there.

Without too much of a stretch, one might say that astrology itself is the *original* twelve step program. But there is more evidence for such a connection, even though some of it is impressionistic and circumstantial.

The founder of Alcoholics Anonymous, Bill Wilson, knew Carl Gustav Jung and had a long correspondence with him. That is a matter of record. Jung was, among other things, an astrologer as well as a student of metaphysical traditions in general.

Jung had also worked with many active alcoholics in his clinical practice. He was generally not very optimistic about their prospects. He felt that the only hope for such a person lay in some kind of spiritual conversion or enlightenment experience – something he felt to be quite rare.

Jung wrote to Bill Wilson that he felt that sobriety could only be achieved through "a higher education of the mind beyond the confines of mere rationalism" – through some kind of enlightenment or conversion experience, in other words. He added that it might also occur through "an act of grace or through personal and honest contact with friends."

Later, Wilson wrote to Jung that "this candid and humble statement of yours was beyond doubt the first foundation stone upon which our Society has since been built."

So here's our trail of breadcrumbs tempting us deeper into the deep, dark forest.

- Jung knew astrology.
- Wilson thanked Jung for "laying the foundation stone" of AA.
- Astrology and Alcoholics Anonymous are both "spiritual programs" in some sense.
- Both involve a staged evolution through twelve sequenced processes

. . . *clues, clues, clues*. What would Sherlock Holmes think? I believe Sherlock would say, "*hmmm . . .*" and go on to look for more evidence.

A scholar or a historian might turn over more stones by carefully perusing the letters that passed between Wilson and Jung. I haven't done much of that beyond a bit of Google searching. But if Sherlock Holmes turned to me looking for suggestions, I would direct him right to the heart of Bill Wilson's whole system of recovery, which is the twelve steps themselves. To me, the fingerprints of astrology are all over them. They uncannily and unerringly mirror the evolutionary logic of the twelve houses.

Anyone familiar with what I have published about the astrological houses over the years will immediately make a lot of multi-dimensional connections here between the twelve houses and the twelve steps. That all goes far beyond what I can cover in a couple thousand words. In this brief newsletter, I just want to point out, one by one, a few highlights that directly and rather obviously link Wilson's twelve steps to the evolutionary processes implicit in the twelve houses.

Did astrology inspire him? Or did he just tune in to one of the universe's most basic laws?

I have no idea . . .

Step #1: *We admitted we were powerless over alcohol – that our lives had become unmanageable.*

When activated by heavy transits or progressions, the first house is always ultimately about reaching one of life's major crossroads. We are required to *make a decision*, often without full information – and invariably without any ultimate certainty about how things will turn out. It is about the right use of Will – which is to say, Will guided by intuition, honesty, and common sense. It is about *making a stand*, turning a corner, and not looking back.

Step #2. *Came to believe that a Power greater than ourselves could restore us to sanity.*

"Oh my God, what have I gotten myself into?" That sense of suddenly finding ourselves on shaky ground is a classic second house sentiment. We have made a new start – on faith alone – in the first house. Now we start to get scared. Do we *have what it takes* to succeed? And actually the answer is no – unless we quickly seek the *right resources* to empower us. Astrologically, might that mean money? Education? Alliances? Or in the case of the twelve steps, "the Higher Power." That is the resource that we need. Only *with God's help* can we possibly succeed – and God's help is available for the asking.

Step #3. *Made a decision to turn our will and our lives over to the care of God as we understood Him.*

The third house is cognitive and mental; it has to do with how we *look at everything* – and how everyone else "looks at things" differently than we do. Inevitably, this leads to a confusion of contradictory data. All we can ever do is continue our inquiries and strive to deepen our understanding. We are sustained by a spirit of faith that there is an answer out there somewhere. In the third step, we literally make a mental commitment – a *decision*. And we come to our best individual, independent understanding of what we are doing and why we are doing it.

A footnote: In the 1930s when the twelve steps first appeared "God" was still a "Him." That language is now dated; hopefully we can all get past that quibble.

Step #4. *Made a searching and fearless moral inventory of ourselves.*

The fourth house is the "midnight house." It is where psychology happens, where we face those *"all alone at 3:00 o'clock in the morning"* kinds of truths about our lives. When it is stimulated, it is time for a long, hard talk with ourselves – time to take our "moral inventory" in a spirit of naked humility. We try to stand naked before the mirror of inner truth – a mirror that is ultimately the reality of the life that we have lived, observed "fearlessly," without any self-serving varnish or comforting rationalizations.

Step #5. *Admitted to God, to ourselves, and to another human being the exact nature of our wrongs.*

In the fifth house, we *express ourselves.* It is about *honest self-revelation.* We put the truth on the table *in a form in which others can see it.* Astrologically, the fifth house is related to *creativity* – and if you have ever sung in front of a group or made a public speech, you know about those butterflies in the belly that come from putting yourself out there with that kind of vulnerability. In the fifth step, we partake of a most ancient human sacrament of recovery: *we make our confession.* For it to count, there has to be an "audience" of at least one other person.

Step #6. *Were entirely ready to have God remove all these defects of character.*

Astrologically, "servants" is a word often associated with the sixth house, and to be "a servant" is to be in a humble position. A servant serves a master, and implicit in that relationship is the comparison of foolishness with wisdom, naivete with experience, the flawed with the perfect. The sixth step is about *humility* and its close cousin, *preparing to surrender* – and the acknowledgment that there is indeed a Higher Power in the universe willing to help us in miraculous ways, if only we are spiritually naked enough to submit to it. That humble submission is the price we must pay.

Step #7. *Humbly asked Him to remove our shortcomings.*

In mainstream astrology, the seventh house is often called "the house of marriage." More accurately, it refers to all sorts of *intimate, interdependent relationships.* In the seventh step, we see the establishment of an intimate bond based on vulnerability and acknowledged need – except that now this intimacy is not about another person, but rather about our personal relationship with the Higher Power. The simplest human analogy would be asking someone whom you love for a hug at a time when you are having difficulty loving yourself – except that now we make that same intimate request of God.

Step #8. *Made a list of all persons we had harmed, and became willing to make amends to them all.*

Astrologically, in the eighth house we see the deepest, most psychologically intimate kinds of relationships. Long-term couples are the best illustration, although a dear friend "with whom you can talk about anything" illustrates the eighth house transaction too. Such connections can sometimes feel almost claustrophobic in their naked emotional intensity. People experiencing that kind of intimacy with each other inevitably wind up revealing their most wounded places even if they don't want to. That self-revelation may happen intentionally – but so often it happens indirectly, via our own hurtful behavior toward each other. At such a moment, all you can do is to apologize. If you have ever looked a loved one in the eye and abjectly pleaded, *"I am sorry. Can you ever forgive me?"* . . . you understand the eighth step. Note that this step is inward, private, and internal. It is about "making a list" and "becoming willing to make amends," not about actually doing it out loud. That step comes next.

Step #9. *Made direct amends to such people wherever possible, except when to do so would injure them or others.*

Classically, the ninth house is about Religion and Law. Those words still work if we let them breathe. All religions deal with questions of right and wrong, and how to behave ourselves in a complicated, ambiguous world. "Law" typically spells out the details – so the Biblical "do not kill" resolves legally into manslaughter, justifiable homicide, and Murder One. In the ninth step, we take what we have admitted to ourselves in the eighth step – or eighth house – and we try to *make things as right with those whom we have offended as we possibly can,* while avoiding making any bad situations worse. Here is the question: *how do we best behave ourselves today in a world that we have already complicated, perhaps irredeemably, in the past?* Right and wrong are slippery concepts, and sometimes the best we can do is to find a middle road. Inevitably we find ourselves in philosophical territory as we contemplate right action and wrong action in the tricky labyrinths of the dance humans do with each other.

Step #10. *Continued to take personal inventory and when we were wrong promptly admitted it.*

In conventional astrology, the tenth house is related to *career* – which on the face of it, doesn't seem to have much to do with the tenth step. In modern society, "career" says a lot about how other people see us and categorize us – or more broadly, it is about how we *reveal ourselves* to the world at large. Similarly, the tenth step is about *not hiding anything;* it is about *authenticity* in terms of our appearance in the world. It is about an ongoing *public* commitment to *moral transparency*. It is not exactly about "never having any secrets," but more specifically, about *never using secrecy as a defense for the ego* nor as a way of staying stuck in the past. The tenth step saves us from the dangers of the fallacious notion of one single "conversion experience" – an error which could slip us into believing that our work on ourselves is now complete and that we can forget about it. That lazy, tempting idea is replaced with "continuing" to take a moral inventory.

Step #11. *Sought through prayer and meditation to improve our conscious contact with God, as we understood Him, praying only for knowledge of His will for us and the power to carry that out.*

In the eleventh step, we *set goals* for ourselves and commit to pursuing them over time. We take the long view. Similarly, in the broader framework of astrology, the eleventh house relates generally to all of our hopes, dreams, and aspirations for the future. It relates to what we *prioritize* in life. Here, in this eleventh step, we commit specifically to a strategy of *spiritual self-improvement over time*. Astrologically, there is also a link between the eleventh house and our *strategic alliances*. That notion is (surprisingly) missing in the wording of the eleventh step, but it is certainly implicit in the whole idea of committing to long-term membership in a healing fellowship.

Step #12. *Having had a spiritual awakening as the result of these Steps, we tried to carry this message to alcoholics, and to practice these principles in all our affairs.*

Astrologically, the twelfth house is, at its best, mystical and spiritual. The reference in the twelfth step to a *spiritual awakening* certainly echoes that notion loudly and clearly. There is more: can we imagine any true spiritual awakening that does not include a simultaneous awakening of *compassion* for the suffering of other human beings? In this step, a caring engagement with the needs of others saves us from the kind of navel-gazing that characterizes more self-indulgent spiritual paths.

So what would Sherlock Holmes think? Did Bill Wilson have some kind of astrological training? I think the evidence that the twelve astrological houses and the twelve steps have a common origin is compelling.

Is it possible that Carl Jung conveyed this ancient metaphysical structure to Bill Wilson? Surely that is a possibility too, but in and of itself, it proves nothing.

Or did Bill Wilson simply plug into one of those ancient archetypal truths that is so basic to the universe that it gets discovered over and over again?

That is easy to believe.

I still don't know the answer, and I am not sure that it really matters. Either way, astrology and the twelves steps are gifts from heaven that help us navigate life in a world that can sometimes be very hard. Those addictive "exit ramps" on the spiritual path can sometimes look very tempting – and, like most exit ramps, once you have taken them, finding your way back to the highway can be difficult.

It might even take you twelve steps to find your way back.

59

*Every couple of years, my Inbox fills with nervous emails from clients
who have just learned that science has now proven that they are not
Sagittarians after all, but rather Ophiuchans. It's one expression of the
larger critical meme that "astrologers have the signs all wrong." In this
intentionally very short piece, which I have often copied and sent to
those nervous clients, we quickly blow all that silliness out of the water.*

AM I REALLY AN
OPHIUCHUS?

(Newsletter – January 2014)

Every two or three years it seems that some scientist will announce the
"discovery" that astrologers have gotten their signs all wrong and that
all of you Virgos have actually been Leos all along. The latest episode also
involves inserting Ophiuchus into the mix – that some of you Sagittarians
are actually Ophiucans.

Now, for the sake of some fun, including Ophiuchus could actually be
worth the price of a little confusion – I'd love to see ten Sagittarians competing over who could best say "Ophiuchus" *three times fast*, all the while
drinking tequila. But, fun aside, here's the simple truth of it: don't worry, all
you Virgos can remain Virgos and there are no Ophiucans among us at all.

There are two issues making themselves felt here. The first one has to do with this scandalous notion that we astrologers have "gotten our signs wrong." *We haven't.* Western astrology is based on the seasons, not the constellations – it's built around the equinoxes and the solstices, not the stars. What we astrologers call "Aries" is different from what astronomers call Aries. *What astrologers call Aries starts with wherever the Sun is on the first day of spring in the northern hemisphere.* That "Aries point" gradually drifts backwards along the track of the zodiacal *constellations*, passing through all of them every 26,000 years or so. (Go back to chapter fifty-four if you want to understand this phenomenon in more detail.)

One effect of all of that is that not every "Aries" was born with the Sun in the *constellation* Aries. No problem – that's because *the constellation Aries has nothing to do with it.* It did, once, many, many years ago. But then the astrologer-astronomers two or three thousand years ago noticed this drift, which is called the *Precession of the Equinoxes*, and began to correct for it. That's when the *sign* Aries decoupled from the *constellation* Aries.

Call me paranoid, but I have the distinct suspicion that when the Internet is ablaze with astronomers "discovering that your sign is not really your sign," that they actually know quite well what they are doing, but they can't resist taking a cheap shot at astrology and astrologers.

What about Ophiuchus? Well, the familiar constellations were all basically folklore, without any formal boundaries or definitions, until fairly recently. In fact, each culture tended to define them differently, connecting the starry dots according to their own local mythology. That's why what's a "big dipper" in the U.S. is a "plow" in the U.K. – or to split the hairs with Virgoan correctness, "a *plough*."

In 1929 and 1930, the International Astronomical Union nailed the constellation boundaries down officially, drawing lines around them, eliminating some of them, while happening to add some new territory to the old constellation Ophiuchus – which now did something no one had ever accused it before of doing: *it now overlapped the ecliptic.* That put it on the zodiac,

Thus did Ophiucus, for the first time in history, become "the thirteenth sign."

Suffice to say that these astronomers are the same people who more recently delivered the brilliant notion that Pluto is no longer a planet. How much authority over astrology do we want to give them? They don't care and neither should we.

I have nothing against astronomers or the I.A.U., but I do quibble with astrologers who feel the need to bow down before their every edict.

Bottom line: there are still twelve signs, not thirteen, Virgos remain Virgos and Ophiucans are unicorns, and that's all you really need to know.

60

The key to true skill in taking in the big, integrative astrological picture lies very much in not being tempted to lose the larger thematic thread of a chart by disappearing down the rabbit hole of seductive details. For that reason, in my client work, I tend to use the major aspects while not paying much attention to the minor ones. One so-called minor aspect often calls me though, and that is the 150 degree quincunx. Here is what I have learned about it.

THE MISUNDERSTOOD QUINCUNX ASPECT

(Newsletter – July 2014)

The quincunx aspect in astrology – two planets separated by 150 degrees; one sign more than a trine, one less than an opposition – what does it signify? It is usually called a *minor aspect,* but many astrologers argue for its power. Personally, I would rate it as the most significant of the minor aspects.

Let's absorb the core principles that underlie this often-misunderstood astrological structure. Let's see how it actually works, in other words

Quincunx – go ahead, admit it: you're having fun just saying the word. But be careful. There's a tendency to pronounce it as "quin" followed by "cunx." But "quinc" then "unx" is more accurate. Those are the Latin words, more or less, for the numbers five and twelve. And astrologically, the quincunx represents 5/12s of the zodiac. Splitting hairs, *quinque* and *uncia* are actually the roots of the term.

The original quincunx, by the way, was a Roman coin, back in the 3rd century B.C. It's value was 5/12s of the standard Roman "dollar" of the day.

So what is the feeling of a quincunx aspect? How does it work? What kind of *relationship* does it establish between two planets?

Remember that all aspects, whether we label them as easy or hard, are always about *integration*. Two energies are trying to figure out how to live together. With a square, that integration might involve *friction*. With a sextile, perhaps *mutual excitation*. A trine? Mutual *enhancement* and *harmony*. Every aspect is about some kind of relationship – and just as with human relationships, they come in a lot of different flavors. Even easy ones have their challenges – they can get very sleepy. Hard ones can turn into World War Three – but they can also breed passion and growth.

What about the quincunx? What kind of dance steps must we master for it to function in a helpful, integrative fashion? The key word we often read is *adjustment*. That's about right, I think – but let me try to make it come more alive for you by telling you about one way that I have experienced it myself. I am going to use my own Sun sign, Capricorn, and my relationship with Gemini as examples – those two signs operate in a quincunx aspect with each other.

By the way, in what I write here I'm going to be thinking like one of the classical Hellenistic astrologers who saw aspects as *existing between the signs themselves* rather than between planets, as we tend to think of aspects today. Those ancient Greek astrologers had a reasonable approach – any planet anywhere in Aquarius, for example, has a certain archetypal "square" argument going with any planet anywhere in Taurus or Scorpio, regardless of exact degree positions.

Cutting to the chase, as a solar Capricorn so I tend to think in a fairly orderly, systematic fashion. Meanwhile, Gemini – *which doesn't* – happens to own much of the real estate in my seventh house, so I've always been drawn to Geminian and Mercury-dominated people.

I might say that I have often found myself *"quincunxed"* by them. Here is what I mean by that.

Maybe I am launched into a speech, busy developing some "complex and eminently rational point" for the benefit of one of my Gemini friends, whom I have cornered. Perhaps, for example, I am expounding upon the parallels between Heisenberg's Uncertainty Principle and the transits of the planet Uranus.

Meanwhile, my Gemini friend appears to be paying enraptured attention. But suddenly she blurts out that *my nose reminds her of the nose of someone she once knew in high school* – someone who had a weird orange cat named Heisenberg that once got lost for six weeks then came meowing back at her high school friend's door, skinny, but with this mysterious, unexplained pink ribbon around his neck, and both the cat and the Gemini woman's friend were Capricorns, she thinks...although maybe come to think of it the cat was an Aquarian . . . with a Sagiattarian Moon . . . yes, definitely the cat had a Sagittarian Moon . . .

What is a good Capricorn to do?
Strangulation crosses my mind, as does bleak despair. *Was she not listening to me?* Does she think I am boring? Does she suffer from ADD? Was I being too pedantic?

Then she mentions how that whole lost cat story *led her high school friend to become a veterinarian.*

And I realize, somewhat awe-struck, what my Gemini friend has actually done. She was indeed listening to me carefully, but she *was thinking in Gemini fashion* – something completely alien to a Capricorn. *The look of my nose led her to the memory of her high school friend and how the "random event" of the cat's misadventure had deepened her friend's fascination with animals and led to his career choice – which illustrated and amplified the very point I had been making in my lecure.*

In so doing, my friend had deftly brought in synchronicity, animal magic, and miraculous Uranian improbabilities whose meaning we can only understand much later. As a good Gemini, she had allowed her mind to slip into *free-association*, wisely trusting that she was probably onto something if she would just let her consciousness *jam* with it for a while.

And she was right.

She didn't follow a linear, logical track, *but her track worked.* That's Gemini, quincunxing Capricorn. No one would mistake that for how Capricorn energy operates. My Gemini friend understood me perfectly well and she was following my point in her own creative, scattershot way.

But our minds worked utterly differently. That's a quincunx in action.

Naturally, every quincunx is a two-way street. There might be times when my Gemini friend could benefit from me helping her "get to the point" or to "remain on track" and to "avoid tempting distractions." Capricorn is good at all of that. Capricorn *stays focussed*. The question is, does that mean Capricorn wears blinders or that Capricorn keeps its eye on the prize – and the answer to that question is *yes*. They're both true, in other words – true, and inseparable.

- The point is that, with a quincunx joining two planets, perhaps in working together their joint intelligence can operate at a more integrative, creative, and effective level than either of them could attain alone, if only they can adjust to each others' natural methods and truly *team up*.

There's the quincunx in action – it represents two perspectives, two methods, two sets of values, *completely widdershins to each other*, and yet stronger together than they ever could be on their own. To get it right, each planet must *stretch* and *adjust* to accommodate the sheer *alien weirdness* of the other one. In reaching that point of *catalytic partnership*, enormous creativity is unleashed. There is a breadth and subtlety of perception.

And there is a tremendous *mutual fascination*.

Meanwhile, if the two planets fail to stretch and adjust, they only manage to drive each other crazy. Mutual frustration arises. Each one simply misses the point which the other one represents. Quincunxes can be very annoying.

My illustration reflects the natural quincunx between Capricorn and Gemini. Similarly, you can put the quincunx into the marrow of your bones by imagining Aquarius and Cancer trying to communicate – or Sagittarius and Taurus, or any of the other quincunx sign pairings. Think of how they can simply *miss each other's meanings and intentions* in expressing themselves – but think too about how the *blind spots* of each can be opened up and illuminated if they make the effort to really listen to each other.

In the example I've used here, I focussed heavily on signs rather than planets. In practical terms in working with quincunxes, I've always found that to be a productive strategy. Signs always imbue planets with specific underlying *values and agendas* – and in looking at the potential for *mutual incomprehension* between one set of values and agendas and the other – looking at the two signs, in other words – you'll often catch the express train to the heart of what's going on between the two planets.

Signs typically make it clearer than the planets do, so they are a good place to start.

An under-reported piece of astrological lore is the great prevalence of quincunx-based human partnerships of all sorts, with a particular focus on coupling relationships and creative partnerships. That shouldn't be a big surprise based on what we've seen so far, but it is an under-utilized point in synastry practice. Astrologer Amanda Owen has done some eye-opening work in that area. Here in the United States, I think of Barack and Michelle Obama, who seem to have an exemplary marriage based on the Leo-Capricorn quincunx. Right here at home, my partner Michelle Kondos and I are in the same boat – she's a Leo and I'm a Capricorn. For you music fans, here's yet another Capricorn-Leo quincunx: *Led Zeppelin's* Jimmy Page and Robert Plant.

John Lennon's prominent Jupiter-Saturn conjunction was quincunx Yoko Ono's Moon, while it also made a quincunx to Paul McCartney's Ascendant. Marilyn Monroe's irresistible Venus made a quincunx to Joe Maggio's Ascendant, while she and John Fitzgerald Kennedy had their Moons in a tight quincunx. Meanwhile, JFK's Venus made a quincunx to Jackie's Ascendant. The list goes on.

The quincunx can be vexing too, even if it is also usually intriguing and compelling. That means that while it's sexy, it is not always a formula for lasting romance – Brad Pitt's Pluto is just one degree away from a perfect quincunx to Angelina Jolie's Moon. A few years ago, you perhaps saw some evidence of the way that aspect worked for them in the tabloid press. Meanwhile, Courtney Love's Ascendant made a quincunx to Kurt Cobain's Venus.

Carl Jung's compelling interest in what Sigmund Freud thought of as "the black tide of occultism" was a famous driver of the rift between them.

Unsurprisingly, Jung's Neptune formed a quincunx to Freud's Mars, while Jung's own Mars was in a quincunx aspect to Freud's natal Uranus.

The price of endless surprise in a relationship is endless adjustment. Surf the waves, and the result is undying fascination as we wonder – usually futilely – what the other person is going to do next.

Whether it's about people or planets, that is the dance of the quincunx aspect.

SECTION EIGHT

THE SKY ITSELF

Picture some ancient intelligent hominid gazing at the vast and shimmering night sky, feeling puzzled, feeling inspired, wondering, breathing it in – that is the moment when astrology was born. That visceral sense of a connection with the sky itself – that "photon connection" – tends to be a chronically missing vitamin in the diet of contemporary astrologers. The lack of simple stargazing makes us too "heady," robbing our work of soul. I got into astrology through that astronomical backdoor myself, looking through telescopes as a young amateur astronomer. I've never lost that childlike sense of enchantment with the starry night. It's one reason I moved out to the dark skies of the southwestern desert. In this section, I take us down two roads. On one of them, we are actually making visual contact with the heavens – stepping out at night and daring to look up at what we spend our lives talking about. Down the other road, I invite us to cross the "great divide" and pay attention to our estranged sisters and brothers: the astronomers. It's long past time for a family reunion. We have so much to teach each other.

61

Amateur astronomy is what got me into astrology in the first place. You don't even need a telescope to do it – just gazing at the milky way from a blessedly dark sky location is enough to make an astrologer out of anyone. Obviously that last line is not exactly true or there would be more astrologers in the world, but what I mean is that no one can look at the night sky without feeling the presence of a magic so vast that it dwarfs our comprehension. That, I think, is the core impulse that turned our ancestors into astrologers. I've stuck with astronomy all these years. As an astrologer too, one thing that has always struck me is the lack of an active synergy between the astrological mind and the astronomical one. The solar system as we understand it today is actually a far cry from the one I learned about in high school – and sadly, that old version of the solar system is still the one upon which most astrologers base their models of human consciousness. By the way, in reading this long article, some of my readers might feel some deja vu – a modified version of it appeared as an early chapter in The Book of Neptune.

THE NEW SOLAR SYSTEM

(The Mountain Astrologer, August 2006)

Pluto's recent demotion to the status of "dwarf planet" upset a lot of us. It shouldn't. We astrologers have been calling the Sun and Moon "planets" for a long time. We have, in other words, a long tradition of using the term "planet" differently than astronomers do.

On top of that, experience has taught us that Pluto simply works like a planet – we know it's a "planet" and we really don't need anyone's approval before we use the term.

Even better, most of us have had some fun thinking about upcoming Pluto transits for those astronomers in the International Astronomical Union who demoted Pluto! How would you like to explain that one to the Lord of the Underworld?

There are deeper, more disturbing issues here though. As astrologers, we need, collectively, to address them. Astrology's bones are being rattled, and it's not just by a bunch of academics quibbling over slippery definitions of the word "planet."

Lately, it's fashionable to say that astrology as we know it goes back only to the 3rd century B.C. in Greece. I laugh at that idea when I think of the hard evidence – evidence as "hard" as the stones of Stonehenge, the Great Pyramids of Egypt, Teotihuacan, and the Venus-temple known as Newgrange in Ireland. Those ancient edifices represent the traditions I personally feel living inside me. Who actually imagines that Stonehenge was merely an eclipse-calculator, and that the people who built it never felt that the sky was speaking meaningfully to them?

Our lineage is ancient, and it is emphatically not limited to the Mediterranean world.

However old astrology may be, it was shaken to its roots just 227 years ago when William Herschel discovered Uranus. Suddenly the venerable system of "seven planets" (counting the Moon and the Sun!) simply didn't reflect reality anymore. "As above, so below" had been astrology's philosophical cornerstone for a long, long time. We either had to abandon it – or deal with this new planet that upset everything.

We dealt with it.

Today, there are astrologers working in Classical, Jyotish, and Renaissance traditions who prefer to ignore Uranus. I am confident that many of them get excellent results. They have my sincere respect. But who could honestly look at the reality of human experience and argue that a transit of Uranus over, say, your natal Sun is a non-event? This "invisible planet" produces results that are quite palpable. Again, kudos to those re-imagining traditional forms of astrology – they have a lot to teach us. But if they try to pretend that the last two thousand years have taught us nothing, I just shake my head. Uranus is real, and it is not the only new astrological reality. *There is a new solar system out there.*

Astrology swallowed the discovery of Uranus whole, and nowadays only a small minority of us would dare ignore it. Interestingly, we found that while Uranus has its own unique energetic signature, it works basically the same way that the other seven planets do. In other words, if someone has Uranus conjunct her Ascendant, that planet's fabled independence or zaniness is strongly visible in her outward character. If someone has Uranus conjunct his Venus, his intimate life will reflect those "peculiar, eccentric, or unusual" qualities we have come to call "Uranian."

Learning to work with a new planet – while it was confusing to the "seven planets" crowd at a theoretical level – turned out actually not to be so difficult. *And of course, the bonus was that the inclusion of Uranus made astrology more accurate.* Before 1781, I am sure that many an astrologer was baffled to see someone's life turned upside down when "nothing seemed to be happening in the chart." Knowledge of Uranus – part of the objective truth of the solar system – made us stronger.

We then had a few decades to reflect. It was another sixty-five years before Neptune entered our vocabulary. That happened in 1846. After that, eighty-four more years (precisely one Uranian cycle!) passed before it happened again: Clyde Tombaugh discovered yet another new planet: Pluto. That was in 1930.

The point is that at a human level, the astrological community had *time for digestion* between these discoveries. By the middle of the last century, finding and absorbing new planets had become almost a routine event – and generations of astrologers had time to chew on the new riddles. For those of you who know modern astrological culture, it was as if Dane Rudhyar put out some theories in 1936, Liz Green commented on them in the 1980s, and Moses Siregar III gave Dane and Liz a Reality Check in 2007.

- Time and collective experience are powerful filters. They separate wheat from chaff very effectively. We astrologers have always been strongest when working as a group, correcting each other, each seeing something the other has not seen.

The critical point is that *astrology stretched to include these three new planets without having to throw away entirely the elemental principles upon which the system had been founded.* By this I mean that these new planets, like the classical ones, seem to have intrinsic meanings which were then modified by sign placements and by aspects to other planets, and then expressed outwardly in houses – they behaved, in other words, just like Mercury or Jupiter. To include them in the system, we didn't have to change the paradigms upon which our thinking was founded. We only had to complicate everything a bit, and wrestle with some hard, ongoing questions about the planetary "rulerships" of signs.

I know that people practicing any of the older traditions may be frustrated by my simplifications here. But what we are facing today is vaster and more vexing than anything we've ever faced before, to the point that I believe these distinctions among the present and former astrological traditions will soon pale before the pressure of emerging astronomical reality.

As a community and as a tradition, we'll "hang together, or we'll hang separately."

First, a bit more history. Just twenty years after the discovery of Uranus, a planetary discovery appeared to happen again: Giuseppe Piazzi. discovered Ceres in 1801. It was at first hailed as a new planet – after all, other than the occasional comet, we'd discovered *nothing but planets* until then, so the assumption was natural. Then, just one year later, Pallas was found – in basically the same orbit as Ceres. Astronomers and astrologers had always understood planets as occupying separate orbits, so something strange was going on here. Then Juno was discovered in 1804 and Vesta in 1807, all in similar orbits between Mars and Jupiter. It was quickly recognized that these bodies were in a different class than Mercury or Uranus. The term "minor planet" was coined, and later our more familiar word, "asteroid."

By the early nineteenth century, the solar system was clearly becoming a more complex place than we'd ever imagined. Do these asteroids have meaning? Yes, for sure – anyone who explores them quickly realizes that they are significant symbols. A lot of astrologers have worked with the so-called "Big Four" asteroids – which actually are only the first four that happened to be discovered. (Hygiea, discovered by de Gasparis in 1849, is actually a lot bigger than Juno.)

My aim here is not really to interpret asteroids. Many astrologers are far more knowledgeable about them than I am. Demetra George's book, *Asteroid Goddesses,* is a great place to get started. I would also like to call attention to Martha Lang-Wescott's *Mechanics of the Future: Asteroids*. If you are drawn to this branch of the astrological world, a practical way of staying right on the cutting edge is to get involved with the Asteroid Special Interest Group (SIG) of the National Council for Geocosmic Research.

The observation I do want to underscore is that, even though asteroids are quite demonstrably real in their astrological meaning, the majority of present-day astrologers do not actually use them. Psychologically, it is easy to understand why. Once we added Uranus, Neptune, and Pluto to the system, charts were already getting crowded! There is a natural, understandable hesitancy to over-complicate the picture. At some point, it becomes too much. We can't stay on top of it. The mind rebels.

And maybe we should trust that hesitancy – as of September 17, 2006, there were a total of 341,328 known asteroids. 136,563 of them have permanent official numbers, and 13,479 have official names.

Many more doubtless remain to be discovered. Current estimates put the total number of asteroids above one kilometer in diameter to be somewhere between 1.1 and 1.9 million. *No astrologer could possibly use them all.* If you tried to do an astrological consultation including all of them and you worked sixteen hours a day, giving each asteroid a single minute, that session would take nearly six years to complete.

This does not mean that asteroids are not real! "As above, so below" still works, down to incredible levels of precision. The larger asteroids are amenable to deeper forms of psychological analysis, while many of the smaller ones seem to add elements of startlingly refined, but ultimately rather minor detail. It's astonishing – but it often only astonishes, without telling us anything we didn't already know.

With thousands of named asteroids and more coming every day, the potential excitement is tempered by the feeling of being overwhelmed by trivial information. One could be forgiven for a feeling of nostalgia about the simpler days of "seven planets." But should we succumb uncritically to that feeling?

This emerging problem of burgeoning, over-abundant celestial symbolism is now over two centuries old. It is, in my opinion, the "elephant in the living room" of the astrological community. We dealt with Uranus, Neptune and Pluto by treating them, more or less, like the classical planets. We jammed them into the old system, made them fit our old paradigms. On the other hand, many of us have essentially dealt with the "asteroid problem" by sweeping it under the carpet.

But the plot continued to thicken. Chiron was discovered in 1977, orbiting out beyond Saturn, far outside the familiar "asteroid belt." It came to be called a "Centaur Object," which is defined as an asteroid-like object orbiting between Jupiter and Neptune. Shortly after Chiron was discovered, another Centaur – Pholus – was discovered. It's even bigger than Chiron. Now we have many more.

You can learn a lot about these discoveries, and stay current, by visiting the web site of astrologer Philip Sedgwick. By the way, I'd like to honor Philip here. He proposed the names for two of the Centaurs, Thereus and Elatus, which were accepted by the International Astronomical Union. Other astrologers have named Centaurs too. Melanie Reinhart contributed Nessus. Robert von Heeren offered Asbolus and Chariklo. With Zane Stein and others, von Heeren also contributed Hylonome. With Philip Sedgwick and others, he named Cyllarus. John Delaney named Echeclus and Crantor.

As an anthropological observation about the "tribe" of astrologers, I find it interesting that while Chiron has caught on in a big way, it is hard to find an astrologer who can even name another Centaur! As I mentioned, Pholus is bigger than Chiron, yet how many of us can even locate Pholus in our own natal charts? Again, the "overwhelm" factor seems to be making itself felt.

- Here is the heart of what I am saying: as a group, *we astrologers are turning away from the objective complexity of the modern solar system, and the reasons are more psychological than rational.*

Maybe we should turn away! Maybe we have to. We can't spend six years sitting with each client. Unlike astrologers who lived before 1781, we must now *edit the solar system.* There is no other realistic choice. It has grown too complex for us. But our unspoken strategy of ignoring that emerging complexity, of pretending that it is not happening, is beginning to unravel.

In 1992 the system blew wide open. The first "Kuiper Belt Object" was found: a *planet-like* body orbiting beyond Pluto.

("Kuiper" rhymes with "wiper" or "viper," by the way).

Astrologers note that in 1992 the paradigm-shifting conjunction of Uranus and Neptune was beginning. Clearly, the basic "myth of the world" was about to change. The cycle of conjunctions between these two planets is 171 years long. The last time it happened, it brought us electricity, fossil fuel-driven mass transportation, and the collapse of European colonialism – the beginning of the modern world, in other words. Uranus-Neptune conjunctions are a long story and not the one I am telling now, although if you are interested, have a look at chapter fifty-one. Suffice to say that the real mythic significance of the early and middle 1990s is not yet fully appreciated. The Internet is surely part of it, but it will likely be decades before anyone has any true perspective on the enormity of the changes rooted in that period of time. I am very confident that the discovery of the first Kuiper Belt Object in 1992 will be remembered by future astrologers as even more pivotal than the discovery of Uranus two centuries earlier.

As I write these words, 1992 was just fifteen years ago. Today, *over eight hundred* Kuiper Belt Objects (KBOs) have been discovered. They are mostly all farther away and generally much smaller than Pluto – which is already pretty little by planet-standards. Astrologers have mostly ignored them all. In a sense, so did the astronomers – until ignoring the KBOs became impossible. That happened in 2003, another KBO was discovered. With this one, now known as Eris, there was a crucial difference: *it was the size of Pluto.*

If Pluto was a planet, then how could Eris not be called one too? Astronomers could no longer ignore the issue. The big question was, *what did the word "planet" actually mean?*

The NASA website ran a headline, *"10th Planet Discovered"* on July 29, 2005. If astrologers felt a little nervous at the thought of yet another planet to add to their consultations, imagine the poor astronomers! They quickly realized that if both Pluto and Eris were truly planets, then there might actually be about eight hundred more of them.

And those were just ones that had been discovered so far. Estimates for the total number of these KBOs with diameters over one hundred kilometers run toward 70,000 – although it is worth noting that the total mass of the Kuiper Belt is probably very low, all together equaling or perhaps just exceeding that of the planet Earth.

Quickly, the International Astronomical Union moved to contain the damage. Meeting in Prague in summer 2006, they famously (or infamously!) downgraded Pluto – and Eris – to the status of "dwarf planets," declaring that there were now a total of eight planets in the solar system.

According to the I.A.U.'s "Prague definition," to be considered a planet, a body must meet three criteria.

- First, it orbits a star. In other words, moons that orbit planets don't count. Fair enough.
- Second, a planet has "sufficient mass for its self-gravity to overcome rigid body forces so that it assumes a . . . nearly round shape."
- Third, a planet has "cleared the neighborhood around its orbit." In other words, its gravity has swept up the local cosmic debris, and it orbits in solitary splendor, unlike the asteroids which often share very similar orbits.

Regarding the second criterion, "roundness," there is much debate. Most of the little asteroids look like potatoes. The asteroid Ceres is massive enough to be fairly round. That's why the I.A.U. upgraded its status to that of a "dwarf planet," like Pluto. But the trouble is, Pallas is pretty round too, and so is Vesta. And if you look at Jupiter through a telescope, you can easily see that it is quite distinctly fat around the middle – not round in any precise sense. Being "kind of round, more or less," hardly qualifies as a rigorous scientific standard. There's just too much slack in the term. "Round" is a word like 'beautiful" or "boring," unless we define it as perfect sphericity. But then none of the planets qualify.

Similar objections exist for the fuzzy third criterion – that a planet "clears its orbit." The Trojan asteroids are locked in gravitational resonance with Jupiter and actually *share* its orbit. More fundamentally, various forms of cosmic debris are simply whizzing around the solar system all the time, cutting in and out of all the planetary orbits. That is why we probably ought to be worried about the "Near-Earth Asteroids," which cross our own orbit regularly. One of them took out the dinosaurs sixty-five million years ago, and who knows what tomorrow may bring?

Earth itself hasn't even "cleared its orbit." Are we not a planet?

Alan Stern, principal investigator for NASA's New Horizons mission to Pluto, put it this way, "Tell me where else in astronomy we classify objects by what else is around them? It's ridiculous." He added, "I just think the I.A.U. has embarrassed itself. . . . If you read the definition that they have adopted in that room today, it is scientifically indefensible."

Some astrologers, eager to defend our own *status quo* regarding planetary definitions, have been eager to criticize the I.A.U. too. We all want to keep Pluto as a planet! But if Pluto is going to remain a planet, then

Eris must surely be considered one too – and probably Sedna and Quaoar, along with Rhadamanthus, Varuna, Orcus, Chaos, Deucalion, Huya, Ixion ... and many others not yet found.

We can kiss the *status quo* goodbye, in other words.

That's over. That was then. This is now.

Here, in my opinion, is the quintessential problem: *the word "planet" is a cultural artifact, nothing more.* It is folklore. It has no final meaning. It is a word left over from the days before telescopes, when the sky we beheld was far simpler. With the discovery of Uranus, the word "planet" began to betray us, although it took us another two and a quarter centuries for us to fully realize it.

Never in the long history of our craft have we faced a challenge of this magnitude. If the word "planet" collapses, what is astrology? How do we begin to think about what we do?

There is a strong temptation to turn away from the enormity of these questions and take safe intellectual refuge in historical forms of astrology. Once again, I am not criticizing those who study such traditions. Again, they have a lot to teach us. That work was rooted in a time when astrology was not marginalized, when it was instead integrated into the bedrock of the then-contemporary worldview. The intellectual cream of society applied its intelligence to its study. I appreciate those who are digging up these traditions. *But I do want to be wary of the reactionary psychological impulse to turn away from complexity and ambiguity, and to take refuge in "the good old days."* The solar system, truth said, is vastly more complex than we astrologers are eager to admit – and vastly more complex than it was conceived to be even just a couple of generations ago, let alone in ancient Egypt, India, or Greece.

A third of a million known asteroids! Eight hundred known "planets" beyond Pluto! No wonder we are nervous. What shall we do?

Our ace in the hole is that we can still rely on our unfailing Hermetic principle: "as above, so below." *The structure of the solar system continues to reflect the structure of the human mind.* There is ample proof of this. Many of us have reflected on the historical synchronicities connected with the timing of the discoveries of Uranus *(the American and French revolutions)*, Neptune *(the Communist Manifesto and Spiritualism)*, and Pluto *(nuclear energy and the widespread cultural integration of psychological language)*.

But the discoveries of those three planets were just the first few drops of rain in the desert. Since 1992, there has been a downpour: not just one new planet, but a deluge of them.

To help us keep the faith, let's run a quick reality check on the continued viability of the Hermetic concept of "as above, so below." The solar system has become more complex. *Has our sense of the complexity of the human mind also deepened in the past two hundred years?* Do we simultaneously entertain many more avenues of perception and belief systems than did our great-grandparents? Is practically everyone identified with some "minority perspective?" Are we now in a multi-cultural era? *Does life simply feel more complicated?*

"Below" is still looking exactly like "above," in other words. Developments in astronomy are still reflecting cultural sociology. Hermes Trismegistus still reigns.

The new solar system is real; it is meaningful; and it is not going to go away. For astrologers, it is the challenge of our Age to figure out not only what it means, but also how to cope with it intellectually in the astrological counseling rooms of the future. Clearly, old styles of piecemeal astrological thinking are not going to succeed.

I don't know the answer, but I'd like to suggest a starting place. Here is a radical suggestion: Let's experiment with dropping the word "planet" at least for a few moments, and see where that leads us. Dump the baggage, and then at least the possibility of clear, new thinking arises.

Furthermore, our customary piecemeal approaches to astrological symbolism are not going to cut that much mustard. We need to think in terms of *integrated systems* rather than separate, compartmentalized planetary categories. Let's look at the solar system with a fresh eye. And let's look at it from a perspective that would literally have been beyond the scope of the imaginations of our ancestors.

- *Let's look at the solar system from the observation deck of a star ship poised a trillion miles above the north pole of the Sun.*

Look down. What do you see? Almost lost in the brilliant solar glare, whipping around it with incredible speed, there are four tiny spheres of rock: Mercury, Venus, Earth, and Mars. Two of them have significant atmospheres. Two don't. But structurally, all four are similar: they are little round worlds made of stone, all sitting close to the central fire, and flitting around it at high speeds.

Next out from the Sun, there's a big, wide haze of dust. That is the asteroid belt. Even Ceres, by far the biggest of them, is less than one-fifth the diameter of the smallest of the stone-worlds, Mercury. It is clearly different from them – Ceres is just part of the haze too.

The haze of dusty stone thins a bit as we continue to head outward, away from the Sun – although we can still see it extending diaphanously beyond the main asteroid concentration.

Our eyes are quickly pulled away from the thinning haze by the spectacle that hits us next. Here, beyond a doubt, lies the solar system's main attraction. Again, it is a second grouping of four spherical bodies – but this time they are gigantic gaudy balloons. One of them even has a flamboyant set of rings around it. As we squint we see that the others have rings too, only fainter. All four of these bright giants are surrounded by retinues of asteroid-sized moons. These four bodies are totally different from the little stone-worlds, and obviously dominant. They move slowly and majestically, unlike the nervous twitter of the inner four. They are made of gas, thickening into a viscous matrix without any true surfaces.

And they are huge.

The very smallest of them (Uranus) is fully four times bigger in diameter than the biggest of the stone-worlds (Earth), while the biggest of them (Jupiter) is *thirty* times the diameter of tiny Mercury. One of them – Jupiter – even has a moon (Ganymede) that is significantly bigger than the entire "planet" Mercury! Another – Saturn –has a moon (Titan) with lakes and a thick, cloudy atmosphere.

There is just no comparison between these gas giants and Earth or Mars. Other than the Sun, these four bodies are clearly the main features of the solar system. In their glare, you might not even notice the little stone worlds.

- Consider: if you were on that star ship, would you use a *single word* to describe both the tiny, frenetic stone-worlds and these gas-giants? If you could see the solar system this clearly and truly, would you have ever invented the single word "planet?"

Let's continue our journey.

Beyond Neptune, we come to another haze of stone, although its texture is more granular than what we saw with the asteroid belt. It is a beach made of pebbles rather than a beach made of grains of sand. And the ocean beyond it is the ocean of deep interstellar space.

If you squint, you can make out tiny spherical Pluto – just half the size of Mercury. Eris, much farther out, is also the size of Pluto, but it's still tiny. And the rest (so far as we now know) are much smaller.

- This is a portrait of the solar system as humanity – at least the astronomers among us – now sees and understands it. *This is the current metaphor-in-the-sky upon which any truly contemporary, state-of-the-art astrology must be based.* This is the actual "above" which we now find ourselves "below."

Human consciousness, after enormous effort, inwardly and outwardly, has attained this pinnacle of clear understanding – and if a few thousand years of astrological experience mean anything, then this new understanding is now holding a mirror before the human mind. It is the task of modern astrologers to make sense of this reality, lest astrology become a museum piece, divorced from the present-day experiential realities of modern human beings. If astrology is going to retain its core philosophical underpinning – that mind and sky are locked in resonance – we simply cannot ignore the sky as we now know it. We cannot pretend that the last two thousand years of observational astronomy have not happened.

Still avoiding the pitfalls of the archaic, misleading word "planet," what exactly do we see out there? Clearly, the Sun is in a class by itself. Then there are two totally distinct, unified groups of major bodies, each composed of four worlds. Separating these two groups like a punctuation mark, there is a dense field of asteroid-haze, which gradually tapers off as we come to the gas giants – and then maybe something a little more complex than asteroid-haze begins again out beyond the gas-giants, finishing off the edges of the system, at least so far as we now know. Synchronicity declares that this "Kuiper Belt" is something we are only beginning to grasp – and not only in outward scientific terms, but also presumably in terms of its mysterious inward human significance.

What can we make of all this? I don't really know exactly. But I have been giving it a lot of thought. Here is a suggestion for a "systems" model of current planetary astronomy. Please question it and argue against it – that's how astrology goes forward. The chances of any one single person, myself included, being "exactly right" about all of this any time in the next century or so are minuscule

THE ROCKY WORLDS

I'm going to start off with something that might be a big mistake. But somebody's got to jump off the cliff . . .

Since we never see the Earth in the sky, it can't be an astrological factor – at least so long as we stick to the geocentric system. Heliocentric systems may have a bright future, but I am going to continue with geocentrism until it is "proven guilty" since it has served us so well for so long.

So, rather than using the Earth in this system, I am going to substitute the Moon. There is at least a good rationalization for this. The Moon is actually half again the size of Mercury, and clearly would be another "rocky world" if it were orbiting the Sun freely. And Earth = Moon is a plausible formula, since they are so bound together in the structural model of the solar system.

And then there's my real reason for doing this: unlike the Earth, *we see the Moon in the sky*. It can be used astrologically, in other words.

In this proposed perspective, we now have four rocky worlds: Mercury, Venus, Moon, and Mars. I believe that these rocky worlds represent primal, foundational "animal" factors in human consciousness.

- MERCURY is simply the senses themselves – the capacity of any organism to perceive and interpret its environment. *Paramecia* do it, gophers do it, and so do we.

- VENUS and MARS are clearly sexual, for starters – again, a clear, compelling "animal" factor in us. But I think we can get even more primary than that. Venus attracts and Mars repels. What can be more basic to human experience than attraction and avoidance? Desire and revulsion? Love and hate? Beauty and ugliness? Joy and suffering? Ask the Buddha. Venus and Mars correlate with these two elemental *organismic motivations*. Venus is the pleasure we seek and Mars is the pain we avoid.

- MOON correlates with the urge to eat and to feed, to heal and regenerate, to rest, to establish a "nest," and to protect the young.

The point is, all these rocky worlds relate to truly primary functions of *organismic consciousness* – functions which are not limited to humans. As the inner animal is part of us, so are these stone worlds. Just for clarity, I would like to emphasize that I am not using the word "animal" pejoratively, but rather in a healthy pagan sense. Hallelujah for the flesh! It's good to be alive. And Goddess help those among us who are ashamed to be animals.

Let me add that, as these "stone-world" functions interact with higher levels of human awareness, they potentially take on loftier coloration. Mercury becomes the entire edifice of language and thus of the collective memory of culture: the stories and ideas that bind us together over millennia. Venus becomes Art, and the self-transcending aspects of love. Mars rises to healthy competitiveness, which breeds excellence, and also to the high warrior's capacity to protect the innocent and the defenseless. The Moon turns into the richness of our psychic lives, and the soulful feelings of our unbreakable commitments to each other.

But these four bodies could not accomplish any of it without the uplifting influence of . . .

THE GAS GIANTS

With the matched quaternity of Jupiter, Saturn, Uranus and Neptune, our "systems" analysis of the solar system moves into new territory. In broad terms, we enter a realm of psychic functions that *seem only to reach their fullest flower in human consciousness, as distinct from animal consciousness* – with one interesting exception I will mention at the end of this section.

- JUPITER. Hope, and a sense that tomorrow might be better than today – that we ourselves might become greater and "more." Humans, some of us at least, consciously seek *self-improvement.* We seek "to be all that we can be." We are status-conscious. We like glory. We like to be "cool." Has an eagle ever consciously prided itself on flying higher than any other eagle in history? Has a tiger ever sought to be declared "Most Ferocious" in its high school yearbook? To be remembered for it? These drives toward *expansion,* and toward earning a place in the *collective memory* are the essence of Jupiter. They are not simply "animal functions."
- SATURN. One very practical definition of Saturn is that it refers to the ability to do what we don't feel like doing – *self-discipline,* in other words. Or self-discipline's cousins: *morality and integrity.* Is the urge toward abstract Excellence part of our animal consciousness? The urge to restrict and constrain ourselves according to *principles?* To *delay gratification?* To achieve self-respect? Animals

don't seem to be much bothered by these matters. Saturn is also connected to our uniquely human *experience of time.* We conjecture about tomorrow. We think about getting older. Do monkeys?

- URANUS. Individuation. The Tibetans teach us that stupidity is a "sin," and that if we indulge in it, we will come back as animals. This is a difficult teaching. By "stupidity," I think they mean "dummying up," which means using intellectual laziness to get us off the evolutionary hook. And they suggest that the results of that error involve our being reborn into the animal kingdom, where the critical element is *endless instinctually-driven repetitiveness* – in a word, what humans would call "boredom." Animals tend to do exactly the same things over and over and over again. We humans, pretty much alone among Earth's creatures, seem to have the Uranian capacity intentionally to change our very natures. If you have self-awareness enough to be reading this magazine, you've probably done that as an individual – changed, consciously and intentionally. We seek to become different from each other, to distinguish ourselves from others of our species. Again, do monkeys? Collectively, we humans are *the apes who learned to fly.* We are the apes who went from Kitty Hawk to the Moon in sixty-six years. There's individuation!

- NEPTUNE. Even the physicists have now confirmed what the mystics have been saying since the beginning of human time: the universe is simply not three-dimensional, and it is logically indefensible to think of it that way. Other dimensions are folded into the ones we see. Neptune represents the capacity to know those facts *in your bones,* to experience those truths directly. It is the place you go when you "let go of yourself." It is about meditation and higher states of awareness. It is about the *mechanisms of conscious dying.* Squirrels and eels show no evidence of engagement with these states of awareness. It's a human thing. Animals, with a few possible exceptions such as elephants, generally don't prepare their beloved dead for another world. This quality of awareness – the notion that beyond the "planetary" realm of ego there lies the "deep space" of consciousness itself – is Neptune's domain.

A couple of modifiers: In writing these words about the distinctions between the stony-worlds and the gas giants, I am aware of being perhaps a little too rigid about the distinction between humans and animals. I personally believe that I have met a few cats who were not only more pleasant company, but also simply more conscious than some humans. I believe there is actually some overlap in evolutionary levels among the species. In writing what I have written, I am simplifying the distinctions between people and animals so that the core principles become more readily visible.

I would also add that animals *who live with humans* quickly begin to take on some of these "gas giant" qualities. We have all seen dogs who seem to feel guilty or ashamed, or cats apparently suffering angry embarrassment after some ill-fated acrobatic move. Further, among cats in the wild, eye-contact is a sign of aggression. But with my own cats, I have sometimes indulged in the quintessential human practice of long, soulful eye-contact. My cats have learned a significant human behavior, and, I think, they've learned its meaning as well. I believe this may be an important key to some of the metaphysics behind the Divine Plan for human/animal friendships. But I am not going to go there in this article – the subject is too vast.

THE TRANS-NEPTUNIANS

Beyond Pluto lie the "Trans-Neptunians." The term comes from the astronomers, and I suspect it has a big future. It may very well replace the term "Kuiper Belt Object."

Personally, I feel that the I.A.U. was totally correct in realizing that Pluto was not a "planet" in the same sense that Neptune or Mercury are – but that they draped themselves in idiocy in the eyes of future historians of science by failing to realize that the real issue is simply that the word "planet" itself needs to become extinct. Like their intellectual ancestors twenty generations ago, they've done the equivalent of bending over backwards to defend an earth-centered solar system. Their definition of "planet" is as tortured as those pre-Copernican "crystalline spheres" that showed the Sun orbiting the Earth.

After Neptune, what is out there? With the discovery of Neptune, we triggered a faculty *of transcendent perception* – but perception of exactly what? *The next dimension, Heaven, the astral world, the dharmakaya* . . . . (no shortage of words here!) . . . . *Tir Na Nog, the deep self, the Happy Hunting Ground, the Bardo, Westernesse, the Land of Faerie* . . . choose your metaphor.

What exactly do we *see* there? Don't answer philosophically. Be an astrologer: let the structure of the solar system itself answer the question. Let "below" be reflected in "above," in other words. Beyond Neptune we come to Pluto. That means that beyond Neptune we enter, essentially, the realm of the unconscious mind. (I quickly add that the soul itself is part of the unconscious mind – the simple proof being that most of us are unconscious of it!)

Another way to express it is that here, starting with Pluto, we enter a realm of "angels" and "demons," of gods, goddesses, archetypes, complexes, alternate realities.

Whatever it is, it's bigger than we are!

- PLUTO is the Guardian of the Gate. How perfect it is that Pluto spends twenty years or so of its two-and-a-half century orbit actually *inside* of Neptune's sphere. Like a shaman, it criss- crosses between our world and the next one. Like Casteneda's Don Juan, it "moves fluidly between the worlds." I suspect that in the future as more trans-Neptunians are discovered and understood, we will realize we that we have made our interpretations of Pluto too broad; that its meaning is more focused than we thought, and that the archetype of the shaman will be seen increasingly as the heart of the Plutonian matter.

In the spirit of Pluto, we step into the unconscious, we step into the shamanic realm – and the first thing we feel is *scared*. We want to resist, to deny, to control. Maybe we "surrender" to those chaotic impulses and we become the darkness we fear – we become evil, or mad. But maybe we are braver. Maybe we can face the dark night of the soul without losing the gifts of integrity that Saturn has given us. If so, then we pass through the Plutonian portal and enter the realm of the *truly sane* . . . that is, those who are then free to explore further.

People are still alive today who were born before Pluto was discovered – that is, before this portal to the unconscious mind opened. How the world has changed! We now live in an Age in which psychological and spiritual work are inseparable. No longer do we idealize "saints" who have not reckoned with their rage, their despair, their mothers, their fathers, their sexuality, their wounds, their shame. That era ended in 1930 when Pluto entered our consciousness.

Just think about asking a celibate, presumably sexually inexperienced – or sexually numb, or horny – *priest* for funky, grounded advice about the challenges of an erotic partnership that's been going on for fifteen years.

Hard to imagine? Welcome to the new paradigm.

I have some thoughts about some of the other Trans-Neptunians beyond Pluto. I am quite excited about them actually. Experience is suggesting to me that Eris has more to say to us than maybe Rhadamanthus (another Trans-Neptunian). But I don't know – maybe I am wrong. That may just be because I personally have a Moon-Eris conjunction, which is beginning to become very meaningful to me as I slowly, nervously, unlock its symbolism.

Is all of this too much? Is this just too weird? I want to underscore that I am convinced that *piecemeal* interpretation of the new planets will only drive us into despair and error – or into labyrinths of arid theory. We need a *macro-view*. We need a new system. We can't do this planet-by-planet. There aren't nine or ten of them anymore; there are millions.

In summary, the New Solar System seems to be presenting us with three basic classes of symbols – plus some interesting "haze."

We've got "rocky worlds." These seemingly correlate with primal "animal" functions.

We've got "gas giants." These represent higher, more expansive possibilities in terms of ego-development or self-realization.

Then there are the trans-Neptunians. Their message is that, if we are not too hung up on the rocky worlds, and we manage to make some progress with the gas giants, it appears that a new possibility arises – one that involves identifying with transcendent functions in ourselves . . . not just "perceiving" higher worlds (that's Neptune, an ego-function), but actually *entering* them directly, however heavy and "psychedelic" that experience may be.

The "haze" of asteroids is something to which I have given short shift here. My guess, inspired by Melanie Reinhart's work, is that these bodies are a kind of "lymphatic system," which is connected with healing and regeneration within the harder structural elements of the "planets."

They also seem to resonate with the "dust" of endless details that constitutes so much of the minute-to-minute focus of mundane experience.

Astrologers, using only their naked eyes, standing atop Pyramids and Ziggurats, surely helped their people. Surely they were as intelligent and wise as ourselves. But, paraphrasing Isaac Newton, "we stand on their shoulders, so we can see a little further." We may celebrate individual genius, but the genius of the human family is slowly moving forward, sharing and remembering, seeing a little more deeply into the cosmos – and thus into ourselves.

I can easily imagine astrologers a hundred years from now laughing out loud at what I've written here – but I feel very confident that the wisest among them will say, "Whatever his errors, these were truly the Questions of the Age."

62

Here I get to toot the horn for my old friend, Jim Mullaney – an astronomer with all the requisite credentials with whom I twice had the honor of sharing the stage at the (very metaphysical) Edgar Cayce center in Virginia Beach, Virginia. That says it all – Jim straddles two worlds with grace and wisdom. He also gave us all the delightful notion of "the photon connection," which really helped me understand how looking through telescopes brought me into the world of astrology. I introduce Jim in this piece, but I also explore the importance of declination in visual astronomy and the meaning of an extraordinarily tight conjunction of Venus and Jupiter in Scorpio.

COMING SOON TO A SKY NEAR YOU – DON'T MISS THE BIG VENUS-JUPITER CONJUNCTION!

(Newsletter – November 2017)

Are any of you out there in the mood to get out of bed before sunrise on November 13th? Or maybe you're a night owl. Then it might be better just to stay up all night and catch the late show that way?

Either way, there's a rare visual treat in store. That night, the two brightest planets in the sky – Jupiter and Venus – will very nearly merge into one single blinding light. This is an unusual astronomical event – if fact, it is actually one of the many possibilities cited for what the famous "Star of Bethlehem" might actually have been.

Despite all that, given the fast orbit of Venus around the Sun, its simple conjunctions with Jupiter are not so unusual. The last one occurred on August 27, 2016. There was one before that on October 25, 2015 and another one a few weeks earlier on August 4, 2015.

You get the picture: Jupiter-Venus conjunctions are not rare things – hardly a reason to get out of bed in the wee hours.

So what's the big deal this time?

In a word, the answer is *declination*. At the moment of the exact conjunction, this time there is only an 11' separation between the planets in terms of declination.

Need a quick definition?

Project earth's equator onto the sky. Planets occasionally cross it, but mostly they are above or below the line, just like London is in the northern hemisphere, while Sydney is in the southern hemisphere. Declination in the sky, in other words, is basically just like latitude here on earth.

On November 13th, Venus and Jupiter form a conjunction in the standard sense of the word – they are in the same degree of the zodiac. Astronomically, that means that they are aligned *along the ecliptic* – a perfect, or "partile," astrological conjunction . . . and, as we just saw, not really such a big deal.

But add that very close *parallel of declination*, and you have a visual feast to remember. In fact, the three wise men may have followed it all the way to Bethlehem.

Here's yet another way to think about it. We astrologers mostly think in two dimensions, while space actually has three. Two cities might have the same longitude – one is directly north of the other – but they might still be many miles apart because one is *way* further north than the other. To know if those cities are really neighbors, you need to know *both* their longitude and their latitude.

Astronomy works the same way. What we astrologers normally think of as "where a planet is within a sign" is actually just its longitude. Declination is what adds latitude.

For two planets to really *look* aligned in the sky, they've got to be aligned according to both measures. That's what we are talking about with this upcoming Venus-Jupiter conjunction. It doesn't happen very often. That's why it's a big deal, in other words.

Working out the geometry, Venus and Jupiter will be only 18 arcminutes apart in the sky. That's less than one-third of a degree. To keep perspective, just hold your pinkie finger up at arm's length. The span of sky it covers is about one degree wide.

One third of that. Close!

By comparison, when Venus and Jupiter formed their conjunction in August 2015, they aligned at the end of Leo – but by declination, they were over *six degrees* apart. Again, hold your arm straight out, this time with four fingers together and pointing up. That's about a six degree spread.

Close, but no banana, in other words.

Cutting to the obvious question: *so what does this conjunction mean?* So far, all this is just about astronomy. The astrologer's task is to read "the will of the gods and goddesses" in the heavens, not to give a planetarium talk. We will read that divine will – in a minute.

But first, here comes one of my favorite rants.

I wonder if any astrologer reading this newsletter will actually get out of his or her nice warm bed and have a look at this glorious sight? I know I will! But I have always been obsessed with the heavens – and also absolutely baffled by how few astrologers ever pay any direct sensory attention to the endless sky-show of the physical universe. I shared the stage at an astrology conference once with a wonderful Muskogee named J.C. Eaglesmith. He told a story about a previous astrology conference in which he had invited the participants simply to go outside and look at the night sky with him. No one wanted to go.

"Mosquitos," said J.C. Eaglesmith, with irony and sadness in his eyes.

Amateur astronomy is what led me into astrology in the first place. I grew up with telescopes, gazing at the starry sky. I've written about some of that in *The Night Speaks*. I won't rehash all that here. Instead I want to talk about an old friend of mine. His name is Jim Mullaney. Growing up, he was one of my heroes. The big amateur astronomy magazine in those days was called *Sky and Telescope*. Jim used to write for it. He also directed an observatory and a planetarium. He was (and is) that rare bird: *the academically-trained astronomer who is wide-open to metaphysics.* Try to imagine Carl Sagan or Neil DeGrasse Tyson meeting at a meditation class and talking about the meaning of transiting Pluto, comparing notes and taking it seriously. That's Jim.

After decades of astronomical observing, Jim Mullaney has come to feel that something mysterious happens to our consciousnesses when we look through telescopes – something that hovers between the realm of magic and the physical realm. He calls it the *photon connection.* What he means is that a literal photon of light leaves Jupiter traveling at about 186,000 miles per second and then crashes into your retina. As it does, it creates biochemical changes in your cerebrum – that's called "seeing" Jupiter.

And just maybe, in so doing, that photon carries a message from Jupiter directly to your soul.

- The photon connection is like catching the eye of a stranger and suddenly, intuitively, you know something very fundamental about that person.
- The photon connection is like listening to Beethoven as opposed to reading about Beethoven.
- The photon connection is like the difference between making love and watching pornography.

The whole point is that, in actually looking at a planet in the sky, the connection is real. There's nothing abstract about it. *It is reality, not a photograph of reality.*

Whatever that "photon connection" brings to you has very little to do with seeing the Jupiter glyph on your computer screen. Instead, it has to do with something *physical,* something that links you directly to the planet, like a mother's touch links her to her baby.

It is so easy for us modern astrologers to forget that the real, true original ephemeris was the sky itself. *That's what made astrologers out of our ancestors.* It can still make us better astrologers today too.

I like writing all of this. It rings true for me. I don't think I would be the astrologer I am today if it were not for hundreds, even thousands, of hours spent with those planetary photons raining into my brain.

You don't even really need a telescope for any of this to happen. Unless we are talking about Uranus, Neptune, and Pluto or beyond, your naked eyes are enough. Just think of stepping out into a moonlit night. Feel something? Feel the veil between this world and the next one growing thin?

That's the photon connection too.

Amateur astronomy is a huge subject and not really what my public work is about. We will get to the astrology of this spectacular Venus-Jupiter alignment in a minute, I promise. But do look at the sky! It is truly our best astrological teacher. And this month it's got some special teaching tricks up its sleeve – tricks that no mortal teacher has.

So, getting to the heart of the matter for our more obvious purposes, what does this Venus-Jupiter conjunction mean astrologically? This month, we all have that conjunction *on steroids* happening somewhere in our charts.

Another hint: It falls in Scorpio, which adds some extra drama – and perhaps even some trauma – to the mix.

In last month's newsletter, I explored the general meaning of Jupiter's passage through Scorpio from October 10, 2017 through November 8, 2018. That will be the foundation of much of what I want to say here, so if you missed that newsletter or need to review it, go back and have a look at it – it's chapter forty-eight in this volume. My plan here is to set the tone by quoting a few lines from last month's newsletter, then to relate it all to Venus.

- Jupiter's principle effect is to expand anything it touches. It symbolizes abundance – hence, its historical reputation as the "Greater Benefic." But before we leap into paroxysms of ecstacy here, let's reflect on exactly what Lord Jupiter is going to be expanding.
- Scorpio embraces all of the "strong energies" in the human psyche – instincts, mammal reflexes, appetites, rage, fear, the wounded places in us all.
- In all cases, the presence of the unconscious mind (Scorpio) will be vividly, even spectacularly, demonstrated (Jupiter).
- Always, in any kind of Scorpionic time, the bottom line is that the unconscious mind is becoming conscious.
- All that is taboo is brought to the surface.
- At the individual level, we need to ask ourselves hard questions – that's the Scorpio process – about what we really want and what is truly good for us. (That's Jupiter) And then, armed with that hard-won self-knowledge, we need to boldly and audaciously make our moves.

- You need a victory – but you had better make sure you "know what's good for you." Thus, Scorpionic inner work clarifies and rectifies the intentions, while King Jupiter leads the charge.
- The lower ground? When Jupiter-in-Scorpio operates unconsciously, the dark and tangled complexes and appetites that animate human madness find extravagant outward expression.

So now let's work integratively. Let's try to place all of those Jupiter possibilities in a Venusian context. As we do that, naturally, our first thought is about *loving relationships*. But let's not forget *beauty* and *artistry* – the human need for aesthetic experience. That's Venus too. And underlying everything with Venus is simply the need for *peace* – that rare and precious state of grace for which we all long and which we occasionally grasp before it slips between our worried fingers.

In terms of loving Venusian relationships, it is always an astrological blunder to think only in terms of sex and romance – and of course an even more terrible blunder to ignore them! Above all, Scorpio wants *genuine connection*, whatever form it might take, erotic or otherwise. In any of your relationships, what might be *blocking* that feeling of direct rapport? What are you afraid to say – or perhaps even *afraid to know?* What do you truly desire?

Hear the voice of Lord Jupiter: don't be afraid to ask for what you need! Be bold. *The aim here is to seize the opportunity to be more Scorpionically transparent, and thus more genuinely connected.*

Meanwhile, be wary of "fool's gold." The most obvious example here would be falling in love with some walking, breathing, butt-wiggling illusion.

Venus links to our *aesthetic sensitivities* as well. Even if you are not an artist, you still benefit this month from investing in anything that adds loveliness to your life. Buy a painting. Improve your sound system. Get that new carpet and cheer up your living space. Jupiter is the King of the Gods – so treat yourself like royalty. Now think about this next question in probingly honest Scorpionic psychological terms: *what exactly is stopping you from doing all that?*

If you are an artist, this could be a big breakthrough month for you. That's especially true if your chart shows some sensitivity to 7 or 8 degrees of Scorpio. To find the vaunted Jupiter "luck," you need to "look higher" –

that means to think in grander terms, to *invest in yourself*, to act as if you believe in yourself, to stop holding yourself back.

Maybe you play classical piano. Is it time to start working on your first original composition?

Maybe you paint. Is it time to hang a public show or knock on a gallery door? Do you deserve a new easel, a finer guitar, or new dancing shoes?

Maybe it's time to get those poems out from their hiding place and read a few to your friends.

Peace is really the ultimate Venusian gift. If you think about what we have just been considering, you'll quickly see the connections. Relationships? *Peace arises pretty much automatically when we get a hug from the right person*, especially after a heart-to-heart or sweet love-making. And, humanly, how could we ever be at peace without our dear friends?

Immersing ourselves in beauty, whether in art or in nature, soothes our souls. So does creativity. There is always a mysterious catharsis and release involved in any act of "making art." It leads to peace too. It does so by *releasing tension*.

In purely Scorpionic terms, dealing honestly and effectively with our convoluted complexes and issues may not be anyone's idea of a good time – but here is an ancient truth: once you've done that, you *breathe easier*. Opportunities abound for that kind of peace-producing inner work this month. In that regard, the Force is with you – so are your friends and your allies.

Claim all these gifts from the Jupiter-Venus conjunction. You deserve them – and *knowing that you deserve them* is pure Jupiter.

Let's get back to the photon connection for a moment: I have a sneaking suspicion that you can boost these energies into the stratosphere by simply getting out of your nice warm bed in the wee hours on or around November 13 and letting those merged Jupiter-Venus photons flow down from the sky and into your heart and soul.

We astrologers often speak blithely of "energy." *That* is energy.

No one – not even the most vehement opponent of astrology – could refute that notion. Those photons are indisputably real. And anyone who claims to understand their mysteries in any final, ultimate, end-of-story sense is wrong – and a pretty rotten scientist, to boot.

I fantasize about an astrology conference in the future. Here we all are, sitting on yoga mats and meditation cushions under the night sky, our hearts open and our eyes on the heavens.

Who needs books? Who needs the collected works of some guy named Steven Forrest? He's just some dinosaur from back in the days when people believed they could learn astrology from a computer screen.

63

A few more thoughts and tips about visual astronomy open this little essay about lunar eclipses. One point I hit pretty hard is that we should all beware of buying into the media hype around so-called "Super Moons" – I explain what they're actually all about here, minus the hype. (Hint: don't sell your house to see one.) Moving on from eclipse-watching, in this piece I also explore the "Saros cycle" of eclipses. I introduce the promising work of one of my Australian students, Murray Beauchamp, who has made some fascinating speculative connections between the lunar Saros cycle and the possible timing of our prior lifetimes, all based on the dance the Moon does with its own nodes over centuries of time.

THIS MONTH'S BIG LUNAR ECLIPSE

(Newsletter – January 2019)

If you live in North or South America, the sky will put on a very fine show on the night of January 20/21. Lunar eclipses are not rare, but ones that coincide with a so-called "Super Moon" are more unusual. And that's exactly what you will be seeing, provided that no clouds get in the way – a somewhat-larger-than-average Full Moon going dark, maybe even turning coppery-red in the process.

Caveat: absolutely guaranteed, the media is going to oversell it, leading to lots of disappointment among people who've been jaded by special effects in space movies. I can see the hyperbolic Internet headlines now: *GIGANTIC MEGA-MOON ECLIPSES ENTIRE SKY!* And of course somebody somewhere will have their fifteen minutes of fame by proclaiming a grand governmental conspiracy to conceal the fact that the Moon will collide with the Earth, probably due to some alleged malfeasance on the part of Hillary Clinton.

Ignore the hyperbole, but please, if you possibly can, have a look at this sky-show! Just keep your expectations somewhere south of seeing *Star Wars* happening up there in the sky that night.

I've always loved astronomy, always had a telescope. That's what got me into astrology in the first place. I've seen a lot of lunar eclipses. They are languorous affairs, to be savored like long, slow winter sunsets or your last piece of chocolate. Totality, for example – the period of total lunar eclipse – lasts about an hour. Compare that with the frantic few minutes of a total *solar* eclipse. That's an entirely different beast, and admittedly a lot more spectacular.

January's Moon-show, from the first nearly-unnoticeable "penumbral" contact of the outer edges of Earth's shadow with the Moon to the final "not-with-a-bang-but-a-whimper" end of it all, runs about five hours long.

The part you really don't want to miss is Totality. That begins at 11:41 PM-EST and ends at 12:43 AM-EST – and if you are in the Pacific Zone, lucky you: it's a far more convenient 8:41 - 9:43 PM on January 20.

Starting maybe an hour earlier, it will be worth a peek – that's when the *umbral* period of the eclipse begins, where the darkest part of earth's shadow hits the bone-white Moon.

So make a thermos of hot tea and bring a blanket . . . unless you're in South America, of course. Then just kick back and enjoy.

Total lunar eclipses happen frequently, and unlike solar eclipses, you can see them from anywhere on our planet, so long as the Moon is in the sky at the time. We'll have another one, for example, on May 26, 2021, then again on May 15, 2022 and yet another on November 8, 2022.

A dime a dozen, right?

What makes this particular lunar eclipse somewhat different is the fact that it coincides with a "Super Moon." The term is unfortunate because of the way it hypes the reality of the thing. But the Super Moon effect is real – and the idea behind it is simple: the Moon orbits Earth in an *ellipse* rather than in a circle. That means that sometimes it's closer to us – and thus looks bigger – and sometimes it's further away, and so it appears smaller. This variation in the Moon's apparent size is significant – a "perigee" (nearest) Full Moon looks about 14% wider than an "apogee" one.

In practical terms though, for two reasons, people generally don't notice the difference: first, Full Moons only happen once a month, so it's a long time to wait between comparisons.

Secondly, and more importantly, *most Full Moons don't coincide with apogee or perigee*, so their size is somewhere in between maximum diameter and minimum.

Here's the point of this astronomy lesson: on January 20, we get the double-whammy: *a nice, big perigee Full Moon that just happens to go into total lunar eclipse.* That combo-platter is obviously rare. I bet even aliens will be setting up their lawn chairs.

Ready for something really cool? Switch your perspective for a moment: *what if you were looking at this event from the surface of the Moon rather than from here on Earth?* Maybe you're an alien sitting in your lawn chair somewhere in the middle of the Sea of Tranquility, not far from where Apollo 11 landed. Well, lunar eclipses occur when Earth lies directly between the Sun and the Moon – so Earth's shadow is cast on the lunar surface. But if you were watching from the Moon, something more like a *solar* eclipse would occur, as Earth blocked out the face of the Sun. It would actually be a magnificent thing to behold. You would see Earth as black disk with a brilliant flickering ring of orange, red, and crimson light surrounding it.

If you think about what you would be contemplating, it'll give you goose-bumps. That flickering ring of orange, red, and crimson light is actually the light of *all of the sunsets and sunrises happening on the Earth at that particular moment, combined.*

Pretty amazing, huh? But you'll need to catch the next bus to the Moon if you want to see it.

Our next step is closer to Earth, and it builds on what we just learned. What you are seeing projected onto the surface of the Moon during a lunar eclipse is actually the light of all those sunsets and sunrises. That's why a lunar eclipse is generally more "coppery" than black.

Of course we all know that sunsets and sunrises come in a variety of shades, ranging from *Ho-Hum* to *Oh My God*. This is why the color of each total lunar eclipse is so unpredictable. Can you predict whether tonight's sunset will be a memorable one? Probably not.

Really, what you will be looking at on January 20 is *Earth's weather*, and even the weatherman gets that wrong a lot.

Less romantically, a lunar eclipse also reflects the level of pollution in our atmosphere. The volcano, Mount Pinatubo, blew its top in June 1991. A year and a half later, a lot of that dust was still in the air – and the next lunar eclipse was nearly black.

What will the eclipsed Moon look like on January 20? No one knows . . . not anymore than anyone can predict the weather that night.

SAROS

Here we get a bit more technical. Read on anyway! For reasons that lie on the other side of a short science class, we just might possibly also be close to a real technical breakthrough in evolutionary astrology – one pioneered by an Australian fellow named Murray Beauchamp.

We will meet Murray in a moment.

There is a Sun-Moon opposition every month – that's just a simple Full Moon. Why then is there no lunar eclipse every month? Simple: Earth's shadow typically misses the Moon entirely because the Moon lies a bit above it or a bit below it. There may be a nearly-invisible *penumbral eclipse*, as the Moon passes through the faint edges of Earth's shadow. Another possibility is that the darker *umbra* of Earth's shadow might just graze the Moon, creating a partial eclipse. Generally, the odds are against it being the Real Deal – a Total eclipse – like what's in store for us this month.

Just as with solar eclipses, for a lunar eclipse to occur, the Moon must lie fairly close to the north node or south node. That assures that the Moon and the Sun are lined up not only in terms of their sign positions, but also in terms of their declinations. That's the critical ingredient.

Each eclipse, whether solar or lunar, has unique properties. *How long does it last? Is it total or partial? How big does the face of the Sun or the Moon look? Is the Moon lined up with its north node or its south node?*

Well over two millennia ago, Chaldean astrologer-astronomers discovered that the conditions that produce *identical eclipses* repeat like clockwork. This enabled them to predict eclipses with great accuracy. They called this cycle the *Saros*. Its length is 18 years, 11 days, 8 hours. After that precise interval, Sun, Earth, and Moon return to approximately the same relative geometry. They are lined up the same way, and a nearly identical eclipse happens.

That last phrase – a nearly identical eclipse – is critical here. Earlier we saw that after this January's lunar eclipse, we will have another one in May 2021. That's only two years and four months later – way short of a Saros cycle. But it will be a different kind of event in terms of length, the visual size of the Moon, and so on.

All of the eclipses linked to a specific Saros cycle are like a family-line, with strands of astronomical DNA held in common. Together, they are called a *Saros Series*.

There are separate solar and lunar Saros series, by the way.

All such series are assigned numbers. Currently, for example, there are forty-one active, distinct lunar Saros series happening. Each such Saros series evolves, and eventually dies. Their life spans vary a lot, but you can think in terms of a Saros series lasting a very long time – say, a thousand years or so.

Are you getting dizzy yet?

Obviously this is complicated territory. Space and format mercifully prevent me from getting "book length-technical" in this newsletter. If you want to learn more, there is a fine article about the Saros cycle in Wikipedia – just Google "Saros (astronomy)" and it will take you directly to Virgo paradise.

You may be wondering what any of this has to do with astrology. Fair enough. "Not much," is a good initial answer. Your mileage may vary, but in my experience lunar eclipses, while visually captivating, have not impacted me much more than the monthly Full Moon – like you, I just grow a coat of fur, sharp fangs, and a compelling jones for human blood.

But, taken as a Saros *series*, these same lunar eclipses just might provide a powerful missing link in the foundational logic of evolutionary astrology. The key is to remember that the nodes of the Moon are critical to eclipses – and that the nodes of the Moon are also the heart of what makes evolutionary astrology a unique discipline within our field. They are what links your chart to reincarnation – the long journey of your soul through human history. And just maybe lunar eclipses – and the Saros series – can focus our attention on certain specific periods in history, perhaps periods which feel inexplicably familiar and real to you.

Earlier, I mentioned Murray Beauchamp. He has been part of my Australian apprenticeship program pretty much from the beginning, and he has developed some intriguing ideas about the lunar Saros series. His book, *The Cryptic Cycle: Astrology and the Lunar Saros* is unfortunately currently listed as "Out of Print – Limited Availability" on Amazon. As of this writing, you can still get it via the American Federation of Astrologers or you can contact Murray directly at lunarsaros@gmail.com.

Murray has lectured quite a lot in Australia and New Zealand, but his work is pretty much unknown in the northern hemisphere. His ideas are still formative, but I already find them extremely intriguing.

Here is his technique in a nutshell:

- Look for the lunar eclipse immediately prior to your birth. It does not have to be total; it can be umbral, or even penumbral.
- Find out which Lunar Saros series that *prenatal* lunar eclipse belongs to.
- Then look for the first *umbral* eclipse in the series. That is the birth of the series. Murray emphasizes making sure that it's the first *umbral* eclipse – not the first eclipse of the series, which is always penumbral and does not count.

By the way, *The Cryptic Cycle* contains tables and Internet links that will help you with all this. Proof of the pudding? Well, it's early to use the word "proof," but here's what got me hooked:

The lunar eclipse that immediately preceded my own birth was part of Lunar Saros Series #116. That cycle began with an umbral lunar eclipse on June 16, 1155 A.D.

What follows is totally subjective and quite possibly meaningless. All I can say in defense of what I am about to convey is that the inevitable first test of all astrological techniques lies in one's own personal experience. I would never teach anything that failed to illuminate my own life.

We must of course soon go beyond our narrow ego-world in order to make sure we are not trying to turn a personal quirk into an entire cosmology. Before we open our mouths, we need to be sure that what we conjecture will be helpful to people in general, not just to ourselves. But everything begins with your own personal astrological experience, and that's natural. No one should ever be ashamed of it.

The 12th century, when my own Saros series began, is the High Middle Ages. For what it is worth, I have always related in a strong, visceral way to that time. The Gothic cathedrals were rising. A kind of humanism entered Christianity, and with it, the onset of many of the very battles that I am still fighting in this lifetime, publicly and personally. When, many years ago, reading Rodney Collin's *The Theory of Celestial Influence*, I first heard of the Christian monastery at Cluny, I got chills. *Was I once there as a literate monk?* I thought so – and Cluny was in active upheaval around the time of the lunar eclipse that started "my" series.

I did not know about my specific *astrological* connection to that time until I met Murray Beauchamp. It was just a subjective, intuitive feeling.

Here's another. In common with most Westerners, my knowledge of Chinese history is pitiful, although it has improved somewhat since I began teaching there a decade ago. Right from the beginning, there has been a weird familiarity about China for me, which leaves me with no doubt that I've had previous lifetimes there. For some inexplicable reason, I lit up the first time I encountered the architecture, style and romantic history of the Song Dynasty – which I had never heard of before I began visiting the country. After learning a few things about it and seeing some of its art and architecture, I felt sure that I'd had a lifetime in that period.

You guessed it: the fingerprints of Saros Series #116 are all over the Song Dynasty. Quoting from Wikipedia: *"The Southern Song dynasty (1127–1279) refers to the period after the Song lost control of its northern half (of China) . . . During this time, the Song court retreated south of the Yangtze and established its capital at Lin'an (now Hangzhou)."*

That line gave me goosebumps. I've spent many happy days in Hangzhou, and felt a compelling sense of *deja vu* there, especially in the Buddhist temples in the hills above the city.

My heart is telling me that Murray Beauchamp is onto something with his research into the lunar Saros series. Did I live in one or both of those times? If I had to formulate a hypothesis, it would be this: *that a lifetime or lifetimes spent around the beginning of the lunar Saros cycle reflected in the lunar eclipse just before your birth represent the roots of the karmic issues with which you are reckoning today.*

I would also like to pursue the obvious conjecture that we might tend to take birth around other subsequent lunar eclipses in "our" Saros series. I've not yet explored that possibility.

Will time prove this hypothesis to be helpful or not?

Like almost everything of lasting value in astrology, the answer will not come from one person, but rather from marrying the idea and the entire astrological community in the alchemical cauldron of time. We may know the answer in a generation or two, in other words – but only if we ask the right questions.

In any case, it is something to ponder as the big-as-it-can-get Super Moon turns to copper on the night of January 20.

One final thought – the Lunar Saros series of which this upcoming eclipse is a member began on July 7, 1694. As time goes by, it will be interesting to see if events around that historical period have any apparent karmic relevance to some of our friends who are *in utero* at the moment.

I also note that The Bank of England was founded in that year and it is the model on which most modern central banks are based. I find this intriguing, especially in light of Uranus crossing back into Taurus on March 6 and the world's economy seeming to be on the verge of major evolution or even revolution as we face what people are increasingly calling "late stage Capitalism."

Is something about our relationship with money that began in 1694 with the founding of the Bank of England coming to a time of karmic reckoning?

We'll see . . .

64

Five years ago as I write, the world of astronomy was electrified by the news that evidence was mounting for the existence of a massive new solar system planet orbiting in deep space, far, far out beyond Pluto and even Eris. The jury is still out on the question of whether or not such a world exists – maybe yes, maybe no. So far, humanity's most impressive telescopes have not turned up a speck of direct evidence for it. As a result, a bit of a scramble is on among astronomers for alternative interpretations of the evidence. We'll see where all this goes. Whatever happens, this newsletter is one more vote for astrologers paying more attention to astronomy – and maybe on some fabled day in the future, the astronomers will return the favor.

"PLANET NINE"

(Newsletter – June 2016)

Wait a minute! Didn't we find the ninth planet eighty-six years ago and name it after Walt Disney's most famous dog?

No, Pluto's now a dwarf, remember? (But who dares mention THAT to Pluto?)

But wait *another* minute! Astrologers have been calling the Sun and the Moon "planets." since the beginning of astrological time – so that makes ten planets, not even counting Pluto. But we all *want to* count Pluto! Ask any astrologer – or at least any modern astrologer.

(On the other hand, some of the Classicists for that matter don't even want to count Uranus or Neptune . . .)

But, then, if we *do* count Pluto, we had better count Eris too. Eris is about the same size and mass as Pluto, and if one's a planet, then the other one must be too.

Like a lot of things in the modern world, such as turning on a television set or adjusting a thermostat, counting planets is a heck of a lot harder than it used to be! And it looks very much like it is about to get a whole lot harder. Evidence is mounting for the existence of what astronomers are now tentatively calling "Planet Nine."

Before we go an inch further, let's keep some lead in our shoes. No one has actually *seen* this alleged "Planet Nine" yet. The evidence for its existence is purely speculative. We don't even know where it is, exactly. No astrologer can plug it into anyone's chart yet to help figure out what it means – that is, if it even exists at all.

I've lived through a lot of false alarms about "new planets" – some from the astronomy side, some from the channeled, metaphysical side. Mostly those predictions have been incorrect. I took this one with several grains of salt too . . . until I began to look more closely at the evidence. I now think it might very well be real. I now think that astrology might be on the cusp of a *very* major paradigm shift.

Since the early 1990s, as we explored in the earlier chapter entitled "The New Solar System," astronomers have discovered literally hundreds of tiny ice-worlds orbiting beyond Neptune. It's usually called the Kuiper Belt (rhymes with "wiper") Eris is one of them. You've probably heard of Sedna or Quaoar or Orcus too. Eventually, astronomers realized that it made the most sense to include Pluto as a member of that same family too. Pluto seems to be the biggest of them and one of the closest – but it's helpful in keeping perspective to realize that Pluto's mass is only *one quarter of one percent* of Earth's mass. So even though it's the largest of these Kuiper Belt objects (or Trans-Neptunians, as they are often called), it's truly tiny, as are the rest of them.

Until, perhaps, now.

What is the evidence for the existence of this new world? Basically, the science that we are about to explore is very much an echo of how we discovered Neptune way back in the middle of the nineteenth century: *by the effects of its invisible gravitational field upon planets whose positions we do actually know.* Uranus was not orbiting "right," and the astronomers of that era realized something further out in the dark must be tugging on it. They used the distortions in Uranus's orbit to roughly calculate the position of the invisible "planet eight." They turned their telescopes in that direction and – *voilà*, there it was: Neptune.

Similarly, something is tugging on the orbits of these little ice worlds of the Kuiper Belt. Their orbits are simply too *organized*. They are marching to the same drummer.

But who is the drummer? No one has seen him yet.

These ice worlds mostly have highly "eccentric" orbits, which just means they swing closer to the Sun, then much further away, orbiting in long ellipses, almost like comets. The big clue about Planet Nine is that an awful lot of these little worlds have their *aphelions* – that's the point where they are farthest from the Sun – all on *one side* of the Sun.

Our question, "who is the drummer" translates into the question of what is balancing them from the other side of the Sun?

Picture it like this. There's a 250-pound farmer square dancing with his 110-pound wife. They're holding both hands and he's twirling her around and around. If he let go, she'd go flying. But loves her so he holds on. If you watched her pelvis, you would see it orbiting her husband's pelvis. He's bigger and heavier, so he's sort of the center of the merry-go-round. But if you watched his pelvis carefully, you'd see it was describing little circles too. So her pelvis is making a big circle and his is making a small one. They are both orbiting a "common center of gravity" *and they are both always on opposite sides of that common center of gravity.*

Now make the farmer invisible. Poof! *Disappearius!!!*

If you were to continue to study the motion of his wife's pelvis, *you would deduce that her invisible partner occupied a position opposite her.* You would know "approximately where he was located."

And you would know he was *a lot heavier* than she was.

That's pretty much what the astronomers are doing. These tiny Kuiper Belt objects are the wife's pelvis. And the invisible farmer must be a giant! *"Planet Nine" is estimated to weigh about ten times what Earth does* – and remember Earth has about four hundred times the mass of Pluto.

For perspective, Neptune has a little more than *seventeen* times Earth's mass – so Planet Nine is no record-breaker. But one thing is sure – if the astronomers do find it, there will be no debate about it being a "dwarf planet," not at ten times Earth's mass. If found, this will clearly be a major addition to the solar system.

Astrologers who are hesitant to accept the burgeoning complexity of the outer solar system can hang their hats on the fact that everything out there is tiny – of course, to pursue that argument logically, they'll have some fancy footwork ahead because of the demonstrable impact of "tiny" Pluto.

But Planet Nine, at ten times Earth's mass, would be impossible to ignore in any way except by simply pretending that its discovery had never happened.

Those tell-tale distorted orbits also tell us that this new world, if it exists, is way out there in deep space. There's only so much the astronomers can learn from watching "the pelvis of the farmer's wife," but it looks like Planet Nine must be fifty or sixty billion miles from the Sun. The number probably doesn't mean much except "big" to you – me either. But for perspective, Neptune's average distance from the Sun is only 2.8 billion miles. Earth is only 93 million miles out.

Fifty or sixty billion miles means deep space: unexplored territory, "where no one has gone before."

Because of Johannes Kepler's inviolable laws of planetary motion, that deep space orbit means two things: Planet Nine is *moving very slowly* and it takes a *really, really long time to get around the Sun*. Current estimates for its orbital period run between ten thousand and twenty thousand years. That's its "year," dwarfing even Pluto's 248 year cycle. By transit, it will barely budge in a lifetime. But what might it mean in the natal chart or by solar arc? "Something" seems like the safest answer anyone could possibly give at this point – again, no one is really sure that Planet Nine even exists, let alone what it might signify.

One more little technical piece. Compared to the plane of Earth's orbit, many of the orbits of these Kuiper Belt objects are tilted 30° "down."

Why might that be true?

Again, the laws of gravitational balance point to something massive orbiting on the other side of the Sun, but 30° "up."

The probability of these patterns occurring by chance is calculated to be about 0.007%. So that's yet another piece of indirect evidence that "something big is moving out there."

Taken together, these clues seem pretty compelling. Telescopes are pointing out into the darkness at the edge of the solar system at this very moment. As the observations of the Kuiper Belt orbits are further crunched, the astronomers will know better where to aim those big eyes.

At this point, no one can come up with an alternative explanation for the observations, except longshot "chance" – but of course science is full of surprises. We can believe in Planet Nine when we see it. Until then, as an astrologer, I can only wait and anticipate . . . and hopefully avoid the pitfall of trying to interpret any of this before we have anything concrete to interpret!

What might Planet Nine mean? I have no specific ideas – but I do know that the discovery of planets has always been a real punctuation mark in human history. Famously, we have the correlation between the discovery of Uranus and the late 18th century revolutions in government and science and culture. We have Neptune's discovery linked to spiritualism, populist revolution, and so on. Pluto linked so obviously to psychology – and the possibility of Armageddon. Big subjects – and no doubt Planet Nine, ten times more massive than Earth, will correlate with a similarly massive paradigm shift.

We astrologers will of course wait with bated breath for the announcement of the mythic *name* of this new world. That's because – with the glaring exception of Uranus – those names have provided one of the most reliable demonstrations of synchronicity available to those who pay attention to such things.

Personally, I'm dying to see where this new planet falls in my own chart. I bet you are too. And that's nothing to apologize for – our own heads and hearts are always the primary astrological laboratory. Then we will start plugging the planet into the charts of famous people. It is so slow in its long, long orbit that it will tend, of course, to barely move over generations. Your whole senior class has Planet Nine in the same few minutes of the same degree. But someone you know will turn out to have it conjunct the Ascendant and for someone else, it is opposed to the Moon. And of course it will be spread out evenly among the houses, and make all manner of different aspects. Together, we, the tribe of astrologers, will figure it out.

And we will give thanks for being alive, and for being astrologers, at such an exciting moment.

Remember: this puppy is *four thousand times more massive* than Pluto! It will change everything – that is, if it is actually there at all . . .

SECTION NINE

THE DHARMA OF ASTROLOGICAL COUNSELING

Read all the astrological books that have ever been written, even memorize them – and there is still no escaping that ultimate moment of truth when you sit down facing the expectant eyes of an intelligent, astrologically-naive client. You need to say something and you've got to start somewhere. In this section, I've collected all of my newsletters that might support you in facing that moment of truth with confidence and grace. Some are about philosophy and attitude – those are perhaps the most important ones. Some are about specific astrological techniques. One is about the essential requirement of staying attuned to shifting cultural realities – specifically, the current trend toward people being "spiritual but not religious," which seems to be a major pattern among contemporary astrological clients.

    I've always had a special affection for my students – people who might keep this sacred flame burning after I am gone. I gratefully dedicate this section of the book to them and to their practices in the individual communities they serve.

65

We can study, read, and learn astrology until age-lines wrinkle on our faces and our friends wonder whatever happened to us – but sooner or later, you have to "cross the Rubicon." It's just you, a chart, and the expectant client, and . . . you've got to start talking. Two bits of advice. Number one, you need an orderly, strategic approach. If you are confused, your client will be totally confused. Number two, you need to remember what you have already said. That line is so simple to say that it might just zoom past you, but it is the key to tying everything together. That quality of integration is what distinguishes you from a computer. This essay is about how to develop that latter skill. Nominally, it is about a relatively trivial set of Mars transits that happened in early 2019, but they only provide the vehicle for illustrating the larger perspective.

REMEMBER WHAT YOU'VE ALREADY SAID . . . OR WHAT MARS IS UP TO IN FEBRUARY

(Newsletter – February 2019)

Facing any kind of crisis or heartbreak in life, most of us would find an eye-to-eye session with a living astrologer to be more satisfying than a computer screen offering us pre-packaged nuggets about our current transits or progressions. There are a lot of reasons for that, most of them rather obvious at the human level. People and machines may be developing an interesting symbiosis, but when the emotional chips are down, human-to-human, heart-to-heart, interactions are still the most appealing option for most of us.

Beyond the obvious touchy-feely realities, there is another level to this distinction – something more cerebral, something that goes beyond empathy and a hug. The human mind can do something that no machine can do. *It can meld all of the symbols together into one clear, coherent, emotionally connected package.* Developments in artificial intelligence may change all that someday, but for now the human heart is still the premier instrument when it comes to pulling the diverse messages of many planets into a single meaningful, coherent statement.

When I am teaching the more advanced kinds of astrological interpretation, I constantly beat the same drum: *integration, integration, integration.* One day I realized that I could boil this critical skill down to one single pithy statement: *always remember what you have already said.*

It is so simple to say, but those words really encapsulate all the critical integrative principles.

Imagine someone is a Capricorn with the Sun-Saturn conjunction. The computer tells him definitively: *you are a loner.* But maybe that person's Moon is in Libra in the seventh house. The computer goes on to explain how *he is a social animal,* with a strong compulsion to be in relationships.

Go figure, in other words.

Learning to make those two statements dance together illustrates the critical interpretive skill about which I'm talking. The part of your brain that likes poetry has more affinity for the process than the part of your brain that thinks like a microchip. Whom should such a man marry, if he chooses to marry? *It had better be someone who does not interpret his need for time alone as a personal rejection.* Absence makes the heart grow fonder. Two can love each other without texting each other fifteen times a day.

In statements such as these, *we reconcile the opposites.* We sit easily with the paradox. In other words, *we remember what we have already said* and take it into account, rather than spewing a memorized package of key words about the Sun, then *forgetting about them* and offering a similar pre-recorded package about the Moon.

Remember what you have already said – the statement is clear enough in principle, but intellectual complications arise after you have said ten different things. What does statement number two have to do with statement number seven? How do they fit together? How can you even remember them all?

This leads me to another line I often use while I am teaching: *you have many planets, but you only have one head between your ears.* Somehow, the messages of all of those planets ultimately merge into one single state of consciousness, like many dyes flowing into one interesting color – a color you have probably never seen before.

Mostly, these integrative principles apply to the way I look at an individual chart. In this month's newsletter my aim is to illustrate them with a living example – one which will bear upon every one of us this month in varying ways. Let's look at the changing sky as it presents itself in February 2019. During these next four weeks, there is, as always, a complex and ever-changing stew of aspects forming and dissolving among the planets.

Out of that stew, I want to extract one theme. It is based on a series of aspects formed by the planet Mars.

The month begins with Mars in its own sign, Aries. When it is there, it simply packs more punch than usual – that's true of any planet when it's in the sign it rules. Speaking of punch, on February 1, Mars squares Pluto. We have the god of war and the god of hell at each other's throats – stand back, in other words. On the seventh, Mars squares the lunar nodal axis. On that same day Mars and Mercury form a sextile. On February 13, Mars conjuncts Uranus. On the fourteenth, Mars crosses into Taurus – the sign ruled by Venus. The atmosphere mellows a bit. What could be more appropriate for Valentine's Day?

After that, there are no more major aspects involving Mars until near the end of the month. On the twenty-seventh, Mars and the Sun form a sextile aspect.

That's a lot of aspects! It would probably be difficult for you to repeat the list from memory without cheating – for me too.

In order to keep a handle on the complexity, there is a great temptation to think of them individually, in atomized fashion. But that's how a computer would do it – spitting out a few lines about Mars square Pluto, then a few lines about Mars square the lunar nodes.

Let's not think like machines. Our Holy Grail is integration. How do we make these events dance together in a meaningful evolutionary sequence?

Our attempts to figure out how to do that are further complicated by the reality of human freedom. How we react to these energies is not determined purely by the planets themselves. Each configuration contains many possibilities. Fortune-tellers ignore our freedom, imagining that aspects mean this or that; that is why their predictive track records are so abysmal. We humans can get any astrological configuration right – and we can get them wrong too. And there are many shades of gray in between. Thus, each one of these Mars configurations represents a *spectrum of possible realities*, further complicating any attempt to predict how they will interact.

Thinking of Mars squaring Pluto at the beginning of the month, many astrologers might express something between caution and horror. And indeed, there are spectacular ways to make a mess out of such an aspect – murdering your boss or your partner in a fit of homicidal rage, for example. But it is also possible to get it right, and how to do that is something we will contemplate in a few moments.

- Our initial key here is the realization that *success with one of these aspects builds a foundation for success with the next one.* Conversely, failure with one renders success with the next one more problematic.

That is one practical effect of our principle of integration – and integration is not just a good idea; it is actually how these things work in real life. For purposes of keeping this essay down to a manageable size, I will do a lot of simplifying here. And of course we are not relating any of this directly to anyone's natal chart, which is how this stuff really works. Here I only want to talk about how February's six big Mars events form an *interdependent evolutionary chain.* Unlike in my normal client work, I will be speaking about all of humanity, not just an individual.

When Mars squares Pluto on February 1, suppressed anger, resentment, and tension come rising up out of the depths. Destructive blow-ups are possible. But Pluto invites us to think deeply and honestly. It asks us to be vulnerable to our own wounded reality.

My mind goes down two roads here. The first one is psychological in tone: *consider, for example, that if you are feeling resentful toward your partner, that perhaps what is unwittingly surfacing is actually an old anger at one of your parents.* Look deeply and honestly at your rage, in other words; reflect upon its actual source. Be wary of *avoiding* those inner processes via the cheap trick of *projecting* these energies onto convenient external targets – don't "kick the dog," in other words. Deal with your own stuff instead.

The second road my mind goes down as I think of the Mars-Pluto square carries us in a very different direction. Is there a legitimate resentment *that you have been afraid to feel,* fearing that expressing it would create more problems than it solved? Under this aspect, letting that resentment fester would be very dangerous. The time has come to deal directly with some of life's darker feelings, and perhaps to share them with someone no more eager than yourself to hear them. That Plutonian gambit takes a lot of a classic positive Mars quality: *courage.*

On the seventh, Mars squares the lunar nodal axis. The north node lies in Cancer, while the south node is in Capricorn. I went into a lot of detail about that particular nodal axis in last November's newsletter, which is included in this volume as chapter twenty. You might want to review that for a deeper understanding of all of this. In a nutshell, what that nodal axis tells us is that we all need to *heal* (Cancer) from some unresolved Capricorn karma of *exhaustion, onerous duty, and long-suffering.*

Now, let's remember what we have already said . . .

Think of the "second road" in what we explored a few lines ago about Pluto and Mars. We spoke there of *suppressed legitimate resentments.* Doesn't that sound like what I just said about that long-suffering Capricorn south node? Self-denial and duty?

See how thinking of Mars squaring the nodes casts light on Mars squaring Pluto? The two events are interdependent. They are working together. How do we know that? We know it *because they are happening at the same time* – we are back to your having only one head between your ears.

Going further, the Cancer north node offers a remedy: perhaps instead of harboring and accumulating resentments, you can just *ask for some kindness and support.* Try visualizing the universe – or your boss or your partner – as a face of the Gentle Cosmic Mother (Cancer) rather than assuming it to be a manifestation of the Harsh Judging Father (Capricorn).

Realizing that your own underlying attitudes are half the problem is a classic Plutonian insight.

On that same day, Mars and Mercury form a sextile. That is part of the picture too, so we need to add it to the mix. Here we have a *supportive* aspect – the sextile – suggesting open doors and abundant possibilities. To take advantage of them, you need to remember that every such door promises benefits from classic Mercury activities: *talking and listening.* Those accumulated frustrations, resentments, and angers need to be put on the table. That is the "talking" part.

Don't forget to listen too!

Thus, conversation supports the nodal breakthrough rooted in the suppressed Mars energies.

Those twelve words illustrate the larger point I am making in this newsletter: we see reflected in them the memory of everything we have said so far. This is what I mean by integration. Again: *conversation supports the nodal breakthrough rooted in the suppressed Mars energies.*

Let's take it further – on February 13, Mars forms a conjunction with the planet Uranus. If we have missed the evolutionary opportunities presented to us during the first half of the month, this aspect is ominous of how our failures finally catch up with us. Mars and Uranus are the two most volatile energies in astrology. Uranus adds a hair trigger – and perhaps an attitude of cold indifference – to the Martial rage. The danger here lies in accumulated frustrations boiling over explosively, and perhaps doing real damage. We might say things we later wish we could un-say.

But that's just the warning. What does it look like if we get this conjunction right? (And remember, getting it right depends on getting all the earlier pieces more or less right too ...) Uranus promises *breakthrough* and *unprecedented insight.* A classic Uranian statement is, *"Wow, I never thought of that before!"*

If you have been building a sane Mars foundation since earlier in the month, mid-month brings liberating insights and new ways of looking at everything. I am using the word "everything" here – but what I really mean specifically is all of these issues of conflict or tension that have been surfacing for the past two weeks. At the time, some of them might have seemed intractable, with no satisfying resolutions possible. And yet, if we have moved forward in good faith, with *openness in our communications* and a *willingness to take responsibility for our own dark shadow,* then we can expect Uranian serendipity around the middle of the month. "Genius answers" arise which we could not have imagined before now.

Again, please note how this particular interpretation of Mars making its conjunction with Uranus *actually derives from everything that went before it.* We have "remembered what we already said." We could not make the comments we made in the last two paragraphs without recalling the big picture.

On Valentine's Day, Mars crosses out of Aries and into Taurus. Traditional astrologers speak of Taurus as the "fall" of Mars. I have never liked that language – it makes it sound as if there is something wrong with Mars being there. Actually, there is nothing wrong with Mars being in Taurus or any other sign – and nothing particularly "good" about it being in Aries. When a planet is in the sign opposite the one it rules, there is only a kind of paradoxical, complicated relationship between the two symbols, which is not necessarily a bad thing. With Mars in Taurus, it is easy to encapsulate the paradox: *Taurus wants peace while Mars is the god of war.* Admittedly, that does not sound like a marriage made in heaven. The good news is that they can balance each other.

Try this and see if it makes any sense to you – *the world would be a happier place if all the warriors let go of the blood-romance of battle and instead fought for peace.*

Our bottom line here, as Mars leaves Aries and crosses into Taurus, is simply that some of the fire goes out of the zeitgeist in time for Valentine's Day. If we have done the evolutionary work I have been describing, then we have *earned the right* to some authentic peace. We have moved to a new level of being. We harvest the fruit of our previous efforts.

If, on the other hand, we have made a weak response to this cascade of Mars aspects, then the dragon only retreats to its cave for a little rest. An ominous calm arises, prelude to the next inevitable – and sadly familiar – storm.

Finally, on the 27th, Mars and the Sun form a sextile. If we have done well this month, this aspect represents the culmination – and reward – of our efforts. It feels adventurous, fresh, and distinctly sexy. It radiates aliveness.

If we have done poorly, then a certain *militant self-righteousness* makes itself felt, and we set the wheels of war turning again.

I hope this little map of February's Mars energies helps to guide and inspire all of us on this short stretch of the evolutionary road that lies immediately ahead. This flow is operating in the collective – that is to say, universally, for all of us. We will all feel it, each in our own particular way.

Still, remember that you are always riding a current of unique transits and progressions in your own natal chart; these Mars energies I have just described are like a tributary to that river, adding something to it, modulating the expression of all the energies that are unique to you.

My main purpose in writing these words is, however, to illustrate our foundational principle of astrological interpretation: *integration*. Again, it is so easy to say it: always remember what you have already said. As you move to understanding an impending transit, try to fold it back into the meaning of the previous ones.

Astrological mastery is absolutely dependent upon this skill. And, so far, humans are far more skillful at it than computers.

66

*Spirituality is eternal – someone sitting in meditation in a cave 8000 years
ago is in the same state of mysterious, luminous transparency as someone sitting
in meditation on a starship orbiting Alpha Centauri half a millennium from
now. But the cultural framework around spirituality – the words we use and
the assumptions we make about it – those are constantly changing. To remain
relevant, astrologers need always to speak the language of their times. And
the times are changing. In this essay, I explore the astrological dimensions
of the shift away from churches and toward yoga, meditation, and spiritual
counseling that is sweeping the world. What role does evolutionary astrology
play in all of that? The short answer is that we are surfing that same cultural
wave, feeling its energy, and drawing inspiration and purpose from it.*

SPIRITUAL BUT NOT
RELIGIOUS
(Newsletter – May 2019)

There is a growing group of humans on the earth who have turned their
backs on religion, but who still feel that they are maintaining an active, personal connection with the divine anyway. Sociologists label them
"spiritual but not religious," which seems like a fair enough term.

The category is an emerging one since there has not been much precedent for it in history – as with so many truly new things, you first have to

imagine it before you can *see* it. For a long while, in other words, there was no "spiritual but not religious" box to check on anyone's sociological survey. It was strictly, are you a Christian, a Muslim, a Jew, or a None of the Above?

Behind this cultural development, there is a lot of astrology, and it is of the momentous kind that suggests we are looking at a lasting sea-change rather than a passing fashion. We will get to astrology in a moment. But first, let's put a few facts on the table. I apologize for the United States bias here, but that is my only source of concrete evidence. We are just using the USA as a launching pad though – I suspect the results are fairly generalizable, at least throughout the industrialized world.

A 2017 survey by the Public Religion Research Institute (PRRI) found that 18% of Americans put themselves in the "spiritual but not religious" category. In 2012, the Pew Research Center announced that the number of Americans who "do not identify with any religion" had grown from 15% in 2007 to 20% in 2012, with that number continuing to grow.

Significantly, while that was true of 21% of so-called "Generation X" folks – those born between 1965 and 1980 – it increased dramatically to 34% among a younger group of "Millennials," born 1990–1994.

Whatever is happening here, the tide is definitely rising.

Behind these numbers I believe that what we are seeing astrologically is the interaction of two factors, one of them is huge – and the other one is even bigger than that.

- Factor number one is the long transit of Neptune through its own sign, Pisces.
- Factor number two is our collective entry into the Aquarian Age.

History demonstrates that the first – Neptune in Pisces – can always be relied upon to trigger a collective spiritual awakening, while the second one promises a strong flow in the direction of individuality, independence – plus a suspicious attitude toward any kind of "group-think."

These are both vast topics and I can only breeze through them in this short essay. For a fuller exploration of Neptune's passage through Pisces, you might try chapter 34 of *The Book of Neptune*, which deals with the same subject in a lot more depth.

The transition into the Age of Aquarius is a complex and controversial topic – and one of my favorites. You can find an introduction to it in chapter thirty-four of this volume, with links to some more in-depth explorations of the same territory.

Let's take these two factors one at a time, starting with Neptune.

Neptune criss-crossed the Pisces boundary in 2011-2012, finally settling solidly on the Pisces side on February 3, 2012. Right now, we are about midway through the transit. In 2025, Neptune moves in and out of Aries, not putting Pisces fully behind it until January 26, 2026.

With all the noise and horror in the world today, it is easy to miss the history-shaping impact of this epochal transit. It happens every 165 years, and it always changes everything.

In a nutshell, when Neptune is in its own sign, its influence simply becomes stronger. A way of saying it is that *everyone on the earth is currently going through a major Neptune transit*, even if that is not obvious through any aspects in their personal chart.

As with everything astrological, Neptune being in the spotlight means good news, bad news, and all the possible news in between. Escapism and addiction abound – there is the astrology behind the *opioid crisis*, for example. Delusion and madness are having a heyday – conspiracy theories are everywhere, world leaders seem to have lost their marbles.

Meanwhile, we are worried about Kim Kardashian's sex life as the Earth's climate reaches the boiling point.

Behind all of those dark Neptunian effects, a *spiritual renaissance* is quietly changing the way we look at the world. It is obviously not about an explosion of peace, love, and understanding sweeping across the earth – rather, it is *a renewal and a reconfiguring of the human relationship with the mysteries*. Spiritual leaders are being empowered, and they are finding receptive, ready students and disciples. Healers and diviners are rising up. Yoga teachers are emerging as lamas. We have shamans in the suburbs and visionaries on street corners. Everywhere, people are hungry, ready for something real, ready for a visitation of raw spiritual energy.

As ever, Neptune must interact with current cultural realities. Each of its passages through Pisces has been a distinct event – but the effects are always palpable, and often dramatic.

Let me prove it to you by quickly hitting just a few historical high points, all coinciding with Neptune in Pisces.

- Neptune entered Pisces in 47 A.D. as St Paul was bringing Christianity to the Roman empire.
- There are various tellings, but the standard version is that in about 58 AD, Emperor Ming-Ti introduced Buddhism to China.
- In either 538 or 552, depending on who you read, we saw the official introduction of Buddhism to Japan.
- Here's a big one, maybe the most impressive event of all. Neptune was in Pisces from May 701 until February 716. The year 711 brought the Islamic invasion of Spain and the establishment of Moorish culture there. A year later, in 712 AD, a Muslim state was established in what we now call Pakistan. The truly amazing thing is that by 715 AD, a Muslim empire stretched all the way from the Pyrenees to China, with Damascus as its capital.
- Neptune was back in Pisces between March 1520 and the end of 1534. Martin Luther had posted his "95 Theses" in 1517, with Neptune still in Aquarius – and in 1521, he was condemned as a heretic and excommunicated, setting into motion the Protestant Reformation.
- The last historical time that Neptune entered Pisces was in April 1847, only crossing finally into Aries in October 1861. The correlations here are dramatic too. *Spiritualism* – which involved communion with the dead and with beings in other dimensions – swept through the English-speaking world. Arthur Conan Doyle, of Sherlock Holmes fame, became a major figure in the movement – a movement that attracted Abraham Lincoln, as well as Queen Victoria and Prince Albert. Numbers vary, but one report I read informed me that in 1850, out of an American population of about twenty-three million people, eleven million of them claimed membership in a spiritualist church.

Now we are in the Neptunian soup again. As ever, it is difficult for a fish to describe the sea – but I think that the "spiritual but not religious" movement is a big part of how it is playing out this time.

Here is another Neptune-in-Pisces idea, one that is closely related: there is an emerging recognition that *beyond all theological differences lies a universal truth* – one that beggars human intelligence and escapes all definitions.

Another way to say the same thing is that increasingly words such as "God," "Allah," "The Force," the "Dharmakaya," and so on, *all mean the same thing.* As the Zen Buddhists say, each one is just "a finger pointing at the Moon." A Muslim at prayer, a Christian at prayer, a Hindu at prayer – all are experiencing a similar Presence.

"Non-partisan" statements such as these naturally still infuriate some people – but try this: *these statements are more likely to infuriate old people than young people.*

Rings true, doesn't it?

"The times they are a-changing," as Bob Dylan astutely observed almost sixty years ago.

Now let's add the Age of Aquarius to the mix.

The position of the Vernal Equinox slowly retrogrades against the starry background, taking 25,772 years to make the complete circuit of the zodiac. One serious complication in thinking about astrological ages is that it is a classic "apples-and-oranges" situation: we are mixing these two kinds of astrology, and they do not mix easily. We are relating the position of the (tropical) Vernal equinox to the (sidereal) starry constellations.

The Vernal Equinox will not enter the constellation Aquarius for another four centuries or so. Who says? The answer is the International Astronomical Union which arbitrarily defined those star-boundaries about ninety years ago.

I am not sure that they were speaking for God.

A further complication is that these official I.A.U. constellations vary enormously in size, while astrology operates as a system with twelve equal signs. When I think of the astrological ages, I take that complete cycle of 25,772 years and divide it up into twelve equal segments, each 2147.5 years long.

So when did the age of Aquarius begin?

Trying to solve the problem astronomically leads directly to confusion, unless we accept the divine authority of the International Astronomical Union – something I see no reason to do. Normally in astrology, we look to the heavens in order to clarify what is happening here on Earth. In this case, I recommend solving our problem by doing it the other way around: in order to try to figure out what is going on in the sky, let us look to events on the earth.

In some of the other "Age of Aquarius" programs I have mentioned, I go into all of this a lot more deeply. But here is my favorite line from those programs: *we went from Kitty Hawk to the Moon in sixty-six years.*

That sure sounds like the Aquarian cusp to me. Without being rigid about it, I like to set the Aquarian boundary around 1903-1905, to coincide with the Wright Brothers first flight and Einstein's publication of the Special theory of Relativity: two events which epitomize the brilliance, rebellion against norms, love of technology, and impatience with boundaries which so beautifully characterize the spirit of the sign Aquarius.

This really is a labyrinthine subject, but for our purposes here, let me make one simple point. While under the sway of the sign Pisces, *there is a powerful urge to dissolve into something greater than ourselves.* As we retrograde into Aquarius, the orientation and underlying agenda shifts dramatically: *no one wants to dissolve into anything anymore.* No one wants to disappear into a nation, a marriage – or a *religion.* It is an age of individuality. We are a salad, not a melting pot.

And what do we see happening? Marriage has become unstable. Families are breaking up or scattering across the landscape. There are far more nations on the earth now than there were a century ago. Societies feel increasingly fragmented. Everyone seems to be part of some "minority group." *And religion is increasingly losing its hold upon individual conscience.*

It would be naïve simply to celebrate all of this; it is far more complicated than that. As with everything in astrology, there is a dark side to the age of Aquarius. There are shadows and there is light. As ever, humanity – and each one of us as individuals – will have to find our way through this tricky new energetic landscape.

- Never before in recorded history has Neptune's *conscious* passage through Pisces coincided with an Aquarian age – remember, the last Aquarian Age started twenty-six thousand years ago. We only became *collectively conscious* of Neptune in the middle of the 19th century.

Spirituality will not die, but it will change, adapting to a new – and far more *questioning, doubting, and individuated* – way of being human. "Spiritual but not religious" is just one expression of this emerging change. Undoubtedly there will be others. I feel quite certain that there are many people sitting in churches, mosques, and temples today who can still identify with these developments I have been describing – these people may still find solace and meaning in the familiar religious rituals, but they have that telltale sense that other rituals may help other people get to the same transcendent place.

Should we call them "spiritual but not religious" too? I will leave that argument to people who enjoy semantic hair-splitting.

How exciting! We are all surfing this breaking wave, creating the roots of a planetary spiritual culture that will last for two thousand more years. Meanwhile, as counseling astrologers working in the evolutionary framework, we are on the cutting edge of this revolution in consciousness. Unlike a pastor in a pulpit exhorting the congregation in a one-size-fits-all way, we are talking about *individual* karmic predicaments and their *unique* resolutions. We're not "better than" that pastor – he or she will still have some role to play, although likely the form of that role will surprise traditionalists.

Bottom line: we evolutionary astrologers are selling individualized downloads, while that poor pastor is trying to sell videotapes for your VCR . . .

. . . . *By the way, do any of you younger folks know what a VCR is?*

67

As counseling astrologers, our aspiration is to be able to help people make wiser choices as they reach life's many crossroads. Those crossroads come in a variety of flavors, but here's a life-altering one that arises for the majority of us from time to time: moving to a new home. Often whether we know it or not, underlying such a geographical change are deep questions about one's soul purpose – questions which are best addressed by the birthchart itself, along with current transits and progressions. But once the decision to move has been made consciously and wisely, the three fundamental techniques of astromapping come into play. They are all detailed here in this essay. Just as with synastry – the astrology of human relationships – we also have a unique relationship with the daemon of the new land we have chosen. How can we understand that energetic interaction between self and place?

RELOCATIONAL ASTROLOGY

(Newsletter – July 2017)

Cue the Rolling Stones playing *Street Fighting Man*, with one minor modification:

Summer's here and the time is right for fighting . . .
. . . with endless Security Clearance queues, homicidal maniacs on the highways, and *lucha libre* family vacations.

I know you know what I mean. Many of us will soon be hitting the road, one way or another. Today traveling is not as easy as it once was, but for most of us it is still often worth the effort and frustration. The next four months will find me personally in New Orleans, North Carolina, Maine, New York, down to Australia, back to New York, back home to the Anza-Borrego desert in California, then over to China.

Obviously I am crazier than most of you.

But not many of us will stay home. We'll hear that Siren call of the open road – or at least the call of familial obligation. *And everywhere we visit, the energy feels different.* Some places just make you feel happy. Some trigger uneasiness. Some feel like home the first time you see them. Some never will.

Many of those reactions are pretty straightforward – no need to look at an astrological chart to help you fathom why a beach looks so good to you on a hot summer day. But sometimes the reasons we react to a place in a particular way are more slippery. That's where astromapping comes into play.

In my practice, I use three different relocational techniques:

• Astrocartography
• Local Space
• Relocated Charts.

Each one is an indispensable tool. Each approach does certain things very well. They don't overlap very much in their functions. If you leave out any one of the three techniques, you will be missing about one-third of the available information and insight. My advice is to use them all, in other words.

In this newsletter, I want to introduce each of these methods, talk about their strengths and their blind spots, and offer a few guidelines about how to best employ them.

Let's start with the simplest and in many ways the most powerful of these techniques . . .

THE RELOCATED CHART

I was born on January 6, 1949 at 3:21 am Eastern Standard Time in Mount Vernon, New York. I moved to Borrego Springs, California, in 2008. *What if I had actually been born there?* That is, what if I had been born at exactly the same moment in time, but here in the desert instead of in New York? What would my chart have looked like?

That's the relocated chart.

Be careful when you are casting it – you've got to make sure that your computer doesn't fool you. Depending on what program you are using, there is a good chance that the machine will see California and "helpfully" turn my birth time to 3:21 am *Pacific Standard Time.*

Wrong! When I was born, it was actually 12:21 am out here in California.

Here's one way to do it: if you simply enter that corrected time, you will have the right chart – that is, January 6, 1949, Borrego Springs, CA at 12:21 am-PST.

Or you perhaps can override the software's insistence on PST and just enter 3:21 am *EST,* even though EST seems weird for the west coast.

Either method works fine, so long as you have the same date, but the new place. 12:21 PST is the same *moment of time* as 3:21 EST. That is the point. The only thing you want to change is the location.

Here's a quick check to make sure you got it right. *Look at the sign position of the Moon* – if it is not in *exactly the same degree and minute as it is in your birthchart,* then something went haywire. At the instant of my birth, the Moon was in 3 degrees 17 minutes of Aries *everywhere in the world.* No matter where you relocate your chart, the Sun, Moon, nodes and planets will remain in exactly the same sign positions. It is only their house positions that change.

Houses of course relate to behavior, circumstances, and events, and that brings us to the practical heart of the matter. The new house positions in the relocated chart will be evident in *what is emphasized in your life in the new place.* Very simply, in my relocated chart for Borrego Springs, there is a strong shift into houses three and six – and I have never *worked so intensely* (6th House) *at writing and teaching* (3rd House), *nor traveled, nor hiked,* so much (3rd House again).

There are deeper things I could say, but again I don't want to "over share."

While all your *planets* always remain in exactly the same signs in your relocated chart, that is not always true for the all-important four *Angles.* Move far enough east or west, and you will have a different Ascendant. Here in Borrego Springs, my Ascendant moves from natal Scorpio backwards into Libra.

That change ripples into *making Venus the ruler of my relocated chart*, taking that honor away from Mars and Pluto. And the biographical signature is quite evident: I live in a beautiful landscape, in a beautiful home full of flowers and paintings, with a beautiful professional artist whom I love – she even has Libra rising herself.

Going a little deeper, what exactly do we see in a relocated chart? How can we understand this tool and use it correctly? What does it mean?

- First question: does the relocated chart replace the birthchart? Absolutely not. Your birthchart is your birthchart, cradle to grave. You can't escape it – and if you are wise, you do not want to escape it. We will say more about that in a moment.

What we have in the relocated chart can be understood – if you will forgive a flagrant oxymoron – as *permanent transits*. Think of it like this: if Mercury transits across your Ascendant, for those few days your email Inbox is flooded, your phone is buzzing, and your friends are so wired on strong coffee that they can't shut up. Then Mercury passes out of the orbs of that aspect and it is all over.

If you move to a place where Mercury *relocates* to your Ascendant, the same kinds of effects and correlations can be expected, except that they do not end. For as long as you are there, that "transit" will be "permanent," so to speak.

Stay long enough, and you might actually write that novel you've been thinking about for years. The longer the exposure, the deeper the effect. But you will even feel it on a week-long vacation.

Your birthchart is your birthchart, cradle to grave, as we said – let's think deeply about that point for a moment. In evolutionary astrology, we understand that there is nothing random about the chart you have. Everything in your present chart is there for a reason – and those reasons *predate your birth*. It is all karmic, in other words – and, stemming from that karma, the chart contains remedies and prescriptions for your evolution. That is evolutionary astrology in a nutshell.

Now, in the light of all that, give the following idea a reality-check:

"I hate my karma! I hate that I was such a snake in a past life!"

Then the cartoon lightbulb lights over the dummy's head. *I've got it!!! I'll just move to Denver and my south node will be in a different house! That's it! Problem solved!"*

You may detect elements of weakness in this reasoning.

Use relocated charts, by all means – but never fall into the illusion that they replace your birthchart.

While we are at it, I would say the same thing about *relocated Solar Return charts.* There's a cottage industry in telling people where to go for their birthdays – go to Tahiti because Jupiter will be conjunct your Solar Return Ascendant there. That is not an entirely misguided notion – but it is bad practice to ignore the Solar Return to your natal place.

If you wonder why I say that, read the last couple hundred words again.

ASTROCARTOGRAPHY

Astrocartographic maps look like straightforward maps of the world or a region of it. The only difference is that they are covered with lines associated with planets, some vertical, some curving across the map. The idea is that when you are near any of these planetary lines, you feel their signature energies.

If you understand the reasoning behind the relocated chart, you can quickly grasp the logic behind Astrocartography – a term coined by the late Jim Lewis. You will also quickly see its major blind spot.

A moment ago, we imagined you moving to a place where Mercury was relocated to your Ascendant. If you looked at your Astrocartography map, you would see that place was on a Mercury line. At the instant of your birth, naturally somewhere on the earth Mercury was rising.

That is your Mercury line.

It is a *line*, rather than a dot on the map, because of course Mercury was on the eastern horizon in more than one place. Here's an easy way to visualize it: think of the familiar image of earth floating in space, half sunlit, half dark. Everywhere along that "terminator" line, the Sun was rising. You've got it – that dividing line between night and day is your *Astrocartographic Sunrise line.* It would show on the map as "Sun conjunct the Ascendant."

If you understand this simple point, you've fully grasped the essence of Astrocartography.

The astrocartography system is ever so slightly more complex than what I just described. Somewhere on the earth, the Sun was *setting* too. Somewhere Venus was on the Midheaven and somewhere Venus was anti-culminating – on the 4th House cusp, in other words. So there are actually four Venus lines, four Sun lines, and so forth – rising, setting, culminating, and anti-culminating.

Look carefully at an Astrocartography map and you will see notations such as this: "Mars/MC." Obviously, that would be the geographical line along which Mars was on the Midheaven at the time of your birth.

As you can see, astrocartography *is all about the four Angles*. And when a planet is relocated to an Angle, it indeed becomes very powerful. That is why Astrocartography often works so well.

Here's the problem: *planets can become powerful in other ways too –* ways that Astrocartography misses.

For example, Mercury rules the 3rd House. If you move or travel, Mercury might be relocated to your 3rd House cusp. It would be strongly emphasized there – just not for reasons of Angularity. Your Astrocartographic map will not show that.

Usually, in the practical realm of astrological counsel, the client is "thinking of moving to Asheville, North Carolina" or some other specific place. In that common situation, I never bother with Astrocartography – I just set up the relocated chart. Relocated charts may lack the digital "bells-and-whistles" of Astrocartography, but they are actually a much more powerful technique. They don't miss anything. You would see that Mercury on the 3rd cusp, for example.

Occasionally people come in for counsel who want to move, but they are not sure where. That is not unusual, for example, when a person is contemplating retirement and has many possible destinations. Then out comes Astrocartography. Using that map, we get a start on scoping out the big picture – but it is not long before we have narrowed the list down to a few appealing places and we are back to relocated charts.

LOCAL SPACE

I am a big fan of this technique. I find it every bit as powerful as Astrocartography, but strangely it is not nearly as well known. Like Astrocartography, Local Space astrology produces a normal-looking map with planetary lines on it, however the way they are derived is entirely different. They are based on *Azimuths.*"

An unfamiliar word? Here's what it means. A child is born. At that moment, *we point to the Moon.* It lies high in the sky, but let us say it bears due east. If we were to drop the Moon directly down to a clear true horizon, we might see that it lies at a bearing of 92° – actually just a bit south of due east.

That line is the Moon's Azimuth.

In the same way, all the planets would similarly have their own Azimuths. It is really almost like pointing a finger at them.

Some planets of course would currently lie below the horizon. No problem – just raise them up until they are on that true horizon and take that bearing.

Now fire a magic bullet at the Moon. It goes all the way around the Earth and hits you in the back of the head. There would, in other words, *be two paths you could go by in order to get to the Moon* – the direct route straight toward it, or the long way around. Either direction would do.

Another way to say it is that Local Space "Azimuth" lines point both exactly toward and exactly away from a planet.

Draw those lines on the map and there's your Local Space map.

It is easy to distinguish Local Space at a glance from Astrocartography because in Local Space you always see lines exploding outward in every direction from your birthplace. In Astrocartography, there is no such epicenter.

In practice, Local Space works just like Astrocartography: *if you travel along those lines, you will experience the energy of those planets.*

Local Space has an important practical advantage: unlike Astrocartography, it can work on very *small distance scales.* Let's say you are planning to move house, but you will remain in the same city. Astrocartography would cast no light on that question at all – it only works on larger geographical scales. In that system, there is no real distinction between the south side of Chicago and the north side.

But maybe in Local Space you see that due north is the direction of your Saturn line – or your Jupiter line . . .

We just learned three things:

- First, that Local Space can be relocated – maybe you were not born in Chicago but your Saturn line is always pointed north anyway.
- Second, we learn that Local Space works over short distances as well as over long ones.
- Third, that the technique can even work as a kind of astrological *feng shui* in your own home. If you have trouble sleeping, don't put your bed on your Uranus line – maybe try moving it to your Moon line.

SOME FINAL THOUGHTS

The practical bottom line in applying all these techniques is that when you relocate, you emphasize an altered set of astrological powers in your life. But you need to think deeply about that. As evolutionary astrologers, we are ever-wary of one-dimensional, "lucky" or "unlucky," interpretations: planets are simply energies. You can use any of them well or poorly.

Saturn locations, for example, imply the need for disciplined effort – and caution us about loneliness or despair. How will you use that energy? *Will you really get your teeth into something or will you just feel isolated and depressed?* It is up to you, not to Saturn. Similarly, Neptune locations support spiritual and creative pursuits – and warn of lassitude, feeling lost, and escapism.

In astromapping, we use all our familiar archetypal planetary imagery, in other words. The translation from the core principles of evolutionary astrology into Astrocartography, Local Space, and Relocation is straightforward.

That is why I groan when I hear of astrologers who suggest that "you should never move to a Saturn line." Maybe you *want to do something difficult* – write a novel, get your doctorate, build a house. Saturn energy can support that kind of focus and discipline. Will it be difficult? Of course! That Is in the nature of those activities.

For similar reasons, I despair when I hear an astrologer exhorting everyone to "move to their Jupiter line." It is really not that simple – I've seen people use Jupiter energy simply to get fat. And of course, all that glitters is not gold.

In applying these relocation techniques in your own life, ask yourself a few penetrating questions:

- What are your intentions behind this move?
- Why are you moving – or taking that vacation in Italy? What do you want out of it?

- What are your historic liabilities connected with the planets you will be emphasizing?
- What has your actual experience been with, say, Venus? Do you really want to underscore that energy in your life?

Your answers are naturally personal, unique, and 100% your own business. There's more – we think of "Venus" and we naturally think of relationships. Fair enough. *But what if your natal Venus lies in Virgo in the 10th House?* Then for you Venus is also charged with the energy of career and mission. Move to your Venus line and you will be electrifying those career potentials in your life – and no astrocartographic "cookbook" would tell you that. Such books can only treat the planets generically.

In other words, to get the full benefit of these mapping techniques, you need to take into account *the specific meanings and possibilities of each planet as it actually fits into the signs, houses, and aspects of your chart.*

In a way, there is really nothing as simple as "pure Venus." You can't separate the planet from its particular conditions.

With those caveats in mind, here follows a quick thumbnail sketch of the high and low potentials of each planet as it operates in the context of both Astrocartography and Local Space.

Meanwhile, happy – and safe – travels this summer!

- *If you move toward a Sun line,* expect heightened self-confidence and charisma, probably greater vitality – and possibly the embarrassment of your ego's "stuff" getting demonstrated to everyone who knows you.

- *If you move toward a Moon line,* expect intensified emotions, nurturing impulses, greater depth, a sense of "being home" – and possibly moodiness, lassitude, and irrationality.

- *If you move toward a Mercury line,* expect underscored intellectual vigor, opportunities to speak or write or teach, restlessness and curiosity – and possibly nervousness, scattered energy, insomnia, and difficulty closing your mouth. *(From a shamanic perspective, your Mercury direction in Local Space is a direction in which to look for omens.)*

- *If you move toward a Venus line,* expect intensified impulses toward intimacy, sexual expression, aesthetic stimulus, and creative enthusiasm – and possibly laziness, romantic complications, and temptations toward addiction.

- *If you move toward a Mars line,* expect emphasized physical vitality, assertiveness, competitiveness, entrepreneurial impulses, and passion – and possibly anger, violence, victimization, and accident.

- *If you move toward a Jupiter line,* expect boatloads of enthusiasm and confidence, big opportunities, more faith in yourself and in life – and possibly over-active appetites, over-extension, and poor boundaries. Yes is a word that can get us in a lot of trouble.

- *If you move toward a Saturn line,* expect peaks of self-discipline, determination, tolerance for solitude, ambition in some sense – and possibly sadness, loneliness, reversals, and low vitality.

- *If you move toward a Uranus line,* expect a drive toward greater independence, rebelliousness, creativity, and a general sense of there being more wild cards in life's deck – and possibly headstrong idiocy and unpleasant surprises.

- *If you move toward a Neptune line,* expect vivid psychic sensitivity, colorful dreams, deeper spirituality, creative inspiration – and possibly spaciness, lack of motivation, poor judgement, and addictive/escapist impulses.

- *If you move toward a Pluto line,* expect intense psychological processes and a deeper sense of "the tides of fate" – and possibly psychological heaviness, existential despair, and catastrophe. In that direction you will encounter the core wounds of your soul, and have a chance to heal them – or to be driven by them.

- *If you move toward a Node line,* you invite the facing and resolution of the basic karmic and evolutionary issues of your life. There is very often a distinct "call of destiny" associated with places along that line. (Note that since the Nodes are an axis in the chart, there is only one Node line – not a separate one for North and South.)

By the way, Ralph MacIntrye who has been involved with my Apprenticeship Program in southern California for a long time has developed software that deftly weaves Astrocartography together with the great advantages of GoogleEarth. Check it out at http://www.astro-map-links.com

68

Astrology's greatest vulnerability lies in our absolute dependence upon accurate times of birth. Even an error of a few minutes can sometimes throw an interpretation into chaos. What can we do when people have no knowledge of their birth time? A process called "rectification" is astrology's ingenious answer. In essence, we work backwards through astrology's predictive techniques, using the dates of known events in the person's life in order to create a chart that would have correctly predicted their timing – voila: that's the right chart. In this little essay about my new kitten, you can get a taste of how these techniques actually work in practice.

WHAT TIME WAS BENNY BORN?

(Newsletter – October 2020)

Michelle and I lost our beloved Norwegian Forest cat, Wally, in January. By summer, we were emotionally ready to invite a kitten into our lives. With Covid-19 raging, the search was mostly on the Internet, which is a shaky place when it comes to falling in love with anyone, including a cat. One little guy did catch our hearts and our eyes though – a kitten named Benny. He was living in a shelter in the city of Hemet a couple hours' drive away. We headed up there on Michelle's birthday, August 12, to have a look at him. We were immediately smitten, and Benny came home with us that same day.

Naturally, as astrologers, we were curious about his chart, but his birth data was not available – he and his four brothers had been dumped unceremoniously at a kill shelter at the tender age of two weeks. They had been picked up by the saints who run a no-kill shelter where it was "estimated" that they had been born "around May 8." That's all we had to go on.

Astrologers are often confronted with situations such as this one, where there is no time of birth available. After all possibilities for finding a recorded time have been exhausted, the final option is to undertake a *rectification*. Basically, one works backwards through astrology's predictive techniques to come up with a chart *that would have predicted events that have already happened* in the person's life.

Rectification is a tricky process, fraught with risks of error.

Would the rectification process work with our Benny? There were many problems, starting with the fact that he was only three months old. That meant that there were not yet many events in his life. Rectification works best with people in midlife. They have longer stories to tell, which means more clues. I also like to have the dates of events widely spaced over time in order to spread out the transits, progressions, and solar arcs a bit. Too many events clustered in the same year tend to generate "false positives."

Benny was so young that many of the planets were still "conjunct themselves."

Just to be crystal clear, let me be the first to admit that in this newsletter I'm going to indulge in some monumentally bad habits when it comes to rectification. I'll at least label them for you. This is a "do as I say, not as I do" situation, for sure. We will come up with a possible chart for Benny – and we will label it "tentative."

As I mentioned, the people at the animal shelter told us that Benny had been born "around May 8." That was all we knew. For rectification purposes, this was an absolute worst-case scenario – not only did we not have a *time* of birth for our kitten, we didn't even have a reliable *date*. Usually with rectifications, you have a birth date, along with at least a hint about the time – "mom says it was in the evening," or something like that. That's not good enough for setting up an actual chart, but it does narrow down the possibilities. We didn't even have that much. So, undaunted (even though we should have been), we set up a noon chart for May 8, 2020 in Hemet, California. That was at least a point of departure.

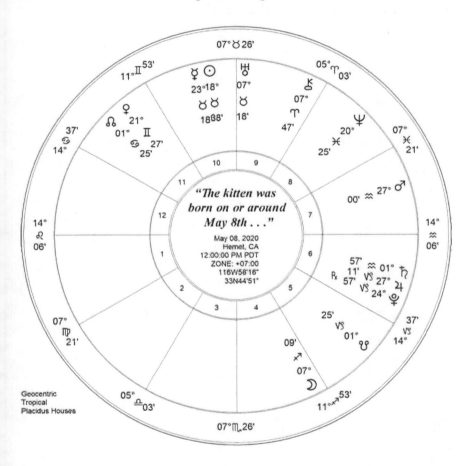

What about *events* in Benny's life? We had only one, and that was our first meeting with him. It was a big day for him as well as for us – not only did he meet his future "parents," but he was also neutered on that same day. In fact, when Michelle and I arrived for our appointment at the shelter, the staff apologized that Benny was at the veterinary hospital and would not arrive back until "around 3:00 pm." We took the delay in stride, did some shopping, and arrived back at 3:00 that afternoon. Benny was still not there. He actually showed up a bit later.

Fortunately, we had sufficient presence of mind to look at our watches. We met him at precisely 3:47 pm-pdt, and that gave us a *timed event chart* in his life. That, plus our initial impressions of him, were all we had to go on – that's not enough, but that was all we had.

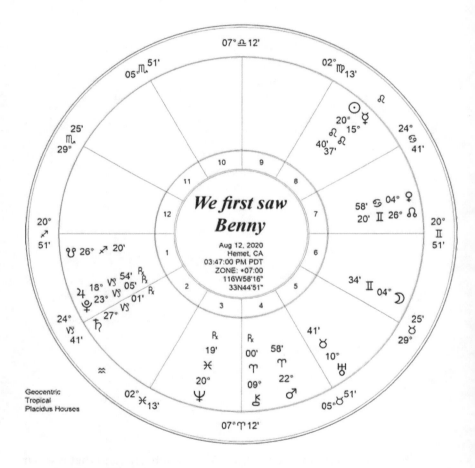

By the way, those "initial impressions" can lie to you with terrible authority. Beginners may "just know" that this person *must* have Leo rising – only to discover a true birth time later on which reveals the Sun or Jupiter conjunct the Ascendent.

Impressions are helpful, but only if you are careful. Never trust them uncritically. Astrologically, there are many different ways to say the same thing. Jupiter can look like Leo. Saturn can resemble Capricorn.

Miss that, and you will resemble a monkey.

Another rectification trick that doesn't involve events is the fact that people (and pets!) who are drawn together usually have strong astrological connections. Would Benny's chart link via synastry to mine or Michelle's? We can safely assume that to be true – but of course that too entails a great many possibilities. In a little while, we will bring that ploy into play as well.

"May 8" being vague and approximate, we didn't even have certainty around the sign of Benny's Moon. It happened to be in Sagittarius on that day, but it easily could have been in Scorpio or Capricorn if May 8 had been off by a day or two.

Synchronicity to the rescue: as we stood there watching Benny in the cage with his brothers, he attempted a bold athletic leap and wound up somersaulting spectacularly into the water bowl. With all due respect to you dignified Sagittarians out there, that did give a point to Sagittarius.

In practice, rectification is all about the four Angles – the endpoints of the horizon and the meridian. They are time-sensitive and so they are what we are looking for. The essence of the rectification process lies in hoping that those Angles reveal themselves through transits, progressions, and solar arcs.

The "event chart" of our first meeting with Benny had 20 degrees 51' of Sagittarius rising – that's very close to my natal Venus, *and for Benny and me, it was love at first sight.* That momentary position of the local Ascendant was my own transit – but could it be Benny's transit too? Might the transiting Ascendant have been triggering his Moon, assuming it too was in Sagittarius as we suspected?

The noon chart for May 8th had the Moon earlier – in about 7 degrees of Sagittarius. We liked the Sagittarian Moon for our kitten, but we wondered if maybe his Moon actually fell later in the sign.

Could Benny's Moon be lined up with the Ascendant of our first meeting, and thus also with my own natal Venus?

That would have him born the next day, May 9, which was of course completely possible.

That "first meeting" chart also had 7 degrees 12' of Libra on the Midheaven. I immediately wondered if the horizon or meridian in that event chart might parallel any of the Angles in Benny's own chart. That didn't narrow things down very much, leaving us with points around the 7th degree of four different signs – Sagittarius, Gemini, Aries, and Libra. They were all possibilities, and all might be wrong and misleading if we weren't careful.

With so little to go on, we next resorted to the perilous practice of cataloging our impressions of Benny. We had already leaned toward a Sagittarian Moon based partly on his behavior when he somersaulted into the water bowl. As you just saw, there were also some astrological arguments to be made in support of that Moon sign based on the event chart of our first meeting.

Nothing to lose, so we took it further by engaging our astrological intuitions. Benny is a really *pretty* kitten – and if you disagree, please don't email me about it or I will have to kill you.

More tellingly, he is *friendly*, even though, being a kitten, he is still half *Velociraptor*. He *likes people* and he *quickly charms them*. From the first day we had him, and every night since, he has slept between Michelle and me, purring away and eager to interact. He doesn't like being left alone, although sometimes for me to get any work done, he needs to be shut out of my office and Michelle's painting studio. He hates that, but he seems to get over it quickly when we emerge. He doesn't seem to hold a grudge.

All of that made me wonder if possibly that Libran Midheaven in the chart of our first meeting might also be Benny's natal Ascendant. We set up that chart, putting that 7-degree Libran Ascendant on a May 9th chart.

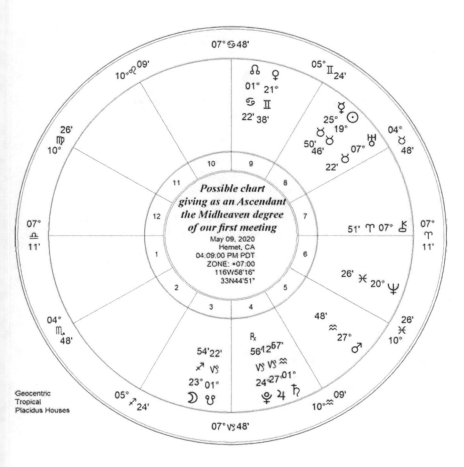

Geocentric
Tropical
Placidus Houses

Next I had one of those serendipity moments that always seem to happen in astrological practice. I noticed that at the instant of our first meeting, transiting Venus was just under five degrees of Cancer. *I realized that if Benny had been born just a few minutes earlier than the chart I had just set up, then Venus would have been transiting his natal Midheaven when he arrived in our arms.*

Perfect!

Additionally, the Sagittarian Ascendant would be triggering his (putative) Moon. Even better, the transiting Moon in Gemini would have been smack on the cusp of his 9th house (long journeys), *and he was just about to embark on a two-hour car trip.*

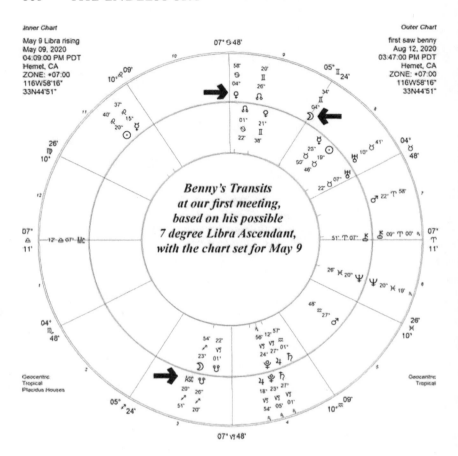

Everything fit perfectly – and that is the most dangerous moment in any rectification. You start to get excited that you have found the answer. And maybe you have. But maybe you have made a fool of yourself by letting your excitement blind you to other possibilities.

In what I have written here, I have based everything on one single event, along with some personal impressions. That is a huge no-no in rectification. My only defense is that I only *had* one event to work with. Another shaky element in what I have done here is to rely heavily on those personal impressions. That is not a no-no, exactly – but it should never be the starting point. The starting point should always be the life event data itself.

So, formally, I would hesitate to declare that this is Benny's true chart. I'd call it plausible speculation – and, as a bonus, a fun way to present something of the real world of astrological rectification in this newsletter.

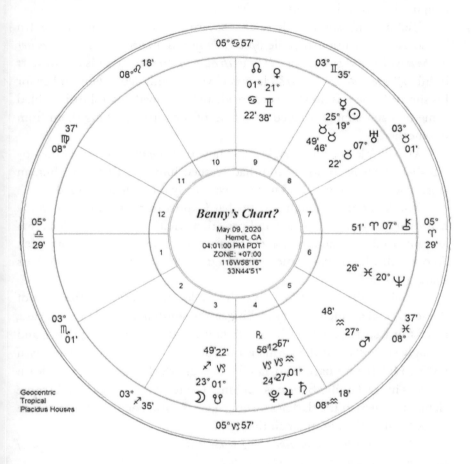

Let me take it one step further. As an evolutionary astrologer, I am always interested in the karma underlying any situation. And cats have karma, as do all sentient beings. We see karma represented most clearly in the south node of the Moon – not to mention in the shape of the person's life, especially when "fate" seems to take a hand in things. That's how karma works. Can a kitten's lunar nodes teach us anything?

Benny was born very close to the time when the south node switched from Capricorn to Sagittarius. His south node (and I always use the Mean node, not the so-called True one) was in 1 degree 22' of Capricorn. (Remember, the nodes are always retrograde.) In my speculative chart, that would place the south lunar node in his 3rd house in a reasonably close conjunction with that Sagittarian Moon.

Tellingly, his south node ruler – Saturn – was in Aquarius in the 4th house. As we mentioned earlier, *poor Benny was dropped off at a kill shelter at the tender age of two weeks, along with his four brothers.* That is a hard start in life. *Where was his mother?* He was obviously still dependent on her for his survival – he was nowhere near ready to be weaned. Had she died? Had some monster simply decided to get rid of the kittens, taking them from the mother?

We don't know the story. We do know that the kind people at the no-kill shelter where we found him had rescued him, and that some human angel had bottle-nursed him until he was ready for regular cat food.

Think about it though – with that Capricorn south node *his karma was hard* and it involved lack and privation. That's Capricorn. His karma also involved *chaos* and *unexpected events* – those are 3rd house correlates. Another 3rd house correlation is *siblings* – and Benny had four brothers sharing his fate.

In discerning karma, we always pay a lot of attention to the ruler of the south node, which is just as telling as the south node itself. In this case, it is Saturn, sitting there in the fourth house. Saturn echoes Capricorn and strongly suggests that the karma is difficult. The 4th house correlates with *family.* Did Benny have hard family karma? Maybe the karma of death and loss in the family? Saturn is conjunct Jupiter, which might imply some element of help in the darkness – but then it is also conjunct Pluto, which deepens all of the nightmarish themes.

Does any of this sound like being separated from your mother at the age of two weeks and sent to a kill shelter to die?

As I mentioned earlier, I rely on the Mean node rather than the True one. Usually they are very close together, and so generally the distinction does not matter very much. But Benny is a test case. His so-called True south node is actually in Sagittarius, not Capricorn. Given the facts of his early life, do you like Saturn or Jupiter as the ruling planet? Which one tells the "true" story? That seems like an easy question to me – and this is a pattern I have seen repeatedly: when someone is born with the True south node in one sign and the Mean one in another, it is the Mean node that tells the deeper story.

Remember: what we see in the south node is a person's *unresolved* karma. It always leaves a mark – and generally a painful one – on the life. Benny is a happy-go-lucky kind of guy – exactly what we would expect in a Taurus with Libra rising and Sagittarian Moon. What the node reveals was the *ripening karma of his early life.*

With that Cancer *north* node of his, Benny has come to a stage in his own evolutionary journey where he needs healing, a loving home, *and something to eat*. I've never seen such a hungry cat. Even the vet was astonished when he gained one full pound in only two weeks. His shelter name, Benny, seems to have stuck with us. But formally he is now *Benito Mangiamo*, which is Italian for "Let's eat."

Once again, I have not only demonstrated some of the fundamentals of rectification here, I have also demonstrated some really bad habits. Beware of relying too much on personal impressions and jumping to astrological conclusions. Always use multiple dates of events, and let the hard facts of astrological reality reveal a pattern.

The work is actually fun in a Virgo sort of way. It's time-consuming though, and for that reason I no longer do it as part of my professional practice. I can recommend people if you need one done.

69

I've always loved this little essay. I wish that every astrologer involved with counseling work could internalize its message. It boils down, on one hand, to a healing mixture that is equal parts humble honesty about what it means to be human and, on the other hand, compassion and self-forgiveness. It's a given that we all make mistakes in life. It's another given that we would all prefer to avoid making them. It's a third given that we simply cannot avoid making them. In the counseling room, we are faced with the reality of talking with our clients about these self-inflicted wounds. What is the right attitude toward them? In this piece, there is no technical astrology at all — just an "attitude adjustment" which I hope enables us to use the fierce power of evolutionary astrology to help us generate liberating insights without shaming or burning anyone in the process.

BOTCHED TRANSITS AND PROGRESSIONS . . .

(Newsletter – September 2019)

I got a terrific question from a client a few weeks ago. I felt it was rich enough territory for a newsletter. Let me open with her words:

> *"When you have come through a major transit or progression and totally fail to get it right, what does the high road look like from there? In prac-*

tical terms, we often just have to live with whatever consequences that may become a non-negotiable part of our lives after a less-than-optimal response. Life goes on, the stars continue to spin, new challenges await. But is it worthwhile to ask if any of the higher potentials of a "botched" transit/progression are actively recoverable? Or is it simply a time to assess, acknowledge the loss and the lesson, and move on? Is it all, you know. . . starlight under the bridge once a transit is over?"

Let me get rolling here with a question that has become a cliché: *is there really any such thing as a mistake?* I'm a Capricorn, so my answer is pretty simple: *yes indeed – mistakes are part of life.* The word serves a useful purpose and we need it in our vocabularies. And when we do make mistakes, there is always a price to pay.

Beyond that practical, grounded perspective, we enter slippery territory.

Mistakes come in a lot of different flavors, for starters. If my airline pilot aspires to never make any aeronautical mistakes, I applaud his or her excellent attitude. But, in the world of astrological counseling, we generally aren't looking at mistakes of such a concrete nature. We are not talking about believing that two plus two equals five. In astrology, we are talking about navigating life itself.

Perhaps you were once partnered with someone. Perhaps you are not in that relationship any more. *Was the whole thing really just a mistake?* Is the question that simple? Maybe, with some relationships, we can just say yes, it was a mistake. But with many, it's a lot trickier.

A moment ago, I promised "slippery territory . . ." *Why* did you marry that person? Retrospectively we can often come up with helpful psychological insights – for example, "Harry represented what I never got from my father." A year of psychotherapy later and you realize that "Harry" was the *clone* of your failed father and that is why the marriage didn't work. You were repeating an old pattern of wounding.

Maybe all that is true – but here's another truth: in marrying Harry, *you were doing your best.* That marriage reflected your actual level of consciousness at the time. Another way to say it is that your marriage was an honest manifestation of how crazy you were then.

That last line doesn't sound particularly flattering, but as we reflect on it, it leads us to dive into some deep waters – waters where we might learn a lot about why we incarnate in this world in the first place.

If I say, "we are all here on Earth in order to grow and learn," everyone agrees and tries not to yawn. We've heard that line too many times before. It's just like wondering if there is really any such thing as a mistake. *But how, exactly, do we grow?* It is possible – maybe even optimal – to sit on a mountain top in meditation and learn everything that way . . . in other words, purely through insight and cognition.

The mind can play tricks on itself though, and often does – maybe what you think you are "learning" on that mountain top has more to do with your defenses and rationalizations than with actual growth. In contrast, by "marrying Harry," you really put the truth about your level of consciousness on the table. No lies were possible there – the condition of your soul was translated directly into outward, existential reality, where you could see it, unvarnished and clear as a bell.

Incarnation works like a charm that way.

In our mistakes, *we make our actual karmic condition visible.* That is a big part of the actual mechanism of our evolution. Mistakes are why we have bodies in the first place. Making them is often the main way that we learn. That is painful and often even embarrassing – but those negatives are balanced by the advantage of sheer naked truthfulness free of our self-protective, delusional "excuses and explanations."

Was "marrying Harry" a mistake? Perhaps that is not even the right question. That marriage was simply an outward manifestation of the truth of your being at the time. None of us can ever do better than that.

The question of mistakes has a place, but it comes along a little later in the time-line.

Let's say that Harry left you for someone else. Let's say you blame the failure of your marriage on "that bitch" instead of learning anything at all from the experience – there's a certifiably 24-karat solid gold mistake.

The marriage wasn't a mistake, *but failing to learn anything from it was.*

People can use astrology to make money, foresee changes in women's fashions, or predict political outcomes. That's all fine, but ultimately, the deepest forms of astrology are about the evolution of consciousness. To be as clear as we can be as astrologers, that is where we need to focus our attention – on consciousness itself. *Did I learn what I needed to learn? What will I keep – for eternity – from this experience?* Those are the truly pivotal questions. Whether you learned about the baleful impact of your father on your psyche by sitting in meditation on that mountain top or by "marrying Harry" is really almost just a footnote.

In this rigorously metaphysical way of thinking, mistakes are a reality – *but an event only becomes a mistake if you fail to learn anything from it.* Otherwise it was just the evolutionary wheels turning in their normal, eternal way.

The glorious German poet, Rainer Maria Rilke, once wrote, ""*The purpose of life is to be defeated by greater and greater things."* The line has a depressing ring to it at first, but it echoes the astrological perspective that I am exploring with you here. When we are living mindfully, we are always up against our own developmental edges. Naturally we make some errors there – how could it be otherwise? Never before have we ever tried anything so difficult! We lack a map. We lack tried-and-true reflexes. We have no hard-won, time-tempered instincts.

If, on the other hand, we "know what we are doing," we are very probably doing what we have already learned how to do in the past. That's fine – but it doesn't have much to do with growth. Where we are truly growing, we are error-prone. We have the most airtight, ironclad excuse for it too: again, *we don't know what we are doing.* We're only beginners.

We all naturally want to "get things right" and to "not make any mistakes." At a practical level, that is a good attitude – but let's not even congratulate ourselves on having it: that drive arises pretty much automatically in the human psyche. As I mentioned earlier, I commend such a "make no mistakes" attitude in my airline pilot. But in life? *If we are unduly afraid of making mistakes, what happens? Do we learn anything at all?*

We can glibly recite the familiar line that "everyone makes mistakes," but the truth is more subtle. *A person, through sheer timidity and conventionality, can resolve to live safely – and die of boredom at a ripe old age, having learned nothing at all.*

Fasten your seatbelts: from the evolutionary point of view, *a life with no mistakes is itself the most terrible mistake imaginable.*

The absolute horror of astrology is, in my opinion, the way it describes *perfection.* None of us can ever reach that golden city. If we hold ourselves to that impossible standard, we tie ourselves in knots of fear and insecurity. Eventually, down that road, shame and self-doubt make us afraid to live.

Your chart, along with your transits and progressions, works the same way the North Star works for a sailor at sea. If he is sailing northward, he aims his bow at that star. It orients him, even comforts him – *but he does not expect to arrive there.*

To not be afraid of life is to not be afraid of mistakes – the two ideas are inseparable.

At a human level, marrying Harry took a bite out of your soul. Even the mistakes we are able to turn into wisdom, even the ones we harness in service of our spiritual evolution, come with a price tag. As we have been seeing, growth and learning are some compensation for the pain and cost of those errors – and, if we choose to learn nothing, all we have left are the pain and the cost, and that is a thousand times worse.

Still, mistakes, while they are inevitable, even purposeful, and we should never be ashamed of making them, *always damage us.* They hurt. That is simply realistic. Blessedly, we have some power of regeneration. With time, we can heal. And most transits and progressions come around again in some other form, so we can take another shot at learning what we needed to learn back then.

Yet the motivation to avoid errors arises naturally in us. It stems from the same source as our desire to avoid getting hurt.

In that quest to avoid unnecessarily damaging mistakes, astrology is a fine ally. It unerringly reveals to us the evolutionary meaning of whatever challenges are pressing at us. It describes precisely what we are learning and how to learn it in the most direct, efficient way. Astrology sometimes asks us to embrace suffering voluntarily – for example, a Pluto transit might invite us to wrestle honestly with some psychological issue that plagues us. Who enjoys being in psychotherapy, for example? It can be awful – but not as awful as the alternative, which generally lies in "living out" our unresolved issues: *marrying Harry,* in other words.

There are many roads in life. Ultimately most of them work. The universe is patient with us, and we are free to make our own choices. The road of mistakes works. So does the faster road which evolutionary astrology reveals before us.

The cosmic message seems to be, "now do as you like."

70

Astrologers don't like talking about this, but sometimes astrology seems simply not to be working at all. With rare exceptions, I think that is generally more the fault of the astrologer than the fault of astrology itself. Still, it is a disconcerting moment for any professional. In this essay, we essentially go through a checklist of possibilities when that situation arises, looking for where our error might lie and how we might help turn the situation around, both for ourselves and for our clients.

WHEN ASTROLOGY FAILS

(Newsletter – September 2017)

I got a worried email from a student of mine this morning. He had a client who had experienced transiting Uranus conjunct her Moon, but "nothing had happened." He was concerned and embarrassed that his predictions had failed. I offered him a few possible explanations. As I responded to him, I realized that his question would be a fine topic for a newsletter. I am sure that this student of mine was not the first astrologer to have had this disconcerting experience.

The first point I want to make will sound pretty dogmatic, but I do believe it to be true: *astrology never fails.* I would quickly add that astrologers themselves often fail, but that is a different issue. Astrology is fundamental to how the universe operates. Astrology failing would be like gravity failing.

I'll temper that remark slightly a little later in this essay, but I really want to put it up there "in lights" before I write another word.

Still, astrologers' predictions sometimes do fail and it behooves us not to be afraid of acknowledging that fact and perhaps learning something from it. There are a lot of potential issues here. Let's have a look at them.

SYMBOLISM IS NOT LITERALISM

I have beaten this drum since long before *The Inner Sky* was a gleam in its daddy's eye, so I don't want to belabor it here. Still, this core point is the heart of the matter when it comes to "astrology's failures." *Symbolism is not the same as literalism.* We don't read an astrological chart in the same way that we read a news feed or a computer manual.

Let me give you an example. An astrologer sees Uranus entering someone's seventh house. The astrologer predicts divorce. No divorce happens.

Has astrology failed? No, it is the astrologer who's now got egg on his or her face. That prediction was too narrow. Its very rigidity would doom it to being wrong more often than it was right. Think about it logically: *the majority of long-term partnerships have survived one or the other of the people experiencing that transit.* That's one painfully obvious point.

The real point, though, is that while divorce is indeed one possible expression of "The Lord of Earthquakes and Lightning Bolts" entering the House of Marriage, *it is not the only one.* What is really happening is that *a pulse of individuation* is in play in the client's personal relationships. That pulse can play out in a lot of different ways.

> *A wife tells her husband that instead of going on their usual vacation with his family this summer, she wants to attend a week-long astrology seminar. She is afraid he will object, but instead he says, "Great! That's actually a relief. I was hoping to skip my family this year, rent a motorcycle, and ride across New Mexico. I was afraid that you would be upset about skipping our vacation."*

What's just happened? *They've given each other some Uranian breathing room.* They are happier and closer because of it. They've probably also set a healthy precedent for "future negotiations" – one that works better for each of them.

That's a far more self-aware response to this transit than divorce.

Our big question: *did "nothing happen?"*

Of course not – the astrologer who foresaw a divorce simply had too narrow a preconception about what a Uranus transit meant. Again, symbolism is not literalism. In this case, the client (not the astrologer!) got the meaning of the transit right. Sadly, this 100% possible *higher response* to Uranus entering the seventh house lay outside the scope of the astrologer's imagination.

That kind of interpretive error alone accounts for the lion's share of situations where "astrology fails." Never under-estimate your clients – and never forget that there is a higher evolutionary meaning in every transit no matter "how bad it looks."

Let's look at another explanation for astrology's apparent failures.

HUMANS LIVE IN TWO WORLDS

We humans naturally walk around in physical bodies, our senses engaged with the outer world. We bounce off each other, dealing with our needs and our appetites, and wrestling with our circumstances.

But we also live in our inner worlds.

Even our understanding of the physical world is conditioned by our inner attitudes and moods. If you doubt that, try reasoning with a depressed person that "life is not really so bad."

On top of that, every night we close our eyes, surrender our engagement with the outer world, descending utterly into the abyss of our inner lives.

That deep psychic underworld we all inhabit is at least as central to our experience as is the outer world of our jobs, the news, and the daily grind.

My point here is simple and it has fundamental relevance to our notion of "astrology failing." *Sometimes an astrological event unfolds 100% on the inner plane.* It is still "an event," except that its nature is purely psychic. It has no direct external behavioral correlates at all.

Again, let's consider our example of Uranus transiting into a woman's seventh house. This time, let's say she is single and has been content to remain that way. Let's say that her attitude toward relationships has boiled down to, "Why buy a cow when milk is so cheap?"

That's a funny line, but it also probably reflects a certain brittleness in this woman.

Let's say that some of her defensive attitude about relationships derives from a fear of being vulnerable. Let's say that *external social conditioning* – always the enemy of the planet Uranus – has forged a resistance in her to trusting anyone. Let's postulate, for example, that her father abandoned the family when she was little.

Let's say that she has surrounded herself with friends who also protect themselves from their own loneliness in that same "sour grapes" fashion – by devaluing relationships.

Uranus entering this woman's seventh house might be about her *claiming her own true individuality back from those external influences.* Sitting on a park bench having a long talk with herself, she realizes that in her true nature, she is potentially a loving partner – or at least she would like to be. She longs for that outward reality to manifest – *and it takes courage for her even to admit it.*

As she sits on that park bench, no knight in shining armor rides up on the proverbial white horse and sweeps her away to a castle on a hill. She is still single. *Outwardly, nothing has changed.* But if we say, "nothing happened when Uranus entered her seventh house," angels laugh and shake their heads. Something enormous has happened. It just happened between her ears – *in the psychic realm* – rather than in the outer world.

Add a little imagination and a little human empathy, and we can quickly realize that this Uranian change of heart in her can be understood as the prelude to some happy intimate possibilities in her future – and that without this change of heart, Prince Charming could fall on his knees before her and she'd turn away thinking, "Nice guy, but he's too short for me."

The message here is that we all live in an inner world as well as an outward one. It is possible for astrology to work on the inner plane without leaving a visible ripple on the surface of life. *A good astrologer must be alert to that reality,* while a bad one thinks only in concrete, outward terms of "predicting what will happen," limiting the scope of that question to the positions of the atoms and molecules in the outer world.

While I stand by the basic point I am making here, I'd like to affirm that it represents a rather rare situation. Generally, because of the way the principle of synchronicity weaves through astrology, there *are* outward expressions of most transits as well as inward expressions. They may be subtle, but they are usually present.

Our protagonist in the previous scenario might, for example, experience *a 30-second flirtation with a stranger*. See the connection with her inner changes? She might click on Match.com, take a nervous peek, and then quickly X-out of it.

These are obviously *microscopic* events, easily ignored. But they are the subtle outward manifestations of the far more dramatic pattern of inner realizations.

An astrologer could be forgiven for not noticing them, but angels notice everything.

Let's move onward to a third reason for astrology's apparent failures.

HOW BADLY DOES THIS TRANSIT NEED TO HAPPEN?

A nearly fail-safe astrological principle is that no transit or progression happens unless it *needs* to happen – they all represent evolutionary necessities. They are all essentially soul-contracts we signed with the universe, right along with our first breaths.

One way to express it is to say that we are all sick – and transits and progressions are the medicine. Calling us "all sick" sounds negative, but ultimately *why are we here, on this earth, in these physical bodies?* Earth is not the most prestigious address in the galaxy. It is good to be alive and there is no shame in being here locked into these vehicles of flesh and bone, but it's just one stage in a larger evolutionary journey – an evolutionary journey is reflected in your birthchart, while transits and progressions simply trigger its unfolding stages. The point is, they always happen when they need to, always at the right time. They arise to expand something in our awareness, to correct something, to heal something.

With those broad philosophical points established, let's recognize that at a given moment, *some of us might need firmer correction than others.* How far off-target are you in your life? How much of a bite has spiritual laziness taken out of your higher potentials? Like the rest of us, you've had your soul-victories and you've probably had your spiritual prat-falls too.

All of this leads to the key point: *the vigor of a transit is connected to how big a "correction" is appropriate for you.* And that is not something that we can see in your chart. The answer has to do with how well you have been responding to your chart all along.

Back to Uranus transiting into that hypothetical woman's seventh house. Even if she is in a happy relationship, she still has her own path to follow in life. *How successfully has she balanced the compromising realities of partnership with fidelity to her own journey and her own nature?* Those are always knotty questions. Naturally we all make mistakes. She is presumably no exception. Out of love for a partner, we might compromise too much sometimes, perhaps without even knowing we are doing it. Or maybe we are so pig-headed, selfish, and stubborn that we find "meeting in the middle" offensive.

Along comes Uranus with this woman's report card.

Illustration: she has been "an obedient, pliant wife," sacrificing herself to the needs of her husband and family to the point that she has become almost a phantom in her own world. Uranus hits her hard. Perhaps it truly feels like "the Lord of Earthquakes and Lightning bolts has entered her House of Marriage."

What happens?

Maybe she finally blows up – abandons the marriage, has an affair, moves to South America under an assumed name. Spectacular stuff! And the fortune-telling astrologer is of course delighted by the accuracy of his or her over-the-top prediction.

More likely, given this woman's passive nature, she experiences the transit internally, but in a dark way. *She gives up.* She withdraws further into emotional *dissociation.* She chooses to become a zombie in her own life. And maybe her husband doesn't notice a thing.

Angels notice, and they weep.

The underlying concept here is that our protagonist badly needed this Uranus transit. The evolutionary requirement it represented was pressing, so the "fault line was locked and loaded" and the earthquake promised to be huge.

And it *was* huge – in one scenario, she divorced. We just have to be sensitive to the notion of an "inner earthquake" as well as the more pyrotechnical outward one.

In these scenarios, we obviously would not be looking at "astrology failing." But what if the initial situation were far milder and the necessary "correction" not so dramatic?

Earlier, looking at the same transit, we imagined one partner telling another that she was "skipping their usual family vacation and going to a week-long astrology seminar." Her partner had no problem with that – he wanted to zoom off on a motorcycle anyway. In that case, the *necessary Uranian corrections* were far smaller and the evolutionary necessity simply less charged. Two wise humans simply make room for more individuality in their partnership. They are both happier and they love each other more for it.

But remember: for the astrologer thinking Uranus in the seventh house "'means divorce," *nothing happened.*

There's yet another reason that astrology can sometimes fail . . . and in this case, *actually* fail.

ASTROLOGY IS A WORK IN PROGRESS

Most modern astrologers shudder at the thought of trying to practice our craft without any knowledge of Uranus, Neptune, or Pluto. And yet up until about a century ago, at least one of those planets was missing.

In parallel fashion, I often think of the plight of our astrological forebears in ancient Greece, Egypt or China, *working before the invention of the clock.* How could they do astrology properly with only a vague sense of anyone's birth time? They found ways to work around the problem – but I'm grateful to have a nice, timed Ascendant and accurate house cusps in any chart I contemplate today.

Going further, I've come increasingly to realize that it is a big mistake to leave Eris – a trans-Neptunian planet the size of Pluto – out of our thinking. But I admit I still don't use it as much as I should – not yet, at any rate. But, like astrology, I am a work-in-progress too.

Up until maybe a dozen years ago, I didn't know much about declination. I shake my head as I think of all the readings I did for people born with the Moon Out of Bounds without my knowing it, understanding it, or mentioning it.

The list goes on. The point is that I am sure there are many undiscovered astrological techniques and factors out there lurking in the future, waiting for unborn astrologers to come along and find them.

The system has always been – and probably always will be – a work in progress.

For our purposes in this little essay, my next thoughts provide a twist on the main subject. What we have been exploring is what is going on when a known transit or progression seems to fail. Here, we look at the mirror-image – *what about when something happens in life, but there doesn't seem to be anything going on astrologically to explain it?*

That's another kind of "astrology fails" scenario.

Any honest astrologer will acknowledge this reality. When it happens, is there some exotic force at play – an undiscovered planet, for example? That is undoubtedly true sometimes – how could it be otherwise? That there are undiscovered planets is a virtual certainty – and, ditto, that they have astrological meaning.

There are "ghosts in the astrological machine," for sure.

Now for a little bit of lead in our shoes – when something happens "without an astrological explanation," the reason might possibly be a lot more prosaic. As an astrological teacher, when a student complains that he or she can't see any astrology to go along with a big biographical event, my mind immediately goes to a less exotic notion than "undiscovered planets." I cannot count how many times I've heard a student say, "Oh, I never use solar arcs" or "Oh, I didn't notice that the Moon had entered its Balsamic phase ..."

When astrology fails, have we just not looked hard enough at what was before our eyes in the chart? Is it a gap in our own technical knowledge rather than some hole in astrological theory that has made a monkey out of us?

Our present arsenal of astrological techniques is certainly incomplete, but it is already quite vast and impressively powerful – and let's just add the obvious corollary: *it requires considerable effort to rise to a high level of skill in this craft.* I believe fervently in free will – but please never confuse it with bad technique! Most of the time when an astrologer can't see the finger-prints of the planets on an accident or a new relationship or whatever, the explanation boils down to not looking hard enough.

When astrology fails, there is still one more serious possibility to consider ...

IS THE CHART ITSELF WRONG?

Astrology depends upon a long, complex chain of principles. By far its weakest link is our dependency on accurate birth information. Even novice astrologers know to mistrust a birth time given simply as "around noon" or to cringe when we hear that "mom says it was around 6:00."

Even a birth time given as "7:22 pm" can be misleading. What does "the moment of birth" actually, specifically, mean? How accurate were the clocks on the walls?

When I was a teenager and starting to get interested in astrology, I asked my mom for my birth time. She confidently told me, "6:15 am."

Later I found my baby book. It turns out that I was born about three hours earlier – but I weighed 6 pounds, 15 ounces.

Never, ever, trust your own mother.

It is always possible that the source of a wrong "prediction" – even if we are wise enough to be predicting questions rather than answers – is simply a *wrong chart*. Garbage in, garbage out, as they say in the world of computing. It is of course an obvious cheap trick to blame "a wrong chart" for our own errors. When it seems that "astrology is not working," do first consider all the points we've already explored. Still, if there is a consistent pattern of errors and the chart simply seems "not to fit the person," then beware: *you might be working with bad data.*

Generally such errors are matters of minutes. As such, they would not have much impact, for example, on the timing of a Uranus transit to the natal Moon – a few minutes isn't going to move the natal Moon very far. But even a few minutes of error can move a house cusp significantly – the average figure there being about one degree of error for every four minutes of error in the time of birth.

It can get a lot worse.

In my experience with birth certificates and other handwritten records, it is not unusual for the numeral "1" to be transcribed in error as a "7." Worse, an "AM" might have been clerically mangled into a "PM," producing a chart that is 12 hours off. Even the position of the Moon would then be wrong by something like six degrees. And of course everything would be in a totally wrong house. Those are "penmanship" mistakes and obviously they are more of a peril for people born before, say, 1985 or so. Nowadays, birth records tend to be more computerized and typically entered via keyboards. Time will tell if the "improved penmanship" balances out the tendency toward sloppy data-entry errors.

I have had experiences where I was left confident that someone's parents had misled a child as to his or her actual birth *date* – for example, to conceal a pregnant bride. This is less of an issue nowadays, but it would be foolish to ignore it, especially with clients born before the social revolutions of the 1970s.

One more source of potential catastrophe: beware that 11/8/68 means November 8, 1968 to an American and August 11, 1968 to a French person. That one has fouled me up more than once too.

The bottom line is always take birth data with a grain of salt. If your predictions aren't working, an error at that most fundamental level could possibly be the cause of your problems. A helpful hint – such errors would have to be *consistent over many transits and progressions* before you take them seriously. If it happens only once in a chart that has otherwise proven reliable, go back and think about the other possibilities we've been exploring.

I'll close by echoing once again that, in my opinion, astrology never fails. The statement might sound arrogant, but I believe it to be true. As I contemplate its meaning, its power actually has the opposite effect on me – I feel humbled by it, not arrogant. I'm the poor astrologer who has to try to live up to that challenge. In my bones, I know that a good answer to a trusting client's most pivotal soul-questions lies there before me on that single sheet of paper. He or she has come to me, counting on my wise counsel. And while astrology never fails, astrologers sometimes do.

Me too.

All I can do is to practice as wisely as I can within my own limits – and to constantly struggle to press those limits further in the direction of wisdom and skill.

Add love, and maybe some humility, and it is a privilege and a joy to practice this sacred craft, even with all my warts.

71

*Most competent astrologers have heard clients exclaim that they've
learned more in two hours with astrology than they did in a year
of psychotherapy. Naturally we're happy to get the praise and the
affirmation, but we need to be careful here. Astrology and psychotherapy
may share similar goals of "soul healing," but they are very different
disciplines. In this essay, I attempt to distinguish one field from the other
and clarify how they might complement each other without stepping on
each other's toes. Some psychological astrologers bang the drum for the
marriage of astrology and psychotherapy. I hope to attend that wedding
someday – but I would not want to be their marriage counsellor. These
two disciplines share many of the same goals, but they are profoundly
different and in many ways, not easily reconciled.*

ASTROLOGY AND PSYCHOTHERAPY

(Newsletter – October2021)

Maybe I am sitting with a client who has the natal Moon on the
Midheaven. The symbols tell me that she has been "called to a mission" in this lifetime – that she has something important to do in her community, something that will touch the lives of people with whom she does
not have any kind of personal karma. With signs and aspects, I can get

a lot more specific, but that's not my point here. I want to write about a very slippery question, and that is the relationship between astrology and psychotherapy. My client with the Moon on the Midheaven is just my launching pad.

We are all responsible for the way we "inhabit" our birthcharts. That element of free will is absolutely central to my understanding of astrology. One dimension of that pivotal principle is that we are all *free to blow it* – free to let fear, bad social conditioning, or sheer laziness take a bite out of our lives. That's true of you, me – and my client with the Moon on her Midheaven too. *The fact that she "has a mission" does not mean that she will rise to it.* Some personal "Moon work" must serve as the foundation of any gift she is eventually able to give to her community. That will require some effort.

My client has been born to play some kind of helpful, healing role in the lives of strangers. They don't know it, but *those strangers are counting on her.* If she does not rise to some approximation of her human potential, she will simply not be there for them. That means that her failure would create suffering for them.

Here's where everything starts to get really sticky. That possibility of failure confronts astrologers with an uncomfortable truth that we cannot escape or sweep under the carpet. *To what extent is it appropriate that we confront this client with the responsibilities that we see in her natal chart?* More is at stake here than her own spiritual well being – other souls are depending on her. Do we have an ethical right to say that? Do we have an ethical *obligation* to say it?

Keep perspective. In your own darkest hours, haven't you sometimes found help? Hasn't anyone ever counseled you or supported you?

What would have happened to you if that person had not shown up?

That's what I am talking about here. That truth about the "soul contract" implicit in her chart is what I am trying to convey to my client. Her own inner work is important, *but not only to her.* Others are counting on it too.

All that is true, if astrology itself is true. If my client hears it as I intend it, she'll be inspired. I hope that my words help to *validate* her "divine orders" – something she knew in her heart anyway. *But what if she's falling short?* What if she's let "fear, bad social conditioning, or sheer laziness" take that bite out of her life? Then, from a psychotherapeutic perspective, my message to her would constitute a serious ethical breach. I have *guilt-tripped* my client and attempted to *manipulate her behavior with shame.*

Yikes! That's harsh, but it is hard to escape. Should I ask her to think of all those poor people she might be failing? *Should I get up her nose about that?*

To be fair, even if that "moral failure" is the basic idea I put on the table, I surely wouldn't say it exactly that way. I would try to be kind and patient and to keep perspective. Evolutionary matters take time, and self-forgiveness, and all of that. But still, that sense of her somehow "falling short" is inevitably part of her takeaway, and there is no easy or honest way around it.

- Never forget: astrology holds the mirror of a "perfectly lived life" before us. That is its horror. None of us can ever fully live up to the standard our chart presents. All we can do is to aspire to it. We are all spiritual "works in progress." Self-forgiveness is an absolutely necessary ingredient in the recipe.

Here's the pivotal point. See how this astrological counseling situation is so different from the tone, and even the ethics, of psychotherapy? *The fierce, stark truth we see in each person's birthchart puts us in a situation no psychotherapist ever needs to face.* It is as if angels have whispered in our ears, and we are burdened by what they have told us. We cannot unhear it. But how do we say it? *Do* we say it?

Let's go further.

Generally speaking, a psychotherapist does a lot more *listening* than an astrologer, while an astrologer does a lot more *talking*. A psychotherapist has to "discover" a client through conversation. An astrologer starts about a lightyear ahead of that, with the ferocious "X-ray vision" of the client's chart in hand.

Further, a client comes to a psychotherapist with a very different set of expectations than he or she would bring to a session with an astrologer. Clients expect the astrologer to "tell them things." The "psychological astrologer" who asks clients how *they* feel about their "Mercury quincunx the Vertex" is a standard joke. The poor client doesn't even know what a quincunx is. Clients come to us for our expertise – expertise which they do not have themselves.

As a counseling astrologer, I naturally want to leave a client feeling empowered and encouraged. I am sure that all decent psychotherapists feel exactly the same way about their work. We're all trying to be *soul-healers* in some sense of the term. There is an obvious complementarity between the two fields. Still, as the old U2 song puts it, "we are one, but we are not the same."

Years ago, I heard Robert Hand give a memorable talk at a conference. The essence of it was about the difference between "healers" and "seers." I think it is a profoundly helpful distinction. We astrologers are *seers*. Psychotherapists are *healers*. The astrologer holds the mirror of truth before the client, then basically says, "now do as you will." Meanwhile, psychotherapists typically work week after week with their clients, holding their hands – and holding their feet to the fire too.

Nina Ortega is both an evolutionary astrologer and a trained psychotherapist. She serves the metropolis where she was born – Mexico City. When I asked her about the questions with which I am wrestling here, she was quite succinct. "Evolutionary astrology brings bright and sharp consciousness about what, when, how to work our issues, but the hard work happens in psychotherapy." Wisely, Nina points out a fundamental dilemma we face as astrologers: "It is easy to forget what the astrologer said because our body *wants to forget*. Remembering is painful, even when our souls want to heal." She adds, "Psychotherapy helps us stay in the presence of the open wound. Sometimes the consciousness that astrology brings is too much to take in one shot."

By the way, Nina's email address is astrologiaevolutiva@gmail.com and she's giving me her blessing about my publishing it. She's been a dear friend for a quarter of a century, and she's a genuine wise woman.

Hadley Fitzgerald is another licensed psychotherapist who also practices as an evolutionary astrologer. She works in Los Angeles here in California and I was honored to have her as a student of mine for many years. She writes, "To me, astrology is the ancient, soul-full ancestor of psychology. Contemporary psychotherapy can provide a dimensional – and, ideally, sacred – container for attending to the myriad dilemmas, gifts, and challenges that the natal chart presents in archetypal terms. When we can stay mindful, there's a cosmic compassion built into astrology, and this has a vital place in the room whether we do a one-time reading or ongoing work."

Like Nina Ortega, Hadley Fitzgerald is also aiming for a synthesis of the two fields. She writes, "I'd had a vision in 1974 that astrology would become an invaluable partner for the therapeutic process. Back then I often said I didn't know if I'd live long enough to see this happen, but I wanted to do my part to be a matchmaker. The concept struck everyone around me as crazy. I'm not sure, but I may have been one of the first graduate students in the country to write a master's thesis about the subject – and to have it accepted. That didn't open – or block – any known roads at the time, so I just kept making a road by walking. And here we are nearly fifty years later."

Hadley is also a dear friend and obviously one of the pioneers forging the future of our field. Her website is HadleyFitzgerald.com. For either astrology or psychotherapeutic work, I'd send my own mother to her. She's that good.

Let's put all of this in a broader context.

Astrology's star may be rising, but "it ain't all the way rose yet." Go to a dress-up party with a lot of high-powered strangers. When someone asks you "what you do," try saying that you are a professional astrologer.

Hallelujah – gone are the days when that would immediately lead to teasing and jokes. But you'll still probably get a few funny looks.

On the other hand, your dignity will be on far safer ground if your response is, "I am a psychologist." To many people, practicing psychology is a "real job," while astrology is more like entertainment. That's all just sociology, not cosmic truth – but it's also the water in which we are all swimming. Again, things are improving. We astrologers are slowly winning the battle for hearts and minds. *Still, the temptation to try to hitch our star to the brighter star of being fellow "mental health professionals" still casts a long shadow over our field.*

Astrologers and psychotherapists can be natural allies. Nina Ortega wrote, "So yes – complementarity is my vote." I am with Nina – complementarity gets my vote too. But I do like to bang the drum for astrology standing on its own two feet. *We are not little "also-ran" faux-psychologists.* Our system of soul-healing is ultimately very different from that of psychology. *We talk more*, for one thing – and that is because we have a lot of answers – at least approximate ones – before our clients even walk through the door. We've seen their charts. That's what they visit us to hear about. And therefore we naturally do much less pure listening, and a whole lot more guiding.

To be "too directive" is a major blunder for a psychotherapist. Ditto really for an astrologer – but we astrologers hit that "too directive" limit a lot further down the road. How, for example, could I ever look at that woman's chart with her Moon on Midheaven and not "guide" her in the direction of finding meaningful work? I *know* she needs a sense of mission in her life or she'll be miserable and feel lost – her chart tells me that in neon lights. A psychotherapist who started by assuming the same thing about her would be guilty of projecting his or her own values or cultural norms upon the client – a major mistake. For all the psychotherapist knows, for that particular woman, the cure for feeling miserable and lost might lie in meditation or in painting. It might lie in having children or grandchildren. It might have nothing at all to do with any sense of mission in the community.

No way around it – *the astrologer knows things that the psychotherapist does not know.* The opposite is true as well, of course. Seers have skills; so do healers. The skills even often overlap, *but they are not the same.*

Many years ago when my practice in North Carolina was getting established, clients would sometimes contact me after a session. They'd start by expressing gratitude for the work, but add that it shook them up and they hoped they could have a further conversation with me. Naturally I agreed – I really didn't see any ethical alternative. Before I knew it, I was "practicing psychology without a licence." Long story, but I went into psychotherapy myself and apprenticed myself to a psychotherapist who was also a client of mine. Perhaps more importantly, I also did something I would recommend to any counselling astrologer – I compiled a list of therapists I knew and trusted and to whom I could refer clients.

I still think making referrals is a splendid idea, but when it comes to 21st century psychology, I currently consider myself the "loyal opposition." I don't mean to overly polarize the issue – quite honestly, some of my best friends are "shrinks." I have enormous respect for the field, along with a few quibbles. I guess what I am really saying here is that, while astrology has benefited enormously from what we have learned from psychology, the shoe can fit the other foot as well – the psychologists can learn a lot from us. I believe that they need to do that.

Let me quote another good friend and colleague – Dan Keusal. He is a trained and licenced psychotherapist with a Jungian bent, and also an evolutionary astrologer. He practices in Seattle, Washington. His website is DanKeusal.com. Dan was one of the founding members of my first astrological Apprenticeship Program back in Kansas over twenty years ago. He's carried the torch ever since. In the Seattle area, he is my go-to referral.

Just as astrology is striving to outgrow its fatalistic, predictive past, psychotherapy needs to resist the current trend toward reductionist approaches that focus on mere symptom relief while ignoring the deeper realms of the unconscious and of the soul. I tell my astrology clients that a birth chart is a symbolic encoding of the next steps their soul is needing to take – and ready to take – in its healing and in its growth, and I work with my psychotherapy clients to help them recognize the unique ways that their own psyche, and its outer-life – the synchronistic mirrors – call them to the day-to-day work of courageously moving into and through those next steps.

Bless Dan for his wisdom here. As evolutionary astrologers – and this statement would also apply equally to any psychotherapist whose work I would recommend or even respect – our goal is not simply "eliminating symptoms." We don't want to be like those medical doctors who prescribe opioids just because your back hurts. We want to get down to root causes and promote the kinds of healing that actually last. Deep psychological work excels at that process. Adding astrology's penetrating insights to its arsenal is like adding Warp Drive to your Prius.

It is not unusual to hear some "science-side" pundit decrying the increasing popularity of astrology as a symptom of the decline of critical thinking and the failure of our educational systems. I'll spare you my retort. Let me just say that the notion that you are *a spiritual being having a physical experience in a meaningful, purposeful universe* is emphatically not a particularly scientific statement, even though I fervently believe it to be true. Just as astrologers have often succumbed to the temptation to model themselves as "little psychologists," I feel that many psychologists have bowed too deeply in the direction of science.

Is psychology really a science?

Let me just say I believe that qualifies as an essay question.

Humans are hungry for a sense of ultimate personal meaning in their lives. Astrology does a far better job of providing that soul-food today than does academic psychology. That's the real reason that we're doing so well in the marketplace lately – I don't think it is about "decline of critical thinking and the failure of our educational systems" at all. I think it is about a widespread spiritual hunger for magic and meaning – something that existentialist psychology fails to provide and which even religion seems increasingly to be failing to offer in any satisfying way.

Like my friends Nina, Dan, and Hadley, I too am excited about the emerging synergy of astrology and psychology – but let's not lose our metaphysical roots in our zeal for public approval. We astrologers are not psychologists. We cannot follow in their footsteps. We need to create our own path.

At this point, if I had to bet, I would bet on astrology's future over that of psychotherapy. That would be my bet – but my *prayer* would be for an emerging marriage of equals. And our theme song would be, "we are one, but we are not the same."

SECTION TEN

EULOGIES

Birth and death, death and birth – the fierce wheels of the world are always turning. Like you, I've lost so many friends and family members, while being blessed with so many new ones along the way. Here in this short section, I put the final amen on The Endless Sky *with eulogies for two men whom I held – and still hold – precious. Tem Tarriktar, creator and publisher of* The Mountain Astrologer *magazine, was one of the first heavy-hitters in the world of astrology to truly recognize the particular value of my work. I'll be forever indebted to him for his support and his kindness toward me over the years, not to mention the enormous gift he gave our community. The final eulogy is for my friend, neighbor, and mentor, the Jungian scholar, Robert A. Johnson, who passed away not long ago at age 97, still Gemini-sharp and twelfth house deep.*

My last words to my father were "see you soon." At the time I meant them straightforwardly, thinking I would see him again in a couple of weeks. Now I often reflect on their actual meaning, which of course merits a goosebump or two.

To these two fine men, Tem and Robert, and to my dad, I repeat those words here: see you soon, my friends.

Life, even if it is long, is very short.

72

GOODBYE TEM

(Newsletter – August 2019)

Tem Tarriktar, the beloved publisher of *The Mountain Astrologer* magazine, passed away last July 8th. He had thyroid cancer. In the Age of
Facebook and Instagram, most of you reading this probably knew of his
illness and his heroic battle against it over the past many months. Likely,
you knew of his passing within hours as well. Astrology is a small world,
and at times such as this, our field and all of us who comprise actually feels
like a family. Death draws us all a little closer to the ancient hearth-fire.

All the standard things one might say in the face of such a loss remain
true, even though familiarity might weaken them to the point that they
sound like cliches: Tem will be sorely missed. Our hearts go out to those he
left behind. We will always remember him. We know he lives on in spirit
and in his legacy of great work.

All true.

All those good words need to be said. All of them are felt deeply
by anyone who knew Tem personally, and by many who knew him only
through his good works. Even if we did not have the joy of knowing him
personally, every one of us in the community benefited from his kindness,
wisdom, and competence in sustaining *The Mountain Astrologer* over all
these years.

It's hard for me to believe, but the first time I met Tem Tarriktar was a little over thirty years ago. Our first encounter happened at the United Astrology Congress in New Orleans, back in 1989. Time flies. I had a couple of books in print with Bantam by then and I had begun to make a little splash in AstroWorld, so Tem knew who I was. At that point, I had never heard of him. If memory serves, he approached me about a possible interview for this crazy magazine he was trying to start. He had rented a booth at the trade show to help promote it.

I liked Tem right away, but his whole enterprise seemed impossibly dubious. The "magazine" was homespun at best – photocopied or perhaps even mimeographed, if I am remembering correctly. He gave me the impression that his total start-up budget for *The Mountain Astrologer* might feed a family of four for a week or two, provided they really liked pizza.

As we got to know each other, Tem confirmed that "wing-and-a-prayer" impression by admitting that he was saving money by sleeping under his table at the Trade Show. He would wait until Security turned its back, then he would duck behind the bunting at the end of the day. He couldn't afford "a room at the inn."

Of course I appreciated Tem's rebel spirit immediately – his massive dose of Leo energy lit up my Aries Moon. And I also knew that with that kind of determination and *chutzpah*, *The Mountain Astrologer* was going to make it despite the long odds and all reason.

And "make it" it did. Two hundred monthly issues later, it is still going strong.

All reports are that the magazine will continue to be published despite the loss of Tem. With the current exponential expansion in public interest in astrology, I suspect it will thrive. If pride exists in the realms where Tem is now soaring, I am confident that he will be proud. And I am also sure he will be phoning in his editorial suggestions from the astral world, whispering pointed suggestions into the dream-ears of those who will take the helm.

In the past, not to mention in the mysterious future, Tem could naturally never have done any of this alone. Reading off the masthead, I want to honor and thank Nan Geary, Linda Kaye, Mary Plumb, Kate Sholly, Frank C. Clifford, Ray Grasse, Janette DeProsse, Sara Fisk, Linda Byrd, Linda Ferencik, and Ann Meigs for their own hard work in the endless effort of cranking out such a high quality magazine – and never missing a publication date, despite hell, high water, and Pluto transits.

There has always been much to love about *The Mountain Astrologer*. The best part, to me, has been the way it has functioned as a kind of collective "watering hole," where partisans of all the different, fragmented branches of our craft could come together as equals and possibly even learn something from each other. Evolutionary astrologers, Hellenists, Cosmobiologists, Uranian astrologers, Jyotish practitioners, Horary astrologers, astro-economists – all were welcome in the pages of TMA.

That inclusiveness addressed a major intellectual problem we astrologers face – trying to maintain some kind of common bond of shared language in the face of our enormous diversity – but more importantly to me, Tem's wide-open welcome mat addressed a spiritual problem: that is simply the risk of partisan intellectual divisions shattering our community. Blithe affirmations that "we are all doing the same thing" may politely defuse arguments – and such affirmations are soul-miles ahead of anyone condemning the other person's house system or zodiac, thus sowing seeds of pointless competition and suspicion.

Still, the various astrological systems are in fact quite different from each other, and truly listening "across the aisle" has never been easy. In the words of U2, Tem always reminded us all that "we are one, but we are not the same." *Tem, in other words, did not try to make the issue of fragmentation any easier than it could honestly be made, but by creating common ground where we could all meet, he at least made addressing it possible.*

Of all Tem's many gifts to the astrological family over the past three decades, it is that one for which I am most grateful. I salute his great soul for bringing that living example of inclusiveness, generosity, and respect for diversity to us all. Perhaps more than any other figure in the landscape of current astrological practice, he embodied the notion of rising above our differences and affirming that we all live under one sky.

I just called this inclusive message Tem's "gift," which is correct. But I also call it his *challenge* to us – a challenge to which we are still rising as a community.

As synchronicity would have it, I am writing these words at the Omega Institute for Holistic Studies in Rhinebeck, New York, where I am currently teaching a five-day class. At the moment, I am sitting in the quiet upstairs of the Ram Dass Library, which has the finest collection of 20th and 21st century "consciousness literature" I have ever seen.

Omega is a dozen years older than *The Mountain Astrologer*, but it is cut from the same cloth. Like the magazine, it too is part of a quiet spiritual revolution that has transformed the world. Like Tem, the founders of Omega did a lot more than simply "have a vision." They *acted* on the vision and they made it real. They created a force of individual transformation that has endured – and will endure, just as *The Mountain Astrologer* will endure, long after the founders are gone.

Standing back even further, Omega and *Mountain Astrologer* metamorphose into individual stars in a far larger cultural galaxy. Conscious yoga, all the various emerging body-mind-spirit therapies, Buddhism coming to the west – they are all part of the same synchronistic wave.

For all the daunting problems that assail the modern world, it is a far more conscious society today than the one into which I was born. Back then, "boys were men and women were girls." Being gay was a disease – or a crime. Atomic tests happened in the open air. The environment existed to be exploited, no questions asked. And our collective spiritual advice boiled down to "be good and you'll go to heaven."

It is hard to convey the magnitude of the awakening that has happened in the past half-century.

My point is that, without Tem Tarriktar, this awakening would have been diminished. He played a part in that pan-cultural wake-up call, and I salute him for that. I am aware that my words might seem hyperbolic – fear not, this not a hyperventilated call to beatify "Saint Tem" . . . I mean, I remember this guy when he was sleeping under a table, hiding from security. But over the years he has touched the lives of many thousands of people, myself included. He has offered countless human beings real hope and practical guidance in times of genuine personal darkness. No one could fully catalog his good works since most of them happened in total privacy – someone, perhaps someone on the edge of despair or worse, sat reading an article in TMA, and perhaps gaining life-saving perspective and some faith that there might just possibly be a future worth living.

We can only surmise about these very private mysteries. But we know they are there. How could it be otherwise, given the quality of the magazine, its healing content, its many readers, and three decades of publication?

Astrologically, Tem was Mr. Leo – a solar Leo with Leo rising and a Leo Moon. His Sun was just a degree and a half above the Ascendant, his Moon conjunct Pluto in the first house, along with a telling Mercury-Jupiter conjunction in Virgo in the first house. Leadership, power, creativity, language – it's all there in simple astrological terms. He made no secret of his chart, so I feel free to speak of it here.

In deeper evolutionary terms, there is implicit in Leo a need to recover from an ancient trauma of rejection, or worse. Saying that "Tem was burned at the stake" in a prior life, while probably not literally true, is a metaphor that at least gets us going. His personal healing path lay in expressing his soul honestly and in a spirit of vulnerability – and in hearing some applause for it this time around. It took real spiritual courage, in other words, for him to stick his neck out "again" by launching *The Mountain Astrologer*.

I honor him for doing that. He could have been an executive in any industry and hidden his soul safely inside a suit.

Tem's lunar south node was in Gemini in the 10th house. Always, once you get used to the evolutionary perspective, you see the same, reliable pattern: *the karmic past always leaves a fingerprint on the present life.* In a prior life, Tem was known *publicly* (10th house) for *what he had to say* (Gemini).

Ditto in this present life, obviously enough. That is how it often works.

Mercury rules that south node from its strong position in Virgo and the 1st house, conjunct Jupiter. That means that in the karmic past, his voice was impactful. He was a leader. He experienced some degree of success, applause and fame.

But Saturn in Scorpio and the 4th house opposes that south node and squares that Mercury. In that same prior life, he hit some kind of "brick wall of reality," probably one of a dark, treacherous or secret nature – that's where Scorpio enters the equations. The betrayal may have even come from his own *family* (4th house).

Mercury (ruler of the south node) squaring the south node implies that he did not see any of this coming. *He was powerful and successful, and then suddenly cut off and silenced.*

Sound familiar?

He thus entered this world in 1956 as a powerful, eloquent voice that had been shocked and traumatized into silence.

Tem took birth to heal that wound – and his healing north node lies in Sagittarius in the 4th house. Thus it is ruled by Jupiter – which, interestingly, is conjunct his south node ruler, Mercury. This is a classic signature of "getting back on the horse that threw him." He came to this earth with a soul-intention of *reclaiming his voice*, of being heard again – but doing it a little differently this time. With the north node in Sagittarius, he came here to "reclaim faith" – but faith in what exactly? A big part of the answer lies in the 4th house – *family*. (Remember: in the prior lifetime, he was probably betrayed by his own family. That hurts!)

No one can heal such a wound all alone. I am on thin ice here, with much that I do not know, but *kudos* to Tem's beloved wife, Kate Sholly, for the soul-healing she offered him by being his loyal and loving companion for, I believe, an entire Saturn cycle.

In a spirit befitting a 4th house north node, Tem's deepest evolutionary work in this life was mostly internal – private, secret, and intimate. We will never know about it, nor should we.

And out of that deep well of healing emerged an ancient, powerful voice, made stronger by what it had endured, rising from its own ashes, and touching the souls of three generations of astrologers.

Thank you for all that, Tem – and godspeed.

73

THE CENTENARY OF ROBERT A. JOHNSON

(Newsletter – May 2021)

On April 22, 2010, at 10:05 AM, as the direct result of an incredible series of "coincidences," I met the late great Robert A. Johnson. Many of us have his books on our shelves – he sold 2.5 million of them, including *He* and *She* and *We* and my personal favorite, *Balancing Heaven and Earth: A Memoir*. He died on September 12, 2018 at the age of 97. I'm writing about him in this newsletter because he would have turned one hundred years old on May 26th of this year – and also simply because I miss him. He was a good friend.

When I was an infant in diapers, Robert was studying directly under Carl Gustav Jung in Zurich. He was also in formal psychoanalysis with Jung's wife, Emma. He's known internationally as a "Jungian author," which I suppose works as well as most labels do. There was a lot more to him than that, but instead of trying to "profile" him, let me tell you one of my favorite Robert stories. He used to travel to India pretty much every year. Once when he was about to present a talk there, he received a lengthy introduction in Hindi, a language which he did not speak. As he stepped up to the podium, he asked what had been said about him. He was told that he had been introduced as "an enlightened being" – which was kind of a shocker to him since he never spoke of himself in those terms. He inquired as to why such a thing had been said. And the man introducing him announced, straight-faced and serious, that the evidence was that Robert *"didn't eat much, didn't say much, and didn't do much."*

It's funny, of course. But those words really did illuminate something deep about Robert A. Johnson. Beyond his piercing intelligence and his profound insights, beyond his public identity as a world-class intellectual, there was simply a kind of magical silence that radiated from him – a quality of sheer *stillness.*

Enlightenment? Your guess is as good as mine.

Funny how most of us can recognize wisdom when we see it. I certainly saw it in Robert, and so cherished my moments with him.

Robert had great respect for astrology. He shared with me that "Dr. Jung" – and Robert always called him that – had once told him that he would "never undertake psychoanalysis with anyone without knowing his or her astrological chart." I had always known that Jung was open to astrology, but I had never heard such a stark statement about it attributed to him.

As Robert and I got to know each other more deeply, he asked me to explain his own chart to him. To me, this was a bit like the Dalai Lama asking me for meditation tips, but I told him that I would take a shot at it. He knew his "early morning" birth time only approximately, so I first had to rectify his chart – something that is always so much easier with an older person since there are so many more timed events to use. I came up with a time of 6:18 AM, on May 26, 1921, in Portland, Oregon.

Here's the chart.

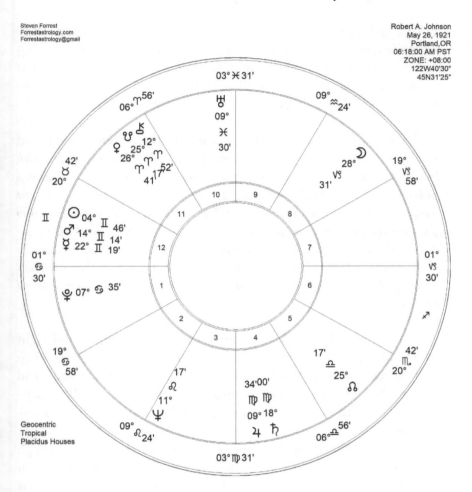

Steven Forrest
Forrestastrology.com
Forrestastrology@gmail

Robert A. Johnson
May 26, 1921
Portland, OR
06:18:00 AM PST
ZONE: +08:00
122W40'30"
45N31'25"

Geocentric
Tropical
Placidus Houses

©2018 Matrix Software Gainesville, FL

Standard Wheel

I'm not going to attempt a full analysis of it – there's just not enough space to do such a process justice. Scanning the chart quickly, we can see that he was "Mister Gemini," obviously – and we note that his Geminian Mercury was also Out of Bounds, suggesting that "maverick" element in his brilliance. *But note too that almost everything else in his chart reflects deeply inward-directed qualities.* That's actually the way it felt to be around him – he "didn't eat much, didn't say much, and didn't do very much." But, Gemini-fashion, he also never missed a thing. His trenchant, penetrating insights could leave you struggling to breathe. To be honest, Robert was not always a gentle man – on more than one occasion, I saw him "rip someone a new one." Generally the trigger was any evidence of egoism.

The reading I did for him went beautifully. Robert wrote to a friend about it, who later kindly shared his words with me. *"My three hours with Mr. Forrest was one of the most remarkable experiences of my life. I hope you will hear it some time. In the last hour, the story broke off into a survey of my last incarnation, which was very sober and full of darkness that has lapsed over into my present life and has accounted for the difficult things I have lived with presently – such things as amputation and loneliness."* Robert later wrote directly to me, *"I have had several charts done in my lifetime, but none of them but yours have escaped the astrologer mistaking so much of the chart as a sounding board for his own ego."*

Coming from Robert A. Johnson, those supportive words sunk right into my soul, giving my battered self-confidence a boost at a time when I really needed it. My long marriage was falling apart. My wife and I had moved to the desert, two thousand miles from my friends and all my support back in North Carolina. The timing of Robert's arrival in my life was providential.

To say that Robert and I became good friends is true, but even though I was sixty-one years old when we met, he was also truly my mentor. In the mystical fashion of any spiritual lineage, his simple presence alone was a powerful teaching. I certainly felt that I understood Jungian psychology far more profoundly after spending time with him. We were far from "wordless" when we were together, but I would still say that most of what I learned from him did not come through language. My Ascendant lined up with his 6th house cusp, so I "presented myself" to him in that classic "house of servants" fashion – as an acolyte or a disciple.

At the same time, each of our natal Suns fell in the other one's 7th house, so a strong natural friendship arose between us too. These two realities actually sat pretty easily with each other. Robert would, for example, often ask me why he was still alive. He wasn't depressed, but he felt his work on earth was done and he was ready to move on. I think one of the reasons he asked me that question so repeatedly is that, as humans go, I'm pretty comfortable with death so I didn't immediately lambast him with spiritual platitudes.

By the way, the best answer I could give him was that I felt he had one more book in him – one about the psychological experience of extreme old age. He never wrote that book, and the world is poorer for the lack of it.

Here's another Robert story. In the little desert town where I live and where Robert had a second home, there's a natural wonder in the landscape called Fonts Point. Getting to it is a bit of a challenge. As a younger man, Robert had visited the place many times, but his disabilities had kept him away ever since. I offered to bring him out there again – which was no mean feat for a man of nearly ninety with an artificial leg. I had a vehicle that could do it. We managed to get Robert loaded into the shotgun seat and we headed out to the big overlook. We brought a folding chair for him. After we arrived at the site, we just sat there and quietly took in the view for an hour or two. Robert slipped into meditation – which led to my then-new partner, Michelle Kondos, painting a portrait of him, which we presented to him on his 90th birthday, and which was later displayed in St. Paul's Cathedral in San Diego on the day of his funeral.

As we were getting ready to leave, Robert turned his soul-seeing gaze on me and simply said, *"If it weren't for your kindness, I would never have seen this place again."* Hearing him say those words was such a powerful experience, such a *transmission*, that I suspect they will come back to me in a future lifetime.

It's the singer, not the song.

My natal Sun is in 15 degrees 43 minutes of Capricorn. On the day and hour I met Robert, the transiting north node of the Moon was in *exactly* that position, to the minute. Karma? No doubt.

A few months earlier, an unexpected knock on our front door had revealed the minister of the church of my soon-to-be-ex mother-in-law. The minister and his wife, from the Pacific Northwest, were here in southern California on vacation. They had been given our address and had decided to pop in and introduce themselves. Robert had once spoken at the minister's church. It was from the minister that I first learned that the fabled Robert A. Johnson had a place here in Borrego Springs, tucked away up by the western mountains. Intriguing – but still far from an introduction.

Two or three weeks later a client happened to email me about scheduling a reading and casually mentioned that he had a friend "named Robert" who also lived in my town. I knew that my client was a Jungian analyst, so I asked him if his friend happened to be Robert A. Johnson. He said yes – and it was through him that arrangements were made for me finally to knock on Robert's door on that morning in April 2010. Transiting Uranus was almost exactly square my natal Uranus – so I knew I should "expect the unexpected." Perhaps even more tellingly, added to that exact transiting nodal conjunction with my Sun, the Solar Arc nodal axis was just seven weeks away from squaring my Moon.

My karmic chickens were coming home to roost – and in this case, little did I know that they were about to lay a golden egg.

One meme in Robert's view of life was how we all need to "follow the slender threads." By that, he meant the subtle clues and other forms of guidance that synchronicity affords us all, if only we are open to them. I am grateful for many things in my life, but the slender threads that wove my life into the life of Robert A. Johnson in his final years are high on the list. In my opening lines, I used the word "coincidence," but I put it in quotation marks. I always do. Basically, I have come to believe that "there ain't no such thing."

So happy 100th birthday to Robert A. Johnson. Thank you for all you gave me and for all you gave to this crazy world. I hope you are enjoying your little rest upon the wind and that you'll be back soon. We miss you. I notice that the cosmos is staging a lunar eclipse on May 26 in honor of your centenary. With your Moon-ruled Cancer Ascendant, that seems appropriate.

The light disappears – but then it always returns.

CONCLUSION

THE LITTLE MIRACLES

S un, Moon, and Ascendant – together they form what I always think of
as the skeleton of the birthchart. If we understand those three symbols,
plus their interactions, we are at least halfway to grasping a person's chart
as a whole. Years ago when I was writing *The Inner Sky*, I coined the term
Primal Triad for them. I still use it today. In fact, the idea is pretty much
the foundation of *Lila*, the astrological cell phone app I've been helping to
develop for the past two or three years – www.heylila.com, if you are interested. In pursuit of that project, we've actually had to Trademark the term.

I'm writing about the Primal Triad here to establish one link in a
chain – the notion that the Sun, Moon, Ascendant blend has been absolutely foundational in my thinking about astrology for the past fifty years.

People criticize astrology sometimes with the cheap shot that it "puts
everybody into twelve little boxes." Give me a break – most of us find the
words "extroversion" and "introversion" helpful, and they divide everybody
into just *two* boxes. Comparatively, even simple Sun Sign astrology is positively granular. Naturally, the deeper rejoinder is that serious astrology is
vastly more complex than Sun Signs . . . and *blah blah blah*. You already
know that or you wouldn't be reading this book.

Dividing people into twelve "types" can indeed be a useful system –
but let's get back to the Primal Triad. As a system, it is much more compel-

ling and precise than mere Sun Signs. The Primal Triad embraces them, but it also adds twelve Moon Signs, along with twelve Ascendants.

Spin the wheel – all of these possible combinations exist in reality. You might be a Scorpio with a Pisces Moon and Gemini rising. Or you might be an Aquarian with a Leo Moon and Cancer rising. None of the possible combinations are rare or forbidden by astronomical logic. Instead of the twelve-box system of popular Sun Sign astrology, we now have twelve times twelve times twelve possibilities. *That works out to 1728 possible versions of the Primal Triad* – and thus a system that, while it may not be quite as unique and individual as fingerprints, moves astrology impressively in that direction. When it comes to specificity, the Sun, Moon, Ascendant blend leaves most other typologies, such as the nine-fold Enneagram or the sixteen-fold Myers-Briggs test, in the dust.

Remember that number: *1728*. It is the second link in our chain.

Now I am going to seem as if I am totally changing the subject. Please bear with me – there's a revelation ahead that left me gasping. Maybe it will leave you gasping too.

Many times here in *The Endless Sky*, I've made reference to my four "Elements" books. In writing them, my guiding star was basically the desire to write down everything I knew about astrology. I wanted to give it all away. Writing those books was *legacy work*, pure and simple. My intention was to record and share many of the stories and metaphors which I had found helpful with my clients over the years. I also wanted to explore astrological theory in a deeper way than I had ever been able to put into a book before. With every possible combination of planet and sign or planet and house, I have always had a kind of "seed idea" ready to go – I wanted to record each one of them and pass them on as well. That meant writing a few paragraphs about each planet in each one of the twelve signs and in each one of the twelve houses.

That's a lot of writing!

This huge project was how I celebrated Saturn's long slog through my Sun Sign, Capricorn. I walked my talk – it was time to move myself to a new level of maturity through the ancient Saturn device of undertaking a "great work." The results were *The Book of Fire*, *The Book of Earth*, *The Book of Air*, and *The Book of Water*. Each volume was a little bit longer than its predecessor.

When the project was complete and I held my four babies in my arms, I breathed a proud sigh of relief – and I casually wondered how many pages long the whole thing had turned out to be . . .

Get ready. I bet you see it coming.

Add up the page counts of the first print editions of those four volumes, and you have 1728 pages – "twelve times twelve times twelve" strikes again. There was the Primal Triad smiling back at me.

Goosebumps.

The Book of Fire – 295 pages. *The Book of Earth* – 396 pages. *The Book of Air* – 507 pages. *The Book of Water* – 530 pages. That page count was not intentional – in fact, I have no idea how I could possibly have made it happen even if I had set out to. After I write a manuscript, it is out of my hands. It goes into pre-production. Someone else makes editorial suggestions, which I review and generally accept. Then the pages are typeset by yet another professional. A decision is made about the font-size, and a 10-point font makes for a shorter book than an 11-point font. What about margins? What about line spacing? Those practical publishing decisions are all in someone else's domain.

What are the odds against the total page count of my four Elements books "happening" to turn out to be equal to the "twelve times twelve times twelve" of the Primal Triad?

As denizens of the 21st century cultural matrix, our next line is inevitably, *That's amazing! What a cool coincidence!*

Detectives in murder mysteries are always saying, "I don't like coincidences."

Me neither. I really don't believe in them at all.

In my understanding, what we have here with "1728" is a classic example of *synchronicity.* Most of you probably know the word, which was coined nearly a century ago by Carl Gustav Jung and physicist Wolfgang Pauli. In essence, they postulated that things happen in this universe for either one of two reasons:

- Something *makes them happen,* and thus we have cause-and-effect.
- Or it would be *meaningful* for them to happen.

My four Elements books turning out to total 1728 pages was shockingly, delightfully *meaningful* to me. It was as if the higher intelligence of the cosmos were saying to me, *"I'm really here. Never doubt my magic. And, by the way, Steve, good job. We've got your back."*

Or something like that. Words don't quite catch it. Maybe it's not about words. Maybe these little miracles are indeed about magic, and an affirmation that magic is a reality in our lives.

A few lines back, I posed the rhetorical question, what are the odds against this "coincidence" actually happening? I'm not sure there would be a rigorously mathematical way of answering, but of course we all know the odds are astronomically long. *And yet it happened.* Calling it a "coincidence" strains credulity to the breaking point. Yet many people would use exactly that word.

- A skeptic hears about an astrologer's prediction coming true. The response? *That's just a coincidence.*

- Two strangers sit next to each other on the flight to Chicago. Against the odds, on the return flight, they find themselves sitting next to each other again. The sheer improbability of that happening starts them talking. Six months later, they get married. The skeptic's explanation? A happy *coincidence.*

- You think of someone you knew in college. Two days later, she sends you a Friend Request on Facebook. Ask the skeptic: once again, that's just another *coincidence.*

- A child remembers a past life as a fighter pilot down to the details of correctly naming a friend and a ship, which are later verified. Ask Mister Science? Once again: a weird *coincidence.*

What got Carl Jung and Wolfgang Pauli thinking about synchronicity was a simple observation: *there are far too many coincidences for "coincidence" to be a plausible explanation for them.* There had to be some kind of invisible organizing principle at work. Jung figured out what that principle was: *meaningfulness.*

Now, from a modern "common sense" point of view, all of this naturally sounds completely insane. "Meaningful" is a word for English class, not for Science class. It's fuzzy and imprecise. It also makes humans seem more important than they are, as if we imagined that the universe revolved around us.

Yet these "incredible coincidences" are part of virtually everyone's actual experience – and for virtually everyone, there are *far too many* of these little miracles for "coincidence" to explain them. It's as if we toss a coin a hundred times and a hundred times it comes up heads – and yet we persist in believing that pattern happened because of random chance, not considering that the coin might be weighted.

Still, the great god Coincidence rules the modern world, or at least the modern mind.

Why?

In the face of the flood tide of reasons *not* to believe that life is random, why do so many people still experience a psychological compulsion to cling to it? Some of that attachment is simply social conditioning – the tyranny of the mass mind. Blame television. Blame social media. *But maybe it is also because people find the alternative explanation even more threatening or even harder to believe.*

What exactly is the alternative model? *Synchronicity* – which boils down to the simple notion that life involves our encountering meaningful patterns in our experience.

- Which means that at the level of the very fabric of the universe, *meaning* is a palpable force. Like gravity or magnetism, *it makes things happe*n.
- Which suggests that saying human life is meaningful is more like stating an objective scientific principle than a pleasant platitude.
- Which means that some intelligence – some "organizing principle" – beyond our comprehension seems to be herding us all in a higher, more mindful direction.
- Which begins to sound an awful lot like what people have been calling "God" since the beginning of human time.

Is any of that actually so frightening? Once we spell it out this way, this perspective is really not frightening at all – just a little weird. Or unfamiliar. Personally, I revel in the amazing *sign* – and that is the right word, not "coincidence" – that the pages of my Elements books totalled that meaningful, magical number, 1728. That otherwise nearly inexplicable fact of my experience simply strengthened my faith in the purposefulness of my life.

Synchronicity is a soul-vitamin.

A little while back, I imagined two people meeting "by chance" on that flight home from Chicago. Later, as a couple, they'll naturally hit some rocky patches – who doesn't? And yet their sense "that God wants them to be together" is going to help them get through whatever their problems are. The point is that the "little miracle" of how they met inevitably becomes woven into their personal mythology, strengthening and supporting their love for each other. How exactly? *By blowing away any rationalizing sense that they are together "by chance," and replacing it with the nearly inescapable intuition that something "bigger than the two of them" was behind their meeting and marrying.*

My point is very simple: *synchronicity is a benign, healing principle.* The misguided "objective, rational, (pseudo-) scientific" enthusiasm with which people hold onto their belief in a meaningless universe still baffles and astonishes me. But then I am an astrologer. I've had front row seats for synchronicity almost every day of my life since I was seventeen years old and lying in my bed reading my first astrology book. *What could possibly be stronger evidence for synchronicity than astrology itself?* Jupiter aligns with the degree of your Midheaven and you get a promotion. Pluto squares your Moon and your poor cat "just happens to die."

We really do not have to mimic the language of science and talk vaguely about mysterious, ill-defined energies coming at us from those distant planets. All we need to do is to talk about synchronicity – Jung's and Pauli's second reason for why things happen the way they do.

In my brief introduction to Section One of this book, you can read these words, "*I delight in this radically subversive dimension of our craft – the dominant paradigm doesn't stand a chance against it.*" Everything I have written here in this concluding chapter is really just the long version of that core idea.

I often call our craft "sacred." I say that for a lot of reasons, and primary among them is the simple fact that we sit with people and talk about the journeys of their souls as they pass through this passion play of a world. That alone qualifies our work as sacred and our craft as a kind of ministry.

We astrologers are doing sacred work for another reason too. The underlying belief systems of modern society legislate against human spirituality. Under the dark dominion of consensual reality, we are all under enormous, relentless pressure to envision ourselves as material objects with expiration dates, making our brief, doomed, appetite-driven way through a soulless, pointless clockwork universe.

We astrologers know that view is simply incorrect. The truth is that we are luminous, ancient spirits, being slowly nurtured by the great incubator of higher consciousness that we call the universe, guided every step of the way by signs and symbols.

You don't believe us?

Don't worry – we can prove it. We have the evidence.

—Steven Forrest
Summer Solstice, 2021
New Orleans, Louisiana